John Tulloch

Rational Theology and Christian Philosophy in England in the Seventeenth Century

In Two Volumes. Vol. I. Second Edition

John Tulloch

Rational Theology and Christian Philosophy in England in the Seventeenth Century
In Two Volumes. Vol. I. Second Edition

ISBN/EAN: 9783337028206

Printed in Europe, USA, Canada, Australia, Japan

Cover: Foto ©ninafisch / pixelio.de

More available books at **www.hansebooks.com**

RATIONAL THEOLOGY

AND

CHRISTIAN PHILOSOPHY

"Take away Reason, and all Religions are alike true—as the Light being removed all things are of one colour."—Preface Gen. to Collection of H. More's Philosophical Writings.

Λόγῳ δὲ ὀρθῷ πείθεσθαι, καὶ Θεῷ, ταὐτόν ἐστι—"To obey right Reason is the same as to obey God."—Hierocles.

RATIONAL THEOLOGY

AND

CHRISTIAN PHILOSOPHY

IN ENGLAND

IN THE SEVENTEENTH CENTURY

BY

JOHN TULLOCH, D.D.

PRINCIPAL OF ST MARY'S COLLEGE IN THE UNIVERSITY
OF ST ANDREWS
ONE OF HER MAJESTY'S CHAPLAINS FOR SCOTLAND

Author of 'Leaders of the Reformation' and 'English Puritanism
and its Leaders'

IN TWO VOLUMES

VOL. I.

LIBERAL CHURCHMEN

SECOND EDITION

WILLIAM BLACKWOOD AND SONS
EDINBURGH AND LONDON
MDCCCLXXIV

TO

THE VERY REVEREND

ARTHUR PENRHYN STANLEY, D.D.

DEAN OF WESTMINSTER

THESE VOLUMES

ARE INSCRIBED

PREFACE.

My aim in these volumes has been to describe a movement hitherto imperfectly understood. In depicting the great struggle of the seventeenth century in England, our historians have very much confined their view to the two chief parties betwixt whom it may be said to have been fought out. The religious forces of the time, which influenced so deeply the national history, have been roughly classified as Prelatical on one side, and Puritan on the other. In point of fact these forces were extremely various and complicated; and we still wait an adequate account of them—a great history of this great period, which shall do justice to all the impulses then moving the national mind, and the powerful characters which they called forth. We may have to wait long. The yet unspent prejudices and passions of the struggle, the necessity of at once sympathising with and yet critically regarding the most diverse religious phenomena, and the vast mass of documentary material which requires to be sifted and illumined, constitute difficulties in the way of accomplishing such a task which only the highest historical genius can surmount.

In the mean time I have endeavoured to sketch in the following chapters one very significant and not the least powerful phase in the religious history of the seventeenth century. At the commencement of the contest betwixt the Parliament and the King, there was a moderate party which was neither Laudian nor Puritan—a party of which the hapless but heroic Falkland was the head, and with which many, if not a majority, of the most thoughtful minds of the country sympathised. This combination—which was even then more intellectual than political—shared the common fate of all middle parties in a period of revolution. It disappeared under the pressure of violent passions and the urgency of taking a side for the King or the Parliament. But the principles with which it was identified, and the succession of illustrious men who belong to it, made a far more powerful impression on the national mind than has been commonly supposed. The clear evidence of this is the virtual triumph of these principles, rather than those of either of the extreme parties, at the Revolution of 1688, which—and not the Restoration—was the natural outcome of the preceding struggle. The same principles, both in Church and State, have never since ceased to influence our national thought and life. Their development constitutes one of the strongest, and—as it appears to me—one of the soundest and best strands, in the great thread of our national history. It is of importance, therefore, that their origin and primary movement should be understood.

I have spoken of the Latitudinarians of the seventeenth century as in some degree a party; but they are rather, as Döllinger somewhere says of their representatives in our own time, a band or group "of spiritually-related Savans," than a party in the strict sense of the term. They pursued common objects, and so far acted together; but their combined action resulted from congruity of ideas, rather than from any definite, ecclesiastical, or personal aims. It is the inevitable characteristic of a moderate or liberal section in Church or State to hold together with comparative laxity. The very fact of their liberality implies a regard to more than one side of any question—a certain impartiality which refuses to lend itself to mere blind partisanship, or to that species of irrational devotion which forms the rude strength of great parties. This characteristic makes the action of such a moderating force all the more valuable; and it may be safely said that no ecclesiastical or civil organisation would long survive its elimination. The "Rational" element in all Churches is truly the ideal element — that which raises the Church above its own little world, and connects it with the movements of thought, the course of philosophy, or the course of science—with all, in fact, that is most powerful in ordinary human civilisation. Far from deserving to be expelled and denounced as merely evil, Rationalism has high and true Christian uses; and the Church which has lost all savour of Rational thought—of the spirit which inquires rather than asserts—is already effete and ready to perish.

The movement which I have described in these volumes appears to me the highest movement of Christian thought in the seventeenth century. I am far from disparaging the theology and literature of Prelacy or of Puritanism during that eventful and fruitful period. There is much in both that still deserves perusal, and may be said to have permanently moulded and enriched our national intellect. There may be single writers on either side of more unique genius than any I have sketched. It is nevertheless true that the stream of Christian thought runs more free, and rises to a higher elevation in the Rational Theologians of the time, than in any others. In the case of the "Cambridge Platonists," it is eminently true that, with all their faults, philosophy in England never reached a more ideal height—a summit of more pure intellectual contemplation—than it did in them. English philosophy became tainted at the Revolution with a certain political bias, and it may be a question how far it is yet emancipated from it. Perhaps it is least emancipated from such a bias in the school which is supposed by many to be the most prevalent and popular amongst us at the present time.

Deeply interested in the principles expounded in these volumes, and the writers who first advocated them in England, I have had sincere pleasure in endeavouring to do some measure of justice to both the one and the other. I have felt this pleasure all the more that some of these writers have hitherto received scanty acknowledgment. It is something of a misfortune for religion and the history of the Church, that the men who secure most attention in their own day, and afterwards, are by no means those distinguished for Christian moderation. Violent and picturesque characters, the fervid and zealous missionary, the eloquent fanatic, the dogmatic and denunciatory theologian, are all apt by their prominence to throw men of quiet thoughtfulness and tempered and rational enthusiasm into the shade. Churchmen like Hales and Whichcote are forgotten, while the noisy champions of extremes are remembered and live in the historic page. I have derived so much pleasure from the repeated study of Hales and Chillingworth, and again of Whichcote and his Cambridge compeers, and cherish so warm an admiration of their great gifts of Christian reasonableness, that I should rejoice if I have done anything to restore the images of men who appear to me the very best types of the English theologian—manly and fearless in intellect, while reverent and cautious in spirit.[1]

In a time like our own I have thought these sketches peculiarly appropriate. The questions discussed by the Liberal Theologians of the seventeenth century, are very much the questions still discussed under the name of Broad-Churchism. Our present parties have all their representatives in the earlier period. The closeness of the parallel, not only in its great lines, but in some of its special features, must strike every attentive reader. We are nearer the seventeenth century, not only in our theological questions—supposed by some to be so novel —but in our scientific theories, than we are apt to think. And if this should incline any to despair of

[1] May I be pardoned for expressing my astonishment that the University of Cambridge has done nothing to give us new or critical editions of any of the Cambridge Platonists. There is a special difficulty in the case of Henry More, whose writings are at once so voluminous and so forgotten; but surely the Pitt Press would not be unworthily employed in issuing critical editions of Cudworth's 'Intellectual System of the Universe,' Whichcote's 'Sermons and Aphorisms,' and, above all, John Smith's 'Select Discourses:' and Cambridge possesses in Mr John E. B. Mayor, of St John's College, a student of the literature of the seventeenth century well qualified to superintend such a task. All the accessible editions of these works are poor, and Whichcote's Aphorisms and even his Sermons in a complete form are scarce. This is hardly fair to writers who did so much to adorn and illustrate this great University at a trying period of its history.

ecclesiastical or theological progress, it may also serve to convince them that the conditions of real advance are only to be found in a wide and intelligent comprehension of all that has gone before, in the spread of a thorough yet wise criticism, and the increase of the simplest Christian virtues in every Church—patience, humility, charity. There are even enlightened men now crying out for a new theology, which shall once more mould into a unity the distracted experiences of our modern spiritual life. But such a theology cannot spring from the ground, nor yet descend as a ready-made gift from heaven. Christian Science has far outgrown the efforts of any single mind. The days of Augustinian dominance are for ever ended. It can only come from the slow elaboration of the Christian Reason, looking before and after, gathering into its ample thoughtfulness the experiences of the Past, as well as the eager aspirations of the Present.

If these volumes shall help any to understand better the spiritual problems which harass our own time, in the attempt which they make to revive the questions of a time gone by, and to restore the faded images of thinkers who deserve to be more remembered than they have been, my purpose will be fully served.

St Andrews, *September* 1872.

PREFACE TO SECOND EDITION.

I TAKE this opportunity of gratefully acknowledging the kindly and appreciative criticisms which these volumes have received, especially in quarters such as 'The Princeton Review' in America, and 'The Guardian' at home, where the tone and object of the volumes might have been supposed to be less likely than in some others to be welcome. Whatever exceptions may have been taken to my manner of treating the "Rational Theology" of the seventeenth century, or even to the name itself, the importance of the subject has been universally recognised, and the volumes admitted to fill up a comparative blank in our theological history. This was my main reason for undertaking the task. I wished to write the history of a movement highly interesting, as it appeared to me, both in itself and in relation to our own time, and which had not been hitherto described—barely, indeed, recognised. I do not think that I have exaggerated the interest of this movement as a distinguishing phase of our national religious thought, nor that I have made more of its significance than it truly deserves.

In some quarters it has been objected that I have been somewhat arbitrary in my selection of men as representatives of the movement, and especially in not including in my list of Rational Divines certain Nonconformist names, such as Baxter. But I had already sketched Baxter at length in a previous volume on Puritanism, to which phase of our religious life and history he far more distinctly, with all his Rational impulses, belongs. Moreover, in both volumes I have confessedly confined myself in the main to groups of men closely associated by personal as well as intellectual ties. Stillingfleet in the first volume is the only exception, and the reasons for including him and Jeremy Taylor (whose connections with the movement are also partial) as pendants to the Falkland School of Divines have been fully given. The second volume is really a monograph. It is devoted to a single school of thought, and includes every name connected with it. I could not have added others without destroying the historical proportions of the subject.

For the same reason I limited my treatment of the antecedent or preparatory influences affecting the movement to a sketch of the Theology of the Reformation, and the rise and import of Arminianism. The relations of the subject to the Scholastic, and still more to the Patristic Theology, were beyond my province. Mr J. Bass Mullinger of St John's, Cambridge, in a careful review in 'The Academy,' has drawn attention to my omission of these relations; but this omission was simply a necessity of my dealing with the subject within anything like the limits I had assigned to myself. I was far from insensible to the fact that the same forms of thought had appeared in the Medieval and Patristic Theology, and indeed distinct allusions to these previous Rational movements will be found in vol. ii. p. 14-24.

This edition has been carefully revised, detailed tables of contents have been added to both volumes, and several minute errata which had remained, particularly in the notes, have been corrected.

St Andrews, *December* 1873.

CONTENTS OF THE FIRST VOLUME.

I.

SPIRIT OF RATIONAL INQUIRY IN PROTESTANTISM.

A.D.		PAGE
	Complex character of the Reformation,	1
	Preceding spirit of religious inquiry—Erasmus, Colet, and others,	2-3
	Dogmatic character of Protestantism—Luther, Calvin, Knox,	3-10
1587 *et seq.*	Rational reaction—James Hermann or Arminius,	10-14
1618.	Synod of Dort—Simon Episcopius,	14-15
	Arminianism as a dogmatic theory,	16-19
	Arminianism as a method of religious inquiry,	19-25
	Three main directions of inquiry,	25-26
	Scripture,	26-30
	Creeds and Confessions,	30-34
	Fundamental and not fundamental articles of belief,	34-36

II.

COURSE OF RELIGIOUS OPINION AND PARTIES IN ENGLAND (1500-1625).

A.D.		PAGE
	Special character of the English Reformation,	37
500-1536.	Rational spirit of the early Oxford movement,	38-41
1571.	Moderate theology of the Thirty-nine Articles,	42
1595.	Exceptional character of the Lambeth Articles,	43-45

A.D.		
	Rational spirit chiefly displayed in ecclesiastical questions,	45
	The Sacraments,	46
	Orders,	47-48
	The Church,	49-51
	Hooker's Christian Rationalism,	52-53
	Growth of "Anglo-Catholicism,"	54-58
	Rival dogmatisms at the end of sixteenth century,	58-59
	The "Anglo-Catholic theory,"	60-64
	The Puritan theory,	64-70
1620-1643.	Rise of a moderate or liberal party,	71-75

III.

LORD FALKLAND—A MODERATE AND LIBERAL CHURCH.

A.D.		
	Question as to Falkland's character—Clarendon's sketch,	76-77
	His distinction as a scholar and liberal thinker,	77-78
1610-1629.	His birth and education,	78-85
	His early friendships,	85
1630?	His marriage—character of Lady Falkland,	87-90
	His visit to Holland and friendship with Grotius,	90-91
1632.	His retirement to Great Tew,	92-93
1633.	His father's death,	94
1635-1639.	Second retirement to Tew—Convivium Theologicum,	95-96
	Literary associates as described by Suckling,	96-98
	Selden,	98-100
	George Sandys,	100-103
	Carew and Davenant,	104
	Ben Jonson,	104-106
	Sir Kenelm Digby,	106-108
	Sir Francis Wenman,	108-109
	Sidney Godolphin,	109-110
	Edmund Waller,	110-111
	Suckling and "Wat Montague,"	111-115
	Falkland's Poems,	115-118
	Theological associates,	120
	Sheldon and Morley,	121-124
	Hammond,	125-126
	Earles,	126-128
	Chillingworth,	128-129
1639.	Falkland joins the Scottish Expedition,	129-131
1640-1643.	His political career,	132

A.D.		
	His activity as a reformer and speaker in Parliament,	134-136
	His speech on the bishops and Episcopacy, . .	137-146
	His acceptance of office, ...	146-149
	His despair of public affairs, ...	149-151
Sept. 1643.	His death, ...	152-153
	His personal appearance, ...	153-154
	His significance as the head of the Rational party in the Church, ...	154-157
	His "Discourse of the Infallibility of the Church of Rome,"	157-167
	His true attitude as a Church reformer and Rational thinker, ...	168-169

IV.

JOHN HALES OF ETON—RELIGION AND DOGMATIC ORTHODOXY.

	His general position—oldest of the Falkland group of divines, ...	170
1584-1605.	His birth and education, ...	171-172
1612.	Greek Professor at Oxford, ...	172
1618.	His visit to Synod of Dort, ...	173-190
	Gradual change in his opinions—" bids John Calvin good-night,"	190-191
1619?	Settled at Eton as Fellow of the College, . .	192
	Correspondence with Chillingworth, . . .	193-194
	Suckling's lines on him, ...	194
	Friends at Eton—Sir Henry Savile, . . .	195
	Sir Henry Wotton, . . .	196-201
	Writings attributed to Hales, ...	202-205
	Charge of Socinianism, ...	205-208
1638.	Connection with Laud, ...	208-214
1656.	His sufferings and death, ...	214-219
	His writings—main principles expounded in them,	219 et seq.
	Dogmatic differences not religious differences,	223-230
	Church authority—Tract on Schism, . .	230-234
	Tract on the Lord's Supper, . . .	235-237
	Fallibility of the Church, . . .	237-242
	Essay on "The Power of the Keys," . .	242-243
	His Rationalism, ...	243-252
	Value of his writings and services to Christian freedom,	254-260

V.

WILLIAM CHILLINGWORTH—THE BIBLE THE RELIGION OF PROTESTANTS.

A.D.		
	Chillingworth's prominence in the history of religious opinion, ...	261
1602-1628.	His birth and education, ...	261-262
1625.	State of religious parties, ...	263-264
	Aubrey's gossip about Chillingworth, . . .	264-269
	Roman missionaries and Chillingworth's conversion to Romanism, ...	269-271
	His reconversion to the Church of England, . .	272-281
1635-1637.	His retirement to Falkland's residence, and studies for his great work, ...	281
	His growing liberality of opinion, . . .	283-287
	His views as to subscription, ...	288-289
	Jesuit pamphlet attacking him, ...	290-292
1637.	'The Religion of Protestants' appears, . .	292
	Appointed Chancellor of Sarum, . . .	293
1643.	Sermon at Oxford before the king, . ' . .	294-295
	Present at siege of Gloucester, ...	295
	Taken prisoner by the Parliamentary army, . .	296
	Treatment by Cheynell—a noted Puritan divine, .	296-302
Jan. 1644.	His death, ...	302
	Character and personal appearance, . . .	304-305
	His great work—its position in literature, . .	308-317
	Its argument, ...	317 *et seq.*
	His disposal of the question of religious latitude, .	333-340
	His services to religious freedom and Protestantism, .	341-343

VI.

JEREMY TAYLOR—LIBERTY OF CHRISTIAN TEACHING WITHIN THE CHURCH.

	Results of the movement as so far described, . .	344-345
	Taylor's partial connection with the movement in respect of his 'Liberty of Prophesying,' . .	345-347
1626-1633.	His education at Cambridge, ...	349-351
1636.	His connection with Laud and transference to Oxford,	352
1638-1642.	His settlement at Uppingham, and treatise on Episcopacy, ...	357

A.D.		
1643.	Driven from his parish by the necessities of the time, .	359
1648-1660.	Various writings, ...	361-365
	Evelyn and Taylor, ...	366-367
	His episcopate in Ireland, ...	368-370
1667.	His death and personal appearance, . . .	371
1647.	'Liberty of Prophesying' published at a crisis, .	372-376
	Its tenor connected with this crisis, . . .	377
	Its general argument, ...	377-380
	Nature of faith, ...	380-388
	Nature of heresy, ...	388-390
	Creeds, ...	392-395
	Remaining particulars of argument, . .	396-406
	Taylor's general position identical with that of Chillingworth, ...	406-408
	Beautiful apologue at the close of the work, . .	409-410

VII.

EDWARD STILLINGFLEET—THE IRENICUM OF A COMPREHENSIVE CHURCH.

	Stillingfleet's life not connected with the subject, .	411
1635-1689.	Brief account of it, ...	413-415
	His general character as a theological writer, . .	415-416
	Keynote of the 'Irenicum,'	416
1659.	Published on the eve of the Restoration, . .	417
	General design of the treatise, ...	417-425
	Two divisions of its argument, ...	425
	(1.) Natural law in its relation to Church government, ...	425-441
	(2.). Scripture in relation to the same, . .	441-444
	Neither Presbytery nor Episcopacy can claim an absolute *jus divinum*, ...	445-460
	The ideal of a Christian Church, . . .	462

RATIONAL THEOLOGY

AND

CHRISTIAN PHILOSOPHY

IN ENGLAND.

I.

SPIRIT OF RATIONAL INQUIRY IN PROTESTANTISM.

I. THE Reformation of religion in the sixteenth century was the product of many influences—intellectual, spiritual, and political. The revival of learning, the rise of modern literature and higher modes of philosophy, the rediscovery, as it were, of the Bible, a widespread excitement and aspiration of faith, the growth of wider social instincts, and the exigencies of political parties, were all powerful. It would be difficult to fix the proportions in which these several influences acted. For they were intermingled in a high degree, and the more we go beneath the surface the more complex and numerous do we find the springs of the great movement to have been.

A spirit of inquiry is especially conspicuous in the religious forces which preceded the Reformation, and helped to forward it. Starting mainly from a revived Biblical interest, and an eager life of freshly-discovered thought, these earlier forces are of a very interesting and enlightened character. They assailed the prevailing scholasticism and superstition, not only with weapons of felicitous criticism and ridicule, but also with a quiet Christian thoughtfulness which went in many cases direct to the truth. They brought the aids both of a new study of Scripture, and of new intellectual methods to the effort which the European mind was making in many quarters to throw off a bondage which had become intolerable. Erasmus is the well-known representative of this rational Christian spirit before the Reformation. But it had many representatives. The "new learning" was widely circulated, and can be traced extensively, not only in Germany and the Low Countries, but also in Italy and England. Along with Erasmus, and in some respects before him, must be reckoned John Wessel, Reuchlin, and Staupitz. The Platonic Academy at Florence, of which Pico and Ficino were the chief ornaments; and again Colet, Sir Thomas More, Tyndale, and others in England, were all more or less Reformers before the Reformation—agents in a movement antecedent to the great movement which was essentially religious, if also a great deal more than religious. The success of the later and more powerful movement has drawn attention away from this earlier impulse of reform. But it was in many respects highly significant, and deserves a closer study than it has yet received. It spoke of harmonising Christianity and natural truth; of interpreting the books of Scripture like other books; of simplifying Christian doctrine to the limits of the Apostles' Creed; of putting the Bible before everything, and being content with the simple truths evidently set forth in it as necessary to salvation. It was broad and tolerant as well as earnest. It aimed at spiritual enlightenment rather than dogmatic change.[1]

When we turn to the great Reformers themselves, these principles of intellectual freedom no longer occupy the foreground. No doubt they too carried forward the higher intelligence of their age. They were the leaders, upon the whole, of its best thought. But their special task was not so much to guide thought as to stimulate religious life. They were, above all, men of faith and of Christian enthusiasm. They were religious before everything else; and what they desired for themselves and others was not primarily rational liberty so much as spiritual salvation. Their hearts and consciences were more awakened in search of peace than their minds in search of truth. They preached yet more earnestly the necessity of deliverance from the burden of guilt and sin than from the oppression of medieval dotage and ignorance. It is impossible to read the writings or study the lives of Luther, Calvin, and Knox, without seeing that their main interests were thus evangelical, and turned round the great question of how

---

[1] See 'Oxford Reformers,' by Frederic Seebohm, p. 112-489—a very interesting volume, describing the earlier movement of reform in England; also, 'Reformers before the Reformation,' by Dr C. Ullmann, *passim*.

the individual soul was to be reconciled with God and find peace in Him. Popery was specially obnoxious to them because it had obscured and perverted the answer to this question. St Paul was specially dear to them because he had given to it such an articulate and satisfactory answer.

And undoubtedly it needed this mightier impulse of faith to break the superstitious sleep of centuries. The earlier spirit of reform, with its quieter intellectual impulses, could not have accomplished the same result. The voice of Erasmus would never have moved Europe as the voice of Luther did. It needed the cry of the evangelist rather than the inquiry of the Biblical critic and rational theologian to penetrate to the popular heart and shake the religious thraldom which had so long oppressed it. It was only by the spiritual forces outrunning the intellectual—the enthusiasm of faith so largely absorbing the mere love of light—that the Reformation grew into such significance and became a power in Europe.

This subsidence of the rational side of Protestantism arose not only from the character of the chief Reformers and the real nature of their work; it was also in the end the natural result of their position. The very strength of the spiritual excitement which they had roused needed by-and-by to be curbed. The tide of religious passion swelled till it threatened to burst all bounds and to subvert the order of society. Luther himself had to struggle against his own headlong impulses, and Carlstadt came in his wake. He was forced to forget the

Pope while he declaimed against his theological colleague and the Zwickau fanatics; and Calvin recognised his most persistent and hated opponents in the Libertines at Geneva, who strove continually to cross his purposes. It was absolutely necessary, therefore, to set a restraint upon the impulses of inquiry, and to break in the spirit of freedom which in its licence menaced the very existence of the Church. And so the very men who had headed the enthusiastic forces of the Reformation, as they broke down the old barriers of authority and spread themselves as springs of religious revolution throughout Europe, are found ere long busy in collecting, consolidating, and placing anew under authority the spiritual energies which they had everywhere called forth.

When we thus look at all the circumstances we have no difficulty in understanding—what may seem otherwise surprising—the extremely dogmatic character which Protestantism soon assumed. This tendency lay in it from the beginning, in its intense assertion of one side of the evangelical principle—what the Germans call the material, in contradistinction to the formal side. If the spiritual life which the movement had evoked was not to be wasted, but to grow into a social and educative power, it must incarnate itself in dogma and take to itself a legislative and controlling, as well as quickening, function towards the human conscience. The national Protestant Churches could never have made a stand against the reviving influence of Rome—could never, in fact, have been formed into stable organisations at all—without a distinctive basis of Christian opinion and a definite power of discipline. And so it came to pass that in the second stage of the Reformation the principle of authority had almost entirely superseded the principle of inquiry. The men of dogma have everywhere come to the front. Luther, always opinionative, grew more violently so from the time of his conflicts with the Anabaptists and his conference with Zwingli (1529). Zwingli himself, of all the leaders of the movement the most candid, rational, and open-minded, perished prematurely. Melanchthon and Castellio almost alone remained representatives of the earlier humanistic spirit. But the former was overborne by the *rabies theologorum*, bred of a hardening Lutheranism; and the latter had no chance with Calvin. The prevailing Protestantism of the sixteenth century set aside both these men. Its scholastic dogmatism repudiated the one, its evangelical earnestness the other. While the fate of Servetus was a terrible warning to all who might attempt to carry the rational spirit to extreme lengths, and to venture into speculations not only beyond the verge of Augustinianism, but of traditionary theology altogether.

In the second half of the sixteenth century, Protestantism is almost stationary in its character as in its progress. It has grown into Churches which from this time make little advance. It has consolidated its theology, which henceforth receives few or no additions. All the great Protestant creeds, with two exceptions, which rather illustrate than contradict our statement, were completed long before the end of the century.[1] The men who formed them had no doubts nor hesitations. They were dogmatists, and not inquirers. They set forth what they believed to be a definite system of truth against a definite system of error. In nothing did they ask, what is truth? and remain in any question whether they had found an answer. They confidently opposed dogmatism to dogmatism. And for a time the questioning intellectual side of Protestantism may be said to have sunk out of sight altogether.

But it was in the very nature of the movement, as well as in the course of events, that the rational side of Protestantism should again ere long emerge. In Lutheranism, indeed, this was not to be the case till after a long while; and then in a form of extreme reaction proportioned to the depression which it had undergone. The miseries of the Thirty Years' War, still more the unhappy influence exerted by Luther's personal name and authority, and the barren controversies arising out of the minuter adjustments of his theological system, destroyed for a time all genuine activity of thought in the Lutheran Church. A more deplorable period of religious contention than that which attended and followed the death of Melanchthon is scarcely to be found. It is spoken of by the Germans themselves as a new scholastic epoch, from the similarity which its absurd and wasteful argumentativeness presents to that of the age pre-

[1] The series of Lutheran symbolic books was summed up by the 'Formula of Concord' in 1577. Of the numerous Confessions of the Reformed Church, all connected with the movement of the sixteenth century were in existence before this, and even early in the preceding decade.

ceding the Reformation. The baleful effects of this dogmatic frivolity and bigotry extended far into the next century. With an exception like Calixtus,[1] there can hardly be said to be a living theological thinker in Germany from Luther to Bengel.[2] This should be borne in mind in connection with the later history of German theology. The home of rational thought was certainly not in Germany in the earlier times of Protestantism. We must look elsewhere for its reappearance.

If Lutheran theology rapidly hardened into dogmatism, Calvinism was intensely dogmatic from the beginning. Calvin was a far more powerful and consistent theologian than Luther. His conceptions of Christian doctrine were at once more clear and more definitely and thoroughly organised. Adopting the same great outlines of Augustinianism, which it never occurred either to him or Luther to question, he elaborated them, if not with a more penetrative and profound insight, yet with far more logical coherence and proportion. He put every relative dogma in its place with legal exactness, and adjusted all the parts of the theological system so completely that he left no room among his followers for the host of minor disputes which infested the Lutheran Church. But this very completeness of the Calvinian dogmatism prepared the way for a reaction. Satisfactory in the highest degree to those who accepted its main principles and identified them without hesitation with the teaching of St Paul, to other minds of a less unquestioning character it left

[1] 1586-1656. [2] 1687-1752.

no scope for the free play of Christian thought, while its stern logical consecutiveness directly tended to grate against the edge of this thought. The system, in short, broke down just where its triumphant logic topped its highest summit. The doctrine of absolute Predestination was the keystone of the whole. Augustine himself had not shrunk from the most extreme consequences of this doctrine, and neither did Calvin. But these consequences were such as to revolt many minds more Christian, so to speak, than logical. The very enthusiasm of spiritual feeling which made their own religious interests so vital to them, drew them back from the results of a logic which seemed harsh and unchristian. They felt there must be a flaw somewhere in a system which, however consecutive, terminated in such results. For, after all, the idea of the divine benevolence is as essential as that of the divine omnipotence; and if we cannot separate from God the thought of absolute will, neither can we separate from Him the thought of absolute good. The same Grace which on one side issues in predestinarian Determinism—saving whom it will according to its own elective arbitration or "mere good pleasure"—on the other side takes the form of divine Love which instinctively desires the good of all, and "wills all men to be saved."[1]

It was inevitable, therefore, that a reaction should spring up against the rigidity of the Calvinian doctrine; and such a reaction was all the more likely the more this doctrine had touched the national life of a people and become one of its mainsprings of

[1] 1 Tim. ii. 4.

action. The very stimulus which it thus gave to the religious and moral consciousness was sure in course of time to call forth opposition. There was only required some free life and energy of thought to develop it. This is exactly as we find the fact to be. No national life, upon the whole, had been so powerfully moved by Calvinism as that of Holland or the Low Countries, where for more than a century before the Reformation evangelical principles had been widely circulated. Calvinism gathered up these principles, and stamped them in the Belgic[1] Confession with its most rigorous and earnest impress. It suited the religious genius of the country; it nursed the heroic character of William of Orange; and inspired the popular mind with that proud desire of national independence which maintained itself unshaken in one of the sternest and grandest struggles which patriotism has ever waged, and in its indomitable enthusiasm proved more than a match for all the intrigue and cruelty of Philip II. Here, where its intellectual and political action was so vigorous, are discovered the first traces of opposition to it, and the ultimate development of a formidable rival system.

II. This opposition did not commence within the universities or among professional theologians, although it speedily spread to both. It was started first of all, or at least first attracted prominent atten-

---

[1] The Belgic Confession was, in the first instance, a private document, composed in French by Guido de Bres in 1562. It was subsequently published in Dutch and German; and in 1566 it was adopted in a condensed form by the Synod of Antwerp. It was finally approved, after revision, by the Synod of Dort.

tion, in the writings of a layman,[1] whose Christian sensibilities were repelled by the doctrine of predestination. Notwithstanding the attempts made to convince him of his errors, he remained obstinate, and was finally proclaimed a heretic. Out of this movement there arose in 1586 a demand for a formal revision of the Belgic Confession. The question was taken up by two ministers at Delft, who in the course of their arguments started a distinction which became in itself a fresh element of controversy. The necessities of logic compelled them to ask whether the divine decree had reference to the fall of man, and specially embraced it, or, so to speak, only came into operation after and dependently upon this great event. The former of these views became known as Supralapsarianism, the latter as Infralapsarianism.[2] It was in these circumstances that James Hermann or Harmensen—better known as Arminius[3]—had his attention specially called to the subject. He was invited to undertake the defence of the doctrine of his master Beza, thus assailed and misinterpreted. But, as sometimes happens, the chosen defender became the most serious impugner of Calvinism. Arminius in the course of his inquiries gradually lost faith in the old doctrine, and passed even beyond the modified position of the Delfian[4] theolo-

---

[1] Theodore Cornheert, who was not alone in his opposition, but his name has come prominently to the front in the movement.

[2] 'Episcopius Instit.' v. thus defines these rival theories: "Prior praedestinationem praeordinet lapsui, posterior eam lapsui subordinet. Illa praeordinat eam lapsui ne Deum insipientem faciat: haec subordinat, ne Deum injustum faciat, *i.e.*, lapsus auctorem."

[3] 1560-1609.

[4] Delf is the old name of Delft.

gians to a more decided attitude of hostility towards it. He became the leader of a distinguished group of Anti-Calvinists, as his name has been taken to stamp the movement which he first made prominent with its enduring historical title.

Whatever may be thought of the system of theology known as Arminianism, beyond question Arminius himself was a man not only of clear head and rare culture, but of earnest practical piety. He had received a singularly elaborate education both in philosophy and in theology, having studied not only at Utrecht and Leyden in his own country, but with Beza at Geneva and Grynaeus at Basle. At the latter place he had so distinguished himself that the theological Faculty wished to confer upon him the degree of Doctor in Divinity, although he was only twenty-two years of age — an honour which he sensibly declined. To his varied mental acquisitions and acquaintance with the state of theological study in these great Protestant centres, he superadded the advantages of travel in Italy. He visited Rome, and resided for some time at the University of Padua chiefly for the sake of pursuing his philosophical studies under the guidance of Zabarella, whose name at this time drew many students to that ancient seat of learning. During all his foreign travels and studies he seems to have lived a frugal and earnest life, carrying with him, we are told, "for the exercise of piety, his Greek Testament and Hebrew Psalter."[1] After a further brief residence at Geneva, he returned to Holland in 1587, and

[1] Funeral Oration by P. Bertius.

became one of the ministers of Amsterdam. At first received with some disfavour on account of his supposed intercourse with the Papal authorities while at Rome, he soon obtained great popularity by his gifts as a preacher. To clearness and force of judgment he united a singularly winning and persuasive eloquence. His voice is spoken of as slender but touching in its modulations and capacity of adapting itself to the varying themes of his discourse. None heard him but confessed themselves moved, enlightened, and sharpened in their religious thoughts. A certain sharpening quality—quick, decisive, and polishing in its effects—like a whetstone or file, seems to have been his distinguishing characteristic.[1] Pastors and preachers, as well as ordinary citizens, flocked to hear him, and welcomed with admiration his instructions.

It was while quietly pursuing this career of usefulness and popularity that Arminius was called upon to adjudicate regarding the doctrine in which he had been taught. And the more he occupied himself with the subject the more did he see cause to modify the conclusions of Calvin and Beza. He corresponded with Francis Junius, then Professor of

---

[1] "Fuit enim in illo incredibilis quædam gravitas lepore temparata, vox gracilis quidem, sed suavis, et canora et penetrans, suada vero admirabilis. Si quid exornandum esse, faciebat ita, ut verum non excederet; si docendum, perspicue, si disserendum distincte. Jam cantus ille et flexus vocis ita erat rebus accomodatus ut ex iis fluere videretur. . . . *Alii tunc ipsum limam veritatis, alli ingeniorum cotem, alii novaculam succrescentum errorum appellabant,* nihilque in Religione, aut sacra Theologia sapere credebatur cui Arminius non saperet."—Oratio P. Bertii de vita et obitu D. Jac. Arminii—Opera Arminii, Leyden, 1629.

Theology at Leyden; continued with unremitting ardour his Biblical researches; and pondered deeply the questions of liberty and necessity. Gradually his change of sentiments began to show itself in his sermons, and he was more than once accused of a defection from Reformed orthodoxy. It was not, however, till his appointment in 1603 to succeed his friend Junius at Leyden, that formal opposition broke out betwixt him and the orthodox party, headed by Francis Gomar, his colleague in the university. Arminius charged Gomar with so teaching the doctrine of predestination as to make God the author of sin; Gomar, on the other hand, accused Arminius of Pelagianism, or, in other words, of so exalting the human element in redemption as to obscure or destroy altogether the doctrine of divine grace. A general synod was convoked in 1606 with the view of settling the controversy; later, a conference was held betwixt the two main disputants themselves,— but all was without effect. Theological rancour had been thoroughly roused; the watchwords of the conflict circulated amongst the clergy and people, and were bandied to and fro in the pulpit, the senate, and the market-place, as in the early days of the Trinitarian controversy. Political interests and rivalries mingled in the agitation and complicated the result. The disturbance prevailed not only in Holland, but spread violently to England and other countries. The Synod of Dort in 1618, while giving an authoritative deliverance on the questions involved, which was accepted by the main sections of the Reformed Church, yet by this very act, as well as by its course of procedure, served to deepen and give consistency to the schism. For the Arminians, or Remonstrants[1] as they were called, were thus driven to form a separate organisation, and to perpetuate their special theological views in schools and institutions of their own. It was not till 1630 that they were fully tolerated, and allowed peaceably to reside in the cities and villages of Holland. Arminius himself soon passed away from the strife—he died in 1609; but his successor, Simon Episcopius, brought all the resources of a marvellous temper and address, as well as a most accomplished erudition, to the aid of the party, while he gave to its principles a more systematic elaboration than Arminius himself was probably capable of imparting to them. It was upon this distinguished leader that the defence of the Remonstrants devolved at the Synod of Dort; and one at least of the addresses which he delivered on this occasion is marked by the highest qualities of enlightened reason and comprehensive charity.[2]

---

[1] They were so called from having addressed a *Remonstrance* in five articles to the States-General of Holland and West Friesland in 1610.

[2] The conclusion of this address, which will be found afterwards alluded to and partly quoted in Hales' Letters, amply bears out what we say. A fairer and more Christian spirit expressed in more sententious and admirable language it would be difficult to conceive.—"Alterum enim duorum censequuturos nos speramus, ut aut probemus causæ nostræ, quam hactenus defendimus, innocentiam, aut illa cadente, reportemus veritatis victoriam : Tam enim accessimus parati vinci, quam vincere; utrum enim ceciderit sine fructu non erit: Non enim vinci pudet eum, qui pro damno erroneæ sententiæ veritatis lucrum quærit, nihilque aliud sibi propositum habet, quam ex veritatis consecutione conscientiæ suæ solidam pacem et tranquillitatem. Quisquis non eo animo accedit, ut quibus minimè favet possit absolvere, et quos unicè amat condemnare, næ ille indig-

The distinctive principles of Arminianism all take their start from the fundamental modification of the cardinal doctrine of predestination initiated by Arminius, and in connection with which the whole movement arose. The divine decree to which human salvation is to be attributed was, according to Calvin's conception, absolute and irresistible. It implied a divine partition of the human race into saved and not saved, originating in the pure will and determination of God. The decisiveness of the decree was quite as real on the negative as on the positive side. The Reprobate, as they were called, were as definitely marked out as the Saved. The whole drama of the moral world, in short, in its antagonism of good and evil, hung upon the absolute fiat of an Almighty Will. The Delfian theologians had so far sought to modify this tremendous doctrine as to exclude from the sphere of the divine Determinism the origin of evil, or, in other words, the event of the Fall. Arminius passed beyond this modification, which merely conditioned the divine

nus est, qui in hoc consessu suffragium ferat. Amicus esse debet Plato, amicus Socrates, amica Synodus, sed magis amica veritas." —Opera Theol. Pars Sec. p. 4.

Episcopius was not only the theological head of Arminianism in succession to his friend and teacher Arminius, but, above all others, its literary and organising genius. Besides various minor treatises all bearing upon the controversy, he was the author of the 'Confessio sive Declaratio sententiæ Pastorum, qui in Fœderato Belgio *Remonstrantes* vocantur, super præcipuis articulis Religionis Christianæ,' with its interesting preface addressed to the general reader; and further, of the elaborate 'Apologia pro Confessione Remonstrantium.' The Confession was composed during his exile in Brabant, following the Synod of Dort, and was published in 1622. The apology appeared after his return to Holland in 1626, with the first remission of the civil persecution against the Remonstrants.

by one inscrutable human act, and extended the conditioning process more or less to all human acts. In other words, he passed out of the pure sphere of the divine to which Calvin and his followers tended to confine their view, and brought prominently forward the free activity of the human will, as a co-determinant in the work of salvation.[1] The essential difference that remained was as to the character and measure of this co-determination, for even the most rigorous Calvinism could not exclude it altogether. Was the primary, preponderant, and truly conditioning element in salvation with man or with God? It was the idea on the part of the Calvinists that the principles of Arminius virtually implied the denial of divine grace, and transferred the work of salvation both in its origin and execution from God to man, that made them accuse him of Pelagianism, and excited such a stormy enthusiasm against the party. The logical suspicion was a justification of religious earnestness, but not of unchristian violence. Again, it was the idea on the part of the Arminians that the Calvinism of Beza and Gomar converted the divine will into mere fate, or an arbitrary instead of a moral and loving activity, and so made God the

---

[1] Bertius thus describes the theological position of Arminius in contrast both with that of Beza and the Delfian theologians: Decretum scilicet Dei æternum in Prædestinatione non esse eligere præcise et absolute ad salutem quosdam, quos nondum decrevisset creare; quod voluit D. Beza: neque vero, posito decreto creationis et præviso lapsu, quosdam, citra antecedentem rationem Jesu Christi, quod volebant fratres Delfenses: sed ex creatis et lapsis eos, qui vocanti Deo vera fidei obedientia responsuri essent, quod ab eruditissimo Melanchthone, et Nicolao Hemingio, et aliis permultis Theologis adsertum est."

author of sin, which kindled the intensity of their opposition, and made them suffer all manner of hardness rather than yield their convictions. They were right in vindicating the voluntary and ethical side of religion, but it does not follow that they were right in their interpretation and denunciation of their opponents' system.

It is no part of our intention, and would be quite beside our purpose, to enter into any consideration of the relative truth or value of these rival theologies. The connection of our subject with Arminianism is entirely apart from the validity or invalidity of its special dogmatic theories. It must be confessed by impartial thinkers that these theories look pale and dubious across the distance at which we contemplate them. Using the same logical weapons, and not shrinking from their application to the deepest mysteries of the divine action, Arminianism does not certainly succeed in explaining these mysteries, or making intelligible the *rationale* of the divine action in the work of salvation, any better than Calvinism; while the latter has the great advantage of being a more powerful and coherent system. It starts from the higher divine side, and argues out courageously and organically its conclusions towards divine ends. If we are to theorise at all about such matters, and not at once recognise that our forms of logic or scientific statement are incompetent to deal with them, then Calvinism may be pronounced the higher theory of the two. Arminianism breaks down in its logic; while it uses with a confidence quite equal to its antagonist the weapon which pierces its own side.

But Arminianism was a great deal more than a dogmatic theory. It was also, or at least it rapidly became, a method of religious inquiry. The method grew out of the necessities of the system, instead of forming the system in the ordinary manner, but soon became its most vital element, and has alone given to it enduring significance in the history of Christian thought. It revived the suppressed rational side of the original Protestant movement, and, for the first time, organised it into a definite power, and assigned it its due place both in theology and the Church.

It was inevitable that Arminianism should make a new appeal to the intellectual side of Protestantism. It could only make good its form of doctrine, and vindicate its position within the Reformed Churches, by Biblical inquiry and argument. Its beginning, we have seen, was in the reaction of the Christian feeling against the oppression of the Calvinistic doctrine. It sprang from the moral rather than from the intellectual side of the Protestant Christian consciousness. But it could not make a movement at all, still less could this movement assume force and significance, without a new and direct appeal to Scripture. And no sooner, therefore, was the spiritual difficulty, started by others, taken up and pursued by Arminius, than it plunged him into a fresh and elaborate course of Biblical inquiry. He felt that he must retrace all his dogmatic theories in the light of Scripture, and bring them again to its test. And this renewed spirit of Scriptural inquiry was more fully taken up by Episcopius. Its rules were worked out, and its applications pursued and methodised.

Protestantism had started on its course with an appeal to Scripture, loudly proclaimed. It had confronted the Pope with the Bible, and the right of all to interpret its contents and search for the truth therein. But the process of inquiry thus initiated had been rapidly arrested by the necessities of the age. Nay, it had never been fairly and fully carried out. Neither Luther nor Calvin had succeeded in approaching Scripture with free and unbiassed minds. Both read it under the influence of Augustinian prepossessions, which directed and coloured all the course of their interpretations. Zwingli and Melanchthon brought more open and truly rational minds to the study of the Bible; but, in the crisis which ensued, neither of them gave the prevailing impress to the confessional theology of the Protestant Churches. This theology, in its main types, was entirely cast in the mould of the great theologian of the fifth century, who had communicated his thoughts to Western Christendom with such force that they have never since ceased vitally to influence it.

But not only was the process of Biblical inquiry thus specially modified and limited in the outset of the Reformation; it was directly hindered and brought to a temporary conclusion by the course of things. The question of authority became so urgent that everything else was comparatively forgotten. An exacting demand was made upon all the Protestant Churches to give an account of themselves—of the definite doctrines which they taught and the principles for which they claimed to exist; not only with reference to the Roman Catholicism which they repudiated, but to the civil communities in which they sought to establish themselves, and the social and ecclesiastical necessities which they professed to satisfy. Hence the multiplicity of creeds or confessions following the Reformation—one of the most extraordinary phenomena in Christian history, the full significance of which has hardly been appreciated. Within a period of about thirty years, Protestant Christendom added upwards of twenty confessions to the three creeds which had hitherto satisfied the Christian Church. Lutheranism was content with one main confession, to which, however, it speedily added four supplementary and explanatory documents. But in the Reformed Churches confession rapidly followed confession till their number reached a goodly volume, less than one page of which would contain the creed which the united Christendom of the East and West in the fourth century judged to be amply adequate for all purposes of Christian communion, denouncing an anathema upon those who should venture to impose anything further upon the Christian conscience.[1]

[1] In Niemeyer's 'Collectio Confessionum in Ecclesiis Reformatis' there are reckoned twenty-eight distinct confessions, some of which, however, are of later date than the period to which we refer.

In addition to the Augsburg Confession, which may be said to begin the series of Protestant creeds in 1530, Lutheranism recognises among its symbolical books the 'Apology of the Confes-

This mass of confessional theology was the result of temporary exigencies. The Churches of the Reformation could not well help themselves or avoid the task thrown upon them. But it exercised at the time, and has continued to exercise, an injurious influence upon the development of Christian thought. It did so then in two ways. It exhausted too rapidly the spirit of religious research, and left the theological mind at the close of the sixteenth century —as the medieval theology had done before—to feed only upon results, instead of carrying on with ever fresh light the study of Scripture. It introduced a new reign of traditionalism. But it not only tended thus directly to diminish the power of religious inquiry; it encompassed its exercise with difficulties, and even dangers. Theologians were warned, as by so many fences, from approaching Scripture save through the medium of dogmatic conclusions already reached. These conclusions speedily came to be identified with Scripture itself, and to take something of its direct authority. Nay, with that natural tendency which lies in all men and all Churches to love and prefer their own things before all others, and to impart the highest religious sanction to the familiar formulæ of childhood and of Christian habit, the dogmas of each Church came to acquire to the popular mind a special sacredness which it has been always comparatively slow to accord to the more simple and concrete statements of Scripture. It was the theory of the Reformation

sion,' the 'Articles of Smalkald,' Luther's Catechisms, and the For- mula of Concord, already noticed as closing the series in 1577.

Churches, no doubt—as it remains the theory of all Protestant Churches to this day—that their confessions only possess authority in so far as they represent the Word of God, and that they are consequently subject to revision with advancing learning and experience. But no theory was ever more inoperative. In point of fact the confession becomes the measure of the Word of God, and not the Word of God the measure of the confession;[1] and no national Protestant Church, so far as we know, has ever ventured deliberately to revise its confession.

Such, then, was the position of Protestantism in the end of the sixteenth and the beginning of the seventeenth century. Its spiritual impulse, on the Continent at least, was already spent. Its theology had become a tradition of Augustinianism, with certain Lutheran and Calvinian ·accretions polemically adjusted to the errors of Popery. Within the German Church there raged a spirit of blind contentiousness, which had wellnigh eaten all heart out of the noble teaching of Luther and Melanchthon. Within the Reformed Churches, such theologians as Beza and Melville and Gomar, all of an essentially polemical temper and an inferior order of spiritual genius, had taken the place of Zwingli and Calvin and Knox. These men were not only not inquirers any more than Luther and Calvin had been, but they were

---

[1] "Immota fidei norma seu doctrinæ regula per eam cuiquam præscribatur quæ scilicet conscientias hominum coram Deo præcise obliget et proinde a qua nemini unquam vel levissime discedere liceat, puta neque in rebus neque in phrasibus, imo neque in methodo aut modo docendi."—Preface to Confession of Remonstrants, Opera Episcopii, ii., Pars Sec. p. 73.

destitute of the elevation of mind and the dignity and grandeur of spirit which made the dogmatism of the great German and Swiss Reformers tolerable. They were confessional theologians—men who had grown up under the shadow of the new dogmatism rather than originated or formed it.

It admits of no question that the confessionalism of the Reformed Churches was already beginning, before the close of the century of the Reformation, to burden Christian minds which had not lost all sense of freedom—in which any trace of the original Protestant spirit survived. This is clearly seen in the writings of the early Arminians. The preface to the Remonstrant Confession, drawn up after the Synod of Dort, is little else than an elaborate apology for the very idea of a new confession; and the apologist only succeeds in his object by virtually abandoning the principle of confessions altogether. He explains at length that there was no intention of placing any further imposition upon the conscience, but only of indicating the sense and meaning in which he and others—the Remonstrants—understood Scripture. In this respect confessions are declared to be useful, as indices or guides of Christian opinion, but not as compulsory enactments. As such they had already done much harm. The setting forth of so many symbols and forms of belief had hindered Christian inquiry, impeded Christian liberty, and opened the way to factions and schisms in the Church.[1] The authority of Scripture had been thereby " more and more weakened, until at length

[1] Ibid., p. 69.

it had fallen away and been transferred to these human formularies as more perfect."[1] All judgments and opinions pertaining to religion had become so associated with these formularies, and dependent upon them, that "men, waiving and undervaluing the sacred Scripture, appealed to them as unexceptionable rules; and he that swerved but a finger's-breadth from them, although moved thereto by a reverence for Scripture itself, was, without any farther proof, accused and condemned of heresy."[2]

Arminianism became the special and formal outlet for all this mental uneasiness in Protestantism. The long-suppressed stream of religious thought burst forth afresh, when once the wall of Augustinian dogmatism was fairly breached. The living waters, not only of a broader spiritual feeling and a conciliatory instead of dividing doctrinism, but of critical and speculative inquiry, began to flow. A rational spirit sprang up, and developed itself rapidly under all obstacles. And although this same spirit has frequently spent itself in arid tracts of mere intellectualism, or wandered into morasses of vulgar and superficial rationalism, it has never since altogether ceased. Its presence may be traced in all the subsequent development of Protestantism, in a nobler and more comprehensive thoughtfulness and freshening life, if also here and there in a weakened and reduced Christianity and defective religious interest.

This renewed manifestation of the rational spirit in Protestantism touched three points, or assumed

---

[1] Ibid., p. 69.   [2] Ibid.

three main directions, all significant and important:
1. Scripture; 2. The authority of the Church in the interpretation of Scripture, or the whole subject of creeds and confessions; and, 3. A point to which we have not hitherto alluded, but which became, as will be seen, one of the most influential in the course of rational religious thought, — namely, the limits of dogma, or the distinction between fundamental and not fundamental articles of Christian belief.

1. The Arminians recognised the supreme authority of Scripture no less than the Calvinists, and equally traced the element of authority in it not to any decree of the Church, or acceptance by the Church of the several canonical books, but to the revealed doctrine itself in its "admirable force and efficacy."[1] The truth of Scripture was held as declaring itself, and in the very fact of doing so, making known to the mind and conscience "its autocratical or absolute and supreme power."[2] It shone forth, in short, as an authoritative light by its own intrinsic lustre. This "divine-like authority" belongs to nothing else; and by the Scriptures alone, therefore, "as by touchstones and firm immovable rules, must all controversies and debates in religion be tried and examined, and according to them decided, so as to leave the judgment of truth finally to God alone speaking in His own Word."[3] So far there was no difference in the Biblical theory of the two parties. There was no question raised as yet by the most forward theological intelligence as to

[1] Confessio Remons., c. i. 7.   [2] Ibid., i. 9.   [3] Ibid., i. 10.

the character of divine inspiration, or the relative divine value of the various books of the Bible. The patristic traditions as to the composition of these books, their organic connection, uniform meaning, and equivalent authority, remained as yet unbroken. Historical criticism in the modern sense was not born till much later, although we can trace its tentative and imperfect beginnings in Episcopius, Grotius, and others. By the time of its birth Arminianism had long ceased to have any significance as a distinctive phase of Christian thought; but it is nevertheless true that a more purely grammatical and historical exegesis, which may be said to be, if not the parent, yet the lineal predecessor of that great instrument of modern thought, took its rise in the Arminian school, and was greatly helped by the intellectual and literary influences which proceeded from it.[1]

But while agreeing in their general theory as to Scripture, the Arminians and Calvinists differed in their application of the theory, and the difference

[1] The Remonstrant Confession emphasises in a very marked manner the necessity of interpreting Scripture in the same manner as any other book, according to its "native and literal sense"—understanding by this not merely the bare sense of separate passages, but the meaning "agreeable to right reason and the very mind and intention of him that uttered the words" (Con., c. i. 16). This is surely something like an anticipation of the critico-historical method. The document proceeds in emphatic language: "But to desire to fetch or take this exposition from any other author, head, or fountain whatsoever—to wit, from any symbol or creed of men's making, or analogy of faith in this or that place received, or any public confession of Churches, or from the decrees of councils, or consent of Fathers one or other, though even the most or greatest part of them—is a thing too uncertain, and oftentimes dangerous." — Confessio Remons., i. 17.

proved very important. The Calvinists recognised in Scripture not merely an authoritative guide to the reason and the conscience, but a coactive and constraining power *over* the reason and conscience. The authority of Scripture, said the Arminians, is merely "directive."[1] It is the witness of the Holy Spirit in the divine Word; but it can only be brought near to the individual and become operative by his own free inquiry and assent. The infallibility of Scripture, in short, to the one was an embodied rule—a "coactive decision,"[2] which the Church was entitled to apply to heretics and dissenters from the common orthodoxy. To the other it was nothing more than a private judgment, which all might reach for themselves—which all honestly inquiring minds did reach for themselves. It was not, and could not be, an external power capable of being wielded by the Church; and any claim to exercise such a power was strongly repudiated. This proved one of the main points of disagreement betwixt the two parties. Such a private liberty of interpreting Scripture—of "prophesying," as it was called—was intolerable to the Calvinists of the seventeenth century;[3] all the more that they felt the logical pinch of the conclusion involved. For where was the right of private judgment at all save in this form? If the truth of Scripture is to be infallibly declared and enforced in the teaching of the orthodox, where is the essential difference betwixt the Protestant and

---

[1] Confessio Remons., i. 10.
[2] Rutherford, Exam. Armin., c. i. 1.
[3] Rutherford's Free Disputation against pretended Liberty of Conscience, in reply to Jer. Taylor and others, *passim*.

the Papal infallibility? The Calvinian dogmatist was ready with the reply that his judgment was "according to Scripture,"[1] and only claimed force as such; and that if such a claim was not allowed there could be no end of controversy in the Church. But then this was the very point in question—which judgment was really according to Scripture? The Arminian was no less sturdy in his dogmatism so far, that his was the truly Scriptural judgment. And so the question was brought back to the point from which it should have started. Was private judgment really the right of all? Were the individual reason and conscience absolutely free in the light of the divine Word? Theoretically Calvinism professed to hold the affirmative, which was a primary postulate of the Reformation; and there is nothing in any of the Protestant confessions at variance with it. But in point of fact, orthodox Protestantism in the sixteenth and seventeenth centuries did not remain true to its own principle, or carry it out consistently to its conclusion. Arminianism attempted to do so, and so far, while elevating Scripture to the same supremacy as Calvinism, differed from it in its estimate of this supremacy.

The supreme authority of Scripture, however nominally recognised, could hardly be maintained practically in the face of the numerous Confessions which had already settled and proclaimed its meaning. A Protestantism which had elaborated and concluded its theology in the most minute points, naturally fell back upon its own work, and in all cases of

[1] Ruth. Exam. Armin., c. i. 5.

controversy interposed the secondary authority, which it had set up, as virtually absolute. The primacy of Scripture remained a dogma among other dogmas, but it ceased to have any living influence. Arminianism sought to revive this influence, and to reassert in its full meaning the principle of private judgment, or the indefeasible right of every man to examine and decide the truth of Scripture for himself. It recognised no other rule of faith even as subordinate [1] —no interpretation of Scripture, however profitable, or invested with whatever sanction, as entitled to come between the soul and the divine Word. In the face of all the opposition which it encountered, it asserted incessantly, and tried to work out in all its practical applications, the great truth—recognised, indeed, but unrealised by other phases of Protestantism—that "God alone is Lord of the conscience."

2. In carrying out this truth it was led to attack the whole system of confessions. It prepared, indeed, a confession of its own; but in doing so, it expressly repudiated any claim to do more than draw out an expository and vindicatory document. Symbols and confessions, it held, according to their true meaning, and even their ancient usage, to have no other design but to testify, *not what was to be believed*, but what the authors of them themselves believed.[2] They were not to be received as "certain indices or discoverers, much less as judges of the

---

[1] Pref. to Confession, Opera Episcopii, ii., Pars Sec. p. 71.

[2] "Et sane si priscos Ecclesiæ annales consulamus, non aliud fuit consilium, non alius scopus aut finis eorum, qui primi ejus modi Symbola, Canones Ecclesiasticos, Confessiones et Declarationes fidei suæ ediderunt, quam ut per eas testatum facerent, non quid credendum esset, sed quid ipsi crederent."—Ibid., p. 71 *et seq.*

true sense or meaning of Scripture, but only as indices of that sense or meaning which the authors of them held for true."[1] They were mirrors of Christian opinion—formulated expressions of the Christian consciousness of the time; and in such a case as that of the Arminians themselves, served to declare and make clear their position and opinions, and so to disperse the accusations and calumnies to which they had been subjected. In their own language, they were "like lighthouses,[2] to show to the unwary and imprudent the shoals and quicksands of error hurtful to piety and salvation; and, moreover, apologies against calumniators, whereby all might understand how false were the charges brought against them." But in no respect were they to be held as limiting the freedom of Christian discussion, or as "fountains of faith." Controversies were not to be "brought to their anvil," but to be fearlessly prosecuted and decided by the Word of God alone, as "the only rule beyond all exception."[3] The private judgment was always entitled to bring these forms themselves under review, and even without scruple to contradict them.[4] This was the only adequate security against their being set up as "idols in the Church," and placed in an equal degree of honour with Scripture, and made fetters for the human conscience.[5] Above all, they were not to be held as limiting the truth of God, so that those who were unable or who refused to receive them were thereby excluded from salvation, or shut out from the kingdom of heaven.[6] In short, they were use-

---

[1] Ibid., p. 71.   [2] "Pharorum instar," Ibid., p. 71.
[3] Ibid., p. 71.   [4] Ibid., p. 72.   [5] Ibid., p. 71.   [6] Ibid., p. 72.

ful as "ensigns or standards" declarative of the belief of those who set them forth; but no farther. No deliverance of synod nor decree of council had or could have in itself, or in virtue of its official enunciation, any sacredness which might not be fairly and fully challenged. Extremes of criticism, or mere licence of opinionativeness, were of course to be avoided. Christian controversy should always be moderate and charitable. It was the part of prudence to weigh things, and the times and places in which this or that opinion might be fitly propounded. It was the part of charity to have a regard to persons, "that they be not offended or troubled who ought to be edified."[1] But no human enactment, however deliberate or formal, had any right to stand between the conscience and God.

No Protestant party ventured to maintain in theory that confessions were in their composition other than human and fallible documents. Yet, in admitting this, the dominant orthodoxy strongly contended for the infallibility of the doctrines taught in them, and their compulsory relation to the individual conscience. The most able and thorough-going exponents of the system held so much beyond doubt. Believing that all controversies were determined in Scripture, they also believed that it was within the power of the Church to declare these determinations with certainty. In other words, they believed that the Church, "though not infallible itself, might determine infallible points," as an earthen pitcher—for thus they ventured to illustrate their

[1] Ibid., p. 71.

position—might "contain gold, and precious rubies and sapphires, although there was no gold in the matter of the pitcher itself, but only clay."[1] The infallible truth, no doubt, may be hidden as treasure in the earthly vessel of the Church, like gems in a pitcher of clay. But then this is not the question. The real analogy is not with the truth thus treasured in the Church, but with the truth expressed and formulated by human argument. Every proposition of fallible men must share in their fallibility; and there is no escape from this save by leaving the divine truth in its original form in Scripture. The gems may remain pure and precious within their enclosure, but not when broken up and mixed with common clay.

Supposing the Church capable of giving infallible decisions "according to Scripture," it may well be supposed also capable of applying and enforcing them. The element of compulsion was ultimately traced to God, yet ministerially it was held to belong to the Church, or to the civil magistrate as the executive of the Church. It was the duty of the magistrate "to take order that unity and peace be preserved in the Church, that the truth of God be kept pure and entire, and that all blasphemies and heresies be suppressed."[2] It was allowed, indeed, that compulsion could not make men religious, or change their beliefs. Conscience, where it did not manifest itself "by elicit acts," was not to be muzzled or enforced.[3]

---

[1] Rutherford's Free Disputations, &c., p. 35.
[2] Westminster Con. of Faith, c. xxiii. 3.
[3] Ruth. Free Dis., p. 23.

This would have been an inquisitorial tyranny too intolerable. But all expressed opinions at variance with those of the Church were not only to be reproved, but forcibly repressed. God has given even to a single pastor, far more to a synod of pastors and doctors, power to rebuke with authority [1]—to lay on burdens and decrees.[2] Whoever will not hear an ambassador, virtually refuses to hear the prince who has sent him. Whoever despises the minister of God, despises God Himself. And when offenders were obstinate, and heretics hardened, they were to be handed over without mercy to the civil magistrate for punishment; if necessary, for punishment unto death. This was a conclusion, as is well known, from which none of the Reformers, not even Melanchthon, shrank, and which was strongly maintained in England even in the middle of the seventeenth century.[3]

All this system of confessional and Church authority was vigorously attacked by Arminianism. The principle of private judgment, consistently carried out and applied without reserve, swept it away, although not without a long-continued and violent struggle.

3. But perhaps the most significant and solvent of all the rational principles enunciated by Arminianism was the distinction betwixt fundamental and non-fundamental doctrines. This distinction not only assailed the narrowness and stringency of the prevailing Protestant dogmatism, but the whole idea upon which dogmatism, whether Roman Catholic or

[1] 2 Tim. iv. 1, 2.   [2] Acts, xv. 28.   [3] Free Dis., p. 177-200.

Protestant, was built. And there is abundant evidence, as in the case of Chillingworth's opponent, Knott, that the Roman Catholics, no less than the Calvinists and Puritans, felt the force of this assault. It raised the vital question as to the essential character of Christianity and the conditions of Christian communion. Did any series of dogmas, after all, constitute Christianity? Was it not rather a personal belief in one or two great facts—"a very few things, which alone are precisely necessary to be known and believed for the obtaining of eternal life?"[1] And has the Church right to insist upon anything beyond the acknowledgment of these facts as its formal basis? Is the profession of any doctrinal belief or theological creed at all necessary to Christian communion? The Arminians inclined to answer these last questions in the negative. The only fundamental truths, they maintained, were the facts lying at the basis of Christianity as contained in the language of Scripture, or, at the utmost, as expressed in the Apostles' Creed. They not only refused to move the sphere of authority beyond Scripture, but they strove to bring the compass of faith within the simple bounds of the primitive Church.[2] As we proceed we shall find ample evidence of the working of this fruitful principle, and of the earnestness with which it was taken up and advocated by our series of rational divines.

These several forces of free opinion, or, more truly, several manifestations of the same right of free inquiry, reappear again and again, sometimes in a de-

---

[1] Pref. to Con., p. 72.   [2] Acts, viii. 37; xvi. 31.

sultory, sometimes in a more organic form. Protestantism found in them its full meaning, and gradually they have leavened the spirit of modern thought. Holland continued their chief home in the seventeenth century; but they found a congenial soil in the minds of a few of the most distinguished members of the Church of England, and grew up, amidst many difficulties, into a party which has never ceased to influence it and the character of English religious opinion. Special causes have also nursed a rational spirit within the bosom of the English Church. It sprang, and continues to spring, naturally out of its constitution. But in its origin it was greatly indebted to the movement of the Dutch Remonstrants, and can only be understood fully in connection with it, and the general course of Protestant thought, which in this chapter we have endeavoured to sketch.

II.

COURSE OF RELIGIOUS OPINION AND PARTIES IN ENGLAND (1500-1625).

I. THE Reformation in England was singular amongst the great religious movements of the sixteenth century. It was the least heroic of them all—the least swayed by religious passion, or moulded and governed by spiritual and theological necessities. From a general point of view, it looks at first little more than a great political change. The exigencies of royal passion, and the dubious impulses of statecraft, seem its moving and really powerful springs. But, regarded more closely, we recognise a significant train both of religious and critical forces at work. The lust and avarice of Henry, the policy of Cromwell, and the vacillations of the leading clergy, attract prominent notice; but there may be traced beneath the surface a widespread evangelical fervour amongst the people, and, above all, a genuine spiritual earnestness and excitement of thought at the universities.

These higher influences preside at the first birth of the movement. They are seen in active operation long before the reforming task was taken up by the Court and the bishops, and bring before us, in truth, one of the most interesting phases of that earlier and more purely Biblical spirit of inquiry which almost everywhere ushered in the Reformation. In England, with the opening of the sixteenth century we find genuine and decided manifestations of an awakening of religious life, of a new tone of religious thought, and of a desire to renovate the Church, and deliver theology and the study of the Scriptures from the bondage of scholasticism. Colet and Tyndale are the most conspicuous representatives of this early movement. The first initiated it by his lectures on St Paul at Oxford,[1] and his active co-operation with Erasmus in the promotion of the "new learning;" the second carried it on by his self-denying devotion and persevering labours in the English translation of the Scriptures till the year of his martyrdom (1536). Around these names there are others less distinguished, such as Bilney and Frith, all earnest students of Scripture, and all animated by an enlightened reforming zeal drawn from its pages.

The spirit of this movement was at once highly rational and evangelical. It is impossible to read Colet or Tyndale without recognising that a deep-seated love of truth and vital power of divine faith moved them in all they did. Not less than either Luther or Calvin they owned the reality of the evangelical principle, of the necessity of penetrating beyond all means of grace or accessories of devotion to the very life of communion with God in Christ. Colet had learned from the study of his beloved St

[1] 1497-1505?

Paul to look up from him to the "wonderful majesty of Christ; and loyalty to Christ was the ruling passion of his life."[1] Tyndale's whole being was inspired by the ardour of self-sacrifice for the holy Evangel. But with all this evangelical enthusiasm and fire of spiritual zeal, there was in both an admirable sobriety, candour, and fairness of theological temper. They approached the study of Scripture with their minds thoroughly cleared of the old formal scholasticism, and desiring simply to read the divine meaning in its own light and purity. They fixed boldly upon the fact that it could only have one consistent meaning, in contrast to the scholastic nonsense of a fourfold sense—" literal, tropological, allegorical, and anagogical." "Twenty doctors," said Tyndale, will "expound one text twenty ways, as children make descant upon plain song. Then our sophisters, . . . with an ante-theme of half an inch, will draw out a thread of nine days long. Yea, thou shalt find enough that will preach Christ and prove whatsoever point of the faith thou wilt, as well out of a fable of Ovid or any other poet as out of St John's Gospel or Paul's Epistles."[2]

Colet in his lectures on the Romans, which Tyndale probably heard at Oxford in the first years of the century, at once threw aside all this scholastic trifling, and tried to bring his hearers face to face with the living mind of the apostle. To a priest who came to him for some hints in his studies, he said, "Open your book and we will see how many

---

[1] Seebohm, Oxf. Ref., p. 105. [2] Tyndale's Works, 1573, p. 168.

and what golden truths we can gather from the first chapter only of the Epistle to the Romans."[1] He loved to point out, more after the manner of the nineteenth than the sixteenth century, the personal traits in St Paul's writings—his "vehemence of speaking," which did not give him time to perfect his sentences — the rare prudence and tact with which he balanced his words to meet the needs of the different classes addressed — his "modesty," "toleration," self-denial, and consideration for others —and the reality of application there was in many of his sayings to the circumstances of the times.[2] He recognised, even largely, a principle of *accommodation* in Scripture—as in the Mosaic account of the creation, and St Paul's statements about marriage. He showed himself in his doctrinal conclusions independent of Augustinianism; and, while emphasising the necessity of divine grace, kept clear of the absolute decree, and the extreme tenet of the bondage of the will.[3] He came at last to find the true sum of Christian theology in the simple facts of the Apostles' Creed. To the young theological students who "came to him in despair, on the point of throwing up theological study altogether, because of the vexed questions in which they found it involved, and dreading lest they might be found unorthodox, he was wont to say, 'Keep firmly to the Bible and the Apostles' Creed, and let divines, if they like, dispute about the rest.'"[4]

Tyndale, if animated by a more profound and

[1] Seebohm, p. 43.
[2] Ibid., p. 35.
[3] Ibid., p. 83.
[4] Ibid., p. 105, 106.

energetic evangelical feeling than Colet, was less liberal in his theology. His leanings were Augustinian, even of a somewhat strong type. Yet he is almost equally clear and rational in his method of Scriptural exposition. "Scripture has but one sense," he says, "which is the literal sense. This literal sense is the root and ground of all."[1] "There is no story, seem it never so simple, but that thou shalt find therein spirit, and life, and edification in the literal sense. For it is God's Scripture written for thy learning and comfort."[2] Of the sacraments, he says, "There is none other virtue in them than to testify and exhibit to the senses and understanding the covenants and promises made in Christ's blood." And therefore, "where the sacraments or ceremonies are not rightly understood, there they be clean unprofitable."[3] The same enlightened spirit is expressed in his general definition of the Church "as the whole multitude of repenting sinners that believe in Christ, and put all their trust in the mercy of God, feeling in their hearts that God for Christ's sake loveth them."[4]

The rational spirit is sufficiently conspicuous in these early traces of the Reformation in England; and although it cannot be said in its subsequent development to have been true to the broader theology of Colet, yet it retained something of its original breadth. This is seen in the doctrinal basis which it finally accepted. The preparation of this basis may be said to begin with the

[1] Works, p. 166.
[2] Ibid., p. 169.
[3] Ibid., p. 441.
[4] Ibid., p. 257.

termination of the earlier movement of reform, and it lasted more or less actively for upwards of thirty years till the settlement of the Articles in their present number and form in 1571.[1] The theology of these Articles is conciliatory and moderate. The great question of predestination, round which the theological thought of the Reformation everywhere circulated, is handled in a strictly Scriptural manner without argument, or any attempt to draw out the divine fact in its negative as well as its positive side.[2] The same thing may be said of the definitions in the Tenth, Eleventh, and Twelfth Articles on Freewill, Justification, and Good Works. An enlightened and clear perception of the truth, and yet a cautious moderation both of thought and language, characterise these significant propositions; and if the darkened tone and exaggerations of Augustinianism may be found in the Thirteenth Article, this is almost the only case in which they occur. Nowhere was the theology of the sixteenth century capable of doing justice to the virtues of the heathens, or of rising to the philosophic comprehension of the ancient Alexandrian school. In this respect, as in some others, the mere dominance of the Western Church had marred its theology, and imparted to it an exclusive and negative character. The definition of the "Church" in the Nineteenth Article is strictly Scriptural, and strikes at the root of all

---

[1] The first series of Ten Articles date as far back as 1536. They were afterwards, in 1552, expanded into Forty-two Articles; and finally, in 1571, reduced to their present number of Thirty-nine.
[2] Art. XVII.

illiberal ecclesiasticism. And if the question of "authority" cannot be said to be fully cleared up in the Article which follows, it is yet stated with admirable balance. The Church has "authority in controversies of faith; and yet it is not lawful for the Church to ordain anything that is contrary to God's Word written, neither may it so expound one place of Scripture that it be repugnant to another." In other words, the Church has power to settle its own doctrine; but this power can only be legitimately exercised in consistency with Scripture and reason.

The same moderate type of doctrine, inclining upon the whole to Augustinianism, but free from many of its exaggerations, is found to distinguish the chief English theologians of the sixteenth century—from Cranmer to Hooker. The "Homilies" are mainly practical, and, where they diverge into doctrine, they are not extreme; and the homily on the reading of Scripture is remarkable for the use of an expression which has since become prominent in connection with the advancement of a spirit of rational religious inquiry. In Scripture, it says, " is *contained* God's true Word."

The most memorable exception to this fair and conciliatory doctrinism of the Church of England in the century of the Reformation, is to be found in the famous Lambeth Articles, prepared at a conference called by Whitgift in the year 1595. Certain attacks had been made both at Oxford and Cambridge upon the tenet of predestination, the effect of which so much alarmed not only Whitgift, but others of the bishops, as to surprise them into the most intemperate and painful expression of predestinarianism anywhere to be found in the shape of a creed.[1] It is true that almost every word of the nine Lambeth propositions is to be found in the Articles agreed upon by the archbishops and bishops, and the rest of the clergy of Ireland, in 1615; and through these Articles, probably, much of the phraseology passed into the Westminster Confession of Faith. But neither in the "Irish Articles," nor in the Confession of Faith, are the logical inferences drawn from the primary predestinarian affirmation presented in so naked, abrupt, and coarse a manner; while the ninth and concluding statement of the Lambeth series stands absolutely alone in its appalling simplicity.[2] It may be an explanation of the Lambeth

[1] There seems at this time to have been a simultaneous excitement at both the universities on the subject of Calvinism. A preacher of the name of Barrett at Oxford had got into difficulties with the university authorities and complained to the Archbishop; while at Cambridge there was a keen controversy on the subject between the two Professors of Divinity. Whitgift himself stated to the Queen that "the design of the Lambeth Articles was only to settle some propositions to be sent to Cambridge for quieting some unhappy differences in that university."—Collier's Eccl. Hist., part ii. b. vii. The Bishops of London and of Bangor, with the Dean of Ely and the Queen's Divinity Professor at Cambridge, and others, concurred with the Archbishop in framing the Articles. The want of moderation so apparent in their language is attributed by Sir Philip Warwick (Mem., p. 86) to Fletcher, Bishop of London. The Archbishop of York, Dr Hutton, was unable to attend the conference, but he afterwards approved of the positions laid down, which, he added, "may be collected from the Holy Scriptures either expressly or by necessary consequence, *and also from the writings of St Augustine.*"

[2] It is briefly as follows: "*It is not in the will and power of every man to be saved.*"

theology that all the successive propositions are strictly deducible from the initiative or major premiss, which is no less virtually contained in the present Thirty-nine Articles; but this is no justification of the attempt to draw out such a theology into the form of a creed, nor does it really alter its harsh, unmoral, and (in the concluding negation) utterly unevangelical character. Happily for the Church of England, the Lambeth Articles never acquired any legal sanction; and, no less happily, they cannot be said to have exercised any influence upon the development of its theology.

It is not on the side of doctrine, however, that we must look for the most active display of rational thoughtfulness in the Church of England at this time. Upon the whole, there was in it, as in the other Churches of the Reformation, a disposition to accept without questioning the doctrines originally elaborated by the great teacher whose influence had been so powerful over the whole of the Western Church, and which had been revived and systematised anew by Luther and Calvin. The spirit of inquiry, even in such a man as Colet, rather transcended or evaded Augustinianism than disturbed it. True to its practical character, the questions which chiefly agitated the Church of England, and preserved the real life of thought in it, were ecclesiastical rather than theological—such questions, for example, as the sacraments, orders, and, above all, the government of the Church. This latter question, which in a sense embraced the others, was the stirring question of all the Elizabethan age, as it was destined, in a significantly altered form, to become that of the succeeding period.

(1.) The early sacramentarian views of the Church of England were substantially the same as those of the Genevan or Reformed Churches. Cranmer, although his language is not free from figure and perplexity, taught that the Eucharist is profitable and edifying, as a means of grace, from its spiritual suggestiveness—not otherwise. It serves to bring before the believing mind the sacrifice of Christ in a vivid and comfortable manner, and so helps it to realise the personal power of redeeming love; but in and by itself it has no saving efficacy. It is impossible in any other than a spiritual manner to eat the body or drink the blood of Christ; for the body of Christ is in heaven, and therefore cannot be also present in the bread or wine of the communion. This phraseology, according to Christ's own witness, means nothing else than "to believe in Him."[1] Christ is present in His sacraments as He is present in His Word, "when He worketh mightily by the same in the hearts of the hearers."[2] But in no other sense is He present in the communion, or to be specially worshipped in it. Ridley held the same views, and claims the authority of the Fathers for them. He as well as Cranmer, indeed, used language which by itself would imply a higher meaning; but this they did on the principle of ascribing to the sacrament or the sign what was only true really of the matter of the sacrament or the thing sig-

---

[1] Cranmer's Works, Park. Soc., i. 207.   [2] Ibid., p. 11.

nified.[1] Such an expression, for example, as "blood in the chalice," he admitted in a certain sense to be true, but only *"by grace in a sacrament."* He clung to the patristic language, and got into confusion and apparent materialism from doing so; but there could be no doubt that he rejected any corporeal presence, or efficacy in the mere rite. The grace of the sacrament, he says, "is not included in it, but to those that receive it well it is turned to grace." Jewel, who alone besides Hooker of the Elizabethan divines can be said to be a systematic writer, is equally, if not more clearly, rational in his sacramentarian teaching. The bread and wine are with him, in the usual language, "the holy and heavenly mysteries of the body and blood of Christ," and Christ Himself is received by them through faith. He is present and given in them, as He is present and given in His Word. But there is no singular or corporeal presence of Him in the Eucharist. "It is not the bodily mouth, but faith alone that receives and embraces Christ's body."[2]

(2.) The question of Orders was freely discussed, and a whole catena of evidence might be adduced to show the liberal direction which, for the most part, the discussion took. Cranmer's opinions are well known. He denied the distinction of presbyter and bishop, and seems even to have questioned the distinctive character and independence of the sacred office altogether.

---

[1] Augustine may be said to have been the author of this principle, which is quoted from him by Jewel (iii. 497, Park. Soc. ed.) as follows: "In sacramentis videndum est, non quid sint sed quid significent."

[2] iii. 488, Park. Soc.

A priest, he contended, might be validly constituted by the supreme civil power, in virtue of the authority committed to it, and also by the people in virtue of their election.[1] Jewel was no less Erastian. Those who speak of themselves as being the only true Church he compares to the Scribes and Pharisees, who cried—"The temple of the Lord, the temple of the Lord," and "cracked that they were *Abraham's children.*" God's grace, he added, is not promised to sees and successions, but to them that fear God. Becon, a voluminous writer, who was chaplain to Cranmer, and the author of one of the "Homilies," no less explicitly denied the distinction between bishop and presbyter, and advocated the old practice of appointing ministers by popular election;[2] while Hooker, in conformity with all the principles of his great work, maintained that "there may be sometimes very just and sufficient reason to allow ordination made without a bishop."[3] But apart from all such special testimonies, the liberal views of the Church of England in the sixteenth century on the subject of Orders are notorious. The correspondence carried on betwixt Cranmer and Parker on the one hand, and the Reformed divines on the other, prove beyond all reasonable controversy that the question of Episcopal

[1] His words are: "A bishop may make a priest by the Scripture, and so may princes and governors also, and that by the authority of God committed to them, and the people also by their election." This is one of his answers to the famous series of questions propounded by Henry VIII. to the bishops. The questions and answers are to be found in Burnet's History of the Reformation, vol. i., and also in Collier's Eccl. History.

[2] iii. 46.

[3] Eccl., B. vii. c. 14, 11. "Ordinarily," however, it is the function of bishops "alone to ordain."—Ibid.

ordination was not regarded as a vital one on either side. There was a sense in which the foreign Churches would not have objected to Episcopacy, while the English bishops were disposed so to modify it as to meet their views. In short, the Church of England had, on this important point, reached in the sixteenth century an attitude more rational and more consistent at once with the spirit of Christianity and the facts of its origin, than it has, unhappily, as a whole, been able to maintain in the course of its history.

(3.) But the main point which then evoked and sustained the rational thought of the Church of England was that of the government of the Church, or the idea of the Church as an institution. What was this idea? Was it definitely fixed in Scripture, and the model or pattern of Church government formally laid down there? No, was the distinct reply of the leaders of the Church of England in the sixteenth century; while strangely enough the affirmative dogmatic side was zealously maintained by the extreme Reformers, known thus early as Puritans, who had brought from abroad not only Calvinian theology but Calvinian Presbyterianism. There are two phases in this great struggle during the Elizabethan age: first, the controversy betwixt Cartwright and Whitgift; and secondly, that betwixt Travers and Hooker, which led to the composition of the 'Laws of Ecclesiastical Polity.' Nothing can be more clear than the attitude of both these distinguished representatives of the Church of England. Whitgift is indeed an infinitely inferior genius; and while his principles are conciliatory, and his tone of argument moderate, his language is often harsh and overbearing. Of his rational position, however, he leaves no doubt. There is, according to him, no "one certain and perfect kind of government prescribed or commanded in the Scriptures to the Church of Christ," and the "only essential notes" of the Church everywhere are "the true preaching of the Word of God, and the right administration of the sacraments."[1] "The substance and matter of government must indeed be taken out of the Word of God," but "the offices in the Church whereby this government is wrought are not namely and particularly expressed in the Scriptures, but in some points left to the discretion and liberty of the Church, to be disposed according to the state of times, places, and persons."[2] Whitgift, in short, vindicates for the Church a rational liberty to order in particulars its frame of government according to the principle of expediency. He met the dogmatism of the Puritan, who could not understand a divine revelation which did not fix everything regarding religion to the minutest particular,[3] by the

[1] Def. of Answ. to Adm., 1573, p. 81.
[2] Ibid.
[3] "And it is no small injury which you do unto the Word of God to pin it in so narrow room as that it should be able to direct us but in the principal points of our religion. . . . Is it likely that He who appointed, not only the Tabernacle and the Temple, but their ornaments, would not only neglect the ornaments of the Church, but that without which it cannot long stand? Shall we conclude that He who remembered the bars there, hath forgotten the pillars here? Or He who there remembered the pins, here forgot the master-builders? Should He there remember the besoms, and here forget archbishops, if any had been needful? Could He there make mention of the snuffers,

simple assertion that in point of fact revelation had left such matters undetermined. He encountered dogmatism by negation, and the sharp and pointed exposure congenial to his somewhat rough, if acute, sense and shrewdness. But he did little more. His mind, as the Lambeth Articles show, was of that limited, pseudo-logical character, which, while sound and rational on such a practical matter as that of Church government, had yet no real power of thought, or penetration of higher principles. It remained to Hooker to carry the controversy into a region of rational light and philosophic comprehension capable of shedding illustration and a new life of meaning, not only upon the constitution of the Church, but upon the whole sphere of theology.

Hooker began, not from negations, but from a positive analysis of the primary and essential principles of all government. Granting, he virtually said, that divine laws are our only immutable guides in the ordering of the Church — which was the Puritan postulate—yet laws are not divine merely because they are found in Scripture. All law, truly so, is no less divine, as forming an expression of the original law, or reason, of the universe. Whether the law is revealed in Scripture, or in the rational constitution of human nature, makes no difference. Its sacredness is the same, as springing out of the same Fountain of all light and order. This unity of nature and life and Scripture, as all equally true, if not equally important, revelations of the

to purge the lights, and here pass by the lights themselves?"—Cart- wright's Reply to Ad., 14-82.

divine will, lies at the foundation of Hooker's whole argument. It is the comprehensive and germinant idea underlying its entire structure, and breathing form and meaning into it—inarticulate sometimes, but not the less powerful. According to this idea, the Church of England, in the Catholic hierarchy of offices which it preserved, was defensible, not merely because it was *there*, and there was nothing in Scripture against it, but because it was in itself a fair, seemly, and rational order of government. It based itself on the divine reason, expressed in the national consciousness, and sanctioned both by the national sentiment and the course of Catholic history. In this, the higher sense, it possessed undoubted divine right. It was conformable to Scripture and the Christian reason, and had its origin directly in the growth and advance of this reason. The Church was to Hooker, in fine, no dogmatic or exclusive institution—as the Puritans would have made it—partitioning by formal lines and boundaries the cosmos of spiritual thought and experience which had sprung from the divine ideal in Christ, and in Him recreated and transformed humanity. It was a spiritual order, capable of diverse forms, and tolerantly comprehensive of all Christian gifts and activities.

If the Church of England had never produced any other writer of the same stamp, it might yet have boasted in Hooker one of the noblest and most rational intellects which ever enriched Christian literature or adorned a great cause. In combination of speculative, literary, imaginative, and spiritual qualities, the 'Laws of Ecclesiastical Polity' stand, as a polemical treatise, unrivalled. The same rich and ample intellect, and the same calm and judicial wisdom, shine through it all, but especially in the first book, where the author rises to his loftiest flight of thought, and expatiates with the most sustained force and compass of reasoning. Nowhere in the literature of philosophy has ethical and political speculation essayed a profounder and more comprehensive task, or sought to take a broader sweep; and never has the harmony of the moral universe, and the interdependence and unity of man's spiritual and civil life, in their multiplied relations, been more finely conceived, or more impressively expounded. The chief characteristic of the work is its elevated calmness of luminous and reasonable thought. Many writers are more acute, subtle, and forcible in detail, and reach their conclusions by more rapid, vivid, and close processes of logic; but no writer ever conducted a great argument in a higher, purer, and more enlightened spirit. None ever dwelt in a more lofty, serene, and truthful atmosphere, or raised himself more directly, by mere grandeur and largeness of conception, above all the petty and vulgar details which beset controversy even on the greatest subjects. The work remains an enduring monument of all the highest principles of Christian rationalism—of that spirit and tendency of thought which everywhere ascends from traditions or dogmas to principles, and which tests all questions, not with reference to external rules or authorities, but to the indestructible and enlightened instincts of the Christian consciousness.

II. In the age following Hooker, or during the reigns of the two first Stuart monarchs, the Church of England lost much of its original breadth and catholicity. The growth of what is known as "Anglo-Catholicism" marks exactly the decay of the more genuine catholic spirit which united the Church of the English Reformation to the other Reformed Churches. It might almost seem as if James I. and Charles I., both of them naturally of a small and irrational type of mind, had impressed something of their own narrowness and pedantry upon the Church and the theology of their day. It is certainly strange that a genius so rich and fine, and a cast of thought so truly noble as Hooker's, should have produced so little result. The Stuart divines, if they read him at all, only read him on one side of his mind—the patristic and controversial—which, when divorced from the higher philosophic side, loses all its life and true meaning. It is impossible to conceive writers with less real affinity to the great Elizabethan divine than Andrews or Donne or Laud, or even Hall, Hammond, or Sanderson.

The Anglo-Catholic theology withal is a genuine development of the Church of England. In some respects it is its most characteristic development; while no theological school has been adorned by a series of higher or more beautiful characters. It is the special line of thought by which the present Church connects itself with the ancient Catholic hierarchy. *Tollatur abusus maneat usus* was the special motto of the English Reformation; and the spirit of the motto was, upon the whole, consistently maintained, notwithstanding the strong desire among some of the bishops, such as Sandys and Grindal, and even Jewel,[1] to carry out more thorough and extensive changes. The patristic element, again, was something different with the English Reformers than with either Luther or Calvin, with all their deference to the Augustinian theology. Not only Augustine, but the Fathers generally—both Greek and Latin—were constantly appealed to in the sacramentarian discussions, and also in the early phase of the controversy with the Puritans. On the former subject, as we have already seen, the greatest anxiety was manifested to adhere to the patristic language, even where it obviously covered a meaning beyond that which the English divine was disposed to accept. This is evident not only in Cranmer and Ridley, but also in Jewel with his wider and more liberal culture. The peculiar force which patristic authority retained over the minds of the English Reformers cannot indeed be better exemplified than in the case of this writer, with all his broad and clearly rational tendencies. His defence of his 'Apology' against Harding bristles with patristic references from all sources, everywhere handled with the utmost reverence. Antiquity was therefore a distinct note of the Church of England from the beginning; and the Fathers were in some

---

[1] In a letter to Peter Martyr, Jewel expresses strong approval of the comparative thoroughness with which the Reformation was carried out in Scotland. "All the monasteries," he says, "are every- where levelled to the ground; ... the altars are consigned to the flames; not a vestige of the ancient superstition and idolatry is left."
—Jewel's Letters.

sort recognised as authorised expositors of divine truth. This position is claimed for them in one of Archbishop Parker's canons in the year 1571, when the Articles were finally settled, and the Reformation may be said to have reached its culminating point. Preachers are there admonished not " to propound anything publicly as an article of faith, save only what is agreeable to the doctrine of the Old and New Testament, *and to what the Catholic Fathers and ancient bishops of the Church have collected out of Holy Writ.*[1]

So far, therefore, the theological tendency of Laud and his school may be traced back to the peculiar character of the Anglican Reformation. As a definite system, however, Anglo-Catholicism did not emerge till the seventeenth century; and the Anglo-Catholics, as a party, have no right to claim the inheritance of the Church of England. They are really the successors, and not the precursors, of the Puritans; and if they followed out certain features of the old national party, and so far became their representatives, they yet did so in a very different spirit. The original advocates of the Church of England *via media*, fought their battle, upon the whole, with the weapons of reason and fair Scriptural inquiry. And nothing more honourable can be said of them in such a time.

---

[1] Parker's canons were subscribed by the bishops of both provinces, and are therefore a valid indication of the state of opinion in the Church. But they never received either royal or Parliamentary assent; and Grindal, then Archbishop of York, in thanking Parker for sending him a copy of them, doubts whether, in default of such sanctions, "they had *vigorem legis*."—Strype's Life of Parker, ii. 57.

They had no exclusive theory of divine right, and their sacerdotalism, so far as it existed at all, was traditionary and not dogmatic. If not latitudinarian, they were never destitute of a certain intellectual breadth. But the age was too troublesome, and men too impatient and violent, to appreciate such an attitude as this. The Puritans were felt to have a certain advantage with the popular and even the ordinary theological mind in the very narrowness of their theory. It was understood of all. That nothing was to be in the Church which was not commanded in Scripture—that an explicit divine command or *jus divinum* must settle everything—was a very obvious, ready-made, and effective, if somewhat coarse, weapon of controversy. It might satisfy men like Hooker, or even Whitgift, to say, —No; rational expediency in matters of Church government is the only law, and the highest law we can have. But men like Bancroft were not content to maintain their cause with such reasoning. They saw how a theory of divine right carried itself with the popular mind, which, in the second decade before the close of the century, was violently agitated by the Martin Marprelate pamphlets against the bishops and the English hierarchy generally. In these pamphlets, the Scriptural theory of Presbyterianism, with many other popular arguments, was ventilated, with a lively if rough and vulgar humour. In such circumstances it was that Bancroft conceived the great polemical idea of turning the tables upon the Puritan Presbyterians, by the assertion of a converse theory of divine right on behalf of Episcopacy, in his famous sermon at St Paul's Cross in February 1588. "The Conformists," it is said,[1] "were amazed at the novelty of the doctrine. The Puritans were confounded with the boldness of the claim. Whitgift said he did not believe the doctrine to be true, but he wished that it were." When this counter-dogmatism was once started it gained rapid ground. It addressed not only the popular intelligence, to which a ready-made dogmatism is always the best form of argumentative assertion ; but it commended itself to higher minds than Bancroft — such as Saravia, Hooker's friend in his later years, and Thomas Bilson, afterwards Bishop of Winchester; and gradually it worked itself into the whole texture of the controversy with the Puritans. Apostolical order—a *jus divinum* of Episcopacy, arising out of the supposed direct sanction of the apostles in the close of the first century—became the watchword of the one party, as Scriptural purity was the watchword of the other. Or, more particularly, the exclusive authority of a threefold ministry (bishops, priests, and deacons) became the special theory, or *raison d'être*, of the Anglo-Catholics, against the tetrarchy or fourfold order (doctors, pastors, elders, and deacons) of the Puritans.

Thus at the end of the sixteenth century emerged the rival dogmatisms which were destined to such fatal conflict. With the accession of James I., these dogmatisms are seen confronting one another in the Hampton Court Conference, as elsewhere ; conscious of their mutual dislike, but as yet unconscious of the

[1] Hunt's Religious Thought, i. 86.

sanguinary issues which were to come from their rivalry. It is not our business to sketch the course of their relations to one another, or to apportion betwixt them the responsibilities of the struggle which ensued. That the deadliest elements of this struggle, however, lay in the womb of these rival theories admits of no question. All the reflective minds of the time felt this, from Hales to Hobbes. Political complications, an insane abuse of the royal prerogative, and a tyrannous exercise of the executive functions both of Church and State, all helped to bring the long-continued struggle to a crisis; but it was the hate and determination engendered by religious fanaticism on both sides that made the fierce background of the struggle, and compelled it to be fought out to its bitter end. Hobbes was wrong in seeking to avenge the national confusions upon the religious principle itself by virtually extirpating it, or—what comes very much to the same thing—by subordinating it entirely to the civil authority; but he was not wrong in ascribing the train of calamities which overtook the country to its aggressive and high-handed violence on the one side and the other.

It remains for us only farther, in this chapter, to describe somewhat more fully the characteristic principles and attitude of the rival dogmatisms, and then to point out the special causes which contributed to the formation of a third or liberal party betwixt the two; or, in other words, to the reappearance, in a definite and progressive form, of the rational religious spirit in which the English Reformation had started, and of which it had already, in Hooker, produced so splendid an example.

(1.) The Anglo-Catholic system, while narrow in theory, and capable both of violent and of vulgar manifestations, yet presents many aspects of speculative and literary interest. It has had the power through all its history of captivating many fine, interesting, and original minds; while in its highest developments it often loses, not indeed its bigotry, but all which makes bigotry offensive and dangerous. It is grounded on a strange illusion of a golden patristic age, when Christian teachers, reverently termed Fathers, enjoyed special advantages of interpreting and declaring divine truth. The Church of England is supposed to inherit the continuous tradition of this golden age, under the name of "catholicity." While protesting, along with the other Reformed Churches, against the abuses and perversions of Rome, it has yet, according to this theory, kept clear of either German or Genevan extremes. It threw off the usurpations of the Papacy, and translated with modifications the old ritual into the common tongue. It remedied various errors of doctrine and of practice which had crept in during the ages of darkness and corruption, but it has preserved unimpaired the sacredness of the apostolic succession, the deposit of Catholic truth, and the sweetness and grandeur of the ancient prayers. The prestige, dignity, and spiritual authority of the Anglican Church descend with unbroken force from the Canterbury mission and the supreme Catholic Church which it represented.

The ideal of Anglo-Catholicism is not the primitive Church as it is seen emerging in its rude simplicities from the synagogue, or as pictured in the touching symbolism of the catacombs. It is the Church of the fourth and fifth centuries, with its elaborated creed and full-grown splendour—the orthodox Athanasian Church, illustrated by great names, and strong in its possession of the truth against the Arians and others who had threatened its life. To ascend to this Catholic time with any doctrine or usage is sufficient, and indeed the most sufficient warrant either can have. The statements of the Christian writers who then instructed the Church possess an exceptional value, and are examined and expounded with a deferential regard only second, if indeed second, to those of Scripture itself. The great Œcumenical Councils which were held during the same period command special admiration, and their decisions are received with special reverence and faith. The great aim of the school is not to reach the primary ideas of Christianity, and trace their growth downwards—to show, for example, how Athanasianism developed from a simpler or less systematised creed—but, reading upwards from the great era of Catholic orthodoxy, to vindicate even the technical subtleties and barbaric exclusiveness of the "Symbolum Quicunque" in the earlier Christian remains. Its method, in short, is essentially and in all things dogmatic, yet with a touch of conciliatory breadth which never fails to come from historic studies, and the recognition of historic difference or dogmatic growth in any form.

The Anglo-Catholic theologian not only rests upon authority, but delights to do so. He works out all his conclusions on assumed data no less truly, if not so entirely, as the medieval theologian did. He starts from recognised principles; he does not go in quest of them. The truth is for him already found and deposited, not *to be* found or inquired after. He is content and proud to inherit the wisdom of the past, and to be the heir of "Catholic" thought and "Catholic" worship through many ages. Christianity is not for him characteristically a divine philosophy, nor yet a spiritual life, but a dogmatic treasure—an heirloom of the ancient divine family, which has gathered the good and orthodox of all generations into its bosom; and he sits reverently at the feet of the great names who have exhibited and transmitted its power, or shone with its beauty since it came into the world. Even when we see in this type of theologian a rare force or charm of mind, it is not so much capacity of inquiry, or pure love of truth for its own sake, that is developed, as largeness of faith and receptive power of thought. That which has come along the golden links of Catholic tradition and association—not the result of his own research, but a consecrated continuity of opinion—he loves and defends. He rationalises little—never if he can help it—even when his sweep of argument is boldest, and his reason takes its highest flight.

This Anglo-Catholic tendency, it is almost needless to say, has more than once in the course of its history shown an inclination towards Romanism. It has, in some of its brightest examples, lost its distinctive national character, and returned into the bosom of the older Catholicism, from whose corruptions it professed to have separated. In times of excitement and agitation of the principles lying at its foundation this is inevitable. But it would, nevertheless, be a grave mistake to confound the general movement with these occasional vacillations. The movement has in itself both a distinct dogmatic and historical life, and is not to be identified with Romanism, even if it be true that its principles lead thither when pushed to their logical consequences. The great lines of religious faith in a country are not to be classified, and still less exhausted, by any applications of logic.

And if, on the one hand, Anglo-Catholicism has sometimes inclined to Romanism, it has also—and never more strongly than in the seventeenth century—shown an inclination towards liberalism. This is one of the strange anomalies with which we meet in religious developments. Puritanism, which began in impulses of liberty, and which, through all its history, has been so associated with the assertion of political independence and the rights of conscience, has yet always been intolerant of dogmatic differences. In the seventeenth century it manifested this intolerance in an extreme degree. From no quarter did the liberal theological spirit receive more discountenance, or more fervent denunciation and resistance. On the other hand, the High Church party, while servile in spirit and tyrannic in the exercise of constituted authority, is found—and eminently so in the case of its most notable representative—extending patronage to the earliest of our rational theologians. All these theologians came out of the bosom of the party, and continued, more or less, closely associated with it. And even in the case of some of the most distinctive of the Anglo-Catholic theologians themselves, there are traces of a certain freedom of thought on purely theological matters—a certain "*libertas opinandi*," as Heylin says, on "points of philological and scholastic divinity." "Some truths," he adds, "are found in each school; but not all in any."[1] The statement has the touch of the liberal and eclectic party. So that if Romanism may be said to lie in wait for Anglo-Catholicism on one side, there is a sense in which Latitudinarianism springs from it on another.

(2.) Puritan dogmatism, again, rests, or is supposed to rest, on direct Scriptural authority. It appeals simply and absolutely to the divine Word, which it identifies with Scripture. Its watchword is not only Scripture as an ultimate authority or rule of faith—for in this respect all forms of Protestantism may be said to agree with it, or at least did agree with it in the seventeenth century—but Scripture as an infallible dogmatic code. It has never fairly faced—and during that century it was not even conscious of—such questions as, What is Scripture? and, What is the relative dogmatic import of its several books? The Bible presents itself to the Puritan as a uniform manual of doctrine and duty, an absolute law of truth and right, in which his own system is plainly and authoritatively laid down. His special dogmas

[1] Introd. to Laud's Life.

are supposed to be mere transcripts of its letter. He ignores, and has always ignored, the idea of dogmatic and ecclesiastical development. St Paul appears to him to speak with as clearly a predestinarian voice as St Augustine, and the Presbyterian platform to be as clearly revealed as the Levitical economy. He has found even the "ruling eldership" in a text of the Pastoral Epistles. All the teaching of life, the experience of history, the accumulations of Catholic ordinance and ritual, have with him comparatively no divine meaning. He is careless of the venerable associations and harmonising beauties which Christian opinion has gathered during the long lapse of the Christian centuries. The Catholic Church and its traditions, if they are regarded at all, are regarded with no enthusiasm. What the Fathers have written is an altogether secondary or irrelevant question. He sets aside all as a dim and imperfect twilight of tradition, to look straight at Scripture; and catch the divine truth in its clear daylight. Its formal enunciations and prescriptions alone are presumed to guide him. "To the law and to the testimony" is his invariable appeal.

It is difficult to conceive a more complete antagonism to the Anglo-Catholic theory. Even when the theological conclusions of the two schools may not greatly differ, their modes of argument and of exposition widely disagree. The Thirty-nine Articles cannot be taken as a characteristic specimen of Anglo-Catholic theology. They were framed before the emergence of its distinctive dogmatic spirit, and have indeed constituted a main difficulty to the most pronounced adherents of the school, who have sought by various glosses to harmonise them with Catholic doctrine. But, such as they are, they exhibit a marked difference to the full-grown type of Puritan theology, as presented, for example, in the canons of the Synod of Dort, or the chapters of the Westminster Confession of Faith. In the one there is present everywhere a touch of moderation, the softening influence of a conciliatory doctrinism which is true to the positive aspects of Augustinianism and the evangelical import of the great questions raised by the Reformation, but which yet shrinks, for the most part, from all negative and extreme deductions. Their meaning is Calvinian; but the logic of Calvinism is sparingly used, and a dogmatic Scripturism does not obtrude itself. In the other, all generality and Scriptural manifoldness have disappeared. The concrete has become abstract; the statement of fact has been transformed into the process of ratiocination; and the negative polemical side of almost every truth is set forth in clearer sharpness and definition than its positive substance. Dogmas are rigorously carried out to their consequences; and the intellect and conscience alike are assailed by the coercive authority with which these consequences, in their most theoretic relations, are expressed and enforced. Above all, the letter of Scripture is itself turned into logic, and the divine idea, living and shapely in its original form, is drawn out into hard and unyielding propositions. Nothing is more singular, nor in a sense more impressive, than the daring alliance thus forced betwixt logic and Scripture. The thought and the letter, the argument and the fact, are inwrought. This identification of Scripture with its own forms of thinking was of the very essence of Puritanism, and gave it something of its marvellous success in an age when argument was strong, and criticism weak.

To do justice to Puritanism, it must be admitted that it did not only bring its ideas to Scripture; but supposed that it found them there. St Paul appeared to speak to it with its own voice, to be a dogmatist of its own type. Calvinism was only Christianity reduced to a system. It was the divine thought articulated in human language. Calvinian speculation has always this true element of sublimity in it. It soars directly to the throne of God, and seeks to chain all its deductions to that supreme height. But it fails to realise how far men's best thoughts are below this height, and how much human weakness and error must mingle in the loftiest efforts to compass and set forth divine truth. Dogmatic Puritanism was the offspring of an uncritical and polemical age, when men theologised, as they fought, with no scruples, and no tenderness towards opponents. And this hard and one-sided spirit survives in it. It barely recognises even now in the sphere of theology that truth is not all on one side. It still looks with jealousy on that more tolerant spirit, both of faith and of criticism, which labours to distinguish the essential from the accidental, and so to penetrate and sift all systems as to lay bare the multiplied influences of time, place, and character,

which have mingled in their production, and stamped
and coloured them with their own impress and hue.
It shrinks from the critical impartiality which exposes everywhere the purely human side of Christian
doctrine, and clings obstinately to ideas of *compensa-
tion, forensic imputation,* and *covenants,* as being of
the very essence of the divine truth—original elements of the primitive Christian consciousness. It
matters not that the origin of such ideas can be distinctly traced outside of Scripture, as temporary
conventionalities, or transitory habits of human
speculation. It delights to identify them with the
divine meaning; and parting with them is as if parting with the very substance of divine revelation.

In its later ecclesiastical or Presbyterian form,
Puritanism cannot be said to connect itself directly
with the English Reformation. For, in the first
instance, there was no question of abandoning the
historical polity of the Church of England. None
of the earliest Reformers entertained this thought,
or supposed that there was anything incompatible
betwixt Scripture and the hierarchy of offices into
which this polity had grown. Yet in such men as
Tyndale, and Latimer, and Hooper, and Ridley, we
see something of the same dogmatic Scripturism of
which Puritanism was only the full development.
The bare text of Scripture is with them a final
appeal; and although they accepted the Anglican
system, there is little doubt that, if they had been
allowed their own way, they would have greatly
modified it. If not enamoured, like Cartwright and
others after the Marian persecution, with the Gene-

van model, they were yet entirely free from Catholic predilections; they cared little or nothing for the external dignity and historical associations of the Church, and earnestly desired a reduction of its medieval ceremonies. They were therefore Puritans before Puritanism, and the name had come into vogue before the party can be said to have been formed. As Anglo-Catholicism links itself with the Church before the Reformation, with a proud sense of its ancient lineage, Puritanism connects itself with the Reformation as its most characteristic outgrowth —although both, in their definite form, were really later developments.

This side of English religious thought grew and hardened by the very means taken to check and destroy it. The Continental experience of the English Reformers, when driven abroad in the reign of Mary, tended greatly to encourage and strengthen it. The hostility of Elizabeth and James I., the vacillations of the archbishops — now, as in the case of Bancroft, violently denouncing and opposing it, and again, in the case of Abbot, temporising with and favouring it — the pettiness and ignorance of the authorities generally, and their small and incessant interferences — contributed to nurse its irritations, foster its surly independence, and give point to its zeal. Whether the two sides of thought, if left alone to their natural working, would have come to understand one another, and so have kept the peace, if not coalesced, it is needless to conjecture. There are some indications that they might have done so. There were statesmen in England like Lord-

Keeper Williams,[1] who could look with indifference on their antagonism, and hold the balance fairly betwixt them. If Williams had not been supplanted by Laud at the accession of Charles, and the dogmatic fever propagated under the unhappy rule of the latter prelate to its fiercest height, affairs might have taken a different course. But Laud forced the evil genius of the time. In him were unluckily concentrated all the intensities of one side, not only in an exaggerated and narrow but in an intensely aggressive attitude. Not destitute of generous and liberal qualities, as he has been sometimes painted, nor even without a certain breadth of dogmatic sympathy, he was yet wholly deficient in largeness of mind, or any real insight into the thoughts of others. The strength and earnestness of spiritual convictions differing from his own were unintelligible to him, and so he hardly realised the difficulties with which he had to deal. Not only his policy — his schemes for procuring "uniformity and decency" of "external worship"[2]— but his very nature, his watchfulness, and the pettiness and persistency of his interferences, proved an irritant of the worst kind. Slowly but surely, during those years when he and his master and Wentworth may be said to have governed alone, the crisis was ripening. The religious consciousness of Puritanism, far from being subdued, deepened to a darker hue,

---

[1] Bishop of Lincoln, and chief ecclesiastical adviser in the last years of James.

[2] "All that I laboured for in this particular," he said, when charged on his trial with introducing Popish ceremonies, "was that the external worship of God in this Church might be kept up in uniformity and decency, and in some beauty of holiness."

and gathered a firmer tenacity. Instead of being weakened, it grew strong under oppression ; and, adding to its strength intensity, deliberateness, and a gradually kindling fierceness, it braced itself for the struggle, and nursed a wrath which was to be terrible in its vengeance.

(3.) It was so far a natural result of the attitude of these respective systems—facing one another in unyielding antagonism—that a third or middle party should spring up. Thoughtful men on either side could not but be visited with misgivings as to the effects of such an antagonism, and the futile and miserable controversies which arose from it. They were driven by the very discomforts of the ecclesiastical position to consider whether there was not a more excellent way than that presented by either extreme. Moreover, it was the direct tendency of the controversies between the two sides to raise fundamental questions as to the constitution of the Church, the nature and importance of doctrinal differences, and the relations of authority and freedom within the limits of the national Communion. So far, therefore, the liberal movement was born naturally out of the oppositions we have described. It came forth a new element out of the theological fulness of the time. A few reflective minds pondering over the distracted condition of the Church and the country, and wearied with the ceaseless contention between Puritan and Anglo-Catholic, struck their line of thought deeper than either, and brought into view a wider set of principles, in the light of which the old antagonisms seemed hollow and false. Getting below the dogmatic basement of both, the structures which had been reared upon them crumbled away, and there was opened up the fair prospect of a higher structure—a Church more true than either had conceived—more divine, because more simple and comprehensive.

But there were two special causes which contributed to the origin of the new movement: (*a*) as we have already indicated, the influence of Arminianism; and (*b*) the aggressions of Popery.

(*a*.) Arminianism was at first by no means welcomed in England. The Church, moderately but decidedly Augustinian in its theology, looked with hostility upon the liberal movement in Holland. James I. professed to be a strong Calvinist; and when the Synod of Dort was convened, sent to it, as is well known, a deputation from the Church of England to countenance and strengthen the Calvinists against the Remonstrants. This they did; but the effect of their visit, and still more the visit of one [1] who was not a member of the deputation, but who had accompanied the English ambassador to the Hague, was different from what was intended. The proceedings of the Synod, however favourable to the Calvinian party, were highly unfavourable to dogmatic peace and Christian concord. The questions supposed to be settled, when transferred to an English atmosphere, were discussed over again with very different results in the case of many of the most active-minded and influential of the clergy. James himself, although he did not formally abjure

[1] Hales—see following Chapter.

his Calvinism, was perplexed by the manifestations of the new doctrinal spirit. Those among the clergy who began to incline to Arminianism were found by him the most favourably disposed to his favourite ideas of royal prerogative, while the Puritans were all strict Calvinists. And much as he loved Calvinism, he loved servility and the principle of passive obedience still more. Thus it was that, even before the accession of Charles and the date of Laud's influence, the current of royal favour had begun to flow steadily towards the novel doctrines and those who espoused them. So far, Arminianism became in England merely another form of dogmatism. It passed in fact into the Anglo-Catholic movement as its theological background, and gave to it a party meaning and consistency which it had not hitherto possessed. It became, along with Popery, a subject of Parliamentary complaint. The High Church and the Puritan parties were henceforth divided theologically as well as ecclesiastically; and the dogmatism of Montague and of Laud himself was more "resolved,"[1] while really less intelligent and devout, than the Calvinism of Abbot. But Arminianism was, we have seen, a great deal more than a mere system of doctrines. It raised, wherever it spread, a new spirit of religious inquiry. It opened up large questions as to the interpretation of Scripture, and the position and value of dogma altogether, and, in short, diffused a latitudinarian atmosphere. The liberal impulses which it thus helped to com-

---

[1] Laud's own expression in speaking of Montague's "alleged heresies." Montague was Bishop of Chichester, 1628-1638.

municate to a few thoughtful minds in England will be abundantly evident in the course of our volumes.

(*b*.) But strangely, also, the very activities of Popery at this time served to quicken in England a new seed of thought. The Roman Church had never lost the hope of winning back the English crown and people to its old Catholic allegiance. It had never, even after the death of Mary, and the defeat of its great champion, Philip of Spain, quite abandoned its intrigues for this purpose; and now in the last years of James, and especially following the marriage of Charles with a Catholic princess, it renewed its efforts with redoubled zeal. Flushed by the success of the Jesuits on the Continent, and well informed of the prevalent ecclesiastical divisions, it sent its emissaries throughout England, under feigned names, everywhere to foment the disunion of the two parties, and to insinuate the claims of Roman Catholicism as the only remedy for the distractions of controversy, and the only means of establishing a stable theology and Church order. Many of the higher classes, as in more recent times, were won over by the seductions of these clever and polished polemics. Buckingham's mother became a pervert as early as 1622; and Buckingham himself seemed on the eve of yielding to "the continual cunning labours of Fisher the Jesuit, and the persuasions of the lady his mother."[1] Laud claimed the credit

---

[1] Laud's own statement in his speech to the Lords, 1643. He mentions no fewer than twenty cases of such perverts or waverers whom, "by God's blessing upon his labours," he succeeded in "settling in the true Protestant religion." See as to the extent

"by God's blessing" of rescuing him as well as many others from their danger, and especially, as is well known, of bringing back Chillingworth to the bosom of the Church of England. The fact that a mind like Chillingworth's was entangled by the thickly-sown sophistries, is enough to show how powerful they were, and how ingenious and seasonable their adaptation to the intellectual and spiritual atmosphere of the time. But the very stress of the Jesuit arguments opened the way for a more rational theory of religion. The necessity of an infallible Church was their great point. How could men believe aright without some "certain guide"? How could the form of the Church be settled without some power to settle it? It was the pressure of such questions that drove minds like Falkland and Chillingworth to examine the whole subject of authority in religion, and to work it out to its only consistent and reasonable conclusion. Thus, as also in later times, the wave of rational and of Jesuit thought met in collision—the aggressions of the one serving to evoke the full strength and life of the other.

of the Romanising influence at this time in England, Hallam's Constitut. History, ii. 66, 67, 10th ed.; Masson's Milton, i. 638 *et seq.*

III.

LORD FALKLAND—A MODERATE AND LIBERAL CHURCH.

I. THE commencement of our movement is associated with a name of romantic interest in English history—that of Lucius Cary, the second Lord Falkland. There are few more charming sketches in English literature—and none more charming in all the attractive series from the same pen—than Lord Clarendon's sketch of this friend of his youth;[1] while his melancholy fate, almost at the opening of the civil war, has deepened the interest of a singular career, and lent to it something of tragic pathos. It is true that Clarendon's portrait is warmly coloured. Not only the magic of his art, but the ideal enthusiasm which lit up the image of a long-vanished friend, may be traced in its glowing lines. Such side-lights of contemporary testimony as we possess regarding Falkland, are also somewhat vaguely admiring and indefinite. There is a sort of

---

[1] Lord Clarendon has sketched his friend's character in his History of the Rebellion, chiefly in Book VII. (ii. 445-455, Clar. Press Ed.), but also, and still more elaborately, in his later work—the Memoirs of his life, written in continuation of his History after his final banishment from England in 1667 (i. 42-50, Clar. Press Ed.)

nimbus about the figure, which prevents us seeing it in the full daylight in which we see many of his contemporaries. But when men like Horace Walpole[1] infer from this that Falkland has been greatly over-estimated, and that his actions by no means equal his fame—they forget how brief his career was, and mistake its true significance. He was only thirty-three when he fell at Newbury; and it is not as a politician that he claims our special admiration, as it is not in this aspect indeed that he is so applausively described by Clarendon. Falkland may not have been fitted for the stormy career in which he had reluctantly embarked. He was incapable of becoming either a Clarendon on the one side or a Cromwell on the other. He lacked the hardy fibre which makes men go straight and unscrupulously at their object—a special source of weakness in such a time. But hardihood of political bias is by no means so rare a virtue that it is to be placed above all others. And Falkland's true portrait is not that of the politician or the soldier, but of the poet, the scholar, the theological controversialist, and, above all, the inspiring chief of a circle of rational and moderate thinkers amidst the excesses of a violent and dogmatic age. Fortunately, also, it is in these aspects that we can now most fairly judge him. His poems, his speeches concerning Episcopacy, and his Discourse on Infallibility survive, and bring before us as living an image of his mind and stamp of thought as we could desire. If Walpole had appreciated— what, indeed, was not to be expected of him—the

[1] Royal and Noble Authors, vol. v.

intellectual significance of Falkland's position, and the true charm of his influence, he would never have spoken of his weakness and mediocrity. A man's contemporaries may not always be the best judge of his character and abilities; but it would indeed have been strange if one who not only has been celebrated by Suckling, Ben Jonson, and Cowley, and lovingly sketched by Clarendon, but who was also honoured by Hales, and consulted in argument by Chillingworth, should not have possessed remarkable powers. The study of Falkland's remains appear to us fully to warrant the distinction which has gathered around his name, and the importance which we assign to him in our history.

Lucius Cary was descended from the Carys of Cockington, in Devonshire—an old knightly family. His grandfather, Sir Edward Cary, appears to have removed to Hertfordshire, where his father, Henry, was born at Aldenham, probably about the middle of Elizabeth's reign. This, the first Lord Falkland, was a man of distinguished, although unsuccessful, political eminence. He was educated at Exeter College, Oxford, which he left without taking any degree, but where he seems to have left behind him a celebrated social name. It is said by Fuller,[1] that his chamber was the rendezvous of all "the wits, philosophers, and divines of the period;" but it has been conjectured, not improbably, that there is some confusion betwixt this traditionary repute of the father as a student, and the subsequent well-known social position occupied by his son in connection

[1] Worthies of England, quoted by Wood and in Biog. Brit., but we have failed to verify the reference.

with Oxford. After being introduced at Court, Sir Henry Cary rose rapidly from post to post till he became a Privy Councillor in 1617, and in 1620 was created Viscount of Falkland, in the county of Fife, in Scotland, in pursuance of a policy begun by James and continued by Charles of bestowing Scotch titles upon Englishmen, with an idea of thereby bringing the two countries into union. Under this title he proceeded to Ireland two years later, where he governed as Lord Deputy till 1629. He was then recalled in disgrace—a victim to intrigues both in Ireland and the English Court. On the one hand, he has been blamed for keeping too strict a rein over the Roman Catholics; and on the other hand, Leland, in his ' History of Ireland,' accuses his government of indolence and weakness. The truth appears to be, that he failed to appreciate Charles's true designs, or to make himself useful in furthering them. He was evidently an ambitious, strong-tempered, and accomplished man, with more address in gaining power than ability in maintaining it. His later position at the English Court, without definite trust or employment, must have been highly uncomfortable. Clarendon speaks of his "broken fortunes;" and his relations to his son, after the latter's marriage without his approval, cannot have added to his happiness. He composed a 'History of the most unfortunate Prince, King Edward II.,' which was not published till 1680; and an epitaph—" not bad," Walpole says —on Elizabeth, Countess of Huntingdon.[1] He was also remarkable, according to the same authority, "for an invention to prevent his name being counter-

[1] This epitaph is also, and more probably, ascribed to the son.

feited, by artfully concealing in it the successive year of his age."[1]

The mother of Lucius was the "sole daughter and heir" of Sir Lawrence Tenfield, Chief Baron of Exchequer. We know little of her beyond the fact of her perversion to Romanism. She was so devoted to her new faith, that she came, in 1634, under the notice of Laud, who, in a letter to the King, dated July in that year, asks leave to bring the "old lady," for her interfering zeal, before the Court of High Commission.[2] She was, like Buckingham's mother, one of the victims of the Jesuit missionaries who then infested England, and seems to have carried with her not only her daughters, but her younger sons. This is to be remembered in connection with Falkland's earnestness on the subject of Infallibility. If himself unmoved by the same influences, he had yet in many ways been brought into contact with the unceasing activity and marvellous seductions of Jesuitism.

Lucius Cary was born, according to the common authorities,[3] at Burford, a market-town in Oxfordshire, about the year 1610. The manor of Great Tew, which afterwards became so associated with his name as his favourite residence, and the rendezvous of his poetical and theological friends, was in the immediate neighbourhood. This and another estate,[4] which is described by Wood as the "priory,

[1] Royal and Noble Authors, v. 72.
[2] Masson's Milton, i. 639, 640.
[3] Biog. Brit., Wood, Ath. Oxon.

There is no record of the birth in the public register of the place, which commences about the beginning of the reign of James I.
[4] Clarendon says that his grand-

with the rectory and demesnes of Burford," were the property of his maternal grandfather, and came to him by direct inheritance. Wood infers that he was born at Burford, because from inquiry at the "ancients of that town," he learned that he was certainly nursed there. Lucius was accordingly about twelve years of age when his father went to Ireland as Lord Deputy in 1622. Immediately thereafter he appears to have begun his studies at Trinity College, Dublin. All contemporary registers have disappeared, and we can only conjecture what his course of education was by its results. Clarendon says that he made better progress in academic " exercises and languages than most men do in more celebrated places—insomuch as when he came into England, which was when he was about the age of eighteen years, he was not only master of the Latin tongue, and had read all the poets, and other of the best authors with notable judgment for that age, but he understood, and spake, and writ French, as if he had spent many years in France." [1]

The religious influences which surrounded him in Trinity College were decidedly Calvinistic, inclining to Puritanism. In the close of Elizabeth's reign, Ireland became the refuge of many of the reforming divines uneasy under the prelatic restraints which

father settled his property "in such manner upon his grandson, Sir Lucius Cary, without taking notice of his father or mother, that upon his grandmother's death all the land, with two very good houses, very well furnished (worth above £2000 per annum), in a most pleasant country, and the two most pleasant places in that country, with a very plentiful personal estate, fell into his hands and possession, and to his entire disposal."—Life, p. 43.

[1] Life, p. 42, 43.

hemmed them about in England; and Trinity College at its foundation in 1593 was supplied with eminent Calvinistic professors from Cambridge. The Irish Articles of 1615 remain the abiding memorial of the hardy predestinarianism of the Irish Protestant Church. Usher, their reputed author, was Provost of Trinity College when young Falkland entered it, and during his time of study here—in 1624—was promoted to the Irish Primacy. It is not improbable that the theological atmosphere which thus surrounded our young student influenced him through life. For, unlike his friends, Hales and Chillingworth, Falkland seems to have remained a Calvinist,[1] and even strongly denounced Arminianism along with Popery in his first speeches in the Long Parliament. Nor is it impossible that he derived from this early time the first impulse towards those latitudinarian views of Church government for which he was afterwards distinguished. For the university authorities in Dublin, and Usher conspicuously — strange as this may seem — were no less remarkable for their liberal ecclesiasticism than for their rigid doctrinal orthodoxy. They strongly rejected that idea of a *jus divinum* of Episcopacy which had been spreading in England from the beginning of the century, and advocated a modified Episcopal organisation which left room for presbyterial action and certain elements of popular or congregational freedom.

On his return to England, it has been alleged that Falkland entered St John's College, *Oxford.* But

[1] See subsequent page as to Aubrey's charge of Socinianism.

there is no evidence of this: his name does not occur in the register of St John's, Oxford; and the story, frequently repeated, has probably arisen from the fact that, so early as 1621, before his father went to Ireland, he appears to have been entered with his brother Lorenzo at St John's, Cambridge. This at least is the inference left to be drawn from a statement in Baker's history of this College, recently printed, as well as from a letter of Falkland's addressed to Dr Beale, the head of the College, in January 1641-2.[1]

[1] The fact remains doubtful notwithstanding, and we have not been able to clear it up. The Biog. Brit. expressly says, "There is no account of his admittance in St John's College registers." If admitted in 1621, it can only have been with a view to future attendance, which never took place—the father's departure for Ireland having led to the abandonment of the plan of his son's studying at Cambridge. The statement in Baker's history occurs in the 'Catalogus Episcoporum qui e Collegio Divi Joannes Evangelistæ prodierunt,' printed pp. 242-80, vol. i. of the volumes recently edited by Mr Mayor of St John's (1869), and is as follows: "Robertus Dawson natus Kendalæ . . . admissus est Socius Coll. Jo. pro doctore Lupton Apr. 6, an. 1609: bach. theol. an. 1620; non diu moram traxit apud nos, *admissus in familiam Henrici Vicecomitis Falkland proregis*, factus illius sacellanus eique (ni faller) *debemus quod Lucius Cary filius primogenitus vicecomitis Falkland admissus est in collegium an.* 1621 (una cum fratre suo Lorenzo Cary) in honorem collegii," p. 263. The following is the letter addressed by Falkland to Dr Beale, the head of the College, in the beginning of 1641-2:—

"Sir,—I received lately a letter from your selfe and others of your noble society, wherein as many titles were given me to which I had none, so that which I shold most willingly have acknowledged and mought with most justice clayme, you were not pleased to vouchsafe me, that is, *that of a St John's man*. I confess I am both proud and ashamed of that, and the latter in respect that the fruites are unproportionable to the seed-plott. Yet, Sʳ, as little learning as I brought from you, and as little as I have since encreased and watered what I did bring, I am sure that I shall carry about with me an indelible character of affection and duty to that society, and an extraordinary longing for some occasion of expressing that affection and that duty. I shall desire you to express this to them, and to adde this, that as I shall never forgett *myself to be a member of their Body*, so I shall be ready to catch at all meanes of de-

It is clear, on other grounds, that academic study cannot have been Falkland's occupation during the years that followed his return to England. Within a year of this event he succeeded to his grandfather's estates. Clarendon expressly says that this took place "about the time that he was nineteen years of age,"[1] or in 1629. About the same time he had begun to form those literary connections which became so great a feature in his life. This is evident from Ben Jonson's verses, in the series of poems which he has entitled 'Underwoods.'[2] The verses are inscribed—"To the immortal memory and friendship of that noble pair, Sir Lucius Cary and Sir Henry Morison." Now Sir Henry Morison was the brother of the lady

claring my selfe to be not only to the Body, but every member of it, S^r, your very humble servant,

"FALKLAND.

"Endorsed: For the President of St John's College in Cambridge, with my humble service."

This letter, with the Latin letter to which it is a reply, and which certainly does not spare epithets such as "Rhetorem, Poetam (vah plebeia nomina) imo vero Philosophum, Militem, Politicum," is found at p. 532, vol. i. of the edition of Baker's history, from which we have already quoted. It was also printed long ago in the notice of Falkland in the 'Biographia Britannica.' Yet in the face of all, and even quoting the above letter in a footnote, Lady Theresa Lewis, in her 'Lives of the Friends and

Contemporaries of Lord Clarendon,' the first volume of which is almost entirely given to Lord Falkland, expressly asserts that it was St John's College, *Oxford*, of which he was a member. "He playfully alludes to this circumstance," she says, "in speaking of himself as 'a St John's man.'" The Parish History of Burford also says that "Lucius Cary completed his education *after Dublin* by a residence at Oxford."

[1] Life, p. 43.

[2] "As the multitude call timber-trees promiscuously growing a wood or forest, so I am bold to entitle these lesser poems of lesser growth by this of Underwood, out of the analogy they hold to the forest in my former book, and no otherwise." — Ben Jonson: "To the Reader."

whom Falkland married "before he was of age;"[1] and, previous to this event, Morison died. We must suppose, therefore, not only his courtship, but the commencement and completion of this memorable friendship in which Jonson shared, to have been embraced within these years. Both Morison and Falkland had plainly made a strong impression upon Jonson and the literary society to which he belonged; and the verses in which he describes their affection for each other, and seeks consolation for Morison's untimely death, are here and there very touching. Nothing, for example, can be more exquisite than the following lines, which might be applied prophetically to Falkland himself:—

> "It is not growing like a tree
> In bulk, doth make men better be;
> Or standing long an oak, three hundred year,
> To fall a log at last, dry, bald, and sear:
> A lily of a day
> Is fairer far in May,
> Although it fall and die that night;
> It was the plant, the flower of light.
> In small proportions we just beauties see;
> And in short measures, life may perfect be."

Thus early young Falkland was launched upon the world, and become known as the friend of Ben Jonson and the bright circle of poetic wits—Suckling, Davenant, Carew, and others—that formed his earliest literary and social connection.

But during this period (1629-31), he was busy not only with such distractions, but with others still more incompatible with quiet academic study. He was a

[1] Clar. Life, p. 44.

prisoner in the Fleet for misdemeanour during ten days in the commencement of 1630.[1] In a letter or petition[2] from his father to the King at this time, Lord Falkland says: "I had a son, until I lost him in your Highness's displeasure where I cannot seek him, because I have not will to find him there. Men say there is a wild young man now prisoner in the Fleet for measuring his actions by his own private fence." This was no doubt the source of Wood's statement[3] that Lucius was "a wild youth;" and the suggestion has been tempting to biographical gossip. The full explanation of the affair, however, is given in the correspondence and extracts from the Council Register presented in the appendix to Lady Lewis's volume. It appears that a "company" of which young Falkland had the command was transferred by order of the King to Sir Francis Willoughby. Willoughby explains at length that he had nothing to do with the act of transference; but our young soldier is highly indignant, and demands satisfaction with the sword. "I doe confesse youe," he says, "a brave gentleman (and for myne owne sake I would not but have my adversary be soe), but I knowe noe reason why, therefore, you showld have my breechez, which yf every brave man showld have, I showld be fayne shortly toe begg in trowses. I dowght not but youe will give me satisfaction with your sworde, of which yf you will send me the lengthe, with tyme and place, youe shal be sure (according toe an

---

[1] January 17-27, 1629-30.
[2] The letter is preserved in the collection called 'Cabala,' and printed in the Biog. Brit., as well as by Lady Lewis.
[3] Ath. Oxon.

appointment) toe meete." He was evidently a fiery and high-tempered gentleman at the age of twenty, and resolved, as he himself says, as he could not " strike at the head, to strike at the stone that lies lower." The result was that a warrant was issued from Whitehall to the warden of the Fleet "to receive into his custody the person of Sir Lucius Cary, and to keep him prisoner until further order." Happily the order for his liberation is dated, as we have indicated, only ten days later,—so that the intervention of his father appears to have been successful. There is no information as to the King's purpose throughout the business, or as to whether the withdrawal of the son's command had anything to do with the father's dishonoured position at Court. Whatever its cause may have been, the slight, it is plain, was deeply resented by young Cary, driving him as it did beyond all reasonable bounds of quarrel with his successor in the command of the company. It may be doubted whether it was ever entirely forgotten amidst all the painful experience which Falkland had of the after-conduct of the King.

Falkland's marriage was not without the romantic interest which attaches more or less to all his life. The lady, we have seen, was the sister of his beloved friend and companion,[1] and he married her in spite of his father's earnest wishes to form a richer and more noble alliance for him. So strongly did the latter resent his son's conduct, that he broke off all connection with him, and refused all offers of

---

[1] The father was Sir Richard Morison, of Tooley Park, Leicestershire.

mediation. The affair, as described by Clarendon, well illustrates the temper of both father and son. " In a short time after he had possession of the estate his grandfather had left him, and before he was of age, he committed a fault against his father, in marrying a young lady whom he passionately loved, without any considerable portion, which exceedingly offended him, and disappointed all his reasonable hopes and expectation of redeeming and repairing his own broken fortune and desperate hopes in Court, by some advantageous marriage of his son, about which he had then some probable treaty. Sir Lucius Cary was very conscious to himself of his offence and transgression, and the consequence of it, which though he could not repent, having married a lady of a most extraordinary wit and judgment, and of the most signal virtue and exemplary life that the age produced,[1] and who brought

---

[1] The character which Clarendon gives to Lady Falkland does not appear overdrawn, and it is somewhat singular that we hear so little of her. For her life had a distinct religious interest of its own. A small volume entitled " The Holy Life and Death of the Lady Letece, Vi-Countess Falkland, &c., by John Duncon Parson (sequestered)," ran through several editions in the period preceding the Restoration. The edition before us is the *third*, bearing the date of 1653. It contains not only a life, but certain letters, all designed to set forth the many excellent virtues of the Lady Falkland, and to present " the figure of a pious soul, with its vicissitudes of comfort and grief." The letters are not her own, but composed, as well as the answers to them, by the author of the volume, thus giving, as he says, "not a strict relation, but a representation." ". Having learned all her objections against herself," he explains, "and having seen the chief sorrow of her heart, I composed them into these letters, and annexed these answers to them, and left them with her." In short, " the lineaments are drawn from the holy lady's soul— not exactly," but with a view to the general purposes of a pious manual. From such a volume it is not easy to glean any clear outline of facts, or indeed of character; yet the

him many hopeful children in which he took great delight, yet he confessed it, with the most sincere and dutiful applications to his father for his pardon that could be made; and for the prejudice he had

somewhat vague "lineaments" which it records, evidently shows that Lady Falkland was no ordinary person. She seems quite entitled to take her place beside Mrs Hutchison, or Evelyn's accomplished and pious friend, Lady Margaret Godolphin, who on opposite sides gave the lustre of their simple, earnest, and unaffected piety to soften and irradiate the miseries of a period of gloomy religious conflict. We are told "She spent some hours every day in her private cloisters and meditations, and these were called her busy hours. . . . Then her maids came into her chamber every morning, and ordinarily she passed about an hour with them in praying, catechising, and instructing them. . . . On the Lord's Day she rose in the morning earlier than ordinarily, yet enjoined herself so much private duty with her children and servants (examining them in the sermons and catechisings), and with her own soul, that oftentimes the day was too short for her. . . . There was near acquaintance between her and some strict Papists, and as near between her and some stricter Nonconformists, and she not only warily avoided the superstition of the one, and the nonconformity of the other, but also earnestly laboured to reduce the one and the other from their erroneous ways. . . . Her young and most dear son Lorenzo (whom God had endowed with the cleverest of natural abilities, and to whom her affections were most tender by reason of these fair blossoms of piety) God takes away from her. This added to her former troubles of the loss of her husband, of her crosses in the world, and her spiritual afflictions."

Enough has been extracted to bring the picture of a fair and high character before the reader; and yet this is the same lady of whom Aubrey, in his sketch of her husband, tells the following ridiculous and unworthy story: "When she had a mind to beg anything of my lord for one of her maids, women, nurses, she would say (however unreasonable the request) 'I warrant you, for all this, I will obtain it of my lord; *it will cost me but the expense of a few tears.*' Now she could make her words good; and this great wit, the greatest master of reason and judgment of his time, at the long-run, being stormed by her tears (I presume there were kisses and secret embraces that were also ingredients), would this pious lady obtain her unreasonable desires of her lord." Those who can believe a story of this kind may also believe Aubrey's further scandal, "that it was the grief of the death of Mrs

brought upon his fortune, by bringing no fortune to him, he offered to repair it by resigning his whole estate to his disposal, and to rely wholly upon his kindness for his own maintenance and support; and to that purpose he had caused conveyances to be drawn by counsel, which he brought ready engrossed to his father, and was willing to seal and execute them, that they might be valid: but his father's passion and indignation so far transported him (though he was a gentleman of excellent parts), that he refused any reconciliation, and rejected all the offers that were made him of the estate, so that his son remained still in the possession of his estate against his will, for which he found great reason afterwards to rejoice."[1]

In consequence of this disagreement with his father, and probably also on account of his unpleasant relations with the Court, and the frustration at home of the military ambition which he had cherished, and which remained one of his strongest impulses,[2] he " transported himself and his wife into Holland—resolving," says Clarendon, " to buy some military command and to spend the remainder of his life in that profession." Here also, however, disap-

---

Moray, a handsome lady at Court, *who was his mistress*, and whom he loved above all creatures, was the true cause of his (Falkland's) being so madly guilty of his own death." In a future page we discuss the credibility of Aubrey's statements, and show how entirely undeserving of trust they must be held in matters of opinion or character, or indeed in any matters save those personal details and recollections which lie within the province of the gossip.

[1] Clar., p. 44, 45.
[2] " In his natural inclination," says Clarendon (History, ii. 453, Def. Press.), " he acknowledged that he was addicted to the profession of a soldier."

pointment awaited him. He found no scope for his military aspirations, and returned again within a brief interval to England. Holland was at this time resting after its long internal conflicts, following the independence which it had so bravely won under the great William of Orange and his son. Maurice's death had brought comparative peace to the raging factions of Gomarists and Remonstrants which had divided it; and in the very year (1631) of Falkland's visit, Grotius had returned from his long exile in France, and been temporarily received with great rejoicing throughout the country which had treated him so shamefully. It is not improbable that our enthusiastic young Englishman, with that singular affinity which he had for whatever was noble and distinguished in character, may have made, during his visit, the acquaintance of the great jurist and divine. The verses which he afterwards inscribed to him,[1] are full, not only of lofty admiration, but of some warmth of personal feeling :—

> " Our Age's warder, by thy birth the fame
> Of Belgia, by thy banishment the shame.
>
> . . . thy age and art seemed to unite,
> At once the youth of Phœbus and the light.
>
> . . . *your acquaintance all of worth pursue,
> And count it honour to be known of you.*"

He had evidently in any case studied Grotius, and felt his own love of truth and clearness of thought developed by contact with this luminous, liberal, and eminently rational intellect.

[1] Prefixed to George Sandys' translation of Grotius' Tragedy of Christ's Passion.

"Though Truth doe naked to thy sight appeare,
And scarce can we doubt more then thou can'st cleare;
Though thou at once dost diferent glories joyne,
A loftie Poet and a deep Divine;
Canst in the purest phrase cloath solid sence,
Scaevola's law in Tully's eloquence;
Though thy employments have exceld thy pen,
Shew'd thee much skil'd in books, but more in men,
And prov'd thou canst at the same easy rate,
Correct an author, as uphold a State.
All this yet of thy worth makes but a part
And we admire thy head lesse then thy heart;
Which (when in want) was yet too brave to close
(Though woo'd) with thy ungratefull countrie's foes.
Since all our praise and wonder is too small,
For each of these, what shall we give for all?
All that we can, we doe—a pen divine,
And differing onely in the tongue from thine,
Doth thy choice labours with successe rehearse,
And to another world transplants thy verse;
At the same height to which before they rose,
When they forc'd wonder from unwilling foes:
Now Thames with Ganges may thy labours praise
Which there breed faith, and here devotion raise."[1]

On Falkland's return to England he abandoned for the time all political and military pursuits, and retired to his residence at Great Tew—"to a country life, and to his books; that since he was not like to improve himself in arms, he might advance in letters." This must have been in the course of 1632; and now for seven years, during all the unhappy period of Wentworth's and Laud's tyrannies, known as "Thorough,"[2] Falkland is to be conceived

---

[1] A reference to Grotius' well-known treatise 'De Veritate Religionis Christianæ'—the original design of which was the conversion of the Indians.

[2] "The word 'Thorough' as de-

in the main as settled on his estates in Oxfordshire, engaged in the study of Greek—classical and patristic—completing his education, pursued in so desultory a manner during the three preceding years—elaborating those religious and political opinions which were to guide his public career—and gathering around him that group of thinkers which, though they exercised for a while but little influence on the course of affairs, were even then acknowledged to be a distinct and significant party. The progress of violence first on the one side and then on the other had its way, and bore down both him and them; but the influence of their opinion survived, and continued to gather force with advancing thought, and the resurgence of excited passions on both sides.

We have no particular information as to the manner in which Falkland and his friends looked upon the doings of Wentworth and Laud. But in the light of his later speeches on Episcopacy there is little difficulty in understanding his feelings, and the deep indignation which the prevalent ecclesiastical cruelties must have excited in his breast. It is strange to

fining the policy of the Government from 1633 onwards, appears first in the correspondence between Laud and Wentworth. 'As for the State,' says Laud, writing to Wentworth, Sept. 9, 1633, 'indeed, my lord, I am for *Thorough*, but I see that both thick and thin stays somebody where I conceive it should not, and it is impossible for me to go *Thorough* alone.' The word once introduced, they play upon it between them in future letters, writing it sometimes in cipher, sometimes openly. Thus Wentworth to Laud, Aug. 23, 1634: 'Go as it shall please God with me, believe me, my lord, I will be *Thorough* and *Thoroughout*, one and the same;' to which Laud replies, Oct. 20: 'As for my marginal note, I see you deciphered it well, and I see you make use of it too: do so still: *Thorough* and *Thorough*.'"— Masson's Milton, p. 620, 621.

reflect on the outrages against religious liberty which were proceeding during the very time that Falkland and Chillingworth were debating over the 'Religion of Protestants.' In the same year in which Chillingworth's great work—which had been argued out betwixt the two friends, and mainly composed at Falkland's residence—saw the light, Prynne, and Bastwick, and Burton, had their ears cut off in Palace Yard, Westminster, for venturing to impugn the prelatic constitution of the Church of England. The period was one in which all wise men were more or less in retirement, and when many, as is well known, would have gladly left England for ever if they had not been prevented—unwittingly detained on the part of those who interfered with them for higher work at home.[1]

The death of his father in 1633 formed a temporary break in his retirement. It took him back to London sooner than he intended, and of course weighted him with cares and duties from which he had been hitherto exempt. The fact of his having been thus obliged to return unexpectedly to London is particularly noticed by Clarendon. He had declared, when he went to the country, that "he would not see London in many years, which was the place he loved of all the world;" but now his father's death by an unhappy accident— a fall which he had from "a stand in Theobald's Park"—"made his repair to London absolutely

[1] Hampden and Cromwell both, it is well known, along with others destined to be conspicuous in the ensuing troubles, had made up their minds to emigrate, when Charles's tyrannic policy—blind in every direction—interfered to prevent them.

necessary in fewer years than he had proposed for his absence." He does not seem, however, with all his fondness for town and its companionships, to have tarried longer in it on this occasion than was necessary. As soon as he had finished the transactions consequent on the death of his father, " he retired again to his country life, and to his severe course of study, which was very delightful to him as soon as he was engaged in it; but he was wont to say, that he never found reluctancy in anything he resolved to do, but in his quitting London, and departing from the conversation of those he enjoyed there; which was in some degree preserved and continued by frequent letters, and often visits, which were made by his friends from thence, whilst he continued wedded to the country."[1]

It is evident that Falkland had two sets of friends among his intellectual contemporaries, and that the graver philosophical and theological set, to which Clarendon specially alludes, came in some degree in succession to the poetic friends of his youth. Gradually he abandoned poetry for divinity; and it is in the later years of his residence at Tew, following his second retirement after his father's death—say from 1635 to the spring of 1639—that we may conceive him to have added divines such as Hammond, and Sheldon, and Morley to his acquaintance, and converted his society into the *convivium theologicum* so well described by Clarendon. Suckling's well-known lines imply this; while, along with his own verses on the death of Ben Jonson, they bring

[1] Clar. Life, p. 47.

before us a vivid picture of that earlier group of the "wits of the town" whose companionship and conversation were so enjoyable to him when in London. It is interesting to notice that Hales and Chillingworth are both mentioned in Suckling's lines; and so we gather that they were amongst Falkland's friends in his earlier as well as his later mood of mind, and were indeed his friends and intellectual associates in a sense which can hardly be supposed true of men like Sheldon and Morley. It was natural for Clarendon writing after the Restoration to emphasise such names, but Falkland himself would probably have dwelt more upon the bright circle of his more youthful years :—

> "Digby, Carew, Killigrew, and Maine,
> Godolphin, Waller, that inspirèd traine."[1]

The list is more fully given by Suckling, and deserves to be transferred to our pages for its own sake, as well as for the pleasant glimpse which it gives us of a bygone literary society, of which Falkland was evidently a conspicuous member.

> "There Selden, and he sat hard by the chair;
> Weniman not far off, which was very fair;
> Sands with Townsend, for they keep no order,
> Digby and Shillingworth a little further:

[1] Eclogue on the death of Ben Jonson. Of the less known names of Killigrew and Maine, it may be mentioned that the first was King Charles's Jester, and the second Dr Jasper Mayne, a dramatist and versifier, as well as preacher of the period. The same names are found associated with Falkland's own in George Daniel's MS. poems :—
"The noble *Falkland, Digbie, Carew, Maine.*
Beaumond, Sands," &c.
—Falkland's Poems, ed. by Rev. A. B. Grossart—1871: note, p. 48.

And there was Lucan's translator too, and he
That makes God speak so big in 's poetry;
Selwin and Walter, and Bartlets both the brothers,
Jack Vaughan and Porter, and divers others.

The first that broke silence was good old Ben,
Prepar'd before with Canary wine,
And he told them plainly he deserv'd the bays,
For his were call'd works, where others were but plays.

Tom Carew was next, but he had a fault
That would not well stand with a laureate;
His muse was hard bound, and th' issue of 's brain
Was seldom brought forth but with trouble and pain.

Will Davenant, asham'd of a foolish mischief
That he had got lately travelling in France,
Modestly hoped the handsomeness of his muse
Might any deformity about him excuse.

Suckling next was call'd, but did not appear:
But straight one whisper'd Apollo i' th' ear,
That of all men living he cared not for't,
He loved not the muses so well as his sport.

Wat Montague now stood forth to his trial,
And did not so much as expect a denial;
But witty Apollo asked him first of all
If he understood his own pastoral.

Hales, set by himself, most gravely did smile
To see them about nothing keep such a coil;
Apollo had spied him, but knowing his mind,
Past by, and called Falkland that sat just behind.

He was of late so gone with divinity
That he had almost forgot his poetry,
Though to say the truth, and Apollo did know it,
He might have been both his priest and his poet."

It is impossible to draw out into the light such a group of names, some of whom have left no impress upon our literature, and no memory of any kind. But, passing by in the mean time Hales and Chillingworth, who will afterwards appear prominently in our pages, there are a few of the others that claim recognition both in connection with Falkland personally and with our subject.

Selden's is the first, and in some respects the most distinguished. He was at this time—say 1637, when Suckling's verses were published—about fifty years of age, and had long enjoyed an exceptional reputation for the extent and variety of his learning. His famous treatise on Tithes had appeared about twenty years before (1618). "By the help of a strong body and a vast memory," says Wood, he had become "a prodigy in most parts of learning, especially in those which were not common. He had great skill in the divine and human laws; he was a great philologist, antiquary, herald, linguist, statesman, and what not." Clarendon[1] is even more enthusiastic: " He was of so stupendous learning in all kinds and in all languages (as may appear in his excellent and transcendent writings), that a man would have thought he had been entirely conversant among books, and had never spent an hour but in reading and writing; yet his humanity, courtesy, and affability was such that he would have been thought to have been bred in the best courts, but that his good-nature, charity, and delight in doing good, and in communicating all he knew, exceeded that breeding." While in his

[1] Life, p. 35.

writings his style "seems harsh and sometimes obscure, in his conversation he was the most clear discourser, and had the best faculty of making hard things easy, and presenting them to the understanding of any man that hath been known." A great friend of Ben Jonson, he belonged himself in a slight way to the poetic fraternity as an occasional writer of verses in English, as well as in Greek and Latin. Falkland greatly admired him, and, according to Clarendon, "knew him so well" that he became on an important occasion, on which Charles wished to influence Selden, the medium of communication between him and the King. He may have learned from the older statesman's cynical thoughtfulness and contempt of extremes, something of his own clearness and liberality in religious matters. Selden's facility during the troubles that ensued has been blamed; but there is no reason to doubt that he was animated throughout by a sincere love of liberty — that liberty which, according to his own chosen motto, was "above everything."[1] He had been early disgusted at the bishops by the treatment to which they subjected him after the publication of his book on Tithes. Their usage "sunk deep into his stomach," and he was heartily glad when the storm swept them away. But while he worked with the Puritan party, he was entirely free from their prejudices. A story is told by Whitelock of the delight which he took in perplexing some of the divines in the Westminster Assembly, of which he was an active member. Sometimes when they had

[1] Περὶ παντὸς τὴν ἐλευθερίαν.

cited a text of Scripture to prove their assertions, he would say, " Perhaps in your little pocket-Bibles with gilt leaves [which they would often pull out and read] the translation may be thus, but the Greek and the Hebrew signify thus and thus," and so would totally silence them. There is something of insolence as well as wit, it must be allowed, in this story. Many of the Westminster divines must have been quite a match for even Selden in Biblical learning. Yet a tradition of this kind serves to show the spirit of the great lawyer. He had evidently no love for the clergy, either Episcopal or Puritan, and especially detested clerical prejudices, the pretensions to special orthodoxy, and the dogmatic opinionativeness so prevalent in his time. One of the best and most characteristic of his sayings in his 'Table-Talk,' which is hardly worthy of his reputation as a whole, clearly and admirably shows this. " 'Tis vain to talk of an heretic, for a man for his heart can think no otherwise than he does think. In the primitive times there were many opinions; nothing scarce but some or other held. One of these opinions being embraced by some prince, and received into his kingdom, the rest were condemned as heresies; and his religion, which was but one of the several opinions, first is said to be orthodox, and so to have continued ever since the apostles."[1]

George Sandys (the " Sands " of the poem) was one of Falkland's choicest friends not mentioned by Clarendon at all. He was the youngest son of the Archbishop of York, whose sufferings in the cause

[1] Table-Talk, p. 105, 106. Singer's ed., 1856.

of the Reformation, and subsequent promotion in the reign of Elizabeth, are well known, and the brother of Hooker's pupil associated with the half-pathetic, half-ludicrous story of the great author of the ' Laws of Ecclesiastical Polity' " rocking the cradle" in his parsonage at Drayton Beauchamp. He was more than thirty years Falkland's senior, having been born in 1577; but peculiar ties of sympathy and affection seem to have united them. Twice he inscribes verses "To my noble friend, Mr George Sandys, upon his excellent Paraphrase on the Psalms;" and again, " Upon his Job, Ecclesiastes, and the Lamentations, clearly, learnedly, and eloquently paraphrased." The lines to Hugo Grotius, from which we have already quoted, are also prefixed to a translation by Sandys. He was a great traveller as well as a translator and versifier, having visited not only the " several parts of Europe, but many cities and countries of the East," extending to the Holy Land. His travels were published in 1615, and widely read with great interest. Falkland evidently felt a special attraction in his fame as a traveller and his stores of foreign observation and experience. He assures Grotius

> " None hath a larger heart, a fuller head,
> For he hath seen as much as you have read :
> The neerer countries past, his steps have prest
> The new-found world, and trod the sacred East;
> Where, his brows due, the loftier palmes doe rise
> Where the proud Pyramids invade the skies ;
> And, as all think who his rare friendship own,
> Deserves no lesse a journey to be known.
> . . . . . . His travels were his choice,

And all those numerous realmes, returnd agen,
Anew he travel'd over with his pen.
And, Homer to himselfe, doth entertaine,
With truths more usefull then his Muse could faine.
Next Ovid's Transformations he translates
With so rare art, that those which he relates
Yeeld to this transmutation, and the change
Of men to birds and trees, appeares not strange :
Next the poetick parts of Scripture on
His loome he weaves, and Job and Solomon
His pen restores with all that heavenly quire,
And shakes the dust from David's solemn lyre.
From which, from all with just consent he wan
The title of the English Buchanan." [1]

In the verses directly inscribed to Sandys there is the same admiring enthusiasm, combined with a genuine warmth of personal feeling. Stress is laid upon the smoothness of Sandys' versification, which has also been highly commended by Dryden. Falkland contrasts it with his own imperfect attempts :—

"Such is the verse thou writ'st, that who reads thine
Can never be content to suffer mine ;
Such is the verse I write, that reading mine
I hardly can beleeve I have read thine ;
And wonder that their excellence once knowne,
I nor correct, nor yet conceale, mine owne." [2]

Again, he pays his friend a compliment, more than once repeated, for the high and sacred strain of his verse :—

"Now thou hast
Diverted to a purer path thy quill,
And changed Parnassus' Mount to Zion's Hill ;
So that blest David might almost desire
To heare his harp thus echo'd by thy lyre.

[1] Poems, p. 75-77.   [2] Ibid., p. 90.

> Those who make wit their curse, who spend their brain,
> Their time, and art in looser verse, to gain
> Damnation and a mistres, till they see
> How constant that is, how inconstant she,
> May from this great example learne to sway
> The parts th' are blest with, some more blessed way." [1]

Occasional allusions may be traced to the questions of the time which seem to indicate a fellow-feeling and coincidence of opinion betwixt the two friends regarding the favourite ideas of the Laudians and the absurd pretensions of Popery. Referring to the site of the early Eastern Churches, described by Sandys in his travels, he says:—

> " In whom these notes, so much requirèd, be
> Agreement, miracles, antiquity,
> Which can a never-broke succession show
> From the Apostles down (here bragg'd of so);
> So but confute her most immodest claime
> Who scorn a part, yet to be all doth aime." [2]

Finally, there is in the closing poem to Sandys, probably the last that Falkland wrote, a fine and touching passage, which seems to forecast his own death, the pathetic beauty of which mingles strangely and solemnly with cheerful anticipations of his friend's future fame:—

> " Howe're, I finish here; my Muse her daies
> Ends in expressing thy deservèd praise,
> Whose fate in this seemes fortunately cast,
> To have so just an action for her last.
> And since there are who have been taught that death
> Inspireth prophecie, expelling breath,
> I hope when these foretell what happie gaines
> Posteritie shall reape from these thy paines,
> Nor yet from these alone, but how thy pen,

[1] Poems, p. 82, 83.   [2] Ibid., p. 80.

Earthlike, shall yearly give new gifts to men;
And thou fresh praise and wee fresh good receive.
. . . The so-taught will not beliefe refuse
To the last accents of a dying Muse."[1]

Of Thomas Carew and Sir William Davenant—the former the well-known author of some exquisite love-verses, and "one of the most celebrated wits"[2] of the time; the latter, poet-laureate after Jonson—it is unnecessary to speak. Both were eminent members of the poetic fraternity with which Falkland mingled; but there is no reason to think that either was among his special friends. With Jonson himself, however, his relations were highly cordial and intimate, while difference of age lent something of respectful admiration to his affection. Jonson had already learned to know and appreciate Falkland in those early years, before 1631, when he and Sir Henry Morison attracted attention by their youthful friendship,—

"Till either grew a portion of the other,
and
. . . . .
lived to be the great sir-names
And titles, by which all made claims
Unto the virtue; nothing perfect done,
But as a Cary, or a Morison."[3]

At that time Jonson was the acknowledged head of English literature. He was also still active and imperial in London intellectual society, although self-

---

[1] Poems, p. 91, 92.   [2] Wood.   [3] Jonson's Poems, Underwoods.

indulgence[1] and a stroke of palsy had made ravages on his massive frame. He held his court in a place well known as the Devil Tavern, near Temple Bar, and hither all aspiring literary enthusiasts flocked. To be admitted to the guild of literature which assembled in the great room in this tavern, called "The Apollo," was to be "sealed of the tribe of Ben," in the literary cant of the day. Whatever may have been his faults, Jonson was, like his later namesake, a powerful and varied genius, whose great qualities are not too highly extolled even in Falkland's verse. The lines upon his death are, upon the whole, our poet's most elaborate performance. They are in the form of an eclogue, in which two shepherds, Hylas and Melybæus, discourse; and this absurd arrangement detracts from the naturalness and simplicity of the feeling. Yet it breaks out here and there in true tones as well as in elaborate eulogy. It is a "doubtful problem," not easy to resolve—

> "Which in his workes we most transcendant see
> Wit, judgment, learning, art, or industry:
> His learning such, no author, old or new,
> Except his reading, that deserved his view;
> And such his judgement, so exact his test
> As what was best in bookes, as what bookes best,
> That had he join'd those notes his labours took
> From each most praised and praise-deserving booke,

---

[1] Jonson's habits of self-indulgence in his later years are well known. Suckling probably alludes to them in the lines—

"Old Ben,
Prepared before with canary wine."

Whatever else he wanted, "he was sure," according to Izaak Walton, "not to want wine, of which he usually took too much before he went to bed, if not oftener and sooner."

> And could the world of that choise treasure boast,
> It need not care though all the rest were lost:
> And such his wit, he writ past what he quotes,
> And his productions farre exceed his notes,
> So in his workes where ought inserted growes,
> The noblest of the plants ingrafted showes,
> That his adopted children equall not
> The generous issue his own braine begot;
> So great his art that much which he did write
> Gave the wise wonder, and the crowd delight.
> Each sort as well as sex admir'd his wit,
> The hees and shees, the boxes and the pit;
> And who lesse lik'd within did rather chuse
> To taxe their judgements than suspect his Muse.
> With thoughts and wils purg'd and amended rise,
> From th' ethicke lectures of his comedies,
> Where the spectators act, and the sham'd age
> Blusheth to meet her follies on the stage:
> Where each man finds some light he never sought,
> And leaves behind some vanitie he brought;
> Whose politicks no lesse the minds direct,
> Then these the manners; nor with less effect.
> When his majesticke tragedies relate,
> All the disorders of a tottering State,
> All the distempers which on kingdomes fall
> When ease, and wealth, and vice are generall."

Of the other special names mentioned by Suckling, and in Falkland's own lines previously quoted—Digby, Weniman, Godolphin, Waller, Montague, and Suckling himself—all, with the exception of Suckling and Montague, live in Clarendon's pages.

"Sir Kenelm Digby was a person very eminent and notorious throughout the whole course of his life, from his cradle to his grave; of an ancient family and noble extraction; and inherited a fair and plentiful fortune, notwithstanding the attainder of his father. He was a man of a very extraordinary person and presence, which drew the eyes of all men upon him, which were more fixed by a wonderful graceful behaviour, a flowing courtesy and civility, and such a volubility of language, as surprised and delighted; and though in another man it might have appeared to have somewhat of affectation, it was marvellously graceful in him, and seemed natural to his size and mould of his person, to the gravity of his motion, and the tune of his voice and delivery. He had a fair reputation in arms, of which he gave an early testimony in his youth, in some encounters in Spain and Italy, and afterwards in an action in the Mediterranean Sea. . . . In a word, he had all the advantages that nature and art and an excellent education could give him, which, with a great confidence and presentness of mind, buoyed him up against all prejudices and disadvantages which would have suppressed and sunk any other man, but never clouded or eclipsed him from appearing in the best places and the best company, and with the best estimation and satisfaction."[1] Digby was a notorious pervert, having been educated a Protestant, although his father was a Catholic, and suffered for his share in the Gunpowder Plot. His perversion took place in France about 1635; and from this time he appears to have made himself conspicuous in the French capital for his constant intrigues with the Jesuits, and parade of his new "persuasion, to the prejudice of the English Church." His doings were the subject of elaborate negotiation betwixt Lord Leicester, then in Paris, and Laud, in the early summer of

[1] Clar. Life, vol. i. 38, 39.

1638.[1] Aubrey says that he was called "the Mirandula of his age," and had "such a goodly handsome person, and so graceful elocution and noble address, that had he been dropt out of the clouds in any part of the world, he would have made himself respected." He admits, however, that the Jesuits, who knew him well, said, "'Twas true, but then he must not stay there above six weeks." The fact seems to be that, with striking superficial qualities and an imposing air of ability, Sir Kenelm Digby was a man distinguished more by a certain restless liveliness of nature than by any higher attributes of head or heart. He belonged to the "Falkland set" before 1633; but there is no evidence of any special or more cordial intimacy betwixt him and Falkland.

With Sir Francis Wenman,[2] however, Falkland was allied by the closest ties. They were not only associates of the same circle in town, but neighbours in the country, and "in so entire friendship and confidence" that Sir Francis had "great authority in the society of all Falkland's friends and acquaintance." Of ancient and noble family, "possessed of a competent estate," and of high repute for "wisdom and integrity," Wenman was greatly esteemed at Court, but he preferred being considered simply a country gentleman. "He was a man," adds Clarendon, "of great sharpness of understanding, and of a piercing judgment; no man better understood the affections

[1] Letter from Leicester to Laud, quoted in Masson's Life of Milton, vol. i. 707.

[2] There can be no reasonable doubt that the "Weniman" of Suckling's lines was Sir Francis Wenman, Falkland's neighbour in Oxfordshire, although Suckling's editor, the Rev. Alfred Suckling, LL.B., does not seem to have perceived this. — Selections from Suckling's Works, 1836, p. 86.

and temper of the kingdom, or indeed the nature of the nation, or discerned further the consequence of counsels, and with what success they were like to be attended. He was a very good Latin scholar, but his ratiocination was above his learning; and the sharpness of his wit incomparable. He was equal to the greatest trust and employment, if he had been ambitious of it, or solicitous for it; but his want of health produced a kind of laziness of mind which disinclined him to business, and he died a little before the general troubles of the kingdom, which he foresaw with wonderful concern, and when many wise men were weary of living so long.[1]

Sidney Godolphin was a youth about Falkland's own age, trained at Oxford, and recently returned from his travels abroad. "There was never so great a mind and spirit contained in so little room; so large an understanding, and so unrestrained a fancy, in so very small a body; so that the Lord Falkland used to say merrily, that he thought it was a great ingredient into his friendship for Mr Godolphin that he was pleased to be found in his company, where he was the properer man; and it may be, the very remarkableness of his little person made the sharpness of his wit and the composed quickness of his judgment and understanding the more notable."[2] He had been abroad on diplomatic employment with the Earl of Leicester, and seems to have coveted advancement with the Court at home; but his constitution was hypochondriacal, and he "loved very much to be alone," and to retire "amongst his books."

[1] Life, p. 51.   [2] Ibid., p. 51, 52.

"He was contented to be reproached by his friends with laziness; and was of so nice and tender a composition that a little rain or wind would disorder him, and divert him from any short journey he had most willingly proposed to himself; insomuch as when he rid abroad with those in whose company he most delighted, if the wind chanced to be in his face, he would (after a little pleasant murmuring) suddenly turn his horse and go home."[1] The outbreak of the civil war, however, roused him to energy, and he embarked with vigour and earnestness in the Royal cause. "He put himself into the first troops which were raised in the west for the King, and bore the uneasiness and fatigue of winter marches with an exemplary courage and alacrity." Like his friend, he fell gallantly fighting in the same fatal year, 1643—the victim of "too brave a pursuit of the enemy into an obscure village in Devonshire."

Edmund Waller we feel almost reluctant to number amongst Falkland's friends. His genius may be held to redeem his weakness. "The excellence and power of his wit, and pleasantness of his conversation," are allowed even by Clarendon, who does not spare him, to have been "of magnitude enough to cover a world of very great faults." But his political cowardice is a reproach to the moderate party, which numbered him amongst its members; and with all his brilliant poetic gifts and social accomplishments, Waller's seems to have been a mean and poor nature —selfish and pleasure-loving in prosperity, and abject and servile in adversity. Society pardoned his

[1] Life, p. 52.

public baseness for his private pleasantries, which had "power to reconcile him to those whom he had most offended and provoked." Having forfeited his life by his treachery to the Parliament, he saved it at the expense of others, "and continued to his age," says our portrait-painter exquisitely, "with that rare felicity, that his company was acceptable where his spirit was odious; and he was at least pitied where he was most detested." Falkland's friendship with him seems to have been chiefly in the earlier years of his literary enthusiasm, before the political struggles which broke down Waller's integrity. Poetic tastes united them; and perhaps a common relation to Dr Morley, who had read and studied with Waller, and who is said[1]—although this scarcely seems likely—to have introduced him to Falkland's society. His lines "To my Lord Falkland" are not distinguished by any particular warmth or poetic skill,[2] but they show a graceful and happily expressed interest in the fate of his friend when he went forth with the King in the first Scottish expedition in 1639,

"To civilise and to instruct the north."

Suckling himself, and "Wat Montague," claim to

---

[1] Clarendon says this, but Waller's first biographer asserts that it was his connection with the Falkland Society that brought him acquainted with Morley.

[2] The following are perhaps the best lines :—

"Ah, noble friend, with what impatience all
That know thy worth, and know how prodigal
Of thy great soul thou art (longing to twist
Bays with that ivy which so early kissed
Thy youthful temples)—with what horror we
Think on the blind events of war and thee!
To fate exposing that all-knowing breast
Among the throng, as cheaply as the rest;
Where oaks and brambles (if the copse be burned)
Confounded lie, to the same ashes turned."

be mentioned in connection with our subject for special reasons. Both were friends of Falkland; but not merely on this account do they deserve notice. Suckling — strange as it may appear to those who only know his career as a poet—wrote a brief religious treatise, entitled 'An Account of Religion by Reason.' There is little of thought or genuine argument in the treatise. It is the work of an elegant *litterateur* handling a subject which he knows imperfectly, and only from the outside. But the mere fact is a testimony to the theological excitement which then everywhere pervaded society, and indicates the desire there must have been in many minds, besides those whose writings and speculations have come to the surface, to examine the subject of religion rationally. Suckling avows that he feared the charge of Socinianism in his undertaking. Then, as in later times, this charge was recklessly applied to all who thought for themselves in religion; or, in other words, who did not take a side with either theological extreme. " Every man," he says, "that offers to give an account of religion by reason is suspected to have none at all;" yet he has " made no scruple to run that hazard—not knowing why a man should not use the best weapon his Creator hath given him for his defence." The treatise itself, if only a meagre and imperfect sketch of the great subjects which it touches—the Trinity, Incarnation, Passion, and Resurrection of our Lord—is substantially orthodox. God is declared "to be one, and but one; it being gross to imagine two omnipotents, for then neither would be so. Yet since this good is perfectly good, and perfect goodness cannot be without perfect love; nor perfect love without communication, nor to an unequal or created—for then it must be inordinate; we include a second coeternal though begotten; nor are these contrary, though they seem to be so."[1] Thus theologised the gay Suckling at Bath, in the year 1637; and although the points of contact betwixt him and Falkland must have been superficial rather than real, we can imagine them not only contending for the " laurel," as depicted in the well-known verses—a contention in which our poet would have had no chance with him—but also trying their strength in religious argument during those stirring years. Suckling's fate was a sad one. Elected along with his friend a member of the Long Parliament, he had so far at first joined in the general outcry against Strafford; but, with a slight hold on the deeper principles at stake in the contest, he had left the popular party even before the impeachment, and madly lent himself to a design for rescuing the great Earl from the Tower. The design having been discovered, a charge of high treason was issued by the Parliament against Suckling and the other conspirators.[2] He fled to the Continent, and there, in disgrace and penury, he terminated his life by his own hand, before the close of 1642. He is said by Aubrey to have been only twenty-eight years of age. The same gossiping authority adds : " He was of

---

[1] Selections from Suckling's Works, p. 131.

[2] The affair is known as " Goring's Conspiracy."

middle stature and slight strength, brisk round eye and reddish face; . . . his head not very big, his hair a kind of sand colour, and his beard turned up naturally, so that he had a brisk and graceful look."

"Wat Montague," we may certainly say, was the same Walter Montague with whom Falkland corresponded on the subject of Popery, and whose letter, with Falkland's reply, is printed along with the 'Discourse on Infallibility.' He was the author of the 'Shepherd's Paradise' — the "pastoral" alluded to so dubiously in Suckling's verses.[1] His letter to Falkland is brief and slight. It goes over the usual ground of the necessity of a continuously visible Church, and the question of Where was the Protestant Church before Luther? Falkland's reply is acute, ingenious, and satisfactory, and contains at least one good hit on the point of the Church's visibility. His patristic studies had convinced him that neither the Roman nor the Protestant Church could find their exact parallel in the early Christian ages. Neither of these Churches, therefore, he argued, "have been always visible" in the sense contended for by Montague; but with this significant difference in the two cases, "that we are most troubled to show our Church in the later and more corrupt ages, and they (the Roman Catholics) theirs in the

[1] Selections, p. 90. The editor adds, in corroboration of our statement in the text, that "Wat Montague was a Papist, and suspected of having been concerned in the perversion of Lady Newburgh. On that occasion," he adds, "it is said in a letter of Lord Conway's, 'the King did use such words of Wat Montague and Sir Tobie Matthew (another of Suckling's poets), that the fright made Wat keep his chamber longer than his sickness would have detained him.'"

first and purest; that we can least find ours at night, and they theirs at noon." So far as his general argument is concerned, it is very much the same as that to be found in his 'Discourse on Infallibility,' and will remain for consideration when we come to examine this discourse and his general position on the subject of religious authority.

Such was the brilliant literary circle in which Falkland mingled in the earlier half of that significant decade which preceded the great constitutional struggle which was destined to end in the civil war. If we add to the background of the picture Hobbes, who returned to England in 1631, and remained till 1634, and of whom it is said that Falkland was a "great friend and admirer,"[1] it would be difficult to conceive a more remarkable intellectual coterie. Poetry and literature in its lighter forms were no doubt its chief interests; and as yet probably these were the chief employments of our intellectual enthusiast. The fact that his own poetic vein is found flowing as early as 1631, on the occasion of the death of Dr Donne, may be held to indicate this. However, with the graver interests which subsequently occupied him, he did not abandon poetry, as some of his verses, such as those to Grotius, and probably the closing lines to Sandys, are at least as late as 1640.

After the extracts which we have already given from Falkland's poems, it is unnecessary that we should quote much further from them. With the exception of the lines on Dr Donne, and a considerably

[1] Aubrey.

longer poem—indeed the longest of the series—
"Upon the death of the Ladie Marquesse Hamilton,"
cast, like the eclogue on Jonson, into the artificial
form of the pastoral dialogue, we have quoted something from them all. There is a peculiar tenderness
in the lines on Lady Hamilton,[1] whose beauty and
high character seem to have specially inspired our
poet, and the rural imagery which abounds in it is
touched sometimes with a graceful and charming
felicity—as, for example, when Cloris, one of the in-
terlocutors of the poem, says of her lover :—

> "His best of wheat and creame before mee poures,
> Brings mee his fairest fruite, his freshest flouers,
> What birds his twigs, what fish his nets can take,
> All that his silkewormes, or his bees, can make,
> The friskingst calves and kids his pastures hold,
> And purest lambes the honour of his fould."

Or again, when she describes the courtiers weeping
for Lady Hamilton, who had been "Lady of the
Queen's bedchamber," and a great confidant of her
royal mistress :—

> "Now wearied with their sorrowes, and their way
> Neere the fresh bankes of silver Thames they lay,
> And wept soe fast as if they meant to try
> To weepe a floud like that they wept it by,
> Whose faces, bow'd, and bright, and moist, did shew
> Like lillies loaded with the morning dew."

The description of the lady herself as she had been
used to walk "by fairest Grenewich" also deserves
to be quoted. "Often in the sun's declining heat
she," Cloris again says,—

---

[1] She was a Villiers, and the first wife of King Charles's friend, James, Marquis, and afterwards Duke, of Hamilton.

"Would view the downes where wee our flockes did keepe,
And stay to mark the bleating of our sheepe;
And often from her heigth hath stoopt to praise
Our countrey sportes, and heare our countrey layes,
Sharing with us, after her ended walke,
Our homely cates and our more homely talke.

. . . .

What beauty did in that faire forme reside!
What any greatness hath, excepting pride!
Eyes of soe modest, yet soe bright a flame,
To see her and to love her was the same:
And if by chance, when shee did neere us stand,
Here bright smooth palme but touch'd my ruder hand,
That did both sences soe at once delight,
The purest swans seem'd neether soft nor white."

But we cannot extend our extracts, or indeed our notice of this aspect of Falkland's life and intellectual activity. As a whole, his poems will hardly bear criticism in comparison with the melodious sweetness and gay sparkling vivacity to be found in the happier efforts of Suckling or Carew; or even with the smoother verse of Sandys, not to speak of the vigorous and more varied muse of such poetic chiefs as Ben Jonson, Waller, and Cowley. Dr Earle, one of his later theological friends, "would not allow Falkland to be a good poet, though a great wit. He writ not a smooth verse, but a great deal of sense."[1] Summary as this judgment is, there is a great deal of truth in it. Falkland's poetic vein does not run smoothly, with that liquid clearness and bright flow of expression without which even a strong and rich genius fails to yield poetry, or at least such poetry as seizes and charms men's hearts, and becomes a possession

[1] Aubrey.

which they do not "willingly let die." And so his poems passed away almost entirely from the memory of his own generation and the generations which followed; and it has remained to our time to draw attention to them, and even to collect them together for the first time.[1] Withal, it must be admitted that they are full of earnest poetic enthusiasm. They glow no less than his prose with a genuine life of thought and feeling; and, as we have seen, there are not a few delightful bits both of imaginative picturesqueness and of vigorous allusive versification which deserve to be remembered in our poetic annals.

Even in this earlier and more purely literary society there are indications that subjects of theology, and the great question of the Church, obtruded occasionally. If a mind like Suckling's did not escape the pressure of such thoughts, it can hardly be supposed that any were free from it; and a company which numbered Digby and "Wat Montague" amongst its members, was not likely to be without some gusts of controversial excitement. But it was Falkland's later society in the neighbourhood of Oxford where the conversation was, as Clarendon says, "one continued *convivium philosophicum* or *convivium theologicum*." After his marriage,

---

[1] Attention was first drawn to Lord Falkland's poems by Mr Mitford, in 1835, in the 'Gentleman's Magazine,' vol. clviii.; and only last year (1871) they have been collected and edited for the first time after the original texts, with "Memorial Introduction and Notes" by the Rev. A. B. Grosart. The slight volume is printed for private circulation; and Mr Grosart deserves the thanks of all admirers of Falkland for his painstaking enthusiasm.

and still more apparently after his father's death (1633), Falkland betook himself, with characteristic enthusiasm, to ecclesiastical and theological studies. Having made himself master of Greek, he passed from the study of the classics to that of patristic antiquity. Clarendon speaks with warm admiration of his "prodigious progress" in learning. "There were very few classic authors in the Greek or Latin tongue that he had not read with great exactness. He had read all the Greek and Latin Fathers, all the most allowed and authentic ecclesiastical writers, and all the councils, with wonderful care and observation; for in religion he thought too careful and too curious inquiry could not be made amongst those whose purity was not questioned, and whose authority was constantly and confidently urged by men who were furthest from being of one mind amongst themselves; and for the mutual support of their several opinions, in which they most contradicted each other; and in all those controversies he had so dispassioned a consideration, such a candour in his nature, and so profound a charity in his conscience, that in those points in which he was in his own judgment most clear, he never thought the worse, or in any degree declined the familiarity, of those who were of another mind; which, without question, is an excellent temper for the propagation and advancement of Christianity. With these great advantages of industry, he had a memory retentive of all that he had ever read, and an understanding and judgment to apply it seasonably and appositely with the most dexterity and address, and the least pedantry and affectation that ever man who knew so much was possessed with, of what quality soever."[1]

These are the studies in which we must conceive him mainly occupied after his permanent retirement to Tew. To what extent his gayer London friends—"Ben Jonson's sons"—mingled with the society there, it is difficult to say. That to some extent they did so, is implied in Clarendon's account. But the main elements of this later society, of which Falkland himself was obviously the chief, and not merely one amongst others, and of which his own residence was the rendezvous, were Oxford men and theologians. All the names are those of well-known Church divines—viz., Dr Sheldon, Dr Morley, Dr Hammond, Dr Earles, Mr Chillingworth. Hales, curiously, is not mentioned. But we may almost certainly conclude that he was one of the number, although probably his distance, at Eton,[2] or London, rendered him a less frequent visitor than those named. Many others—both Oxford and London men—must have been occasionally present. Clarendon's addendum to the names given by him plainly supposes this—" and indeed all men of eminent parts and faculties in Oxford, besides those who resorted thither from London." Falkland's house, "within ten or twelve miles of the university, looked like the university itself, by the company that was always found there." And all "found their lodgings there as ready as in the colleges; nor did the lord of the house know of their coming or going, nor who were in his house,

[1] Life, p. 48, 49.   [2] Since 1613 he had been one of the Fellows there.

till he came to dinner or supper, where all still met; otherwise there was no trouble, ceremony, or restraint, to forbid men to come to the house, or to make them weary of staying there; so that many came thither to study in a better air, finding all the books they could desire in his library, and all the persons together whose company they could wish, and not find in any other society."

With the exception of Chillingworth, all the divines mentioned survived to the Restoration. Not only so, but their lives became so identified with the later movements which followed first the temporary overthrow of the Church of England, and then its re-establishment, that it is comparatively difficult to conceive of them in that early time when they were Falkland's guests and joined in his favourite discussions. This is especially true of the two first mentioned, Sheldon and Morley. After the Restoration, Sheldon was appointed first Bishop of London, and then in 1633 Archbishop of Canterbury. He was not only active but zealous in the disgraceful legislation which issued in the ejectment of St Bartholomew's Day [1] and the Five-Mile Act.[2] While others were for leniency, Sheldon, according to Burnet, "pressed the execution of the law," and "undertook to fill all the vacant pulpits that should be forsaken in London better and more to the satisfaction of the people than they had been before." [3] According to the same authority, "he seemed not to have a deep sense of

---

[1] 24th August 1662.
[2] 1665.
[3] Burnet's Hist. of his Own Time, i. 349.

religion, if any at all, and spoke of it most commonly as of an engine of government and a matter of policy."[1] Whatever credit may be due to this statement of Burnet—and it can hardly be received without confirmation [2]—it is beyond question that Sheldon's whole career proves him to have been more of a politician than a divine. He cannot, therefore, be supposed to have added much to the purely intellectual side of the debates which interested Falkland and Chillingworth. But his clear and firm judgment—Burnet admits that he had "a very true judgment"—and direct vigorous sense, even then gave him special influence over his friends. Chillingworth's correspondence with him on the subject of subscription plainly shows this. His remarkable powers of conversation

---

[1] Burnet's Hist. of his Own Time, i. 320.

[2] Burnet's statement is supposed to receive confirmation from certain remarks of Dr Samuel Parker, Bishop of Oxford, who had been Sheldon's chaplain, to the effect that the Archbishop, "though very assiduous at prayers, yet did not set so great a value on them as others did, nor regarded so much worship as the use of worship, placing the chief point of religion in the practice of a good life." But while Parker tells this, he at the same time says that Sheldon "was a man of undoubted piety;" and the real import of all such remarks can only be fairly judged from a knowledge of all the circumstances—the point of view of the speaker, and the character of those whom he is addressing. The same thing is to be said of his alleged "advice to young noblemen and gentlemen, who by their parents' commands resorted daily to him, was always this : ' Let it be your principal care to become honest men, and afterwards be as devout and religious as you will. No piety will be of any advantage to yourselves or anybody else, unless you are honest and moral men.'" Outspoken manliness, and an intense aversion to all religious pretence, may explain such sayings without supposing any lack of true religious feeling in the speaker.

contributed to give weight to his opinions. "He had a great pleasantness of conversation; perhaps too great. He had an art that was peculiar to him of treating all that came to him in a most obliging manner."[1] He was also, according to uniform testimony, generous and charitable; and it was no doubt his agreeable politeness and a certain munificence of nature which led Sir Francis Wenman to say of him, when he resorted to the conversations at Tew, that "Dr Sheldon was born and bred to be Archbishop of Canterbury." He was twelve years older than Falkland; and having been elected Warden of All Souls in 1635, when the meetings at Tew were in full vigour, he was probably one of the most regular visitors there.

Of Morley we have already heard in connection with Waller. He, too, survived the Restoration, and became Bishop, first of Worcester and then of Winchester, where, like Sheldon, he distinguished himself by his munificence. He was less active and prominent in promoting the repressive measures of the Restoration; but he must also be held accountable for them, and the shadow of their disgrace so far also covers his name. Baxter says [2] that he was the "chief speaker of all the bishops" at the Savoy Conference, and frequently bore down objections by his "fervour" and "interruptions." Strangely, with all his enthusiasm for the royal cause, with which he became identified in many special ways, he was very zealous against Popery, and had the reputation of

[1] Burnet's Hist. of his Own Time, i. 320.
[2] Life and Times, Part II., 363.

being a great Calvinist. On this latter account he seems to have suffered somewhat at the hands of Laud in the early years of his intimacy with Falkland. The story is told of him at this time, that on being "asked by a grave country gentleman (who was desirous to be instructed what their tenets and opinions were) 'what the Arminians held,' he pleasantly answered, that *they held all the best bishoprics and deaneries in England,*—which was quickly reported abroad as Mr Morley's definition of the Arminian tenets."[1] Morley appears to have been an eminently sensible and vigorous-minded man—a hard student, "usually rising about five o'clock in the morning, both in winter and in summer," and a hard thinker, extremely fond of argument—"of great wit, readiness, and subtlety in disputation," says Clarendon, "and of remarkable temper and prudence in conversation, which rendered him most grateful in all the best company."[2] What was "temper and prudence" in agreeable society, may have readily passed into heat and vehemence when he was contradicted and crossed in argument. And so may be explained the "hot spirit" ascribed to him by Baxter—and Burnet's words, that while "a pious and charitable man, of a very exemplary life, he was extreme passionate and very obstinate." Burnet adds that Morley first became "known to the world as a friend of the Lord Falkland's; and that was enough to raise a man's character."[3] In comparison with Sheldon, he thinks

[1] Clarendon, Life, i. 56. [2] Ibid., i. 56.
[3] Burnet, i. 321, 322.

him to have been the honester, but the less able man of the two.

Henry Hammond was a higher character, and certainly a much higher divine than either Sheldon or Morley. Sheldon's ability, so far as we know, never took the form of authorship; and Morley only became an author after the Restoration, or in his old age, as he himself cynically said, when he published a few sermons and tracts chiefly of an official character. Hammond was a voluminous author; and his 'Practical Catechism' (1644), and 'Paraphrase and Annotations on the New Testament' (1653), give him special rank in the list of Anglo-Catholic theologians. His life has been drawn at length by one of his own contemporaries,[1] and presents a beautiful picture of self-devotion, simplicity, and saintliness. His friendship with Sanderson is well known; and the likeness yet the contrasts betwixt the two friends—their equal enthusiasm and earnestness of piety—with the more compliant temper and less rigorous practices of Sanderson, and the stiffer Anglican Churchmanship of Hammond, give a curious and graphic insight into the character of Episcopacy during its time of persecution. At this time Hammond was reduced to great poverty, but his meek and quiet spirit never murmured. His gentleness under suffering is especially commemorated. He had learned to make the best of all circumstances, saying with Epictetus, "that everything had two handles—if the one prove hot and not to be touched, we may take the other

[1] Life by Bishop Fell, 1661.

that is more temperate." "He delighted," he said himself, " to be loved rather than reverenced ;" and one of his sayings, memorable for its solemnity, may be taken as the key-note of his lofty Christian earnestness : "Oh! what a glorious thing, how rich a prize for the expense of a man's whole life, were he to be the instrument of rescuing one soul ! " It was in the view of Charles II. to appoint him to the bishopric of Worcester, but he died in the spring of 1660, before the King's arrival.

Dr Earles, or Earle, as the name is also written, is perhaps the least remembered of all the divines mentioned by Clarendon; but in 1630 he was the only one who had really distinguished himself as an author. He had then written a very clever series of sketches entitled, ' Microcosmography ; or, A Piece of the World discovered; in Essays and Characters.' The sketches were published anonymously in 1628, and ran through six editions betwixt that date and 1633. They bore to be printed for " Ed. Blount," and so are known by many as " Blount's Characters." But their authorship is beyond question. Clarendon says, in evident allusion to them, that " some very witty and sharp discourses " were " published in print without his consent," and that when known to be his " he grew suddenly into a very general esteem with all men."[1] And this is not to be wondered at. The sketches which compose the ' Microcosmography' are extremely clever, and to this day highly amusing. They are everywhere marked by a lively incisive wit, a proverbial felicity of expression, and an inge-

[1] Life, i. 57.

nious, compact, and sarcastic turn of portraiture which, notwithstanding some crudeness of arrangement, keeps the attention alive throughout, and seizes it with unexpected surprises of humorous pleasure. A perfect anthology of good sayings might be selected from it—sayings both rich in themselves, and richly illustrative of the manners and tendencies of the time.[1] It is easy to understand the affinity betwixt such a man as Earle and Falkland. "He was an excellent poet," it is said, "both in Latin, Greek, and English," though he suppressed many of his

---

[1] We can only give a few here, and these, perhaps, not the most telling or descriptive. Of a child the author says: "He is nature's fresh picture, newly drawn in oil, which time and much handling dims and defaces. . . . The elder he grows he is a stair lower from God; and, like his first father, much worse in his breeches."

Of the sermon of a "young raw preacher:" "The labour of it is chiefly in his lungs; and the only thing he has made in it himself is the faces. He takes on against the Pope without mercy, and has a jest still in lavender for Bellarmine; yet he preaches heresy, if it comes in his way, though with a mind, I must needs say, very orthodox. . . . He preaches but once a-year, though twice on Sunday; for the stuff is still the same, only the dressing a little altered."

Of a grave divine: "He makes more conscience of schism than a surplice. He esteems the Church hierarchy as the Church's glory, and however we jar with Rome, would not have our confusion distinguish us."

Of a mere formal man: "His religion is a good quiet subject; and he prays, as he swears, in the phrase of the land. . . . He apprehends a jest by seeing men smile, and laughs orderly himself when it comes to his turn."

"An idle gallant is one that was born and shaped for his clothes; and if Adam had not fallen, had lived to no purpose. . . . He is one never serious but with his tailor."

The devotion of a female hypocrite "is much in the turning up of her eye, and turning down the leaf in her book, when she hears named chapter and verse. She loves preaching better than praying, and of preachers, lecturers. . . . She overflows so with the Bible that she spills it upon every occasion, and will not cudgel her maids without Scripture. . . . She is an everlasting argument, but I am weary of her."

English pieces "out of an austerity to those sallies of his youth." "He was very dear," adds Clarendon, "to the Lord Falkland, with whom he spent as much time as he could make his own; and as that lord would impute the speedy progress he made in the Greek tongue to the information and assistance he had from Mr Earles, so Mr Earles would frequently profess that he had got more useful learning by his conversation at Tew (the Lord Falkland's house) than he had at Oxford."[1]

After the Restoration, Earle became Bishop of Salisbury, and, unlike both Sheldon and Morley, showed himself extremely favourable to the Nonconformists. He laboured, "with all his might" against the Five-Mile Act.[2] He was evidently a sweet-natured and tolerant man, of unaffected piety and goodness. Walton says of him, that since the death of Hooker none had lived "whom God hath blest with more innocent wisdom, more sanctified learning, or a more pious, peaceable, primitive temper."

But of all the divines mentioned by Clarendon, Chillingworth is of course the most significant; and there is abundant evidence that he was Falkland's friend, and the frequenter of his house in a more intimate sense than any of the others. "Here"—at Tew—says Clarendon, "Mr Chillingworth wrote, and formed, and modelled his excellent book against the learned Jesuit, Mr (K)Nott, *after frequent debates* upon the most important matters,—in many of which," it is characteristically added, "he

[1] Life, i. 58. [2] Conformist's Plea, p. 35.

suffered himself to be overruled by the judgment of his friends, though in others he still adhered to his own fancy, which was sceptical enough, even in the highest points." There is a tradition that Falkland actually assisted in the composition of Chillingworth's great work. Of this, however, there is no evidence, and it may be said to be contradicted by the internal character of the work. Yet evidently the two friends were associated to the mind of their generation in a quite peculiar manner. " Mr William Chillingworth, of Trinity College in Oxford," Aubrey says, "was his most intimate and beloved favourite, and *was most commonly with my lord.*" " They had such extraordinary clear reasons, that they were wont to say at Oxon, that if the Great Turke were to be converted by natural reason, these two were the persons to convert him."

All this intellectual companionship was broken up with the first mutterings of war in 1639. Before this, Ben Jonson was dead, and the meetings in the " Apollo " discontinued. The *convivium theologicum* probably met at Tew for the last time in the spring of that year before Falkland went away with the royal army, then raised to suppress the rebellion in Scotland. This expedition is known as the first " Bishops' war." Troops were collected by a circular letter in the King's name addressed to all the English nobility, who were invited to assist his Majesty in recalling his northern subjects to a sense of their allegiance. Falkland considered himself bound by the royal summons, or the old soldierly inclinations may have returned upon him irrepressibly with renewed opportunity of gratifying them. Clarendon's language rather implies this latter view, and, moreover, that a further disappointment befel him in reference to the command of a troop of horse which he had been promised. Thwarted in this ambition, "he went a volunteer with the Earl of Essex."[1]

The history of the expedition to Scotland is aside from our purpose. It came to nothing—ended, in fact, in a somewhat ignominious manner for Charles and his army; and all the success remained with Henderson and the Scottish Covenanters, who arranged a temporary settlement with the King in sight of Dunse Law, where the armies lay facing each other. There is no account of Falkland throughout the expedition. He cannot be supposed to have entered upon it with any enthusiasm, notwithstanding his military ardour. "A crusade in favour of Episcopal power and a compulsory liturgy,"[2] however it temporarily secured his sword, cannot have enlisted his sympathy. But we have no means of estimating his judgment of what proved so hapless a movement of the royal policy.

It was this event of his life which is commemorated by the verses of Waller and Cowley inscribed to him. To the former we have already alluded. Cowley's verses, upon the whole, have more nature and life than Waller's, while they show even more strikingly the extraordinary impression which Falk-

---

[1] Hist. of the Rebellion, b. vii. vol. ii. 453—Clar. Press, 1816.
[2] Lady Lewis's Life of Lord Falkland, p. 18.

land's character and abilities had made upon the more intellectual men of his time. And Cowley's testimony is all the more remarkable, that we have not hitherto encountered him among Falkland's special friends. It is hardly possible, notwithstanding Walpole's sneers, that such a combination of judgments could have been mistaken. We give but a few of Cowley's lines :—

> " Great is thy charge, O North; be wise and just;
> England commits her Falkland to thy trust,
> Return him safe; learning would rather choose
> Her Bodley or her Vatican to lose.
> All things that are but writ or printed there,
> In his unbounded breast engraven are.
> . . . .
> And this great prince of knowledge is by Fate
> Thrust into th' noise and business of a State.
> . . . .
> Such is the man whom we require, the same
> We lent the North; untouch'd as is his fame,
> He is too good for war, and ought to be
> As far from danger as from fear he's free."

The Scottish expedition had ended, and the King was again at Whitehall by the midsummer of 1639. We hear nothing, however, of Falkland till the following spring, when he was elected to sit for Newport, in the Isle of Wight, in the "Short Parliament," which then met for three weeks (15th April—5th May 1640). There is no record of his having spoken during this brief Parliamentary experience, but the impression produced upon him was fruitful and important, according to Clarendon's statement : "From the debates, which were there managed with all imaginable gravity and sobriety, he contracted such a reverence for Parliaments that he thought it really impossible they could ever produce mischief or inconvenience to the kingdom, or that the kingdom could be tolerably happy in the intermission of them. And from the unhappy and unreasonable dissolution of that convention, he harboured, it may be, some jealousy and prejudice to the Court, towards which he was not before immoderately inclined."[1]

It is no part of our intention to sketch, even in the most summary manner, the series of political events which now followed each other in rapid succession. It will be enough to indicate very briefly the part taken by Falkland, first on the popular side, and then—evidently after great hesitation and misgiving —on the side of the King. To do justice to the political side of his character, or to attempt any vindication of his political action, would far outrun our space, besides leading us away from our special subject. Falkland's brief but busy public career may be divided into three parts : first, from the opening of the Long Parliament (3d Nov. 1640) to the execution of Strafford (12th May 1641); second, from this great event to his acceptance of office under the King about eight months later (1st Jan. 1641-2); and lastly, the twenty months—from Jan. 1642 to Sept. 1643—of his official life.

During the first of these periods Falkland is entirely at one with the popular party, and amongst the most active in urging their measures of redress

[1] Hist. of Rebellion, b. vii. vol. ii. 447.

and punishment. Within six months the whole system of "Thorough" had not only been swept away, but its authors committed to the Tower, and the most conspicuous of them, after a trial of fourteen days in Westminster, brought to the scaffold. Others—the Secretary Windebank and the Lord Keeper Finch—only escaped the same fate by flight. No one ventured to say a word for the delinquents, or to stop the current of events. Falkland appears most notably in the case of Finch, but he and Hyde also joined in Strafford's condemnation. Even in his severity his fairness and sense of justice appear. He bore no love to the great Irish Viceroy, not only for his political delinquencies, but "from the memory of some unkindness, not without a mixture of injustice, from him towards his father"—some old score, no doubt, arising out of Strafford's relation to his father as his successor in the government of Ireland. Yet he was the only member of the House of Commons who, when the proposition was made for immediate impeachment, ventured to suggest any delay. He desired the House to consider "whether it would not suit better with the gravity of their proceedings, first to digest many of those particulars which had been mentioned by a committee before they sent up to accuse him, declaring himself to be abundantly satisfied that there was enough to charge him."[1] The suggestion was opposed by Pym, and rejected by the House under apprehensions of Strafford's influence with the King, and the risk of his

[1] Hist. of Rebellion, b. iii. vol. i. 239.

being induced once more to try the policy of dissolution.

From the first Falkland appears to have taken an active part in the discussions of the Parliament. The impeachment of Strafford took place almost within a week of its meeting; and on the 4th of December (1640) he is found speaking at length on the subject of the illegal exaction of ship-money. Here, as everywhere, it is the sense of justice—in this case of outraged justice—which animates him and inspires his eloquence. " The constitution of this commonwealth," he said, " hath established, or rather endeavoured to establish, to us the security of our goods, by appointing for us judges so settled, so sworn, that there can be no oppression. . . . But this security, Mr Speaker, hath been almost our ruin, for it hath been turned, or rather turned itself, into a battery against us; and those persons who should have been as dogs to defend the sheep, have been as wolves to worry them. These judges," he continued, " have delivered an opinion and judgment in an extrajudicial manner—that is, such as came not within their cognisance, they being judges, and neither philosophers nor politicians." He desired to vindicate the King while condemning the judges. " A most excellent prince hath been most infinitely abused by his judges telling him that by policy he might do what he pleased;" and as " these men have trampled upon the laws which our ancestors have provided with their utmost care and wisdom for our undoubted security, we must now be forced to think of abolishing of our grievances, and of taking away this judgment and these judges together, and of regulating their successors by their exemplary punishment." Having then alluded to the accusation of Strafford " for intending to subvert our fundamental laws, and to introduce arbitrary government," he implies that whatever doubt might exist as to his conduct, none can exist as to the conduct of the judges—" No law being more fundamental than that they have already subverted, and no government more absolute than that they have really introduced." In conclusion, he concentrates his eloquent indignation upon Lord Keeper Finch. " Mr Speaker," said he, "there is one that I must not lose in the crowd, whom I doubt not but we shall find, when we examine the rest of them, with what hopes they have been tempted, by what fears they have been assayed, and by what and by whose importunity they have been pursued, before they consented to what they did ;—I doubt not, I say, but we shall find him to have been a most admirable solicitor; but a most abominable judge : he it is who not only gave away with his breath what our ancestors had purchased for us by so large an expense of their time, their care, their treasure, and their blood, . . . but strove to make our grievances immortal, and our slavery irreparable, lest any part of our posterity might want occasion to curse him ; he declared that power to be so inherent to the Crown, as that it was not in the power even of Parliaments to divide them."

This speech was fruitful in results. The system of illegal imposts, which had produced such a flame in the country, was not only swept away, but Falkland, assisted by Hyde, was appointed to prosecute the chief delinquent at the bar of the House of Lords. Finch, as we have seen, did not wait to face the trial, but fled in disguise to Holland. Thanks, however, were voted by the House of Commons on the 14th of January " to Mr St John and Mr Whitelock, the Lord Falkland, and Mr Hyde, for the great services they have performed to the honour of this House and the good of the commonwealth in their conduct of this business."[1] It is in reference to Falkland's conduct in this matter particularly that Clarendon observes : He was " so rigid an observer of established laws and rules, that he could not endure the least breach or deviation from them; and thought no mischief so intolerable as the presumption of Ministers of State to break positive rules for reasons of State, or judges to transgress known laws upon the title of conveniency or necessity."[2]

But Falkland's attitude in the great series of debates which followed on the Church is more interesting to us. Here also, at first, he was entirely on the popular side, and in his zeal against the bishops even separated himself for a time from his friend Hyde, with whom he had hitherto acted in all things. His friend afterwards remembered the circumstance, and has touchingly signalised it in his ' History.' We shall confine ourselves at present to a rapid review of the different stages of the subject as it came before the Parliament, and the part taken by Falkland in the course of the debates. His special position in the matter of Church government will again come before us in the closing discussion of his opinions.

[1] Rushworth, iv. 141.   [2] Hist. of Rebellion, b. vii. vol. ii. 447.

The conduct of the bishops came before Parliament very early after its opening. Immediately following Strafford's accusation, Wren, Bishop of Ely, was impeached; and on the 18th December Laud was voted a traitor by the House of Commons, and conveyed to the Tower. Falkland disliked the Archbishop; and the dislike was probably reciprocal. It is true that Laud, while baiting the Puritans with merciless severity, maintained kindly personal relations with men like Hales and Chillingworth. He did this probably from mixed motives, but certainly from no sympathy with their opinions; and any toleration he was disposed to give to old friends, whom perhaps he thought it possible to win over to his own side, he was not at all likely to extend to one in the position of Falkland, who showed both readiness and ability to put himself at the head of a moderate or liberal party in Church as well as State—who had, in fact, already become distinguished as the leader of such a party. The instinct of the genuine sacerdotalist is still more true to hatred of liberalism than of Puritanism. It was all the more creditable to Falkland that he seems to have taken no part in the impeachment of the Archbishop. But numerous petitions having been presented in December, alleging the manifold grievances of the country from the oppression of the bishops, and praying for their abolition, Falkland made his first great speech on Episcopacy on the 9th of February following, when the petitions were taken up and discussed. The whole of this speech apparently has been preserved, and is marked throughout, in the highest degree, both by eloquence and sense—the enthusiasm of patriotic sentiment, and yet the moderation of a reflective intellect. It commences as follows: " Mr Speaker,—He is a great stranger in Israel who knows not this kingdom hath long laboured under many and great oppressions both in religion and liberty; and his acquaintance here is not great, or his ingenuity less, who doth not both know and acknowledge that a great if not a principal cause of both these have been some bishops and their adherents. Mr Speaker, a little search will serve to find them to have been the destruction of unity, under pretence of uniformity—to have brought in superstition and scandal under the titles of reverence and decency—to have defiled our Church by adorning our churches—to have slackened the strictness of that union which was formerly between us and those of our religion beyond the sea: an action as impolitic as ungodly. We shall find them to have tithed mint and anise, and have left undone the weightier works of the law. . . . It hath been more dangerous for men to go to some neighbour's parish when they had no sermon in their own, than to be obstinate and perpetual recusants; while masses have been said in security, a conventicle hath been a crime; and which is yet more, the conforming to ceremonies hath been more exacted than the conforming to Christianity." He deplores the check thus given to Christian instruction and the consequent "ignorance, which would best introduce that religion which accounts it *the mother of devotion.*" He continues: "The most frequent subjects, even in the most sacred auditories, have been the *jus divinum* of bishops and tithes, the sacredness of the clergy, the sacrilege of impropriations, the demolishing of Puritanism. . . . Mr Speaker, to go yet further, some of them have so industriously laboured to deduce themselves from Rome, that they have given great suspicion that in gratitude they desire to return thither, or at least to meet it half-way. Some have evidently laboured to bring in an English, though not a Roman Popery; I mean not only the outside and dress of it, but equally absolute, a blind dependence of the people upon the clergy, and of the clergy upon themselves, and have opposed the Papacy beyond the seas that they might settle one beyond the water. Nay, common fame is more than ordinarily false if none of them have found a way to reconcile the opinions of Rome to the preferments of England, and to be so absolutely, directly, and cordially Papists, that it is all that fifteen hundred pounds a-year can do to keep them from confessing it."

So far, and further, in reference to many particulars carefully detailed, but for which we can find no room, Falkland's enthusiastic patriotism breaks forth against the bishops. But before the close of his speech, he recalls the fact that the order, and the men who had so abused it in England, were not to be confounded. "We shall make no little compliment to those, and no little apology for those, to whom this charge belongs, if we shall lay the faults of these men upon the order of the bishops—upon the Episcopacy. I wish we may distinguish between those who have been the stream that carried them." He remembers that "the first planters and spreaders of Christianity," and the "main conducers" to its resurrection at the Reformation, were bishops; "and that even now, in the greatest defection of that order, there are yet some who have conduced in nothing to our late innovations but in their silence—some who, in an unexpected and mighty place and power, have expressed an equal moderation and humility, being neither ambitious before nor proud after, either of the crosier's staff or white staff—some who have been learned opposers of Popery and zealous suppressors of Arminianism—between whom and their inferior clergy infrequency of preaching hath been no distinction—whose lives are untouched, not only by *guilt*, but by *malice*, scarce to be equalled by those of any condition, or to be excelled by those of any calendar;—I doubt not, I say, but, if we consider this, this consideration will bring forth this conclusion — that *bishops may be good men;* and let us give but good men good rules, we shall have both good governors and good times."

Falkland argues, therefore, even in this first speech, for the maintenance of the order of Episcopacy cleared of its abuses. If "temporal power," or "employment," or the extent of their revenues, interfered with the usefulness of bishops—let these things, he urged, "be considered and taken care of;" but he can hardly deem it possible that the House of Commons should "think it fit to abolish, upon a few days' debate, an Order which hath lasted (as appears by story) in most Churches these sixteen hundred years, and in all from Christ to Calvin." And even in proposing to cut down the proportions and income of the Episcopal office, he is strongly opposed to doing this to such an extent as would interfere with "the dignity of learning and the encouragement of students"—which, as he puts it, would "invert" the policy of Jeroboam, "and, as he made the *meanest* of the people *priests*, make the highest of the priests the *meanest* of the people." Episcopacy, to his mind, in short, was not a divine, though an ancient and primitive order. "I do not believe them (bishops) to be *jure divino*—nay, I believe them not to be *jure divino.*" But neither did he hold them to be "*injuriâ humanâ.*" He considered them, in fine, as neither "necessary nor as unlawful, but as convenient or inconvenient;" and drew his thoughtful eloquence to a conclusion in words weighty with wisdom for all time, and which it would have been well if the Long Parliament had remembered and acted upon: "Since all great mutations in government are dangerous (even where what is introduced by that mutation is such as would have been profitable upon a primary foundation); and since the greatest danger of mutations is, that all the dangers and inconveniences they may bring are not to be foreseen; and since no wise man will undergo great danger but for great necessity,—my opinion is that we should not root up this ancient tree, as dead as it appears, till we have tried whether by this or the like topping of the branches, the sap, which was unable to feed the whole, may not serve to make what is left both grow and flourish."

Many speakers followed on this occasion, and the subject was referred to a committee "formerly appointed for the London and other petitions." It was destined to reappear before the House in many forms, and to test and dissolve the unanimity with which its members had hitherto worked. Gradually it became evident that there were two distinct parties—one for a moderate reform of Episcopacy and all other abuses, and a "root and branch" party, which desired not only the overthrow of the Church, but were prepared for still more extreme measures. Falkland advanced a step, but only a single step further, with the anti-Episcopal party. He voted, not only for the exclusion of the bishops from judicial functions,[1] but also at first for their exclusion from the House of Peers. It was on this last occasion that he separated from Hyde, and hope seems to have been temporarily cherished that he might throw himself heart and soul into the extreme movement. Hyde and he had been noted as "inseparable." They sat together in the House beside Sir John Colepepper, member for Kent—so soon to be associated with them in office—"on the left-hand side at entering." This "was so much taken notice of, that, if they came not into the House together, as usually they did, everybody left the place for him that was absent." When the bill for excluding the bishops from the Upper House first came under discussion, Hyde spoke earnestly for throwing it out on the ground of its involving a grave constitutional change. Suddenly Falkland

[1] 11th of March (1641), when the discussions as to the position of the bishops in the House of Lords seem to have begun.

rose from his seat beside his friend, "and declared himself to be of another opinion; and that, as he thought the thing itself to be absolutely necessary for the benefit of the Church which was in so great danger, so he had never heard that the constitution of the kingdom would be violated by the passing that Act, and that he had heard many of the clergy protest that they would not acknowledge that they were represented by the bishops." At the same time, he implied the matter was one for the House of Peers itself ("amongst whom the bishops sat and had their votes") rather than for the House of Commons to determine. "If they could make it appear that they were a third estate" then that House "would reject" the Bill. "And so, with some facetiousness answering some other particulars, he concluded for the passing of the Act." It was a marvellous delight to many, adds the historian, "to see the two inseparable friends divided in so important a point — and the more because they saw Mr Hyde was much surprised by the contradiction, as in truth he was."[1] But Clarendon is here forgetful of the real sentiments of his friend expressed in his previous speech. He had then plainly stated that the position of the bishops in the House of Peers—or "their lordships," as he called it—was no essential part of the Episcopal authority; and that if their usefulness demanded it, they might well be deprived of this position.

Falkland was in truth substantially consistent throughout all the discussions on the subject of

[1] History, i. 315.

the Church, even where his consistency is most open to challenge. It is perfectly clear from the tenor of his speeches, even when denouncing the bishops, that he desired to uphold Episcopacy, and for this purpose was willing to sacrifice all that was merely adventitious in the office, and which seemed to him, upon the whole, rather to mar than to add to its usefulness. He looked at the substance and reality of Church order — which was plainly dear to him—and for the sake of securing this, was ready to yield whatever seemed to him unnecessary and unimportant. But when he discovered that the enemies of Episcopacy were not to be satisfied by such concessions, but were determined on its overthrow, he immediately took his stand against them. This is the simple explanation of his having opposed, six months later, or in the following October, a bill of the same character—for "depriving the bishops of their votes"— as that which he had formerly supported. Hampden taxed him on this occasion with a change of opinion; but Falkland quite pertinently retorted " that he had formerly been persuaded by that worthy gentleman to believe many things which he had since found to be untrue, and therefore he had changed his opinion in many particulars as well as to things and persons."[1] The truth was, that in the

---

[1] It was on this occasion apparently that he made his further extended speech "concerning Episcopacy" — "a draught" of which was afterwards found amongst his papers in his own handwriting, and printed at Oxford in 1644. This speech is by no means so vigorous and eloquent as the first, from which we have already quoted in the text, but it is also very interesting in relation to

interval the course of events had rapidly advanced. The "root and branch" Bill, for abolishing Episcopacy, had been introduced in June. And not only had the movement against the Church gathered strength, but, more significantly still, the extreme party had prepared, although not yet presented, the "Grand Remonstrance" in the face of the desire of all moderate politicians to consolidate the reforms already obtained, and open up the way for reconciliation with the King, instead of further aggravating differences. In short, by the autumn of 1641, the patriots of the Long Parliament had already separated into two divisions. The Constitutionalists, with Falkland and Hyde and Colepepper, at their head, had taken their stand against further encroachments; while the Radical reformers, headed by Pym, Hampden, and others, were determined upon still more extensive changes and an increased weakening of the royal prerogative. Falkland had plainly been let understand by Hampden, that if the Bill for the exclusion of the bishops from the House of Lords were carried, nothing further would be attempted against the Church. And when he found that he was deceived in this, he felt himself quite warranted in revising his original decision upon the point. To some extent probably Hampden himself was deceived. For Clarendon mentions that at first

---

Falkland's ecclesiastical views. It is chiefly taken up with urging the inconvenience of a radical change of Church government, especially in favour of the "Scotch ecclesiastical government"—whose *jure* *divino* pretensions, "to meet when they please, to treat of what they please, to excommunicate whom they please, even parliaments themselves," are somewhat scornfully set forth.

he did not feel inclined to the introduction of the
"root and branch" Bill, although he afterwards gave
his assent to it. The current of events hurried him
and others away; and the tide for the time was running so strongly against the very name of bishops
that he and Pym, and no doubt others, who professed themselves favourable to the doctrine and
discipline of the Church of England, reformed of its
abuses, were swept away with the general stream.

A crowd of stirring political events now rapidly
succeeded each other,—the debates on the Grand
Remonstrance, the attempt of Charles to arrest
the five members, the retirement of the Court
from London, the assumption of military powers
by Parliament, and, finally, the raising of the royal
standard at Nottingham (23d Aug. 1642). Falkland had plainly drawn himself off from the extreme party during the summer of 1641; and when
the attempt was renewed, which had been unsuccess-
fully made at an earlier stage, of attaching certain
of the parliamentary leaders to the King's service as
ministers, he was at length induced to accept the office
of Secretary of State, along with Colepepper as Chancellor of the Exchequer. Clarendon has told all the
story of his hesitation, and yet his ultimate acceptance. "No man could be more surprised than he was
when the first intimation was made to him of the
King's purpose; he had never proposed any such
thing to himself, nor had any veneration for the
Court, but only such a loyalty to the King as the law
required from him."[1] Whatever we may think of

[1] Hist. of Rebellion, b. iv. vol. i. 444.

Falkland's judgment in accepting office in the circumstances, with his obvious distrust of the King's character, and the evident dislike which existed betwixt him and that inner circle of councillors, with the Queen at their head, who guided Charles far more than any minister, it is impossible to doubt the purity of the patriotism which animated him now, as in all preceding stages of his career. The study of his character and speeches reveals his deep devotion to the English constitution, both in Church and State. With all his love of liberty, religious and political, he had a genuine enthusiasm for the Church and for royalty. For Charles himself he may have had little affection or esteem. He dreaded the demands which a character like his was sure to make upon a minister. He feared "lest the King should expect such a submission and resignation of himself, and his own reason and judgment, to his commands, as he should never give, or pretend to give." Withal he was ardently loyal. His attachment was "to a principle, and not to a man;"[1] and he allowed all his personal scruples to be overcome by the enthusiasm of his belief in the reconciliation of royalty and constitutional government—of Church order and religious freedom.

It has been lately insinuated,[2] notwithstanding Clarendon's express assertions to the contrary, that Falkland, along with Hyde himself and Colepepper, were privy to Charles's attempt to arrest the five

---

[1] Lord Lytton in an admirable essay, "Pym *versus* Falkland."— Miscell. Prose Works, vol. i.

[2] Forster's Arrest of the Five Members.

members. But there is really not a tittle of evidence in favour of this suggestion, which is at the same time opposed to all we know of Falkland's character, his transparent truthfulness, and hatred of rash and crooked courses—features so transparent in all his career, that, Mr Forster himself admits, " he could as easily have given himself to steal as to dissemble." We cannot, therefore, conceive him entering upon office with such a stain of evil secrecy in his mind, or such a purpose of ill-concerted vengeance towards men with whom he had been lately acting. To some it may be equally difficult to conceive his going on after the event with the negotiations which were then in progress, and accepting office at all in the circumstances. But there is all the difference in the two cases betwixt a man, it may be, unwisely impelled by a sense of duty to enter the service of his sovereign for the sake of his country, and a man clearly committing himself from the first to a course which neither patriotic nor moral judgment can approve. The gravest doubts may be raised as to the wisdom of Falkland's policy in identifying himself with a cause which, however great and beautiful it appeared in his own eyes, was in hopeless and impracticable hands—in hands with many of whose doings he could have no sympathy. It must have been a bitter humiliation to him, on many occasions, to find himself associated with " the Digbys and the Jermyns," and the general crew of ultra-royalists which gathered around the royal standard. It may also be true that he had misgivings as to his position from first to last—that there were even points on which his heart was as much with the Parliament as with the King; for he was a man of infinite " self-questionings." But it is impossible to doubt that he had chosen what appeared to him to be the right side in a great crisis, in which he felt he could not stand aloof, or fail in service to his country.

The result was not what he expected, and he soon began to despair. He had hoped to conciliate opinions, and they grew every month more irreconcilable; to mitigate party feeling, and the exasperation between the Parliament and the King every day increased. And when civil war became inevitable, and blood was shed on both sides, his heartbreak proved intolerable. He lacked the firmness or coarseness of fibre which gathers strength in the face of opposition, and rises in proud defiance to meet menace with menace. " From the entrance into this unnatural war," says Clarendon, " his natural cheerfulness and vivacity grew clouded, and a kind of sadness and dejection of spirit stole upon him which he had never been used to." And even after hostilities had begun, he hoped and hoped that peace would ensue after a decisive trial of strength. When this hope perished, and negotiations with the Parliament seemed finally broken off, " those indispositions which had before touched him grew into a perfect habit of uncheerfulness; and he who had been so exactly easy and affable to all men that his face and countenance were always present and vacant to his company, and held any cloudiness and less pleasantness of the visage a kind of rudeness or incivility, became on a sudden less communicable, and thence very sad, pale, and exceedingly affected with the spleen. In his clothes and habit, which he had minded before always with more neatness and industry and expense than is usual to so great a soul, he was not now only incurious, but too negligent; and in his reception of suitors, and the necessary or casual addresses to his place, so quick and sharp and severe that there wanted not some men (strangers to his nature and disposition) who believed him proud and imperious, from which no mortal man was ever more free. . . . When there was any overture or hope of peace he would be more erect and vigorous, and exceedingly solicitous to press anything which he thought might promote it; and sitting among his friends, often, after a deep silence and frequent sighs, would, with a shrill and sad accent, ingeminate the word '*Peace, peace;*' and would passionately profess that the very agony of the war, and the view of the calamities and desolation the kingdom did and must endure, took his sleep from him, and would shortly break his heart."[1]

To those disposed to idealise the one party or the other, Falkland's attitude may not appear magnanimous. But to others, looking below the surface to the real horrors of the fratricidal war in which Parliamentarians and Royalists were engaged, and to the blows inflicted upon liberty, civil and religious, by the exasperated passions of both sides, there may

[1] Hist. of Rebellion, b. vii., vol. iii., 453-54.

be pardoned some feeling, not only of pathos but of enthusiasm, for this martyr of moderation. Moderation may have its heroes, surely, as well as fanaticism; and if Pym's political daring and Cromwell's rude and powerful genius claim our admiration, we may reserve some share of it for one, inferior to both in statecraft and firmness of purpose, but greatly their superior in elevation of personal character and range of intellectual and spiritual thoughtfulness. The drooping figure of Falkland may seem weak as he sits ingeminating "*Peace, peace,*" but all the while his heart was wellnigh broken by the calamities he could not avert, his intellect was cool and luminous in council, and his spirit courageous to recklessness in the hour of danger. We cannot think less of a man that his patriotism was tender as well as intrepid, and that he mourned for a broken ideal of order and peace which his higher intelligence assured him could never come from the excesses of either side.

Of the cause which he thus nobly but sadly served, Falkland was destined soon to be the victim. The war was begun on the 23d August 1642. In the September of the following year, after varying alternations of success and defeat, the Parliamentary forces moved to the relief of Gloucester, which had been invested by the Royalists, and the siege of which is memorable to us in connection with Chillingworth's attempts at engineering. Having succeeded in raising the siege, the Earl of Essex gradually advanced to Newbury, where the Royalist forces had already established themselves two hours before his arrival. Falkland accompanied the King on his march from Gloucester, but Hyde was detained at Bristol. From thence he is found remonstrating with his friend for the indiscreet manner in which he had been exposing himself to danger. It was not, Hyde said, "the office of a Privy Councillor and a Secretary of State to visit the trenches, as he usually did; and conjured him, out of the conscience of his duty to the King, and to free his friends from those continual uneasy apprehensions, not to engage his person to those dangers which were not incumbent to him." Falkland replied that, as the trenches were at an end, there would be no further danger there; but "that his case was different from other men's; that he was so much taken notice of for an impatient desire of peace, that it was necessary that he should likewise make it appear that it was not out of fear of the utmost hazard of war."[1] He was evidently sensitive that his personal courage should be suspected in his eagerness for peace, and this may have given a touch of recklessness to his gallantry, which had been conspicuous throughout.

On the morning of the battle, there are different accounts of his bearing. A well-known story is told by Whitelock, of his having "called for a clean shirt," saying that "if he were slain he should not be found in foul linen;" and, further, that "he was weary of the times, and foresaw much misery to his own country, and did believe he should be out of it ere night." Clarendon, on the other hand, who is much more likely to have been well informed, says that

[1] Life, i. 202.

he was "very cheerful," as he usually was in the prospect of action. He put himself at the head of Sir John Byron's regiment, and as he was advancing to the charge of a body of foot—the hedges on both sides being lined by the enemy's musketeers—he fell, mortally wounded by a musket-shot. His body was not found till next morning, and having been transferred to Great Tew, was so hastily interred that its exact resting-place remains unknown.

Thus perished, in his thirty-fourth year, one who seemed to many in his age "incomparable," both for his virtues and his talents. For many days Hyde was so absorbed in grief for the loss of his "dear friend"—his "sweetheart," as Falkland had affectionately addressed him[1]—that he was unable to attend to any business; and long afterwards, when twenty-six years of an eventful life had passed, he felt that time had in no degree effaced the "love and grief" with which he cherished the image of his friend. I had with him, he said to his children in his will, "a most perfect and blameless friendship."[2] It could only have been some rare charm of character which thus fixed so much love and admiration—which not only drew forth encomiums from poetic friends, and the applause of literary and theological associates, but the memory of which melted to tenderness the hearts of two such men as Clarendon and Chillingworth.

Like his friends Hales and Godolphin, Falkland was of low stature—"a little man," with "no great strength of body, blackish hair, something flaggy,

[1] Letter, March 1641. [2] Written at Jersey, 1647.

and, I think, his eyes black." Such is Aubrey's portrait; and Clarendon's account confirms the impression that Falkland was not in any degree indebted for his remarkable influence to external attractions. His " motion" was ungraceful, his voice " untuned," and " his aspect so far from inviting that it had somewhat in it of simplicity." " Sure no man was less beholden to nature for its recommendation into the world ; but then no man sooner or more disappointed this general and customary prejudice." But his " little person was quickly found to contain a great heart" and a fearless nature—his untuned voice to be the organ of an understanding and wit so excellent as to need no ornament of delivery; while his disposition " was so gentle and obliging, so much delighted in courtesy, kindness, and generosity, that all mankind could not but admire and love him."[1]

II. It now only remains to estimate more distinctly the significance of Falkland's position as the head of the moderate or rational party in the Church of England at the outbreak of the civil war. We have already quoted at length his views concerning Episcopacy. He believed in its antiquity and utility as an Order of Church government. He proved its ardent supporter in the hour of trial, and earnestly repudiated the attempts to subvert it. But his defence of Episcopacy was the defence of an ancient Christian institution, and not of an exclusive divine system. His own studies had convinced him that the Order of Bishops was coeval with the organisa-

[1] Life, i. 38.

tion of the Christian Church. It had lasted, as he said, "these sixteen hundred years;" and it was contrary to all his instincts as a student and a statesman to change "in an instant the whole face of the Church like the scene of a mask." But in the very same breath in which he advocated this rational conservatism he repudiated with a terse emphasis, which may bear to be repeated, the *jus divinum* of Bishops. "Mr Speaker," he said, "I do not believe them to be *jure divino*—nay, I believe them not to be *jure divino*." In short, while vindicating the Reformed Church of England, he rejected on its behalf not only the arbitrary impositions of the Laudian Bishops, but all sacerdotal pretensions, and all idea of radical distinction betwixt it and the other Churches of the Reformation. It was one of his express charges against Laud and his coadjutors that they had "slackened the strictness of that union which was formerly between us and those of our religion beyond the sea—an action as impolitic as ungodly."

The same enlightened principles which guided his attitude towards Episcopacy appear in his estimate of other forms of Church government. He objected to the "Scotch Ecclesiastical government" not because it was Presbyterian, but because of its *jure divino* pretensions and arbitrary interferences with social manners and the course of civil government.[1] He recognised in its advocates the same "desire of uniformity" which in the Laudian Bishops had led to such disastrous results—"the destruction of unity,"

[1] Speech concerning Episcopacy prefixed to Discourse of Infallibility, p. 7, 2d ed., 1660.

as he said, " under pretence of uniformity." He saw the intolerance which lay beneath the aggressive Puritanism of the time, and reprobated it as strongly as he had done the aggressions of Anglicanism. It appeared to him worse than the *jure divino* pretensions of " some bishops," because more " likely to be believed by the people." This is very much the strain of his second speech concerning Episcopacy, in which he points out the inconveniences of abolishing, without any satisfactory substitute, a form of government which " hath very well agreed with the constitution of our laws, with the disposition of our people," and under which "we have lived long happily and gloriously." The conclusion of this speech is less pointed and eloquent than that of the former, but scarcely less significant of his position as a liberal churchman :—" For us," he says, " to bring in any *unlimited*, any *Independent* authority, the first is against the liberty of the subject, the second against the right and privilege of Parliament; and both against the protestation. If it be said that this *unlimitedness* and *independence* is only in spiritual things, I answer first that arbitrary government being the worst of governments, and our *bodies* being worse than our *souls*, it will be strange to set up that over the second of which we were so impatient over the first. Secondly, that M. *Sollicitor*, speaking about the power of the Clergy to make canons to bind, did excellently inform us what a mighty influence spiritual power hath upon temporal affairs. So that if our Clergy had the one, they had inclusively almost all the other. And to this I may adde (what all men may see) the vast temporall power of the Pope allow'd him by such who allow it him onely *in ordine ad Spiritualia:* for the fable will tell you, if you make the Lyon judge (and the Clergy, assisted by the people, is Lyon enough) it was a wise fear of the Foxe's, lest he might call a knubb a horn. And sure, Sir, they will in this case be Judges, not onely of that which is Spirituall, but of what it is that is so: and the people, receiving instruction from no other, will take the most Temporal matter to be Spiritual, if they tell them it is so."

His "Discourse of the Infallibility of the Church of Rome" explains most clearly and fully his religious position. In this brief discourse, and in his more lengthened "Reply to the Answer thereto," we see how vital was his interest in religious questions, and especially in the great question of religious certitude or authority, which invariably, in a time of spiritual excitement, comes to the front. He had a special interest in the question, like his friend Chillingworth, on account of the insidious activity of the Jesuit missionaries; but his thoughts naturally ran in the same direction. The necessity of looking into the whole subject for himself was one of the special reasons which led to his retirement to Tew, and the theological reunions which he encouraged there. For, " in religion, he thought too careful and too curious an inquiry could not be made." Above all others, this was the intellectual interest which united him with Chillingworth, and in the discussion of which they both sharpened their reasoning faculties. A good deal in the general argument of the Discourse reminds us of "the Religion of Protestants." There are passages, and especially turns of reasoning, which are a distinct echo of its great author—we seem almost to catch his voice; but there does not seem after all, on the one side or the other, any formal traces of indebtedness. With a common tone of argument, the individuality of each writer is sufficiently manifest.[1]

The position of the Church of Rome is clearly stated in the outset. This Church defends herself against all allegations of error by saying that she cannot err. She has no errors, because she never can have any. She appeals, in short, to her infallibility. But this, as Falkland points out, is the very point to be proved, and "so much harder is it to be believed than the first, that it needs more certain proof." A claim to infallibility can never be accepted on its own authority. It must be vindicated on the clearest and most indubitable grounds. And so,

---

[1] Falkland and Chillingworth and Hales are supposed to have been indebted in their "revolt against Church authority" (Hallam's Lat. Hist., ii. 421, 6th ed.) to Daillé's well-known Treatise "concerning the right use of the Fathers," published in 1628. There can be no doubt that Falkland greatly admired Daillé's book, and partly translated it, although the papers whereon this translation was half finished were *long since* lost, even in 1651. (Testimonies of the Lord Falkland and others to Daillé's book, prefixed to its translation printed in that year in London.) But beyond a certain tone of speaking as to the inconsistencies of patristic tradition, and the difficulty of finding its meaning, there is no evidence of his having made much use of it, and none at all of his having borrowed from it. Daillé's treatise, we can imagine, was a welcome assistance to both Chillingworth and Falkland in their researches; but the value of their writings is quite independent of any assistance which it could have given them. In Hales we have not found any trace of indebtedness to Daillé.

under pretence of escaping argument as to religious truth, we end in an infinite regression of argument. We can never get out of the shadow of our own reason, nor rest on any surer grounds than those of rational conviction in some form or another. "We can never infallibly know that the Church is infallible." And if Romanists say "that an argument out of Scripture is sufficient ground of divine faith, why are they offended with the Protestants for believing every part of their religion upon that ground, upon which they build all theirs at once? And, if following the same rule, with equal desire of finding the truth by it (having neither of those qualities which Isid. Pelus.[1] saith are the cause of all Heresie, Pride and Prejudication [2]), why should God be more offended with the one than with the other, though they chance to erre?"[3]

The alleged ground of infallibility is the necessity of "some certain guide" in religious matters. But supposing such a guide to exist, of what use is it unless it be plainly manifest? An infallible church which does not "plainly appear to be so," is as if God "were to set a ladder to Heaven, and seem to have a great care of my going up, whereas unless there be care taken that I may know this ladder is here to that purpose, it were as good for me it never had been set."[4] And what, he asks, is to be made of the case in which the Church of Rome contradicts

---

[1] Isidorus of Pelusium, a Christian writer of the fifth century.
[2] αὐθάδειαν καὶ πρόληψιν.
[3] Discourse, 2.
[4] Ibid., 2, 3.

herself? Here, surely, the principle of infallibility plainly breaks down. "For to say, I am to believe the present Church, that it differs not from the former, though it seem to me to do so, is to send me to a witness, and bid me not believe it."[1]

This suggests to him the further question, which is the church? Supposing the idea of infallibility granted, all that this imports is, "that God will have a church always which will not err, but not that such and such a succession shall be in the right." The Greek Church may be the true church; or it may have been the church, although it has now fallen into error. To maintain the Church of Rome to be the true church because its opinions are more consonant to Scripture or antiquity, is to "run into a circle, proving the Romanist tenets to be true; first, because the church holds them, and then theirs to be the church because the church holds the truth—which last, though it appears to me the only way, yet it takes away its being a guide, which we may follow without examination, without which all they say besides is nothing."[2]

This necessity for examination brings him back to the centre of the subject. The right of private judgment or examination is repudiated by the Romanists, because when differences arise as to the meaning of Scripture, "there is no way," as they say, "to end them." But whereas the assumption of infallibility itself is no security against difference of opinion—as Falkland shows by various instances of such difference in the Church of Rome—the

[1] Ibid., 3. [2] Ibid., 4.

only reasonable inference to be drawn from the fact of such difference is, that it is not hurtful in itself nor displeasing to God. Where God has not clearly and indubitably revealed His will, " it will not stand with His goodness to damn man for not following it." To those "who follow their reason in the interpretation of the Scriptures, God will either give His grace for assistance to find the truth, or His pardon if they miss it. And then this supposed necessity of an infallible guide (with the supposed damnation for the want of it) fall together to the ground."[1] These words, in their trenchant force and magnanimous confidence, closely resemble those of Chillingworth; and there is a good deal of the same hunting of the adverse argument from point to point, in which this great writer delights—leaving no loophole of escape, and no ground on which to rest. The idea of infallibility is looked at in every aspect, and its futility exposed unsparingly, though without much logical arrangement or clear advance of reasoning. There is a lack of definite arrangement, and we find ourselves frequently returning upon the same path. As a whole, however, the subject is well conceived, and its handling worthy of Falkland's argumentative ability, and fairness and vigour of mind, while it shows throughout a firm grasp of the rational principles lying at the basis of Protestantism or any form of intelligent religious faith.

The details of the treatise, from its want of connection, do not readily fall into order. It is enough to indicate its main ideas, and to quote such passages as

[1] Ibid., p. 5.

may throw an additional light on the thought and position of the writer. Having shown, first, that infallibility itself must be proved before it can be erected into a principle of religious authority; and, secondly, that it must be located, or, in other words, proved to belong to the Church of Rome, and no other Church—in all the steps of which proof there may be uncertainty and mistake;—he proceeds to point out, that even admitting these two points, the principle is after all of no practical utility. For every Christian in the end must rest on his own understanding of the supposed infallible dogma or decree. Let the voice of the Church be ever so authoritative, it can only reach me through my intelligence, and after all I may misunderstand it. Of its sense I can have no better expounder than my reason, and should I fail with all my efforts to understand it, surely I shall not be damned for my failure? Why then "shall I, for mistaking the sense of the Scripture, or why am I a less fit interpreter of the one than of the other"—of the Bible than of the Church? " And when both seem equally clear, and yet contradictory, shall not I as soon believe Scripture, which is without doubt of as great authority?"[1]

Falkland enters into many special questions with the Church of Rome, particularly in his 'Reply;'[2]

[1] Ibid., p. 7.
[2] Falkland's 'Reply' is considerably longer than his original essay, but it is mainly an expansion of its general line of thought. The 'Answer' to which he replied is said to have been written by a Roman Catholic priest of the name of Holland, who had been a Cambridge student. It is distinguished by great courtesy of tone towards Falkland, and is well and temperately written, but not otherwise remarkable. The Discourse, with 'Answer,' and his Lordship's 'Reply,' are all found in

but his argument mainly interests us, and is in itself most luminous and interesting, where it keeps the level of general principles, or deals with his own personal convictions. Like his friend Chillingworth, he kindles into indignation at the idea of persecution for religious opinions. Dogmatic differences, however vital, can never justify intolerance. He refers to Constantine's famous letter on the Trinitarian controversy, as showing that even on a question so great as this, neither side was deemed without the pale of the Church. "Punishing for opinions" was entirely foreign to the best ages of Christianity, and was in fact "a mark to know false opinions by." "And I believe," he adds, "throughout antiquity you will find no putting any to death, unless it be such as begin to kill first, as the Circumcellians, or

a single volume which seems at first to have been published in 1651, and afterwards in 1660 with one of Falkland's speeches on Episcopacy prefixed. The volume is edited by a Dr Thomas Triplet, who appears to have been tutor to Falkland's son Henry, and who says in an introductory letter of dedication, addressed to his pupil, that he had received the manuscripts, not long before her death, from Lady Falkland. Triplet afterwards became a prebendary of Westminster, and is said to have been "a man of great wit, and a great companion of Lord Falkland."

Henry the third Lord Falkland was a man of considerable distinction, no less than his father and grandfather. He inherited apparently their literary ability, without the earnestness of character that might have been supposed due to him both from father and mother. A good story is told of him by Walpole ('Royal and Noble Authors,' v. 121), that "being brought early into the House of Commons, and a grave senator objecting to his youth, 'and to his not looking as if he had sowed his wild oats,' he replied with great quickness, 'Then I am come to the properest place, where are so many geese to pick them up.' He wrote," Walpole adds, "'The Marriage Night, a Comedy.'" Henry was the second son, the eldest, Lorenzo, having died in youth, to the great grief of his mother. See p. 89.

suchlike. I am sure the Christian religion's chiefest glory is, that it increaseth by being persecuted; and having that advantage of the Mohammedan, methinks it should be to take ill care of Christianity to hold it up by Turkish means—at least, it must breed doubts, that if the religion had always remained the same, it would not now be defended by ways so contrary to those by which at first it was propagated. I desire recrimination may not be used; for though it be true that Calvin had done it, and the Church of England a little (which is a little too much), yet she (confessing she may err) is not so chargeable with any fault as those which pretend they cannot, and so will be sure never to mend it. . . . I confess this opinion of damning so many, and this custom of burning so many, this breeding up of those who knew nothing else in any point of religion, yet to be in a readiness to cry, *To the fire with him, to Hell with him*—these, I say, were chiefly the causes which made so many so suddenly leave the Church of Rome."[1]

The right of rational inquiry appears to him more sacred and truly religious than any blind faith whatsoever. "Grant the Church," he says, "to be infallible, yet methinks he that denies it, and employs his reason to seek if it be true, should be in as good case as he that believeth it, and searcheth not at all the truth of the proposition he receives. For I cannot see why he should be saved because by reason of his parents' belief, or the religion of the country, or some such accident, the truth was offered

[1] Ibid., p. 13, 14.

to his understanding, when, had the contrary been offered, he would have received that. And the other damned that believes falsehood upon as good ground as the other doth truth, unless the Church be like a conjuror's circle, that will keep a man from the devil, though he came into it by chance. They grant no man is an heretic that believes not his heresy obstinately; and if he be no heretic, he may sure be saved. It is not then certain damnation for any man to deny the infallibility of the Church of *Rome*, but for him only that denies it obstinately. And then I am safe, for I am sure I do not. Neither can they say I shall be damned for schism, though not for heresy, for he is as well no schismatic, though in schism—that is, willing to join in communion with the true Church, when it appears to be so to him, as he is no heretic, though he holds heretical opinions, who holds them not obstinately—that is (as I suppose), with a desire to be informed if he be in the wrong. . . . I have the less doubt of this opinion, that I shall have no harm for not believing the infallibility of the Church of *Rome*, because of my being so far from leaning to the contrary, and so suffering my will to have power over my understanding, that if God would leave it to me which tenet should be true, I would rather chuse that that should, than the contrary. For they may well believe me that I take no pleasure in tumbling hard and unpleasant books, and making myself giddy with disputing obscure questions." To believe, he continues, that there must always be "a society of men whom I might always know, whose opinions must be certainly true,

is a more agreeable way than to endure endless volumes of commenters, the harsh Greek of Epiphanius, and the harder Latin of Irenæus."[1]

To the objection that it is mere pride of reason that is at the bottom of all doubts about the Church's infallibility, he retorts that "too much impatience and laziness of examining is the cause that many do not doubt it." What pride, he says, can there be in desiring to have a rational foundation for belief, since even the Infallibilist must pretend to some reason for his position, and that the writer himself is willing to be led wherever Truth may lead him, "remembering that Truth in likelyhood is, where her author God was, in the *still voice*, and not the *loud wind*"? His mind, he professes, is open to every reasonable influence—prayer as well as argument. He would neither be "wilfully blind," nor "deny impudently" what he sees. But save Reason herself, he can imagine no ultimate guide to the Truth. Every intelligence in the end must incline to the side of the greater reason. "For to be persuaded by reason, that to such an authority I ought to submit it, is still to follow reason, and not to quit her. And by what else is it that you examine what the apostles taught, when you examine that by ancient tradition, and ancient tradition by a present testimony? Yet when I speak thus of finding the Truth by Reason, I intend not to exclude the Grace of God, which I doubt not (for as much as is necessary to salvation) is ready to concur to our instruction; as the sun is to our sight, if we by a wilful winking chuse not to

[2] Ibid., p. 15, 16.

make, not it, but our selves guilty of our blindness. ... Yet when I speak of God's Grace, I mean not that it infuseth a knowledge without reason, but works by it, as by its minister, and dispels those mists of passions which do wrap up Truth from our understandings. For if you speak of its instructing any other way, you leave visible arguments to fly to invisible; and your adversary, when he hath found your play, will be soon at the same locke; and I believe in this sense, infused Faith is but the same thing, otherwise apparelled, which you have so often laught at in the Puritans under the title of private spirit."[1]

These quotations are enough to indicate Falkland's religious attitude, and to show what claims he had, apart from his mere social and political position, to lead the group of rational thinkers, who, amidst the conflicts of the seventeenth century, sought to take a middle course, and to fix the minds of their countrymen upon a broader and more tolerant view both of the Church and of Christianity. It is evident that Falkland added to his general intellectual accomplishments and political sagacity a deep and serious interest in the religious questions which really lay at the root of all the national difficulties of his time. He had pondered these questions thoughtfully, and worked out for himself clear and definite conclusions in favour at once of religious liberty and the national Church. While professedly arguing against the infallibility of the Church of Rome, his argument is equally valid against the Prelatic sacer-

[1] Reply, p. 118, 119.

dotalism which had more or less oppressed England since the accession of the Stuarts, and the Puritan dogmatism which sought to take its place. His plea against infallibility is really a plea in favour of freedom of religious opinion in a sense which neither Prelatist nor Puritan in the seventeenth century understood. It seemed to him then, as it has seemed to many since, possible to make room within the national Church for wide differences of dogmatic opinion, or, in other words, for the free rights of the Christian reason incessantly pursuing its inquest after truth, and moulding the national consciousness to higher conceptions of religious thought and duty. The frame of the Church of England was admirably suited for such a purpose as linking together in its Catholic order the Christian ages, and being in itself both apostolic and rational. He would have reformed but preserved and purified it, as the flexible and appropriate vehicle of the nation's religious progress. This was the conservative side of his thought, where he separated entirely from the "root-and-branch" men, on the principle succinctly expressed by him, that "where it is not *necessary* to change, it is necessary *not* to change." His mind, like all higher minds, sought not so much outward as inward change. He shrank from revolution in Church or State; but he would have liberalised both, in a truer and nobler sense than his contemporary revolutionists, ecclesiastical or political. His ideas were born out of due time; and the extremes, first of destruction and then of reaction, were destined to run their course. In all times of excitement this is more or less likely to be the case. The voice of reason is unheard amongst the clamours of party. And a Falkland dies broken-hearted when a Cromwell and a Clarendon take their turn of success. But the seed of wise thought never perishes; and Falkland's ideal of the Church, no less than of the State, may yet be realised when bigotries, Christian and anti-Christian, have more thoroughly consumed themselves in their internecine heat, and men have learned that the patient search for truth is better than all dogmas, and that the charity that thinketh no evil and rejoiceth in the truth is a higher Christian gain than the most definite opinions, or even the faith that could remove mountains.

IV.

JOHN HALES OF ETON—RELIGION AND DOGMATIC ORTHODOXY.

I. JOHN HALES—often dignified as the "ever-memorable Mr John Hales of Eton"—deserves the first place in our series of Theologians. He was the oldest of the group that surrounded Falkland, and although the quiet tenor of his life brought him into few prominent points of contact with the great events in England through which he passed, his temporary residence in Holland during the very crisis of the struggle betwixt the Calvinists and Arminians, the influence which this struggle evidently had upon his thought, and the interesting account which he has left in his Letters of the meetings of the Synod of Dort, all connect him directly with the origin of the rational movement which it is our aim to sketch. Hales's writings, moreover, were amongst the first, as they remain in some respects the best, expression of the principles inspiring and guiding the movement. They present a very complete picture of a singularly fresh, acute, and boldly ingenious and reflective mind, whose influence has been felt far beyond the circle of those more intimately associated with him, or who joined with him in a common object.

Of the man himself, unhappily, we have not the same full means of information as we have of the writer. There is no record of his life of any value. We must glean, as we best can, its particulars and their connected significance from Maizeaux's meagre and somewhat confused volume,[1] Wood's 'Athenæ Oxonienses,'[2] and the Biographical Dictionaries. So far, indeed, his own Letters from the Synod of Dort, which are full of life and meaning, will help us, and we shall weave their personal and descriptive touches, with some detail, into our sketch. Clarendon's lively but brief portraiture, and Aubrey's gossip, will also furnish some points of interest.

John Hales was born at Bath (Aubrey says Wells) in 1584. His father was "steward to the family of the Horners in Somersetshire."[3] He was educated in his native city in "grammar learning," and at thirteen years of age entered a scholar of Corpus Christi College. Here he took his degree in July 1603, and very soon began to attract attention by

---

[1] 'An Historical and Critical Account of the Life and Writings of the Ever-Memorable Mr John Hales,' a thin volume published in 1719 "as a specimen of an *Historical and Critical English Dictionary*," by P. Des Maizeaux, author of a similar volume of a more elaborate and valuable character on Chillingworth. The volume contains few facts beyond those given by Wood, but it throws some light upon the accessory features of his later life.

There is also a life written in Latin, with care and appreciation, by the well-known Mosheim (*Jo. Halesii Celeberrimi Britannorum Theologi Vita, Fata, et Labores*), prefixed to a Latin translation of Hales's Letters, and published in 1724; but it is almost entirely founded on Maizeaux's volume.

[2] Vol. iii. 409-416. Bliss's ed. Wood's notice of Hales is interesting, but inaccurate and misleading.

[3] Athen. Oxon., iii. c. 409. Bliss's ed.

the remarkable character of his attainments. "The prodigious pregnancy of his parts," says Wood, "being discovered by the hedge-beaters of Sir Henry Savile, he was encouraged by them to stand for a fellowship of Merton College." He obtained this fellowship in 1605—" in which election he showed himself a person of learning above his age and standing." "Through the whole course of his scholarship," Wood adds, "there was never any one in the then memory of man that ever went beyond him for subtle disputation in philosophy, for his eloquent declamations and orations; as also for his exact knowledge of the Greek tongue." His Greek scholarship formed a special bond betwixt him and Savile, who was then engaged in his famous edition of Chrysostom, in which he found the young scholar eminently serviceable. Their friendship was a lasting one, and the friends were afterwards associated at Eton as they had been at Oxford.

Shortly after obtaining his fellowship he appears to have entered into orders, and obtained some fame as a preacher. In 1612 he was appointed Greek Professor; and the founder of the Bodleian Library, Sir Thomas Bodley, having died in the following year, Hales was appointed to deliver his funeral oration. The oration is published among his writings, under the title of "Oratio Funebris habita in Collegio Mertonensi, a Johanne Halesio. Anno 1613. Martii 29, quo die Clarissimo Equiti D. Thomæ Bodleio funus ducebatur." In the month of May[1] of the same year he was admitted a Fellow of Eton.

[1] The date of his admission was the 24th May 1613.

This is all that we learn of his life during these years. It is not till November 1618 that we see him in the full daylight of his own letters written from Holland. Thither he accompanied Sir Dudley Carleton, ambassador to the Hague, as his chaplain; and when the Synod met at Dort, he went there to report the proceedings for the interest and benefit of his "right honourable and very good lord." He held no official commission to the Synod, and took no part in its doings along with the deputation from the Church of England. He is only as an interested onlooker. But this very fact gives a certain piquancy and liveliness to his letters, and our readers will not regret to have their attention called to them. Moreover, the attitude of the Remonstrants or Arminians, and the arguments employed by them in their conflict with the majority of the Synod, have a significant bearing upon our general subject.

He was commended to "Mr Bogermannus,"[1] the president of the Synod, who gave him facility for making himself acquainted with the business transacted day by day, and reporting it. His letters open on a scene more edifying than much that otherwise engaged the Synod — the appointment of a committee to translate the Scriptures. This is on Monday the $\frac{16}{26}$ November 1618. On the following day we have a curious glimpse of the state of practical religion in the provinces in the midst of all the doctrinal disputes which had so long rent them asunder. The Synod gave itself to consider the prevailing "defect of the afternoon sermons and catechising,

[1] John Bogermann, a zealous opponent of the Remonstrants.

especially in the country villages."[1] This was attributed to three causes — pastoral negligence, pluralities, and the "difficulty of reclaiming the country people on the Sundays, either from their sports or from their work." Various stringent remedies were proposed and adopted; among others, that "the ministers should give good example by bringing their own family to church." The several deputies from England and Switzerland were "desired to deliver their custom in this behalf." "My Lord Bishop" (Carleton, Bishop of Llandaff)[2] stated that the "magistrate imposed a pecuniary mulct upon such as did absent themselves from divine duties; which pecuniary mulct generally prevailed more with our people than any pious admonitions could." The deputies from Geneva said that "every Sunday they had four sermons"!

He then describes,[3] on the $\frac{19}{29}$, a sermon preached by "Mr Dean of Worcester" (Hall, afterwards Bishop of Norwich), "a polite and pathetical Latin sermon, made in the Synod house," from Eccles. vii. 16, "Noli esse justus nimium, neque esto sapiens nimis." "After a witty coining upon his text, how it should

---

[1] Letters from the Synod of Dort. Hales's Works, vol. iii. 7.

[2] George Carleton, who does not appear to have been in any way connected with the ambassador, had also been of Merton College, and is said by Wood to have been a severe Calvinist (vol. ii. p. 423). The other deputies from England were, besides Carleton, Dr John Davenant, Professor of Divinity at Cambridge; Dr Samuel Ward, Master of Sidney College; and the well-known Dr Joseph Hall, mentioned in the text, afterwards Bishop of Norwich. Dr Hall's health after a short period requiring his return, he was replaced by Dr Thomas Goad.

[3] Ibid., p. 20.

come that righteousness and wisdom which are everywhere commended unto us should here seem to receive a check, he showed how men might seem to be too just by too strictly keeping the letter of the law when sitting in places of justice, or by inflicting too heavy punishment; next, in the second word *sapiens nimis*, he taxed the Divines by presuming too far in prying into the judgments of God, and so came to reprove the curious disputes which our age hath made concerning predestination; that this dispute for its endlessness was like the mathematical line *divisibilis in semper divisibilia*, that it was in divinity as the rule of Cos is in arithmetic."

It is pleasing to recognise thus early Hall's mild and liberal spirit. His earnest exhortations to peace and union were taken in good part. "The Praeses," it is said, "gave him thanks for his good pains." It would have been better, no doubt, if the Synod had taken his words to heart, and acted upon them.

During this time the Remonstrants, or Arminians, had not yet arrived; and for some days still their coming, or at least their appearance at the Synod, was delayed. In the interval the Synod busied itself with various practical questions as to the best manner of catechising, and whether there should be one or several modes adapted to different classes of persons, the education of the clergy, and the celebration of baptism. In reference to this last question, the chief difficulty was as to the baptism of children born of those who were called "ethnic parents." It was decided that the children of such parents should "by no means be baptised till they came to the years of discretion"—"a strange decision," says Hales, "and such as, if my memory or reading fail me not, no Church, either ancient or modern, ever gave. When it was objected, 'What if they were in danger of death?' their answer was, that the want of baptism could not prejudice them with God, except we would determine as the Papists do, that baptism is necessary to salvation. Which is as much," he adds, "to undervalue the necessity of baptism as the Church of Rome doth overvalue it."[1]

It is obvious in this, as in other matters, that there was considerable difference of opinion, and still more of spirit, between the representatives of the Anglican Church and the dominant party in the Synod.[2] On the great question at issue, however, with the Remonstrants there was at first apparently perfect unanimity. Of all connected with the Church of England, Hales himself—not excepting Hall—was probably the most liberal-minded, and it is impossible to mistake his bias against them when the Remonstrants are first introduced, and Episcopius makes his first appeal in opposition to the competency of the Synod. Before the end, however, and under the force of certain arguments of Episcopius, or of others, a considerable change passed upon his sentiments.

It was on the 6th December,[3] that the Remonstrants, headed by Episcopius, appeared at the

[1] Letters, p. 42.
[2] The Synod was not a numerous body. The Dutch and Walloon clergy numbered thirty-eight. There were five University Professors and twenty-one "Seculars," or Lay Elders. The foreign divines numbered twenty-eight, and of these the English had the precedence.
[3] "Stylo novo," as he says, and we shall henceforth adhere to this simpler reckoning.

Synod.[1] "In the midst of the Synod-house a long table was as if set apart for them, for it had been hitherto void, no man sitting at it. Here chairs and forms being set, they were willed to sit down." Whereupon Episcopius, standing up, made a short speech, in which he prayed God "to give a blessing to this meeting, and to pour into their minds such conceits as best fitted men come together for such ends; then he signified that, according to their citation, they were now come 'ad collationem instituendam' concerning that cause which hitherto with a good conscience they had maintained."[2]

On the 10th of December, Episcopius opened the conflict of his party with the Synod; and the letters of our author assume a higher interest. He characterises, by no means in a complimentary manner, the speech made by the leader of the Remonstrants on this occasion, and the opinions expressed by him. Episcopius recited, he says,[3] "*e scripto*, a long and tedious speech of two hours at the least, consisting of two general heads : first, of exceptions they had against the Synod, 'tanquam in judicem incompetentem;' secondly, of a conceit of their own, what manner of a Synod they thought fit it should be which was to compose these controversies in hand." The Remonstrants objected to the Synod as entirely composed of the adverse party, and "it was against all equity and nature that the adverse party should be judge." They objected also because this dominant party had schismatically separated themselves from

---

[1] Letters, p. 45, 46.   [2] Ibid., p. 58.
[3] Ibid., p. 46.

VOL. I.   M

their brethren. They desired a Synod composed of "certain select men who had taken part with neither side,"—a mere " chimæra saltans in vacuo," he continues; "such a Synod as never was nor can be." "I think it could scarcely be found in the Netherlands, though the sun itself should seek it." Failing this, they wished that a Synod should be formed of "an equal number of both parties, each with their several præses and assessors, who should debate the matter betwixt themselves;" and if they were unable to agree, the civil magistrate, as a " Deus e machina," was to be called in and " prescribe the moderamen," from which there was to be no appeal. " Of the same thread was the whole of their speech," says Hales, contemptuously adding, " When they had well and thoroughly wearied their auditory, they did that which we much desired—they made an end."

Obviously our author has no bias towards the Arminian side. According to his own representation of the purport of their demands, his judgment seems severe and one-sided. But on the next appearance of Episcopius he expresses himself more favourably. "Standing up," he says,[1] " Episcopius required that a little time might be granted to them, and forthwith uttered an oration ' *acrem sane et animosam*,' about which, by reason of some particulars in it, there will grow some stir." He gives an abstract of the speech, which it is impossible to read without being struck by the wisdom, ability, moderation, and courtesy it displays. Hales himself, in some parts, might be supposed speaking according to the

[1] Letters, p. 69.

wisdom of his later writings, for example, in the following statements :—" They (the Remonstrants) thought it sufficient if the chief points of religion remain unshaken. That there had been always sundry opinions even amongst the fathers themselves, which yet had not broken out into separation of minds and breach of charity. That it was impossible for all wits to jump in one point. It was the judgment of Paræus, a great divine, that the greatest cause of contention in the Church was this, that the schoolmen's conclusions and cathedral decisions had been received as oracles and articles of faith. That they were, therefore, unjustly charged with the bringing in of a sceptic theology ; they sought for nothing else but for that liberty, which is the mean betwixt servitude and licence."

Episcopius then described the points against which he and his friends had set themselves :—" First, against those conclusions concerning predestination, which the authors themselves have called *horrida decreta ;* secondly, against those who for the five articles, so called, have made a separation ; thirdly, against those who cast from them all those who in some things dissent from them ; and lastly, against those who taught the magistrate should, with a hoodwinkt obedience, accept what the divines taught without further inquiry."

He maintained that " the smaller part does not necessarily make the schism, nor the major part the right." Although they had been overborne, they were not defeated :—" The Scriptures and solid reason shall be to us instead of multitudes. The conscience rests not itself upon the number of suffrages, but upon the strength of reason. *Tam parati sumus vinci, quam vincere.* He gets a greater victory, that being conquered gains the truth. *Amicus Socrates, amicus Plato, amica Synodus, sed magis amica veritas.*[1]

Such are fragments of this remarkable oration of Episcopius, "delivered with great grace of speech and oratorical gesture." It is not wonderful that it impressed Hales, and that he should have been at pains to report it. It remains to this day a splendid specimen of eloquent, moderate, and Christian argument. The lay members particularly were much affected by the candid enthusiasm of the speaker, and had they not been powerless in the hands of the political party that was really guiding the movement, good might have come from it. As it was, no result worthy of such an effort followed. The President, with characteristic rudeness, rebuked Episcopius for having spoken at such length without special leave; and then demanded a copy of the speech, in reference to which he subsequently sought to fix a charge of falsehood upon the speaker. Our author gives us a vivid glimpse of all these personal details, and also of various altercations between the Synod and the Remonstrants as to the order of proceeding, and the delivery of what are called the "considerations" of the latter, by which are meant certain proposals of change, particularly in regard to the confession and catechism, which on former occasions had been urged by the Remonstrants.

[1] Letters, p. 73, 74.

Various incidents of interest follow. The reception of the Scottish commissioner, Waltar Balcanqual, who reports that "the king, at his coming away, did charge him, *verbis sublimibus*, to exhort them unto peace," is described in a separate letter on the 20th December:—"The Scotch nation," according to their Commissioner, "had evermore so linkt itself to this people (the Dutch), that it hath always laboured to endeavour the peace of this state, and now it was ready to do as much for the peace of the Churches amongst them. They had very straitly bound unto them the Scottish Church (*demeruistis ecclesiam Scoticanam*) by so kindly welcoming him."

The lighter humorous aspects of the Synod are not forgotten :—" Old Goclenius (one of the foreign divines) could not let the Remonstrants pass without a jest, such a one as it was; for being asked for judgment, he put off his hat, and told us that the Remonstrants were '*Canonici irregulares*, regular irregulars,' and put on his hat again. Where the sap of the jest is, I know not; but the gravest in the Synod had much ado to compose their countenances."[1]

These glimpses, like all real insight into ecclesiastical assemblies, excite our astonishment at the importance which subsequent generations have attached to them and their decisions. All such conventions are found more or less to present aspects ridiculous from their absurdity or shocking from their violence and unfairness, when the veil is once lifted, and we see them for a moment as they appeared to an onlooker. If old Goclenius play the fool, the "*præses politicus*"

[1] Letters, p. 87, 88.

('Mr Bogermannus') plays the tyrant. Upon a decree of the States being read to the Remonstrants, Episcopius required a copy of it:—" The Præses asked him why? '*Ut pareamus*,' said Episcopius. 'No,' said the same Præses, 'it is only that you may find some words to cavil at; and, therefore, they should have none. It was sufficient that they knew the meaning of it.' This at first," Hales adds, "seemed to me somewhat hard; but when I considered that these were the men which heretofore had, in prejudice of the Church, so extremely flattered the civil magistrate, I could not but think this usuage a fit reward for such service."[1]

Our author is far from himself here. He forgets his charity as well as lays aside his judgment. In appealing to the civil magistrate the Remonstrants may have been mistaken; but they only consistently maintained an opinion which they were entitled to hold as a party, which many good men have held in every age, and which both parties—Calvinists and Remonstrants alike—held when it suited them. But supposing that they had thereby judged wrongly, this would be no justification of a clear wrong done them by the "*Præses politicus*" of the Synod in refusing them a copy of a decree directed against them. The truth appears to be that Hales was somewhat wearied with the importunity and calm resistance of the Remonstrants. The slowness and delays of the business troubled him; for he speaks of the session at which these things took place, Friday 21st, as "a long, a troublesome, and a fruitless session." He is puzzled

[1] Letters, p. 90.

also about his movements. The Synod is adjourned to Thursday of the following week, and his honour the ambassador had evidently wished him in the interval to return to the Hague ; but he excuses himself as a poor traveller :—" I am but a silly traveller, and conveniently I cannot travel without a guide. The days being short, and the tide coming somewhat late, night would quickly come. Now for me to go by night, having neither language nor any to conduct me, must needs be very inconvenient."

During the next three weeks or so—that is, from 27th Dec. to 15th Jan. (1618-19)—the business of the Synod came to "a great crisis," as it is described by our author. He sets forth the main details in a very graphic way, still showing, upon the whole, strong sympathy with the dominant side. So far evidently the foreign deputies tried to mediate between the parties, but without success. The Remonstrants continued firm in their attitude of resistance. The points in dispute were, *first*, as to the order to be held in discussing the articles ; whether the question of reprobation were to be handled after the five articles, or whether it should be handled in the first place, as the Remonstrants desired. "They pretended," says Hales, "their doubts lay especially there ; and that being cleared, they thought they could show good conformity in all the rest." The *second* difficulty was the objection of the Remonstrants to be assailed with "interrogations, which they very much disdained as pedagogical." The *third* was as to their " liberty of disputation," whether it was to be limited by the discretion of the Synod, or large and unlimited, according as it pleased them.

The first of these points particularly excited a very vehement discussion, in which Episcopius, as usual, on the side of the Remonstrants, and ' D. Gomarus,' on the side of the Synod, are the prominent figures.

" The point of reprobation is that," said Episcopius, " ' quod maxime nos ægre habet,'—he could not endure that doctrine concerning the absolute decree of God; that God should peremptorily decree to cast the greatest part of mankind away only because He would. Corvinus answered that he could not ' Salva conscientia versari in ministerio,' till that point was cleared ; Isaacus Frederici that ' præcipuum momentum' was in that question; others that on the question of election they had no scruple ; all their doubt was on the point of reprobation ; and therefore their conscience would not suffer them to proceed further in disputation till that matter were discussed."[1]

On the other hand, Gomar,[2] " that saw that his iron was in the fire (for I persuade myself that the Remonstrants' spleen is chiefly against him), began to tell us that Episcopius had falsified the tenet of reprobation; that no man taught that God absolutely decreed to cast man away without sin ; but as He did decree the end, so He did decree the means ; that so as He predestinated man to death, so He

[1] Letters, p. 94, 95.
[2] Francis Gomar was the great opponent of Arminius at Leyden, where they were colleagues as Professors of Divinity in the first decade of the 17th century. In the year 1618, at the close of which the Synod of Dort opened, he was settled as Professor of Hebrew and Divinity at Groningen, where he died in 1641. He was partially educated in England, and was a Calvinist of the extreme school.

predestinated him to sin, the only way to death; and so he mended the question," adds our author, whose sympathies cannot stand such a strain as this, "as tinkers mend kettles, and made it worse than it was before."[1]

Reiterated discussion was of no use; the Remonstrants were "called in," and the president, "after a short admonition," requested to know whether they would proceed according to the order desired by the Synod; but as invariably they declined to do so. Evidently they saw that their cause was prejudged. In truth, they had been summoned, not as Episcopius signified on his first appearance, "ad collationem instituendam," not to conference, but merely to give in an account of their opinions, and leave them to the judgment of the Synod. This was urged quite fairly against them, according to the terms of their summons.[2] They could not claim to be exempted from these terms, and yet they would not yield without a free discussion in all things, and especially on the point of reprobation, which they knew was the weak point in the Contra-Remonstrant's doctrine. They had no alternative but ignominiously to submit to condemnation, or to take up an attitude which they should have taken up primarily, and refused to appear under such a summons at all. Virtually they declined the judgment of the Synod as *pars adversa*. When driven to it, Episcopius said, "We are resolved, *agere pro judicio nostro non pro judicio Synodi;*[3] words which one of the seculars or political members

---

[1] Letters, p. 96.
[2] With the exception of Episcopius, who had been originally summoned in the same terms as the other Professors of Divinity to take his seat in the Synod. See Calder's Life, p. 242-75.
[3] Letters, p. 100.

of the Synod "willed should be noted." At length, on the 14th January, they were dismissed with bitter reproaches by the Præses:—"'I will dismiss you,' he said, 'with no other elogy than one of the foreigners gave you—*quo coepistis pede eodem cedite*—with a lie you made your entrance into the Synod, with a lie you take your leave of it, in denying lately that ever you protested yourselves provided to give answer on the articles, or to have had any such writing ready, which all the Synod knows to be false. Your actions all have been full of fraud, equivocations, and deceit. That, therefore, the Synod may at length piously and peaceably proceed to the perfecting of that business for which it has come together, you are dismist. But assure you, the Synod will make known your pertinacy to all the Christian world ; and know that the Belgic Churches want not *arma spiritualia* with which in time convenient they will proceed against you. *Quamobrem vos delegatorum et Synodi nomine dimitto, exite.*' So with much muttering the Remonstrants went out ; and Episcopius going away, said, 'Dominus Deus judicabit de fraudibus et mendaciis ;' Sapma, ' Exeo ex ecclesia malignantium.' And so the Synod brake up." [1]

Thus were the Remonstrants thrust from the Synod of Dort. The issue was probably inevitable. The Synod was entitled to vindicate its jurisdiction and the terms on which it had been convened, which the Arminians had so far accepted by obeying the summons. Yet the result was unhappy, and the mode of their dismissal in the highest degree undignified

[1] Letters, p. 123, 124.

and unbecoming. It was very soon felt that a great mistake had been committed. Hales gives expression to this feeling: "The most partial spectator of our synodal acts," he says, "cannot but confess that in the late dismission of the Remonstrants with so much choler and heat, there was a great oversight committed." There appears to have been some idea of trying to repair the mistake. But this was found to be impossible. As our author remarks, such mistakes of public action are "with less inconvenience tolerated than amended." The Synod could not retrace its steps without loss of dignity; and so another example was presented of the folly of ecclesiastical assemblies convened under the impulse of sectarian zeal, rather than of enlarged Christian enlightenment, and an honest wish to deal fairly and charitably with questions which must always divide men so long as they are serious subjects of thought.

After the dismissal of the Remonstrants from the Synod of Dort the interest of Hales's letters very much diminishes, although they continue for about a month longer. Then, on the 9th of February 1619, they suddenly terminate. After about three months' attendance he was evidently well wearied of the business. Several causes contributed to this. His own interest in the dogmatic distinctions under discussion, never very keen, grew languid with the apparently interminable altercations and delays. He was no zealot; and while approving, upon the whole, of the position of the dominant party, he was clear-sighted enough to see the unfair violence with which men like Gomar maintained their opinions and assailed those of others. Martinius of Breme, having, after the departure of the Remonstrants, ventured to state some scruples " about the manner of Christ's being *fundamentum electionis*, Gomar started up and exclaimed, ' Ego hanc rem in me recipio,' and therewith cast his glove, and challenged Martinius with the proverb, ' Ecce Rhodum ecce Saltum,' and required the Synod to grant them a duel." The Synod was glad by fair words to pacify the combatants, and according to custom the session was concluded with prayer. But, slyly adds our author, " zeal and devotions had not so well allayed Gomarus his choler, but immediately after prayers he renewed his challenge, and required combat with Martinius again ; but they parted for that night without blows." Hales plainly felt himself less and less at home amidst such scenes of polemic violence.

Another feature of the proceedings shocked his sense of justice, while it necessarily abated his interest. The main business of the Synod was transacted, not in public, but in private. The real conclusions were prearranged at private sessions, and the " evening sessions," which appear henceforth to have been the only public ones, he says, " are only to entertain the auditory, not to determine anything at all."[1] It had been at first debated in the Synod " whether they should admit of hearers, or do all in private." Old Sibrandus[2] was very hot against the

---

[1] Letters, p. 148. In the same letter he says, "All this business of citing, referring, examining, must needs seem only as acted on a stage, if the Synod intempestively beforehand bewray a resolution," p. 149.

[2] An old and irascible opponent of Episcopius at Franeker.

auditory, and thought it not fit that any care should be had of them, as being only "*mulierculæ et pauculi juvenes incauti;*" a complaint in which our author admits there was some reason; "for many youths, yea, and artificers, and I know not what rabble besides, thrust in and hurtle the place; and, as for women," he somewhat ungallantly adds, "whole troops of them have been seen there, and the best places for spectators reserved for them; while they must needs expose the Synod to the scorn of those who lie in wait to take exception against it." The decision, however, was in favour of the public, as it generally is in such cases.

Hales's language, in speaking of the auditory, almost implies some feeling of personal affront, for we must remember that he was not, like his brother divines from England, a member of the Synod. He was merely there himself as an auditor and reporter, seated, probably, among the "youths, artificers, and I know not what rabble besides," without even the means of light to carry on his reporting, as he says in a letter a few days later. "I would willingly," he writes, on the 29th January, "have given your honour an account of his speech" (a speech by Altingius, one of the Palatine professors, whose discourse appeared to him "the most sufficient" of any he had yet heard); but "it was in the evening, and the auditory are allowed no candles, so that I could not use my tables." We do not wonder, therefore, that a few days further we find him intimating that if he had his lodging discharged he would willingly leave. He inquires, like a prudent man, whether his "honour was to answer the charge of his lodging, or the public purse." "I would willingly be resolved of it," he continues, "because I have a desire to return to the Hague; first, because the Synod proceeding as it doth, I do not see that it is *operæ pretium* for me here to abide, and then because I have sundry private occasions that call upon me to return."

So after a single letter more, which contains no further hint of his movements, he returned, and we hear no more of him in connection with the Synod of Dort. His presence there, however, was not without a lasting influence on his opinions. His letters help us but slightly to trace the progress of this influence, but his subsequent writings make it plainly manifest. There is a story told by his "intimate friend," Farindon,[1] according to which he himself attributed a distinct change in his theological sentiments to a speech of Episcopius in handling St John, iii. 16. "There he *bid John Calvin good-night*, as he often told." There is some confusion, but probably also some truth in this story. The only reference we find, in his letters, to John, iii. 16, is not in regard to Episcopius, but Martinius of Breme, to whom allusion has been already made, and who founded much on this famous text. Martinius was evidently an able man, of liberal and at the same time evangelical sentiments, and it is possible that his arguments drawn from this passage of the Gospels may have moved our author. There is, on the other hand, no evidence from his

[1] Maizeaux, Acc. 3.

own correspondence that his opinions were at the time much affected by anything Episcopius said.

Of the gradual change in his sentiments there can be no doubt, and there were probably many concurring causes for it. Of a calm, reflective, and patient temper — gifted with a shrewd, quiet insight, and a great natural love of fairness—he could not be an auditor for three months of an assembly like that of Dort without feeling that the truth did not all lie on one side. The spectacle presented to him—of extreme orthodoxy with unchristian choler, of contentious zeal aiming at triumph, rather than of earnest thoughtfulness anxious for light — could not but start new trains of inquiry in a mind so open and candid as his. It naturally forced upon him the general question of the value of theological dogmatism, and the grounds on which men seek to control each other's opinions and beliefs. All his writings prove that this was the form in which a theological change matured in his mind. His was no passage from one extreme of opinion to another. If he bade John Calvin good-night, he did not say good-morning to Arminius. He did not pass from one side to another. His mind was of far too high an order, his gift of spiritual insight far too delicate and subtle, to admit of his doing this. When he left the narrowness of Calvinism, he did so not because he became possessed by some other narrowness, but because he saw from a higher field of vision how little dogmatic precision has to do with spiritual truth, and how hopeless it is to tie and confine this truth under definite creeds and systems. We shall find abundant evidence of this immediately.

Hales returned to England in the beginning of 1619 (Feb.), and appears to have settled at Eton in the quiet enjoyment of his Fellowship. He passed his time probably betwixt Eton and London, patiently working out the deeper thoughts about religion which had been quickened in him by his experience in Holland, and occasionally joining in the more stirring social life of the metropolis. It was in the years following that Ben Jonson gathered around him the brilliant set of intellectualists and young poets known as the "Apollo," whom we have already described. He was appointed Poet Laureate in the very year of Hales's return, and, we are told, "was frequently received at Windsor, where he was on familiar terms with the royal family." It may have been during one of these visits that he and our author became acquainted, for it is also said of the latter that "when the King and Court resided at Windsor, he was much frequented by noblemen and courtiers, who delighted much in his company, not for his severe and retired walks of learning, but for his polite discourses, stories, and poetry."[1] This is not inconsistent with Clarendon's description of his living a life of studious seclusion "amongst his books," but "very well pleased with the resort of his friends to him, who were such as he had chosen, and in whose company he delighted," and only making at rare intervals—"once in a year"—a journey to London to enjoy the conversation of his friends there.[2] Falk-

[1] Wood.   [2] Life, i. 59.

land, it is to be remembered, had not yet, nor for nearly ten years after Hales's retirement to Eton, joined the Jonson set of wits—nor Suckling either; and it is in connection with them especially that we hear of him in this society.

From the time that Falkland appears in London, or during the significant decade that preceded the meeting of the Long Parliament, we can hardly suppose Hales's life at Eton to have been so extremely secluded as Clarendon's words suggest. His mind, for one thing, was by this time actively at work regarding the alarming state of the Church and public affairs in general. He was maintaining an active intercourse or correspondence with Chillingworth as to the composition of his great work.[1] We are told,[2] moreover, that "his company was much desired" by the wits and poets in town, amongst whom Falkland and Suckling, with Ben Jonson himself, are particularly mentioned—and that "he used *often* to meet with them, and held very well his part in those ingenious conversations." Suckling's allusion to him in the 'Session of Poets' and some interesting lines which he has directly addressed to him, imply the same thing. Hales was evidently at this time no stranger in the poetic fraternity, although coy of his visits. He loved his quiet ease at Eton and his books. He required to be tempted to town; but the attractions there were evidently sufficient to draw him not infrequently from his retreat. Suckling writes as a pleasant genial friend who often met him and enjoyed his

---

[1] Wood. [2] Maizeaux.

company. The lines give a very pleasing picture of our author's mingled sweetness and gravity—his retired studiousness and fondness for subtle argument, and yet his appreciation of "wit and wine," and the claims of good-fellowship. Whatever may be his theological preoccupations,—

> "Whether these lines do find you out,
> Putting or clearing of a doubt;
> Whether predestination,
> Or reconciling three in one;
> Or the unriddling how men die,
> And live at once eternally,"—

he is exhorted to "leave Socinus and the schoolmen," and, "bestriding the college steed," to "come to town:"—

> "'Tis fit you show
> Yourself abroad, that men may know
> (Whate'er some learned men have guess'd)
> That oracles are not yet ceased:
> There you shall find the wit and wine
> Flowing alike, and both divine:
> Dishes, with names not known in books,
> And less amongst the college cooks;
> With sauce so pregnant, that you need
> Not stay till hunger bids you feed.
> The sweat of learned Jonson's brain,
> And gentle Shakspeare's easier strain,
> A hackney-coach conveys you to,
> In spite of all that rain can do:
> And for your eighteen pence you sit
> The lord and judge of all fresh wit.
> News in one day, as much we've here
> As serves all Windsor for a year,
> And which the carrier brings to you,
> After 't has here been found not true.
> Then think what company's design'd
> To meet you here: men so refin'd,

> Their very common talk at board
> Makes wise or mad a young court-lord,
> And makes him capable to be
> Umpire in's father's company.
> Where no disputes, nor forc'd defence
> Of a man's person for his sense,
> Take up the time; all strive to be
> Masters of truth, as victory:
> And where you come, I'd boldly swear
> A synod might as easily err."

Agreeable, however, as Hales's occasional visits to London and its "refined" and sparkling society may have been, his life at Eton was, after all, his main business. It would have been interesting to lift the veil upon him "amongst his books"—as he pursued his studies in the seclusion of the college, or meditated amidst the rich and peaceful glades around. But we have no adequate means of doing this. That old scholastic life has not been preserved in any clear traces that can be set before our readers. Yet we can tell something of Hales's companionship also at Eton, and see that it must have been not only pleasant, but in a high degree congenial and stimulating.

During the period of his residence as a Fellow there were two provosts, both of them his special friends, of marked character and distinction. One, Sir Henry Savile, has been already mentioned. He was Hales's patron and friend at Oxford, where they belonged to the same college (Merton), and worked together at the edition of Chrysostom, so well known under Savile's name. After his own transference to Eton, it was probably his influence as provost that procured Hales's later appointment to a fellowship there. This is indeed expressly affirmed.[1] Savile was a man of solid and fine acquirements, devoted to science no less than scholarship, as his grants to Oxford abundantly testify. His liberality was on a truly munificent scale. His edition of Chrysostom, in eight folio volumes, is said to have cost even then £8000, and for the purpose of completing it, he himself visited all the public and private libraries of Britain, and sent learned men for similar research into France, Germany, Italy, and the East. A much older man than Hales —having been born in the middle of the previous century— their relation throughout was probably somewhat of the nature of patron and pupil; but their joint labours on Chrysostom had brought them into very cordial fellowship, and their tastes and spirit of thought were in many respects suited to one another.

But Hales's theological as well as personal sympathies found more to engage them in Savile's illustrious successor, after a brief interval, in the provostship of Eton College. Of all who have adorned this high position, no one has brought to it more distinction, or displayed in it a more wise and exalted mind, than Sir Henry Wotton. Belonging to an accomplished family, all the members of which more or less distinguished themselves, he had been carefully educated at Oxford, and then for six[2] years

---

[1] Chalmers's Biog. Dict., XXVII. Wotton, has *nine* years, but a
[2] Walton, one of whose charm- comparison of dates shows this is
ing lives is that of Sir Henry a mistake. From a letter, of date

abroad, in intercourse with Beza, Isaac Casaubon, and "the most eminent men for learning and all manner of arts." He became both a great German and Italian scholar, and an "amateur and most excellent judge of painting, sculpture, chemistry, and architecture." His introduction to political life in connection with the famous Earl of Essex—Elizabeth's favourite—was unfortunate. But he escaped from this connection, went again abroad, and entered into the confidential service of the Grand Duke of Tuscany. It was while in this service that he was employed in a remarkable mission which prepared the way for his future advancement. Letters having been intercepted by the Grand Duke, which discovered a design of taking away the life of James VI. of Scotland, Wotton was sent secretly into that country, disguised as an Italian, obtained a private conference with his Majesty, and, in return for his information, received high marks of favour. " He departed," says Walton, "as true an Italian as he came."

On James's accession to the English throne, Wotton came home, was knighted, and obtained an important diplomatic appointment as ambassador to the republic of Venice. A series of similar posts, culminating with that of the embassy at the Court of Vienna, occupied him till the year before James's death, when he finally returned to England; and

---

July 1592, it appears that he had been then abroad three years, and about three years later he was at home, and appointed secretary to the Earl of Essex. It has been supposed that the mistake had arisen out of a transposition of the figures 9 and 6.

in 1624 was appointed Provost of Eton. The statutes of the college requiring the provost to be in holy orders, he resolved to comply with them, and was ordained deacon, notwithstanding his advanced years and long political career.[1] This change in his mode of life gave a turn to his whole thoughts, and he betook himself earnestly to the study of divinity and the spiritual exercises becoming his new position. "After his customary public devotions his use was to retire into his study, and there to spend some hours in reading the Bible and authors in divinity, closing up his meditations with private prayer: this was, for the most part, his employment in the forenoon. But when he was once sat to dinner, then nothing but cheerful thoughts possessed his mind, and those still increased by constant company at his table of such persons as brought thither additions both of learning and pleasure; but some part of most days was usually spent in philosophical conclusions. Nor did he forget," Walton characteristically adds, " his innate pleasure of angling, which he would usually call 'his idle time not idly spent;' saying often, 'he would rather live five May months than forty Decembers.' "[2]

To his divinity studies Wotton brought the varied experience and wide thoughtfulness which he had acquired in intercourse with learned and religious

---

[1] Born in 1568, he was, of course, when appointed Provost of Eton, fifty-six years of age.

[2] Walton's Life. The place where Sir Henry Wotton and Isaac Walton were accustomed to angle in company is known as the "Black Pots." It is close to the college, in a bend of the Thames, where the South-Western Railway now crosses the river.

men throughout Europe. He had seen what Christian good there may be in very different forms of religious faith and worship; and so, like Hales, he disliked greatly the prevalent spirit of religious contentiousness.[1] Numerous stories have been preserved of his catholicity of feeling, and the successful repartee with which he would retort on troublesome questioners. To one that asked him, "Whether a Papist may be saved?" he replied, "You may be saved without knowing that: look to yourself." To another, who was railing against the Papists, he gave this advice: "Pray, sir, forbear till you have studied the points better; for the wise Italians have this proverb, 'He that understands amiss concludes worse.' And take heed of thinking the farther you go from the Church of Rome the nearer you are to God." But he had no less something pointed to say to the disputatious Romanist. Being at Rome, "a pleasant priest" invited him one evening to hear their vesper music at church. The priest seeing Sir Henry stand obscurely in a corner, sent to him by a boy of the choir the question, written on a small piece of paper, "Where was your religion to be found before Luther?" To which question Sir Henry presently underwrit, "My religion was to be found then where yours is not to be found now, in the written Word of God." His testimony to Arminius is as creditable to his Christian fairness as anything recorded of him. "In my

---

[1] He directed the following inscription to be put upon his tombstone:—

"Hic jacet hujus Sententiæ primus
Author
Disputandi pruritus Ecclesiarum Scabies
Nomen alias quære."

travel toward Venice, as I passed through Germany I rested almost a year at Leyden, where I entered into an acquaintance with Arminius—then the professor of divinity in that university—a man much talked of in this age, which is made up of opposition and controversy. And, indeed, if I mistake not Arminius in his expressions—as so weak a brain as mine is may easily do—then I know I differ from him in some points; yet I profess my judgment of him to be, that he was a man of most rare learning, and I know him to be of a most strict life, and of a most meek spirit."

These stories, and others of a similar import, are told us on the best authority by Walton; and all serve to show how entirely Sir Henry Wotton must have been a man after Hales's own heart. Their intercourse could not fail to have been frequent and pleasant in those afternoons which the provost was wont to give to his friends, and "such persons as brought additions of learning and pleasure." "He was a great lover of his neighbours," and there was no one "like-minded," who could enter into his thoughts, or share his learning, or "care for his state," like his erudite, acute, and bright-witted colleague. Hales may have learned something of his breadth and freedom of opinion from one to whose experience and knowledge of the world he would be disposed to defer. Wotton's cast of mind and large charity would certainly help the development of his own thoughts. Their intercourse is said to have been particularly frequent in the latter part of Wotton's life, when he became "more retired and contemplative." In one of those visits, when he felt his end drawing near, he is said to have addressed Hales to the following purpose: "I have in my passage to my grave met with most of those joys of which a discursive soul is capable. . . . Nevertheless, in the voyage I have not always floated on the calm sea of content, but have often met with cross winds and storms, and with many troubles of mind and temptations to evil. Yet Almighty God hath by His grace prevented me from making shipwreck of faith and a good conscience, the thought of which is now the joy of my heart, and I most humbly praise Him for it. . . . And, my dear friend, I now see that I draw near my harbour of death; that harbour that will secure me from all the future storms and waves of this restless world; and I praise God I am willing to leave it, and expect a better—that world wherein dwelleth righteousness—and I long for it."[1]

Wotton died in the autumn of 1639, and before this Hales had in some degree emerged from his retirement, in connection not only with the London *littérateurs*, whose feasts he occasionally graced, but with the great Church questions of his time. His famous 'Tract concerning Schism and Schismatics' was certainly written before this, although not printed till some time later (1642). There is no reason, indeed, to doubt the statement that it was written about 1636, at Chillingworth's request, to assist him in the composition of 'The Religion of

[1] Walton's Life.

Protestants,' absurd as are Wood's comments in connection with the statement. It has the air of being intended for such a purpose, and Hales himself says that it was written "for the use of a private friend." But there are at least two other and very characteristic writings of Hales which belong to this important period—namely, his tracts 'Concerning the Power of the Keys,' and 'On the Sacrament of the Lord's Supper.' The former bears the date of 1637; and the latter, which is particularly interesting, must be concluded to be as early, if not earlier. It was evidently written in the heart of the Romanist controversy, which was then violently agitating England, and more or less engrossing all inquiring minds. Like all his writings at this time, it was elicited from him by the application of some correspondent or friend, whose name is not disclosed. The following significant allusion to the influence of the Romish teachers closes the tract: "If you shall favour me so much as to carefully read what I have carefully written, you shall find (at least in those points you occasioned me to touch upon) sufficient ground to plant yourself strongly against all discourse of the Romish *corner-creepers*, which they use for the seducing of unstable souls."

Besides these acknowledged writings of Hales at this period, there are two brief Latin treatises which have been attributed to him, one of as early a date as 1628, and the other published in 1633. The first bears the general title, 'Anonymi Dissertatio de Pace et Concordia Ecclesiæ,' and the second is spoken of as the 'Brevis Disquisitio.'[1] The question of the authorship of these treatises, at least of the second of them, is important in its bearing on Hales's general position, and his honesty as a religious thinker. Wood may be considered the chief, and in a sense the only definite authority, for attributing these writings to our author. He enumerates them among the " things written" by him; but, not to insist upon the suspicious source[2] on which he evidently relied in

[1] The full title of this tract is as follows: ' Brevis Disquisitio, an et quomodo vulgo dicti Evangelici Pontificios, ac nominatim Val. Magni de Acatholicorum credendi regula Judicium, solidè atque evidenter refutare queant.' Maizeaux has examined with patience, and not a little critical acumen, the external evidence as to the authorship of these tracts, and concludes decidedly, not only that they are not the production of Hales, but that they belong to the writers to which they are respectively attributed in Sandius's 'Bibliotheca Anti-Trinitariorum;' the 'Dissertatio de Pace,' &c., having been written by a Polish knight, Samuel Przipcovius, and the 'Brevis Disquisitio,' &c., by Joachimus Stegmannus, a celebrated Socinian minister. Both pamphlets may be found by the English reader, admirably translated, in the second volume of the Phenix, a collection of rare pamphlets, chiefly of the seventeenth century.

[2] The original source of the rumour which connected Hales with the 'Brevis Disquisitio' seems to have been ecclesiastical gossip in the heyday of Laud's power, revived by Heylin, his biographer, after the Restoration (see p. 208), and emphasised by a somewhat reckless and coarse writer, Dr Samuel Parker, who became Bishop of Oxford in the reign of James II. Parker, whom we may afterwards meet in the course of our history, in connection with the Cambridge Platonic school, had a famous controversy, in 1673, regarding the Separatists from the Church of England, with Andrew Marvell, Milton's friend, in which the latter introduced Hales's name, with commendation, and appealed to his tract on Schism. He ventured to contrast the spirit of the writer with that of Parker, and to add, " I could not but admire that majesty and beauty which sits upon the forehead of masculine truth and generous honesty, but no less detest the deformity of falsehood disguised in all its ornaments."—Rehearsal Transprosed, p. 134, 135. The comparison seems to have excited Parker's coarse temper; and in his reply, 'A Reproof to the Rehearsal Transprosed,' he fell foul of Hales

making his statement, the obvious prejudices and frequent inaccuracy of the worthy author of the 'Athenæ Oxonienses' deprive his evidence of any value on such a point. The examination of the tracts themselves is sufficient to convince every student of Hales's writings that he is not their author, and beyond all question not the author of the 'Brevis Disquisitio,' which chiefly warrants the charges of Socinianism made by Wood, and repeated by others. With a certain likeness of tone in speaking of the general subject of reason—a likeness, after all, more superficial than real, as the writer of the Disquisition lacks the finer temper and balance of mind with which our author always expresses himself on this subject—there is otherwise no resemblance whatever betwixt the writers. The dogmatic attitude of the author of the Latin treatise is a clearly defined one—equally opposed to Lutherans, Calvinists, and Papists. He distinctly separates himself from the two former—"those who follow Luther and Calvin for their guides in religion"—as well as from the latter; and objects not only to the superstitions of Popery, but to the distinctive tenets

as well as of his admirer. "The next time," he said, "you nose the Church of England with Mr Hales, let the 'Disquisitio Brevis' be your book."

Wood speaks of this "pen-combat" between Parker and Marvell as "briskly managed, with much smart, cutting, and satirical wit on both sides;" but he admits that it was "generally thought, even by many of those who were otherwise favourers of Parker's cause, that he (Parker), through a too loose and unwary handling of the debate (though in a brave, flourishing, and lofty style), laid himself too open to the severe strokes of his sneering adversary, and that the odds and victory laid on Marvell's side."—Ath. Oxon., c. 619, quoted by Maizeaux.

of evangelical Protestantism—the Trinity, the Incarnation, the meritorious satisfaction of Christ, and even original sin and infant baptism—as unreasonable and unscriptural. This is entirely inconsistent with the spirit of Hales, and the characteristic tendencies of his mode of thought.

The earlier treatise on the 'Peace and Concord of the Church' might more possibly be conceived to have proceeded from his pen. It is in some respects a beautiful and striking composition, and in its general character highly consistent with his enlightened and tolerant Protestantism. It has nothing of the hard, dogmatic, and somewhat flippant tone with which the 'Brevis Disquisitio' opposes orthodox dogmatism. But it too bears clear internal marks of foreign authorship. It is evidently written by one with the miseries of the Thirty Years' War before his eyes, and with more information as to the state of religious opinion and religious parties on the Continent than Hales, even with the advantage of his residence at Holland, can well be supposed to have. While an auditor at the Synod of Dort, he was still, we have seen, a Calvinist; and although he may have afterwards "bid Calvin good-night," he never took up a line of definite antagonism to Calvinism, and it may be said with confidence, would never have written regarding the doctrine of predestination as the author of this dissertation does. Still less was he likely to do this anonymously at so early a date after his return from Holland in 1628, and in the first writing deliberately given by him to the world.

We are freed, therefore, from the necessity of examining these writings, and we might be excused from considering the charge founded on them, did it not crop out so frequently in the literature of the century, and reappear in ignorant comment on our author's acknowledged writings, such as the tract on Schism. Aubrey, of course, repeats it, in his usual gossiping manner. "He" (Hales) "was one of the first Socinians in England, I think the first," is his confident statement; and Professor Masson quotes Aubrey apparently without any consciousness that he is doing Hales a gross injustice.[1] The charge, moreover, recurs in the case of Chillingworth in a still more definite and

---

[1] Aubrey, ii. 363, 1813; Life of Milton, i. 500. There can be no doubt that it is a real injustice to writers of acknowledged theological eminence, and who have been at pains to make their religious views and position clear to the world, to have talk like that of Aubrey's quoted against them. In matters of religious opinion, Aubrey's judgment is of no more value than that of any social gossip-monger would be in our own day. The phrase, "the first Socinian in England," seems to have been a favourite catchphrase with him, borrowed probably from his gossiping circle. He applies it in an exactly similar manner, and with the same wantonness, to Falkland — although Falkland, we have seen, placed the encouragement even of Arminianism on the same level with that of Popery as a charge against the Laudian bishops. The worth of Aubrey's statements about Socinianism may be guessed by his further statements in the same page — almost in the same breath. Hales was something of a Familist as well as a Socinian, if he is to be believed. For he adds: "I have heard his nephew, Mr Sloper, say that he much loved to read . . . Stephanus, who was a Familist, I think that first wrote of that sect of the Familie of Love: he was mightily taken with it, and was wont to say, that sometime or other these fine notions would take in the world." Even Wood, whose own accuracy and insight are frequently to be questioned, speaks of Aubrey—in words quoted by Professor Masson—as a credulous person, "roving and magotie-headed," who was in the habit of stuffing his letters with "folliries and misinformations."

flagrant form. It thus forces itself upon the attention of the historian of the rational school of thought in the seventeenth century, and deserves a passing notice. The truth is, that there is not the slightest ground for suspecting either Hales or Chillingworth of Socinianism, beyond the fact that they argue vigorously and directly for the claims of reason in the interpretation of Scripture and the criticism of dogma. To carry out in this manner Protestantism to its legitimate conclusions, and vindicate consistently the right of private judgment, has been always adjudged by certain limited dogmatists—supposed heroes of Protestantism, but really traitors to its essential principles—to partake of the nature of Socinianism. As if it were a matter of course that the conclusions of Scripture and reason must be opposed, and that to rest finally in the arbitration of enlightened Christian thought must be to rest in something short of, or contrary to, the conclusions of evangelical theology! But this is to be unfair at once to evangelical theology and to reason. We may surely ask with a candid Roman Catholic author of the seventeenth century, "Does the making private reason judge of the true sense of Scripture infer that neither Christ nor the Holy Ghost are God? that the pains of hell are not eternal? that separate souls have no being, or at least no perception? &c. God forbid: for then how many innocent persons would be guilty of blasphemies unawares to themselves? Then not only Mr Chillingworth, but Dr Stillingfleet, and besides them, God knows how many more in London and in the universities of England, would be Socinians."[1]

As to Hales, the charge of Socinianism is peculiarly unwarrantable, for he has left us of his own free thought his confession of the Trinity, which is as clear, full, and explicit as any Trinitarian can desire. We cannot quote the whole of it, but the following statements will be allowed to leave his orthodoxy beyond question : " God is one, yet so one that He admits of distinction ; and so admits of distinction that He still retains unity. As He is one, so we call Him God, the Deity, the Divine Nature, and other names of the same signification : as He is distinguished, so we call Him Trinity; persons, Father, Son, and Holy Ghost. In this Trinity there is one essence. . . . The one essence is God, which with His relation, that it doth generate, or beget, makes the person of the Father : the same essence with this relation, that it is begotten, maketh the person of the Son : the same essence with this relation, that it proceedeth, maketh the person of the Holy Ghost."[2]

It is in connection with this question of orthodoxy and his tract on Schism that we find our author brought into significant connection with Laud in 1638. Heylin's account of his visit to the Archbishop is extremely graphic, and so far characteristic of the two men ; but, like many other graphic stories, it is probably more interesting than accurate. It is introduced with an allusion to the ' Brevis Disquisitio,' which appears to have been the foundation of all

[1] Cressy's Epist. Apologetical, 1674. [2] Works, i. 76, 77.

subsequent statements connecting Hales's name with this treatise. It was ascribed to him, it is said, "in common speech;" but Heylin does not venture on his own authority to say that he knew anything of the authorship. Of Hales himself, he speaks with the generous admiration with which almost all mention him. He was a man, he says, "of infinite reading and no less ingenuity—free of discourse, and as communicative of his knowledge as the celestial bodies of their light and influences." (Such a man, it might have occurred to Heylin, was not likely to "insert cunningly some of the principal Socinian tenets" in a discourse really and professedly on another subject.) The tract on Schism, although not printed at this time, had passed from hand to hand "in written copies," and evidently excited much attention both amongst Hales's friends—who are spoken of as "our great masters of wit and reason"—and the ecclesiastical authorities. The tone of it must have been far from pleasing to Laud. It struck, in fact, at the root of his whole system of Church authority. But he could not, even if he had been disposed, act harshly towards one who was so intimately associated with Chillingworth, his own friend—and, moreover, to do him justice, he seems to have had no disposition to do so. He hoped rather, as Heylin says, "that he might gain the man whose abilities he was well acquainted with when he lived in Oxford." Accordingly he sent for him to Lambeth, and had a long conference with him, thus described by his biographer : "About nine of the clock in the morning, he (Hales) came to know his Grace's pleasure, who took him along with him into his garden, commanding that none of his servants should come at him upon any occasion. There they continued to discourse till the bell rang to prayers, and after prayers were ended, till the dinner was ready, and after that too till the coming in of the Lord Conway and some other persons of honour put a necessity upon some of his servants to give him notice how the time had passed away. So in they came, high coloured, and almost panting for want of breath, enough to show that there had been some heats between them, not then fully cooled. It was my chance to be there that day, and I found Hales very glad to see me in that place, as being himself a mere stranger to it, and unknown to all. He told me afterwards that he found the Archbishop (whom he knew before for a nimble disputant) to be as well versed in books as business; that he had been ferreted by him from one hole to another, till there was none left to afford him any further shelter; that he was now resolved to be orthodox, and to declare himself a true son of the Church of England both for doctrine and discipline."[1]

Such is Heylin's story, and we must judge of its credibility according to our knowledge of the persons concerned.[2] Maizeaux is very indignant at its mis-

---

[1] Cyprianus Anglicus, or Life and Death of Archbishop Laud, 1671.

[2] Clarendon's description of the same visit deserves to be placed beside that of Heylin, and probably gives a more accurate account of what really passed:— "Laud," he says, "sent for Mr Hales, whom, when they had both lived in the University of Oxford, he had known well; and told him that he had in truth believed him to be long since dead; and chid him very kindly for having never come to him, having been of his old acquaintance: then asked him whether he had lately written a

representations, and sets forth at length the grounds on which he conceives a man like Heylin is not to be trusted in his account of such a matter. He was a violent sacerdotalist, and "constant assertor of the Church's right," like the subject of his biography. He had also much of the blind confidence and narrow intensity of spirit characteristic of his class, which frequently passes with others, and even with themselves, for spiritual zeal. Of Hales's mode of thought, and of the real significance of his attitude on the subject of the Church, he had evidently no conception. Such men never have of anything which transcends the bonds of party, or the lines of accustomed tradition. It would be almost certain, therefore—even if we had only his own story—that he had misinterpreted the natural and complimentary deference of Hales's remarks into an expression of his submission to the supreme superiority of the Archbishop's arguments. Hales, moreover, was a wit, and may have delighted in playing with a man like Heylin, whose mind would not readily catch the

short discourse of Schism, and whether he was of that opinion which that discourse implied. He told him, that he had for the satisfaction of a private friend (who was not of his mind), a year or two before, writ such a small tract, without any imagination that it would be communicated; and that he believed it did not contain anything that was not agreeable to the judgment of the primitive Fathers: upon which the Archbishop debated with him upon some expressions of Irenæus, and the most ancient Fathers; and concluded with saying that the time was very apt to set new doctrines on foot, of which the wits of the age were too susceptible; and that there could not be too much care taken to preserve the peace and unity of the Church; and from thence asked him of his condition, and whether he wanted anything: and the other answering that he had enough, and wanted or desired no addition, so dismissed him with great courtesy."

subtler aspects of a subject. In reporting what passed between him and the Primate, he may have put his own case very much at a disadvantage. There might seem to him humour as well as humility in representing himself as overcome by his Grace's searching logic. He may have even jocularly owned that he was henceforth resolved to be "orthodox, and a good son of the Church"—as good as Heylin himself!

But we have happily the means of testing to what extent Hales submitted or in any degree owned himself in the wrong on this occasion. After his interview he addressed a letter to Laud on the subject of their conversation, or, as the letter bears, "upon occasion of the tract concerning Schism," in which he acknowledges regret that what he had written had "given offence," and professes his desire to repair any mischief that may have arisen from "a scribbled paper dropt from so worthless and inconsiderable a hand as his." The apologetic tone of this letter is not to be admired. It is altogether too deprecatory. It would have been much better if he had stood up manfully for his "abortive discourse," as he calls it, and not have spoken of any of its statements as the "issues of unfortunate inquiry" over which the sponge might be passed. But, after all, he nowhere recalls any of the principles he had laid down. There is nothing throughout of the nature of a recantation suggested by Heylin, and caught up and repeated affirmatively by subsequent writers.[1] And so far as even his tone is concerned,

---

[1] Hallam agrees strongly that there is no evidence of Hales's recantation, although we cannot say with him that "his letter is

it is impossible not to recognise in it something of that humorous irony which we suppose to have lain under his conversation with Heylin. He apologises for the style of his tract as in some things "over-familiar and subrustic," as sometimes "more pleasant than needed," and sometimes "more sour and satirical." But his Grace is to be pleased to remember what "the liberty of a letter might entice" him to, and that he was by "genius open and uncantelous, and therefore some pardon might be afforded to harmless freedom and gaiety of spirit." Yet all the while he is conscious of a higher spirit, and in a noble passage speaks of the earnestness and single-mindedness with which he has sought the truth. Like many a man, he was willing to concede for himself any deference to existing authority. He would gladly live at peace; but he felt at the same time the instinctive necessity of a true mind only to yield to what he felt to be the truth. "For the pursuit of truth," he says, "hath been my only care, ever since I first understood the meaning of the word. For this I have forsaken all hopes, all friends, all desires, which might bias me, and hinder me from driving right at what I aimed. For this I have spent my money, my means, my youth, my age, and all I have, that I might remove from myself that censure of Tertullian—*Suo vitio quis quid ignorat?* If, with all

---

full as bold as his treatise on Schism." The story, he adds, is one of Heylin's "many wilful falsehoods;" and the idea of Laud having the superiority of Hales in argument "is ludicrous, considering the relative abilities of the two men."—Constit. Hist. of England, ii. 77, 16th ed.

this cost and pains, my purchase is but error, I may safely say, to err hath cost me more than it has many to find the truth : and truth itself shall give me this testimony at last, that if I have missed of her, it is not my fault, but my misfortune."

This glimpse of Hales in connection with Laud is almost the only occasion in which he can be said to emerge into the light as a Churchman during those troubled and ominous years which preceded the great outbreak. His, it must be confessed, was a nature little fitted for conflict, or for carrying forward, in the face of opposition, a cause however dear to him. The idea of ecclesiastical turmoil—"of the brawls grown from religion"—was hateful to his whole soul, and on no account would he have added to them. He had confidence in the quiet growth of higher thought. He had none, apparently, in party action or agitation, even for the higher side. From this time forward, therefore, he may be said to disappear from view. It is to be remembered that even now he was no longer young. At the time of his interview with Laud he was fifty-four years of age. In the following year he accepted the only Church preferment that seems ever to have been offered to him—a canonry at Windsor;[1] but he had hardly entered on his duties when the storm came; and for many years afterwards, as wave after wave of Revolution broke upon the Church that he loved,

[1] According to Clarendon—who calls the preferment "a prebendary of Windsor"—the Archbishop could not, "without great difficulty, persuade him to accept it; and he did accept it rather to please him than himself, because he really believed he had enough before."

and the college where he had lived so pleasantly amongst his books, there is hardly any trace of him. All that is known is, that he was driven from his offices and his residence in the college, and reduced to great penury. Yet we may be sure that, in so reflective and generous a nature, his own straits were by no means the worst that he endured in those years. The miseries of his country, and the rapid loss of all his friends in the wretched struggle, must have inflicted upon him still deeper pangs. One by one they perished within a brief period—Suckling in exile and disgrace—then the "blameless" Falkland—and lastly, within a few months, Chillingworth. The times were very hard, and it is somewhat pitiful to think of the loneliness, as well as the poverty, of the aged scholar. He had been used to say in his prosperous days that "he thought he should never die a martyr," playfully alluding to his lack of zeal and the comprehensiveness of his theological opinions; but he seems to have suffered scarcely less than the severities of martyrdom. He was left alone without friends, or nearly so,[1] and even at length without books. "He was soon forced to dispose of the only thing left which could afford him some satisfaction in the world—I mean, one of the best collections of books that a person of his station ever enjoyed. All that his charity and his generosity had allowed him to spare, he had con-

---

[1] A kind lady in the neighbourhood of Eton—the Lady Salter—is said by Aubrey to have shown him attention in his last years—after his "sequestration." "He was very welcome to her ladyship," says Aubrey, "and spent much of his time there."

stantly employed towards the completing of it.[1] But the same charitable and generous temper that had prevented his acquiring any other estate besides those books, would not permit him to keep long the produce that had arisen from the selling of them. He shared it with several ministers, scholars, and others, who had been also deprived of their substance, whereby this resource soon failed him. He might have found it supplied by a gentleman, who invited him to come to his house, had he not declined to accept that generous offer. He rather chose to take upon him the education of a youth who lived near Eton. But the fury of the ruling party would not suffer him to continue in that family, so that he at last retired to Eton, and lodged in the house of a widow, whose husband had been his servant. In this obscure retreat he was reduced to extreme want; and a celebrated author,"[2] continues Maizeaux, " very justly observes, that 'it is not one of the least ignominies of that age, that so eminent a person should have been, by the iniquity of the times, reduced to those necessities under which he lived.'"

Some few months before his death, his friend, Mr Farrindon,[3] found him in this retreat. His lodgings were " mean ; " he had only a few books of devotion

---

[1] Clarendon also mentions his fine collection of books. " A greater and better collection than was to be found in any other private library that I have seen— as he had sure read more, and carried more about him in his excellent memory, than any man I ever knew, my Lord Falkland only excepted, who, I think, sided him."

[2] Andrew Marvell.

[3] Farindon, or Farringdon, as the name is sometimes written, was one of those moderate Episcopalian divines, and who, though ejected

in his chamber—the remnant of his magnificent library; and "for money about seven or eight shillings; and besides," said he, "I doubt I am indebted for my lodging." Yet his temper was "gravely cheerful," and he was able to offer his friend some refreshment. "After a slight and very homely dinner, suitable to the lodgings, some discourse passed between them concerning their old friends, and the black and dismal aspect of the times." At last he asked his friend to walk out with him to the churchyard, where, after some communications as to his circumstances, he added, "When I die—which I hope is not far off, for I am weary of this uncharitable world—I desire you to see me buried in that place of the churchyard" (pointing to the place). "But why not in the church?" asked Mr Farrindon, "with the Provost, Sir Henry Wotton, and the rest of your friends and predecessors?" "Because," says he, "I am neither the founder of it, nor have I been the benefactor to it, nor shall I ever now be able to be so, I am satisfied." This is the last glimpse we get of him. He died at Eton on the 19th of May, 1656, and was buried according to his desire, "in plain and simple manner without any sermon, or ringing the bell, or calling the people together." So he had enjoined in his will, which is a very quaint and characteristic document.

from his vicarage at the commencement of the Civil War, found employment by abstaining from the use of the formularies of the Church. He became minister of St Mary Magdalene, Milk Street. He was an admirable preacher, and held in high esteem.

It is hardly necessary to sum up the features of Hales's character. We can readily realise from the whole tenor of his life, as well as of his writings, the picture suggested by Clarendon of a modest, sensitive, yet profound and discerning spirit—hating religious controversy, yet apt and keen in religious argument when once engaged in it—honest and open-minded to a fault, yet with a great power of reserve in him before the unwise and unreflective—loving peace, yet detesting tyranny—and severe to himself, while kind and charitable in all his thoughts of others. "He was a very hard student to the last," according to Wood,[1] "and a great faster; and though a person of wonderful knowledge, yet he was so modest as to be patiently contented to hear the disputes of persons at table, and those of small abilities, without interposing or speaking a word, till desired." "He was," says another authority,[2] "of a nature so kind, so sweet, so courting all mankind, of an affability so prompt, so ready to receive all conditions of men, that I conceive it near as easy a task for any one to become so knowing, as so obliging." There is an interesting story preserved of his special appreciation of Shakespeare's genius, which should not be forgotten. He is reported to have said, in the course of "those ingenious conversations" which he had with Sir John Suckling, Ben Jonson, and others, that if "any topick" was produced, "finely treated by any of the ancient poets, he would undertake to

[1] 3. c. 411.   [2] Bishop Pearson.

show something upon the same subject, at least as well written by Shakespeare."[1]

In personal appearance, he is said by those who "remembered and were well acquainted" with him, to have had "the most ingenious countenance they ever saw; it was sanguine, cheerful, and full of air."[2] His stature was "small," but "well proportioned, and his motion quick and nimble." Aubrey, who saw him at his retired lodging at Eton shortly before his death, and who may be safely trusted for personal characteristics, speaks of him as "a prettie little man, sanguine, of a cheerful countenance, very gentle and courteous. I was received by him with much humanity; he was in a kind of violet-coloured cloath gowne, with buttons and loopes (he wore not a black gowne), and was reading Thomas à Kempis; it was within a yeare before he deceased. He loved Canarie; but moderately to refresh his spirits. He had a bountiful mind." Altogether a pleasant picture of a large, thoughtful, affable, and devout soul, whom adversity had not soured, and whose piety blended with, without absorbing or discolouring, the genial warmth of his humanity.

II. The acknowledged writings of Hales are contained in three small volumes, edited by Lord Hailes (Sir D. Dalrymple), and published at Glasgow about

---

[1] The story is given by Rowe in his account of Shakespeare's life, and quoted in the notes to Maizeaux's Life of Hales, p. 60. It is also told in a still stronger form by Dryden in his Essay of Dramatic Poesie, p. 32 (1693). But neither Rowe nor Dryden mention the authority on which he gives the story.

[2] Wood, 3. c. 413.

the middle of the last century by the well-known printers of the name of Foulis. During his lifetime he published, or permitted to be published, only one or two sermons which he had preached at Oxford and St Paul's Cross, and a sermon on duels which he had preached at the Hague. The tract on Schism was also published during his lifetime, apparently in an unauthorised form. After his death, his friend, Mr Farrindon, undertook to prepare a collection of his writings, and to prefix to it a memoir; but in writing to the London bookseller who had urged him on the subject, he says,[1] "I am like Mr Hales in this, which was one of his defects, not to pen anything till I must needs." The result was that he died before he had completed his preparations. Dr Pearson, the well-known Bishop of Chester, so far took up his unfinished task, and the " Golden Remains of the Ever-Memorable Mr John Hales of Eton College," &c., appeared in 1659, but without any memoir. The Bishop prefixed, however, an Epistle to the Reader, in which he drew a careful character of the author, from which we have already quoted. Nothing can exceed the enthusiastic admiration of this well-known and highly orthodox divine for Hales's genius, learning, and theological capacity. He was a man, he thinks, " of as great a sharpness, quickness, and subtility of wit, as ever this or perhaps any nation bred." And "as a Christian," none was "ever more acquainted with the nature of the Gospel, because none more studious of the knowledge of it, or more

---

[1] Maizeaux, p. 69.

curious in the search."[1] Second and third editions of the "Remains" appeared in 1673 and 1688, and also in 1677 a new volume containing several additional tracts without preface or advertisement. In Lord Hailes's edition, which professes to be complete, all these writings are collected and presented in a uniform shape, prefaced by various "Testimonies" concerning the author.

The value of Hales's writings consists not in any elaborate treatment of theological questions, but in the singular spirit of enlightenment, and calm, penetrating, comprehensive wisdom which pervade them. They contain no special treatise to which subsequent ages have appealed as a model of theological exposition or argument. They are only tracts, sermons, or letters; and the sermons are neither rich with the jewelled eloquence of a Jeremy Taylor, nor weighty with the solid reasoning and systematic power of a Barrow. But there is in all our author's writings exactly that which so many theological writings want, the light of a bright, open-eyed, candid intelligence, which sees frequently far beyond the range of the most powerful systematic intellect straight to the

---

[1] The following additional sentences from Bishop Pearson's "elogium" on Hales—to which allusions will be found in the text—may be quoted:—

"His industry did strive, if it were possible, to equal the largeness of his capacity, whereby he became as great a master of polite, various, and universal learning, as ever yet conversed with books. Proportionate to his reading was his meditation, which furnished him with a judgment beyond the vulgar reach of man, built upon unordinary notions, raised out of strange observations, and comprehensive thoughts within himself. So that he really was a most prodigious example of an acute and piercing wit, of a vast and illimited knowledge, of a severe and profound judgment."

truth—"an acute and piercing wit," a wise, calm, and "profound judgment." A great reader and student, versed in a various and even (according to Bishop Pearson) a "universal" erudition, he is yet entirely free from the pedantry of learning, a rare attainment for his age. His accumulated knowledge of books and systems never encumbers him. He never, or rarely, uses it as materials of exposition, or stuff for dilating and parading arguments in themselves worthless, after the prevailing fashion. But all his knowledge has become an enriching basis of his own thought, and raises him above "the vulgar reach of man" to see for himself clearly and widely. It has entered into the very life of his quick and genial intellect, and contributes to the wealth of his meditative insight, and his tolerant, comprehensive, and sweetly-tempered genius. The simplicity and breadth of his religious thought are astonishing for his time. He goes to the heart of controversies, and distinguishes with a delicate and summary skill the essential from the accidental in religion as in other things.

Hales's works may be said to be of two classes—miscellaneous tracts and pieces, such as mostly fill the first of the three volumes to which we have adverted; and sermons, which compose the greater part of the two remaining volumes. About the half of the third volume is occupied by his "Letters from the Synod of Dort." These letters, of course, with the exception of his "Oratio Funebris" on the founder of the Bodleian Library, are the earliest of all his writings. As to the others, it is impossible to fix their relative chronological position. We have already given our reasons for believing that the most significant of his undated tracts—that on the Lord's Supper—belongs to about the same period as his tract on Schism; and most of his sermons probably belong to the same or a still earlier period, although not collected, nor with a single exception [1] published, till long afterwards. There is no evidence of his writing anything after the commencement of the troubles in which he and his friends were so directly involved; and no trace in the volumes of allusion to subsequent events, or the special controversies which they called forth.

It is impossible, therefore, and unnecessary, to attempt any further arrangement of his writings. His favourite ideas are scattered here and there through them all—now simplified and popularly illustrated in a sermon, and now urged with more brevity, sharpness, and incision in a tract. We shall accordingly draw our quotations from them as may suit our purpose, and endeavour to present his ideas under some sequence of thought or subject rather than in any order of growth or time.

1. The first aspect of his teaching which deserves attention is his clear exposition of the principle more or less underlying all his thought—that theological or dogmatic differences are not really religious differences, and should not break the unity of common faith and worship. All theological opinion implies certain human additions to the reli-

---

[1] The Sermon "Of Duels," which he preached while resident at the Hague.

gious element — certain "conceits of men," which in their very nature provoke and admit of diversity of criticism; but this diversity is no ground of religious separation. There is no reason why men of very differing opinions in such matters should not worship together. The "liberty of judging," which Hales took to himself, he not only extended to all, but he felt that such liberty was an inherent Christian right, which it was the business of the Church not only to tolerate, but, so to speak, to educate and find room for. It was not difference of opinion which the Church had to fear, but the hardness and perversity of will which turned such difference into a cause of unchristian estrangement. Truth and error were, after all, each man's own responsibility, and even those who fell into error might be nearer the truth in spirit than those who professed to hold it. "He thought," says Clarendon, "that other men were more in fault for their carriage towards them than the men themselves were who erred; and he thought that pride and passion, more than conscience, were the cause of all separation from each other's communion, and he frequently said that that only kept the world from agreeing upon such a liturgy as might bring them into one communion." This is the key-note of a great deal of his writing.

"It is not the variety of opinions," he says in one of his sermons, "but our own perverse wills, who think it meet that all should be conceited as ourselves are, which hath so inconvenienced the Church. Were we not so ready to anathematise each other, where we concur not in opinion, we might in hearts be united, though in our tongues we were divided, and that with singular profit to all sides. It is 'the unity of the Spirit in the bond of peace' (Eph. iv. 3), and not identity of conceit, which the Holy Ghost requires at the hands of Christians."[1]

Then he gives an instance in which there is plainly a reminiscence of the Synod of Dort. "I will give you one instance, in which, at this day, our churches are at variance; the will of God, and His manner of proceeding in predestination, is undiscernible, and shall so remain until that day wherein all knowledge shall be made perfect; yet some there are, who, with probability of Scripture, teach that the true cause of the final miscarriage of them that perish is that original corruption that befel them at the beginning, increased through the neglect or refusal of grace offered. Others, with no less favourable countenance of Scripture, make the cause of reprobation only the will of God, determining freely of His own work as Himself pleases, without respect to any second cause whatsoever. Were we not ambitiously minded, every one to be lord of a sect, each of these tenets might be profitably taught and heard, and matter of singular exhortation drawn from either; for on the one part, doubtless it is a pious and religious intent, to endeavour to free God from all imputation of unnecessary rigour, and His justice from seeming injustice and incongruity: and on the other side, it is a noble resolution so to humble ourselves under the hand of Almighty God, as that we can with patience hear, yea, think it an honour that

[1] ii. 94.

so base creatures as ourselves should become the instruments of the glory of so great a majesty, whether it be by eternal life or by eternal death, though for no other reason but for God's good will and pleasure's sake. The authors of these conceits might both freely (if peaceably) speak their minds, and both singularly profit the Church: for since it is impossible, where Scripture is ambiguous, that all conceits should run alike, it remains that we seek out a way not so much to establish an unity of opinion in the minds of all, which I take to be a thing likewise impossible, as to provide that multiplicity of conceit trouble not the Church's peace. A better way my conceit cannot reach unto than that we would be willing to think that these things, which with some show of probability we deduce from Scripture, are at the best but our opinions, for this peremptory manner of setting down our own conclusions, under this high commanding form of necessary truths, is generally one of the greatest causes which keeps the Churches this day so far asunder; when as a gracious receiving of each other by mutual forbearance in this kind might peradventure, in time, bring them nearer together."[1]

This mode of thought is now sufficiently familiar. But it was far from familiar in Hales's time, and it may be inferred from his letters that it had only gradually grown up in his mind as the fruit of much reflection and experience of religious controversy. His spiritual insight, his sense, moderation, and candid deference to facts, had borne him out of the

[1] ii. 94, 95.

current of religious partisanship, and opened up to him a higher vision than was common to his contemporaries. His mind was evidently in continual quest of truth. He did not take up his opinions and then no more trouble himself to examine them. He was continually going deeper in search of principles, and mastering them with a clearer sight, so as to recognise their true meaning and bearing, and the modifications which they undergo. A healthy modesty, and constantly penetrating and subtle delicacy in consequence, mark his conclusions. He is reverential in the highest sense, and yet keenly original. He is reserved, and yet he speaks out his mind in the face of what he must have known to be cherished prejudices.

There is a highly important passage from the tract on Schism on the same subject. "It hath been the common disease of Christians from the beginning not to content themselves with that measure of faith which God and the Scripture have expressly afforded us; but, out of a vain desire to know more than is revealed, they have attempted to discuss things of which we can have no light, neither from reason nor revelation; neither have they rested here, but upon pretence of Church authority, which is none, or tradition, which for the most part is but figment, they have peremptorily concluded and confidently imposed upon others a necessity of entertaining conclusions of that nature, and to strengthen themselves, have broken out into divisions and factions, opposing man to man, synod to synod, till the peace of the Church vanished, without all possibility of recall. Hence arose those antient and many separations amongst Christians occasioned by Arianism, Eutychianism, Nestorianism, Photinianism, Sabellianism, and many more, both antient and in our time, all which indeed are but names of schism, howsoever in the common language of the Fathers they were called heresies. For heresy is an act of the will, not of reason, and is indeed a lie, not a mistake, else how could that known speech of Austin go for true, *Errare possum, hæreticus esse nolo?* Indeed, Manichæism, Valentinianism, Marcionism, Mahometanism, are truly and properly heresies; for we know that the authors of them received them not, but minted them themselves, and so knew that which they taught to be a lie. But can any man avouch that Arius and Nestorius, and others that taught erroneously concerning the Trinity, or the person of our Saviour, did maliciously invent what they taught, and not rather fall upon it by error and mistake? Till that be done, and that upon good evidence, we will think no worse of all parties than needs we must, and take these rents in the Church to be at the worst but schisms upon matter of opinion. In which case what we are to do is not a point of any great depth of understanding to discover, so be distemper and partiality do not intervene. I do not yet see that *opinionum varietas, et opinantium unitas*, are ἀσύστατα, or that men of different opinions in Christian religion may not hold communion *in sacris*, and both go to one church. Why may not I go, if occasion require, to an Arian church, so there be no Arianism expressed in their liturgy? And were liturgies and public forms of service so framed as that they admitted not of particular and private fancies, but contained only such things as in which all Christians do agree, schisms on opinion were utterly vanished. For consider of all the liturgies that are or ever have been, and remove from them whatsoever is scandalous to any party, and leave nothing but what all agree on, and the event shall be, that the public service and honour of God shall no ways suffer; whereas to load our public forms with the private fancies upon which we differ is the most sovereign way to perpetuate schism unto the world's end. Prayer, confession, thanksgiving, reading of Scripture, exposition of Scripture, administration of sacraments in the plainest and simplest manner, were matter enough to furnish out a sufficient liturgy, though nothing either of private opinion, or of church pomp, of garments, of prescribed gestures, of imagery, of music, of matter concerning the dead, of many superfluities, which creep into the churches under the name of order and decency, did interpose itself. For to charge churches and liturgies with things unnecessary was the first beginning of all superstition, and when scruples of conscience began to be made or pretended, then schisms began to break in. If the spiritual guides and fathers of the Church would be a little sparing of incumbering churches with superfluities, and not over rigid, either in reviving obsolete customs or imposing new, there were far less danger of schism or superstition, and all the inconvenience were likely to ensue would be but this, they should in so doing yield a little to the imbecillities of inferiors, a thing which St Paul would never have refused to do. Meanwhile, wheresoever false or suspected opinions are made a piece of the church liturgy, he that separates is not the schismatic, for it is alike unlawful to make profession of known or suspected falsehoods, as to put in practice unlawful or suspected actions."[1]

2. The great practical question of Church authority here suggested, is the next under which we may sum up Hales's views. He thus briefly speaks of bishops and their due position. "They do but abuse themselves and others that would persuade us that bishops by Christ's institution have any superiority over other men further than of reverence, or that any bishop is superior to another further than positive order as agreed upon amongst Christians hath prescribed. For we have believed them that hath told us 'That in Jesus Christ there is neither high nor low, and that in giving honour every man should be ready to prefer another before himself' (Rom. xii. 10); which saying cuts off all claim most certainly to superiority by title of Christianity, except men can think that these things were spoken only to poor and private persons. Nature and religion agree in that neither of them hath a hand in this heraldry of *secundum sub et supra; all this comes from composition and agreement of men among themselves.*"[2]

This and the preceding passage are amongst the most decisive in the famous tract on Schism, which only extends in all to twenty ordinary pages. It is somewhat astonishing to reflect now how much noise this tract made, not only when first written and circu-

[1] i. 125, 128. [2] i. 131.

lated amongst Hales's friends, but afterwards when republished amongst his 'Golden Remains' on the eve of the Restoration. The "pen-combat" betwixt Andrew Marvell, and Parker, Bishop of Oxford, on the subject, was only one of several manifestations of the interest which it excited at this later period, and the significance attached to its utterances. Stillingfleet quotes it at length,[1] and with high appreciation, in his 'Irenicum;' and as late as 1678, a prebendary of Exeter, Thomas Long, B.D., published an elaborate examination and censure of it. Its very brevity, and the light felicity and sense with which it touched a thorny subject, contributed to its circulation and influence. The opening sentences very well represent these characteristics of the writer: "Heresy and schism, as they are in common use, are two theological Μορμῶς, or scarecrows, which they who uphold a party in religion use to fright away such as, making inquiry into it, are ready to relinquish and oppose it if it appear either erroneous or suspicious. For as Plutarch reports of a painter who, having unskilfully painted a cock, chased away all cocks and hens, that so the imperfection of his art might not appear by comparison with nature; so men willing for ends to admit of no fancy but their own, endeavour to hinder an inquiry into it by way of comparison of somewhat with it, peradventure truer, that so the deformity of their own might not appear."

He defines schism as "an unnecessary separation of Christians from that part of the visible Church of which they were once members." It is

[1] See following page.

"ecclesiastical sedition," or a wilful and open violence against "that communion which is the strength and good of all society, sacred and civil." Yet, "the great benefit of communion notwithstanding," there are occasions on which "consent were conspiracy, and open contestation is not fraction or schism, but due Christian animosity." And these occasions are "when either false or uncertain conclusions are obtruded for truth, and acts either unlawful or ministering just scruple are required to be performed." While therefore, speaking generally, it is a crime hardly pardonable "to break the knot of union" amongst Christians, yet in speaking of schisms in particular, many things are to be considered, and the judgments of antiquity by no means to be accepted without hesitation. There may be a schism where the real schismatic is not he that separates, but he that causes the separation; and again, there may be a schism where both parties are the schismatics.

He then explains, with some detail, that all schisms have crept into the Church by one of three ways,—"either upon matter of fact, or matter of opinion, or point of ambition." He takes, in illustration of the first mode of schism, the question of Easter as controverted in the early Church. "This matter," he says, "though most unnecessary, most vain, yet caused as great a combustion as ever was in the Church; the West separating and refusing communion with the East for many years together. In this fantastical hurry, I cannot see but all the world were schismatics; neither can anything excuse them from that imputation, excepting only this, that we charitably suppose that all parties out of conscience did what they did."[1] In the Donatist schism, on the other hand, the blame is found to lie on one side. The Donatists were plainly the schismatics. Yet he sees no reason why either of these questions should have broken the unity of the Church. " For why might it not be lawful to go to Church with the Donatist, or to celebrate Easter with the Quartodeciman, if occasion so require? since neither nature, nor religion, nor reason doth suggest anything to the contrary: for in all public meetings pretending holiness, so there be nothing done but what true devotion and piety brook, why may not I be present in them, and use communication with them?"[2]

The two further grounds of schism—variety of opinion, and Episcopal ambition—he expounds with special interest; but we have already quoted the main passages of this exposition. From the general purport and tone of the tract, it seems hardly possible to avoid the conclusion that Hales had in view the state of the Church of England at the time he was writing, and that he condemned by implication the arbitrary exercise of ecclesiastical authority then so prevalent. In so far, therefore, as he yielded to the personal influence of Laud, or turned aside the obvious application of the great truths laid down by him, he must be accused of timidity. To some extent, no doubt, he merits the accusation. The apologetic tone of his letter on the occasion has been already condemned. Yet it is only fair to him to show that, notwithstanding all the

[1] i. 130.   [2] i. 123.

deference of his personal attitude, and his lack of courage, he did not in any respect compromise his principles. While having no wish for himself to dispute the fact of ecclesiastical authority, he still claimed to have his own opinion as to the origin of this authority, and only to yield to it in so far as his conscience and reason dictated. His language plainly enough implies that he did not abandon his position as to the *natural* source of ecclesiastical power, although he did not choose to urge it further. " Let titles of honour and dominion go as the providence of God will have, yet quiet and peaceable men will not fail of their obedience: no more will I of ought, so be that God and good conscience command not the contrary. A higher degree of duty I do not see how any man can demand at my hands : for whereas the exception of good conscience sounds not well with many men, because ofttimes, under that form, pertinacity and wilfulness is suspected to couch itself; in this case it concerns every man sincerely to know the truth of his own heart, and so accordingly to determine of *his own way, whatever the judgment of his superiors be, or whatsoever event befal him.* For since in case of conscience, many times there is a necessity to fall either into the hands of men or into the hands of God; of these two whether is the best, I leave every particular man to judge : only I will add thus much, it is a fearful thing to trifle with conscience ; for most assuredly, according unto it, a man shall stand or fall at the last." [1]

3. His rational attitude and clear sober-minded-

[1] i. 142.

ness are especially marked in the two tracts on the "Lord's Supper" and on the "Power of the Keys." In both he goes very plainly and directly at his point. The first has been already characterised as one of the most significant of Hales's writings. It is so in its treatment of the sacrament of the Supper, but particularly in what it says of the relation of general councils or assemblies to Christian dogma, or the settlement of Christian truth. The full title of the tract is, " On the Sacrament of the Lord's Supper, and concerning the Church's mistaking itself about Fundamentals."

Hales controverts equally the Romanist and current Protestant view of the Lord's Supper. The latter no less than the former appears to him to imply that the words of consecration are "not a mere trope," but really add something to the nature of the rite. In his view, the words are entirely figurative, and the rite complete without them. In instituting the holy ceremony, our Lord commands us to do what he did, but "leaves us no precept of saying any words. Neither," he adds, "will it be made appear that either the blessed apostles or primitive Christians had any such custom; nay, the contrary will be made probably to appear, out of some of the ancientest writings of the Church's ceremonials. Our Saviour indeed used the words, but it was to express what his meaning was. Had He barely acted the thing, without expressing Himself by some such form of words, we could never have known what it was He did. But what necessity is there now of so doing? for when the congregation is met together, to the breaking of bread and prayer, and see bread and wine upon the communion-table, is there any man can doubt of the meaning of it, although the canon be not read? It was the further solemnising and beautifying that holy action which brought the canon in, and not an opinion of adding anything to the substance of the action. For that the words were used by our Saviour to work anything upon the bread and wine, can never out of Scripture or reason be deduced; and beyond these two, I have no ground for my religion, neither in substance nor in ceremony."[1] St Ambrose seems to be responsible for the prevalent mistake. It was he who said—and posterity have too generally applauded the maxim: *Accedat verbum ad elementum, et fiat sacramentum.* But this is "an unsound, ungrounded conclusion," and implies the false persuasion that "to make up a sacrament, there must be something said and something done; whereas, indeed, to the perfection of a sacrament, it is sufficient that one thing be done whereby another is signified, though nothing be said at all."

The Genevan view[2] of receiving in the Supper the body and blood of Christ — "not after a carnal but after a spiritual manner" — finds no favour in his eyes. To speak in any real sense of the flesh of Christ in connection with the bread appears to him as unmeaning as the Roman Catholic phraseology as to the blood of Christ being sacrificed

---

[1] i. 53, 54.
[2] This view owes its authority, he thinks, to Calvin and Beza, who "have spread it over the face of the Reformed Churches," i. 60.

and shed in the sacrament—but only *incruente*—
"unbloodily." According to him, there is nothing
whatever given in the communion "but bread and
wine." "Jesus Christ is eaten at the communion-
table in no sense—neither spiritually, by virtue of
anything done there, nor really; neither metaphori-
cally, nor literally. Indeed that which is eaten (I
mean the bread) is called Christ by a metaphor; but
it is eaten truly and properly." And in this sense,
"the spiritual eating of Christ is," as he says, "common to all places as well as the Lord's table."
Finally, he adds: "The uses and ends of the
Lord's Supper can be no more than such as are
mentioned in the Scriptures, and they are but two:
(1.) The commemoration of the death and passion of
the Son of God, specified by Himself at the institution of the ceremony; (2.) To testify our union with
Christ, and communion one with another—which end
St Paul hath taught us. In these few conclusions
the whole doctrine and use of the Lord's Supper is
fully set down, and whoso leadeth you beyond this
doth but abuse you: *Quicquid ultra quæritur, non
intelligitur.*" [1]

Passing to the further question—Whether the
Church may err in Fundamentals?—he concludes,
first, "that every Christian may err that will."
Otherwise there could be no heresy—"heresy being
nothing else but wilful error." But admitting this,
his supposed questioner still asks—Can Christians
err by whole shoals, by armies meeting for defence
of the truth in synods and councils, especially

[1] i. 62, 63.

general?" He answers emphatically, some may suppose brusquely,—"To say that councils may not err, though private persons may, at first sight is a merry speech; as if a man should say, that every single soldier indeed may run away, but a whole army cannot, especially having Hannibal for their captain. And since it is confessed that all single persons not only may but do err, it will prove a very hard matter to gather out of these a multitude, of whom being gathered together, we may be secured they cannot err. I must for mine own part confess, that councils and synods not only may and have erred, but considering the means how they are managed, it were a great marvel if they did not err; for what men are they of whom those great meetings do consist? Are they the best, the most learned, the most virtuous, the most likely to walk uprightly? No, the greatest, the most ambitious, and many times men neither of judgment nor learning; such are they of whom these bodies do consist. And are these men in common equity likely to determine for truth? *Sicut in vita, ita in causis quoque spes inprobas habent*, as Quintilian speaks. Again, when such persons are thus met, their way to proceed to conclusion is not by weight of reason, but by multitude of votes and suffrages, as if it were a maxim in nature that the greater part must needs be the better; whereas our common experience shows that *Nunquam ita bene agitur cum rebus humanis, ut plures sint meliores*. It was never heard in any profession that conclusion of truth went by plurality of voices, the Christian profession only excepted; and I have often mused how it comes to pass that the way which in all other sciences is not able to warrant the poorest conclusion, should be thought sufficient to give authority to conclusions in divinity, the supreme empress of sciences." [1]

This is one of the passages quoted by Hallam to illustrate his allegation that Hales's language is "rough and audacious, and that his theology has sometimes a scent of Racow." [2] From the charge of Socinianism, we have already sufficiently vindicated our author; and Hallam's theological perceptions, if occasionally acute and subtile, are too deficient in penetration and compass to make it at all necessary to renew the subject. What appears to him "scent of Racow," is merely the strong odour of common-sense and reason. With his usual instinct this historical critic shrinks from directness and earnestness of speech, and his cold, bald refinement takes offence at the plainness of Hales, as at the warmth and natural robustness of Luther. A rhetorical sword-master like Bossuet is his model of a divine. But a touch of nature, we confess, even if it be somewhat rough, is of more value than any degree of mere external polish, even in a theologian. The passage which provokes his criticism in the present case is a forcible, but by no means too forcible, statement of an important truth. For surely there are few things more extraordinary than the prevalent confidence of all Churches, Protestant as well as Catholic, in the formal decisions of general councils or assemblies. Is it not astonishing that such decisions, attained by mere plurality of votes,

i. 65, 66.   [2] Int. to Lit. of Europe, ii. 425.

should be supposed to impart a special stamp of authority, a sort of sacredness, to spiritual truth? The survival of such a confidence in the face of the facts of human history, and the common experience of the motives which more or less rule all such assemblies, show how strong are the roots of reverence in the human mind. And the delusion is all the more remarkable that it seems to rest for its only justification on a still deeper delusion as to such assemblies being specially under the guidance of the divine Spirit. "It is given out," as Hales says, "that Christian meetings have such an assistance of God and His blessed Spirit, and let their persons be what they will, they may assure themselves against all possibility of mistaking." . . . "I should doubtless," he continues, "do great injury to the goodness of God, if I should deny the sufficient assistance of God to the whole world, to preserve them both from sin in their actions and damnable errors in their opinions; much more should I do it if I denied it to the Church of God; but this assistance of God may very well be, and yet men may fall into sin and errors. Christ hath promised His perpetual assistance to His Church; but hath He left any prophecy that the Church should perpetually adhere to Him? If any man think that He hath, it is his part to inform us where this prophecy is to be found. That matters may go well with men, two things must concur—the assistance of God to men, and the adherence of men to God: if either of these be deficient, there will be little good done. Now the first of these is never deficient, but the second is very often: so that the promise of Christ's perpetual presence made unto the Church infers not at all any presumption of infallibility."[1]

In order to show this more fully, he analyses the term "spirit," "which is so much taken up" in such cases, and shows how it must signify either "a secret elapse or supernatural influence of God upon the hearts of men, ... or that in us which is opposed against the flesh, and which denominates us spiritual men. ... Now of these two," he concludes, "the former it is which the Church seems to appeal unto, in determining controversies by way of council. But to this I have little to say: (1.) Because I know not whether there be any such thing, yea or no. (2.) Because experience shows that the pretence of the Spirit in this sense is very dangerous, as being next at hand to give countenance to imposture and abuse, which is a thing sufficiently seen and acknowledged both by the Papist and Protestant party; as it appears by this, that though both pretend unto it, yet both upbraid each other with the pretence of it. But the Spirit, in the second sense, is that I contend for; and this is nothing but reason illuminated by revelation out of the written word. For when the mind and spirit humbly conform and submit to the written will of God, then you are properly said to have the Spirit of God, and to walk according to the Spirit, not according to the flesh. This alone is that Spirit which preserves us from straying from the truth: for he indeed that hath the Spirit, errs not at all; or if he do, it is with as little hazard and danger as may be, which is the highest point of infallibility

[1] i. 67, 68.

which either private persons or churches can arrive to."[1]

The brief "Essay concerning the Power of the Keys" is also highly characteristic. It is a clear, sharp, sensible treatment of a subject which hundreds of pens have obscured rather than illuminated. A single passage will sufficiently show this, and indicate its line of interpretation. The "Power of the Keys" is simply the privilege of declaring or opening the message of divine love to mankind. It has no relation to any priestly or judicial function in the Christian ministry. And all who themselves have received the divine message, or to whom the kingdom of heaven has been opened, have equally with the clergy the keys of this kingdom committed to them. "Every one, of what state or condition soever, that hath any occasion offered him to serve another in the ways of life, clergy or lay, male or female, whatever he be, hath these keys, not only for himself, but for the benefit of others : . . . to save a soul, every man is a priest. To whom, I pray you, is that said in Leviticus, 'Thou shalt not see thy brother sin, but thou shalt reprove, and save thy brother'? And if the law binds a man, when he saw his enemy's cattle to stray, to put them into their way; how much more doth it oblige him to do the like for the man himself? See you not how the whole world conspires with me in the same opinion? Doth not every father teach his son, every master his servant, every man his friend? How many of the laity in this age, and from time to time in all ages, have, by writing for the public

[1] i. 69, 70.

good, propagated the Gospel of Christ, as if some secret instinct of nature had put into men's minds thus to do. You conceive that forthwith upon this which I have said must needs follow some great confusion of estates and degrees; the laity will straightway get up into our pulpits, we shall lose our credit, and the adoration which the simple sort do yield us is in danger to be lost. Sir, fear you not, the sufficient and able of the clergy will reap no discountenance, but honour by this; for he that knows how to do well himself, will most willingly approve what is well done by another. It is extreme poverty of mind to ground your reputation upon another man's ignorance, and to secure yourself, you do well, because you perceive perchance that none can judge how ill you do. Be not angry then to see others join with you in part of your charge. 'I would all the Lord's people did preach,' and that every man did think himself bound to discharge a part of the common good, and make account that the care of other men's souls concerned him as well as of his own.'"

4. Hales is not only always rational in spirit—he has a very definite system of thought. He sees clearly the drift of his principles, and is satisfied that the ground on which he stands is the only satisfactory ground of religious conviction. The following extracts from a very significant sermon "Of Enquiry and Private Judgment in Religion," will set his rational theory of Christianity, in its systematic relations, fully before the reader. The central question with him, as with Falkland, is Infallibility. He

describes the craving of men after it, and shows them where alone it is to be found—with themselves and with God. "An infallibility there must be; but men have marvellously wearied themselves in seeking to find where it is. Some have sought it in general councils, and have conceived that if it be not there to be found, it is for certainty fled out of the world. Some have tied it to the Church of Rome and to the bishop of that see. Every man finds it, or thinks he finds it, accordingly as that faction or part of the Church upon which he is fallen doth direct him. Thus, like the men of Sodom before Lot's door, men have wearied themselves, and have gone far and near to find out that which is hard at hand. We see many times a kind of ridiculous and jocular forgetfulness of many men, seeking for that which they have in their hands; so fares it here with men who seek for infallibility in others which either is, or ought to be, in themselves: as Saul sought his father's asses, whilst they were now at home; or as Œdipus in the tragedy sent to the oracle to inquire the cause of the plague in Thebes, whereas himself was the man. For infallibility is not a favour impropriated to any one man; it is a duty alike expected at the hands of all—all must have it. St Paul when he gives this precept (Gal. vi. 7) directs it not to councils, to bishops, to teachers and preachers, but to all of the Galatian Churches, and in them to all of all the Churches in the world. Unto you, therefore, and to every one, of what sex, of what rank or degree and place soever, from him that studies in his library to him that sweats at the plough, belongs that precept of St Paul, ' Be not deceived.' . . But if any man should reply upon our blessed apostle, and tell him, ' Am I like God that I should look not to be deceived?'—this cannot excuse him; for behold, as if he had purposely meant to have taken this objection away, the apostle joins together both God and us, and tells us, as God cannot, so we must not, be deceived."[1]

He amplifies the subject in a decisive manner, well conscious of the novelty of his views. A man must know, he argues, not only *what* he has to believe, but *why* he is to believe. " I comprise it all in two words, *what* and *wherefore*. They that come and tell you what you are to believe, what you are to do, and tell you not why, they are not physicians, but leeches; and if you so take things at their hands, you are not like men but like beasts. I know that is something an hard doctrine for the many to bear, neither is it usually taught by the common teachers. But it is, nevertheless, true, that every man must bear his own burden, and this burden consists not merely in the substance of what we believe, but the reasons why we believe. That part of your burden which contains *what*, you willingly take up; but that other which comprehends *why*, that is either too hot or too heavy, you dare not meddle with it; but I must add that also to your burden, or else I must leave you for idle persons; for without the knowledge of *why*, of the true grounds or reasons of things, there is no possibility of not being deceived. Your teachers and instructors, whom you follow, they may

[1] iii. 149, 150.

be wise and learned, yet may they be deceived; but suppose they be not deceived, yet if you know not so much, you are not yet excused. Something there is which makes those men not to be deceived; if you will be sure not to be deceived, then know you that as well as they. Is it divine authority? you must know that as well as they. Is it strength of reason? you must know it as well as they. You can never know that you are not deceived until you know the grounds and reasons upon which you stand; for there is no other means not to be deceived, but to know things yourselves.—I will put on this doctrine further, and convince you by your own reason. It is a question made by John Gerson, sometime Chancellor of Paris: 'Wherefore hath God given me the light of reason and conscience, if I must suffer myself to be led and governed by the reason and conscience of another man?' Will any of you befriend me so far as to assail this question? for I must confess I cannot. It was the speech of a good husbandman, 'It is but a folly to possess a piece of ground, except you till it.' And how then can it stand with reason, that a man should be possessed of so goodly a piece of the Lord's pasture as is this light of understanding and reason, which He hath endowed us with in the day of our creation, if he suffer it to lie untilled or sow not in it the Lord's seed?"[1]

He then inquires into reasons why "men are so generally willing in points of religion to cast themselves into other men's arms, and leaving their own reason to relie so much upon another man's." He

[1] iii. 152, 153.

finds the explanation partly in the natural sloth of men, who "are well content to take their ease and call their sloth 'modesty,' and their neglect of inquiry 'filial obedience;' partly in the fault of the ministry, who are afraid to advise men 'to search into the reasons and grounds of religion,' in case it 'breed trouble and disquiet,'—in this manner acting as the Sybarites, who, 'to procure their ease, banished the smiths because their trade was full of noise;'" but also in the fact that "the dregs of the Church of Rome are not sufficiently washed from the hearts of many men." He feels that the Protestantism around him of the "common teachers" is but a poor and imperfect Protestantism, which does not reach to "the uttermost grounds" on which religious knowledge, like all other knowledge, must rest. There is no other way than going to the root of the divinely-planted reason and conscience in each of us. "David found this by his own experience. 'I am wiser than my teachers,' said he, in his Psalm cxix. v. 99. Why? because he believed them? this would never have made him so wise, much less wiser;—why then? 'For thy testimonies,' saith he, 'are my studies.' Therefore is he wiser than his teachers, because that, knowing all that they could teach him, he stayed not there, but by his own search and study he arrives at a degree of knowledge beyond his masters. St Basil, in his sermons upon some of the psalms, taxes a sort of men who thought it a sin to know more of God than the traditions of their fathers would give them leave; and would not advance or improve the knowledge of the truth by any faculty or industry of their own. Beloved, there is not a more immediate way to fall into the reproof of St Basil, and to hinder all advancement and growth of Christian knowledge amongst the common sort of men, than this easy and slothful resolution to rest themselves on others' wits."[1]

Having thus vindicated personal inquiry and individual thoughtfulness as the basis of all true religion, he considers, in conclusion, the various substitutes on which men repose when they put off the care of their faith and religion from themselves on other men; and condemns them in succession.

"I will show it you by the particular examination of every one of these; which I will the willinger do, because I see these are the common hackney reasons which most men use in flattering themselves in their mistakes; for all this is nothing else but man's authority thrust upon us under divers shapes. For, first of all, education and breeding is nothing else but the authority of our teachers taken over our childhood. Now there is nothing which ought to be of less force with us, or which we ought more to suspect; for childhood hath one thing natural to it, which is a great enemy to truth, and a great furtherer of deceit; what is that? Credulity. Nothing is more credulous than a child; and our daily experience shows how strangely they will believe either their ancients, or one another, in most incredible reports. For, to be able to judge what persons, what reports are credible, is a point of strength of which that age is not capable. 'The chiefest sinew and strength of wisdom,' saith

[1] iii. 160.

Epicharmus, 'is not easily to believe.'[1] Have we not, then, great cause to call to better account, and examine by better reason, whatsoever we learnt in so credulous and easy an age, so apt, like the softest wax, to receive every impression? Yet notwithstanding this singular weakness, and this large and real exception which we have against education, I verily persuade myself that if the best and strongest ground of most men's religion were opened, it would appear to be nothing else.

"Secondly, Antiquity, what is it else (God only excepted) but man's authority born some ages before us? Now for the truth of things, time makes no alteration; things are still the same they are, let the time be past, present, or to come. Those things which we reverence for antiquity, what were they at their first birth? Were they false? Time cannot make them true. Were they true? Time cannot make them more true. The circumstance, therefore, of time, in respect of truth and error, is merely impertinent. Yet thus much must I say for antiquity, that amongst all these balancing and halting proofs, if truth have any advantage against error and deceit, it is here. For there is an antiquity which is proper to truth, and in which error can claim no part; but then it must be an antiquity most ancient. This cannot be but true, for it is God, and God is truth. All other parts of antiquity, deceit and falsehood will lay claim to as well as truth. Most certain it is, truth is more ancient than error; for error is nothing else but deviation and swerving from the truth. Were

[1] Νῆφε, καὶ μέμνησ' ἀπιστεῖν, ταῦτα γὰρ ἄρθρα τῶν φρενῶν.

not truth, therefore, first, there could be no error, since there could be no swerving from that which is not. When, therefore, antiquity is pleaded for the proof of any conclusion commended to you for true, be you careful to know whether it be most ancient, yea or no : if it be so, then is it an invincible proof, and pleads for nothing but the truth; if otherwise, though it be as ancient, I say not as Inachus, but as Satan himself, yet it is no proof of truth.

"Thirdly, Universality is such a proof of truth, as truth itself is ashamed of; for universality is nothing but a quainter and a trimmer name to signify the multitude. Now human authority at the strongest is but weak, but the multitude is the weakest part of human authority; it is the great patron of error, most easily abused, and most hardly disabused. The beginning of error may be, and mostly is, from private persons, but the maintainer and continuer of error is the multitude. Private persons first beget errors in the multitude, and make them public; and publicness of them begets them again in private persons.[1] It is a thing which our common experience and practice acquaints us with, that when some private persons have gained authority with the multitude, and infused some error into them, and made it public, the publicness of the error gains authority to it, and interchangeably prevails with private persons to entertain it. The most singular and strongest part of human authority is properly in the wisest and most virtuous; and these, I trow, are not the most

[1] Ubi singulorum error fecerit publicum, singulorum errorem facit publicus.

universal. If truth and goodness go by universality and multitude, what mean then the prophets and holy men of God everywhere in Scripture so frequently, so bitterly, to complain of the small number of good men, careful of God and truth? Neither is the complaint proper to Scripture; it is the common complaint of all that have left any records of antiquity behind them. Could wishing do any good, I could wish well to this kind of proof; but it will never go so well with mankind that the most shall be the best.[1] The best that I can say of argument and reason drawn from universality in multitude is this— such reason may, perchance, well serve to excuse an error, but it can never serve to warrant a truth.

"Fourthly, Councils, and synods, and consent of Churches, these indeed may seem of some force; they are taken to be the strongest weapons which the Church had fought with; yet this is still human authority after another fashion. Let me add one thing, that the truth hath not been more relieved by these than it hath been distressed. At the Council of Nice met 318 bishops to defend the divinity of the Son of God; but at Ariminum met well near 600 bishops to deny it. I ask, then, What gained the truth here by a synod? Certainly in the eye of reason it more endangered it, for it discovered the advantage that error had among the multitude above the truth; by which reason truth might have been greatly hazarded. I have read that the nobility of Rome, upon some fancy or other, thought fit that all

[1] Sed nunquam ita bene erit rebus humanis, ut plures sint meliores.

servants should wear a kind of garment proper to them, that so it might be known who were servants, who were freemen; but they were quickly weary of this conceit, for perceiving in what multitudes servants were in most places, they feared that the singularity of their garment might be an item to them to take notice of their multitude, and to know their own strength, and so at length take advantage of it against their masters. This device of calling councils was but like that fancy of the Roman gentlemen; for many times it might well have proved a great means to have endangered the truth, by making the enemies thereof to see their own strength, and work upon that advantage; for it is a speedy way to make them to see that, which for the most part is very true, that there are more which run against the truth than with it."[1]

These are but a few of the numerous passages full of wise and truthful thought to be found in Hales's three volumes. We have confined ourselves mainly to one aspect of his writings, but they possess many independent merits. He is before his age, not only in his reach of thought on general religious questions, but also as an expositor of Scripture. Some of his expositions are fine specimens of exegetical argument—as, for example, that " Of the Sin against the Holy Ghost," in the first volume. It is quite singular how the loads of technical difficulty by which such a subject has been obscured disappear under his clear, quiet, direct analysis, keeping close to facts, and laying them bare in the face of the pseudo-interpretations

[1] iii. 161-166.

which have turned attention away from them. He is strong for the "literal sense" of Scripture,—"the literal, plain, and uncontroversable meaning, without any additions or supply by way of interpretation."[1] His elaborate sermon in the third volume of "The abuses of hard places of Scripture" is a mine of wise and just criticism, which it is strange to think has produced so little effect as it has done. This is a reflection, indeed, which constantly occurs in the perusal of such a writer as Hales. The reader is constantly coming upon remarks and trains of thought which astonish him by their coincidence with the last lessons of Christian criticism and philosophy. That "the Bible must be interpreted like any other book" would not have been any novelty to him, only he would have added, that with all our pains in interpreting it, there would still remain "hard and intricate texts," in regard to which our duty is to wait and pray for light, and not rashly to attempt any solution. It is the craving of men for certainty in matters which God has left in obscurity, and which no wit of man can penetrate, which is the chief source of controversy in the Church. "I verily persuade myself that if it had pleased those who in all ages have been set to govern the Church, to have taught men rather not to have doubted than to have expected still solutions of their doubtings; to have stopped up and dammed the originals and springs of controversies, rather than by determining for the one part to give them as it were a pipe and conduit to convey them to posterity; I persuade myself, the

[1] ii. 36.

Church would not have suffered that inundation of opinions with which at this day it is overrun."¹ "When we seceded from the Church of Rome our motive was, because she added unto Scripture her glosses as canonical, to supply what the plain text of Scripture could not yield. If in place of this we set up our own glosses, thus to do were nothing else than to pull down Baal and set up an ephod; to run round and meet the Church of Rome again at the same point in which at first we left her."²

Again, in the same sermon, which abounds in pertinent and choice sayings which a reader instinctively notes as he proceeds:—" If he that abases the prince's coin deserves to die, what is his desert that instead of the tried silver of God's Word, stamps the name and character of God upon Nehushtan—upon base brazen stuff of his own?"³

There are few theological writers who present more scattered "beauties," both of thought and expression—sayings which surprise the reader for their quiet profundity and ripe store of meaning. A quaint humour plays along his page at times, and a quick, frequent variety of illustrations, which make his sermons and tracts as fresh and interesting as when they were written. If one reflects how difficult it is to read some of the best theological writers of the seventeenth century—men like Andrews or Hammond on the High Church side, or Owen, or even Howe on the Puritan side—this will seem no ordinary praise. It is the complete rational activity of the man,—the life of thought within him,—which fuses

[1] ii. 43, 44.   [2] Ibid., p. 36.   [3] Ibid., p. 27.

together his stores of knowledge, and gives them forth in breathing and not dead forms. This interest animates all he does. His wealth of illustration, if sometimes excessive and occasionally irrelevant, is never tiresome. Drawn from a copious and diversified learning, it is never put forward for the sake of effect; it has no air of ostentation or pedantry; it is the natural play of a richly-cultured mind. His patristic and classical allusions come in rapid and easy succession, nimbly tripping up one another in their course, as if they ran a race in his fertile brain. It is no uncommon thing to find Aristotle, Chrysostom, and Cicero or Horace, all studding a single page of a sermon, and fitly lending point or beauty to the thought. A happy phrase or sentence from one Father suggests a happy phrase or sentence from another, and both are wrought with felicitous touch into the texture of his own composition,—as in the following example, which strikes us as quite a *curiosa felicitas:* " Prayer added unto diligent labour is like a sweet voice to a well-tuned instrument, and makes a pleasing harmony in the ears of God. 'The good housewife,' saith Chrysostom, 'as she sits at her distaff and reaches out her hand to the flax, may even thus lift up, if not her eyes, yet her mind unto heaven, and consecrate and hallow her work with earnest prayer unto God.'[1] 'The husbandman,' saith St Jerome, 'at the ploughtail, may sing a hallelujah; the sweating harvestman may refresh himself with a psalm; the gardener, whilst he prunes his vines and arbours, may sound some one of David's sonnets.'"[2]

[1] De Anna, Serm. iv. § 6.   [2] Epist. lib. ii., ad Marcellum.

But our criticism is sufficiently extended. We have quoted enough to show what Hales was as a writer, especially as a thinker — what a genuine breadth of reason and of spiritual apprehension there was in him. The combination which he presents of simplicity and grasp of view—of modesty and depth—of sobriety, and yet freedom of judgment, is particularly attractive. Liberal as are his opinions for the age, he exhibits no rashness or intemperance of statement. He sees the folly of mere deference to authority in religion. He exposes the main vice of theology in all ages — the substitution of human opinion or "conceit" in the place of divine truth. He expresses himself "bluntly" at times, but never coarsely, and his intellectual temper, upon the whole, is admirably balanced. In a true sense his mind is "unshackled;"[1] he has thrown himself loose, that is to say, from many prejudices. But he is nevertheless always reverent, earnest, and moderate. He sees very well that it is not the clergy or any particular class of men that are mainly to blame for prevailing bigotries; it is rather the natural sloth and prejudice of human nature. He is content, therefore, to unfold the evil and point the remedy. He knew human nature too well, and had studied human history too intelligently, to suppose that he could speedily enlarge men's thoughts on such a subject as religion. He held up a higher light in his own teaching, but he was aware how many, from weakness of reason or strength of passion, would

[1] Hallam, Hist. of England, ii. 77, 10th ed.

continue to turn away from it. He was no more fitted to be a reformer than a martyr. His reason was too wide and large, and he felt all the difficulties of a subject too keenly, to thrust his own views impatiently or violently upon others. He was, Clarendon tells us, fain to keep his opinions to himself, as being far from confident that they might not harm others less calm and sensible than himself, "who might entertain other results from them than he did." This led him to be "very reserved in communicating what he thought himself on those points in which he differed from what was received." And there is something to be said in behalf of this spirit of reserve. A constant experience makes it evident that there are certain minds constitutionally incapable of any freedom of opinion in religious matters. They neither desire it for themselves nor understand it in others. A freedom of speculation like Hales's startles and confuses them without awakening in them any higher thoughts. They seem only capable of receiving the truth in some partial half-superstitious form; and if the superstitious vesture is stripped away, truth itself is apt to follow. They have none of our author's power of discriminating the essential from the accidental in religion. And Hales knew this very well. He knew, also, the violent and harmful prejudices which persons of this contracted turn are apt to entertain towards men of a more liberal thoughtfulness. He had heard both himself and his friend Chillingworth denounced with coarse violence as Socinians. To a man of quiet, scholarly temper, such things are odious. It is not only that they feel them unmerited, but that they also feel that no vindication they could make would be intelligible to the men who urge them. For those who deal in such charges are invariably incognisant of the deeper grounds of religious opinion. They judge of religious differences from the outside—from superficial resemblance or antagonism. With no finer edges either to their intellect or their conscience, with no subtlety or depth of spiritual imagination, they cannot penetrate below the most obvious distinctions of belief; and especially they cannot understand minds which, like Hales's, are constantly seeking a unity of religious conception,—which delight in search after such a unity to strip off the scholastic folds in which religious opinion has been swathed, and to see divine truth according to the "simplicity which is in Christ."

But, reserved as Hales was as to some of his opinions, there was one point on which he expressed himself with frank boldness: "Nothing troubled him more," says Clarendon, "than the brawls which were grown from religion. And he therefore exceedingly detested the tyranny of the Church of Rome, more for their imposing uncharitably upon the consciences of other men, than for the errors in their own opinions; *and would often say that he would renounce the religion of the Church of England tomorrow, if it obliged him to believe that any other Christian should be damned; and that nobody would conclude another man to be damned who did not wish him so.*"

It is sufficiently obvious that, quiet and unobtrusive as Hales's life may have been, he was a man of marked influence upon a few higher minds. Personally he had no ambition, and apparently but little activity. He kept aloof from the fierce practical controversies of his time. It was his nature to do so —to brood and meditate on the principles underlying religious controversy, rather than to take any active part in it. His intellectual refinement—his sympathies with the Past—his love of the concrete, and tolerance of the historical results to which Christian usage and opinion had gradually grown in England—made him incline to the Royalist party, with which he ultimately threw in his lot, and whose misfortunes he shared. In no circumstances can he be conceived a Puritan. Those instincts of political liberty which were the highest and most aggressive element of Puritanism, if not uncongenial, could only have feebly influenced him, while his ideas of religious freedom were plainly of a more thorough and comprehensive—in a word, of a more rational—character than Puritanism has ever shown itself capable of attaining. The importance attached by the Puritan party to minute matters, details of worship, or special interpretations of doctrine, were scarcely intelligible to a mind like his. Their dogmatic handling of Scripture, their love of formal theory and abstruse logic, openly repelled him. Like his friend Falkland, therefore, he stands significantly aside from both extremes. He is a Churchman without narrowness; a friend of authority, who must yet have hated in his heart and deeply felt the folly of Laud's tyranny. In freedom of thought and clearness of faith, he greately excels the mere professional divine of any age. He is evangelical without dogmatism, and preaches grace without despising philosophy. At once conservative in feeling, and liberal in opinion, he hates all extremes, as of the nature of falsehood, and a prolific source of wrong. He is the representative—the next after Hooker—of that catholicity yet rationality of Christian sentiment which has been the peculiar glory of the Church of England.

V.

WILLIAM CHILLINGWORTH—THE BIBLE THE RELIGION OF PROTESTANTS.

I. WILLIAM CHILLINGWORTH is a more prominent figure in the history of religious opinion than John Hales. His name is widely known to English Protestants, and his great work, if not really read and studied so much as it deserves to be, is yet generally acknowledged as a bulwark of Protestant argument, and one of its chief trophies in the long-waged, still unfinished conflict with sacerdotal theory and ecclesiastical exclusiveness.

Chillingworth was eighteen years younger than Hales, having been born in Oxford in October 1602. His father was Mayor of Oxford; and William Laud, afterwards Archbishop of Canterbury, then a Fellow of St John's College, was his godfather.[1] This connection was a significant one in his after-history. He was "educated in grammar learning under Edward Sylvester, a noted Latinist and Grecian;" and at the age of sixteen "became a scholar of Trinity

---

[1] Wood's Ath. Oxon., vol. ii. Our main authorities for the facts of his life are Wood's 'Athenæ Oxonienses,' and the 'Historical and Critical Account of the Life and Writings of William Chillingworth,' by Maizeaux, the latter a work of a more elaborate character than the memoir by the same author of Hales.

College, under the tuition of Mr Robert Skinner." He was admitted Master of Arts in 1623, and Fellow of the same College in 1628.[1] " He was there observed," says Wood, " to be no drudge at his study; but being a man of great parts, would do much in a little time when he settled to it." According to the same authority, he was also noted thus early for his keenly intellectual and argumentative disposition : " He would often walk in the college grove and contemplate; but when he met with any scholar there, he would enter discourse, and dispute with him purposely, to facilitate and make the way of wrangling common with him, which was a fashion used in those days, especially among the disputing theologists, or among those that set themselves apart purposely for divinity." Aubrey's version of the same circumstance is characteristic : " He did walk much in the college grove and there contemplate, and meet with some *cod's-head* or other, and dispute with him and baffle him. He thus prepared himself beforehand. . . . He was the readiest and nimblest disputant in the university; perhaps none hath equalled him since."

He did not confine his studies to divinity, but applied himself with great success to mathematics, and even obtained some reputation as a poet. He finds a place along with his friend Hales in Sir John Suckling's "Session of the Poets."

When Chillingworth was thus engaged studying and disputing at Oxford, the country was in a state

[1] Wood's Ath. Oxon., vol. ii.

of great controversial excitement. The anti-Papal fever, of which we have already spoken, was in full vigour. Even before the death of King James, in 1625, the Court had shown signs of a leaning to Rome. The Calvinistic enthusiasm, which found vent in the patronage of the Synod of Dort, had passed away. The High Church party, mainly Arminian in its doctrinal tendencies, was acquiring power. The Romanists began to raise their heads once more, and priests traversed the country without molestation. On the accession of Charles I., and his marriage with the Princess Henrietta, sister of Henry IV. of France, Popish influences were permitted still greater scope. The Queen, as a Roman Catholic, had stipulated for the free exercise of her religion, and a due attendance of its ministers—a bishop, with twenty-eight priests or monks, and a chapel wherever she might happen to reside. The children of the marriage were to be trained under her care till they were thirteen. The natural consequence of all this was great party activity and excitement. It seemed then, as on so many subsequent occasions, that England might be once more gained to the Catholic fold. Several Jesuits and "Seminary Priests," as they were called, were very active among the youth of the universities, and made not a few converts, who were generally conveyed to English seminaries abroad. The attention of Parliament was aroused to this evil, and it petitioned the King on the subject in 1628, the same year in which Chillingworth obtained his fellowship. The words of the petition are emphatically descriptive of the state of feeling in the country. They pray that his Majesty "would be pleased to command a surer and straight watch to be kept in and over his Majesty's ports and havens, and to commit the care and charge of searching of ships for the discovery and apprehension, as well of Jesuits and seminary priests brought in, as of children and young students sent over beyond the seas, to suck in the poison of rebellion and superstition, unto men of approved fidelity and religion : and such as should be convicted to have connived or combined in the bringing in the one or conveying of the other, that the laws might pass upon them with speedy execution."[1] The King agreed to grant the prayer of the petition, and to give orders to see it fully executed. But nothing came of the royal promises, and the Parliament continued its complaints. The Popish missionaries were intrepid and persevering, and easily succeeded in eluding the feeble attempts that were made to search for and apprehend them.

It is in connection with the state of religious and political excitement that we come across a story which casts discreditable reflections upon Chillingworth as a young man. The story, we need hardly say, is partly attributable to Aubrey, although it has assumed in later hands a more definite form than can be found in his pages. We have already given our reasons for discrediting Aubrey's scandals. It is plain in reading them that they are often the veriest gossip, without any evidence, or even the pretence

[1] Rushworth, Hist. Collections.

of evidence. It was enough for him to have heard anything from anybody to lead him to commit it to paper. His professed authority in the present case is Sir William Davenant, Poet-Laureate, whose word certainly cannot be held to give any weight to statements otherwise incredible—inconsistent with all we know of Chillingworth's character, both from his friends and as depicted in his own writings.

The story is that Chillingworth, "notwithstanding," in Aubrey's language, "his great reason, was guilty of the detestable crime of treachery." He acted, in short, according to the insinuation, as a sort of spy for Laud, "his godfather and great friend," giving him "weekly intelligence of what passed in the university." And special trace of this spy system is supposed to be found in connection with information lodged against a certain Mr Gill, a son of the head of St Paul's School, and one of Milton's preceptors. This younger Gill—friend and correspondent as he was of Milton—seems to have been something of a fool. He had been bred at Oxford, taken orders, and afterwards become usher in the school under his father, where he had come in contact with Milton, and apparently assisted in his education. All this might be supposed a guarantee of respectability, but there was a mad humour in the man that might have proved fatal to him. Not content with writing letters to his friends at the university stuffed with dangerous nonsense about the Court, he was in the habit of running down to Oxford on a visit to his old haunts there. On one of these occasions, in the autumn of 1628—following the assassination of the Duke of Buckingham by Felton—he was in Trinity College cellar drinking with "divers others," when the talk fell upon the events of the time. Gill became boisterous over his cups, and is reported to have said that "our King was fitter to stand in a Cheapside shop with an apron before him, and say, 'What lack ye?' than to govern a kingdom;" and further, that "the Duke was gone to hell to meet James there." He is further represented as having drunk Felton's health, saying " he was sorry Felton had deprived him of the honour of doing that brave act."[1] All this nonsense was communicated to Laud; Gill was arraigned and tried before the Star-Chamber, and condemned, as the consequence of his folly, to be degraded from his ministry and degrees in the university, to be fined heavily, and to have his ears taken off, the one at London, and the other at Oxford. The fine and corporal punishment were remitted on the earnest petition of "old Mr Gill" to his Majesty; and the son lived, as such braggarts often do, to change entirely his political tune. He became a very servile courtier, and even a literary lackey to the Archbishop.

Professor Masson has told this story of Milton's friend in his 'Life of Milton;'[2] and the question occurring of how the report of Gill's escapade could have reached Laud's ears, leaves it to be inferred that Chillingworth may have been his informant. Putting together Aubrey's scandal and the state-

[1] See account quoted, Masson's Life of Milton, i. 177.
[2] Ibid.

ments of certain documents in the State Paper Office that "one Mr Shillingworth," along with others, was present when "Alex. Gill spake his lewd words," it appears to him "that Aubrey had got some true inkling of the fact," though, he hopes, "in a form unnecessarily discreditable to Chillingworth." The whole affair seems altogether too paltry to be mentioned with the name of Chillingworth, who, whatever may have been his faults, was a true and generous-minded man, incapable of such meanness as the story implies. Clarendon, who, in some respects, has by no means drawn a flattering portrait of him, emphasises the "conspicuous sincerity of his heart," and the "innocence and candour of his nature." The whole structure of the scandal, moreover, falls to pieces when closely examined. Aubrey, in his more detailed statements, not only does not say anything of Gill's mad freak and speeches at Oxford, but gives a version of his conduct quite different from and inconsistent with the story repeated by Mr Masson. He says that young Gill and Chillingworth "held weekly intelligence one with another for some years, wherein they used to nibble at State matters," and that "in one of his letters" Gill called "*King James and his sonne* the old foole and the young one, wch letter Chillingworth communicated to W. Laud, A.B. Cant." Now any grain of truth there may be in this story cannot well refer to an event which happened in 1628, three years after King James's death. The only thing which can be said to be proved in the whole matter is Chillingworth's presence, along with three other persons, when Gill made his mad speeches. There is not the slightest reason—apart from Aubrey's malice—for supposing him to have been Laud's informant. And if it be necessary to make any supposition about the informant, there is a person of the name of Pickering mentioned amongst those present whom Gill jeers or insults on the occasion, because he refuses to enter fully into his wild humour, and drink the toast to Felton's health. This Pickering may have taken his revenge by having some hint of the matter conveyed to the Archbishop. And on such a supposition it is further conceivable that the Archbishop, from his personal relations with Chillingworth, may have asked him as to the truth of the story. This is all that can possibly be imagined.

Aubrey's charge of treachery stands entirely by itself on the authority of Davenant; and when the question lies betwixt a man, as his letters show, and all his friends testify, of even sensitive honour—and "a roving, magotie-headed" gossip reporting the speech of one who, besides his looseness of character, may be supposed to have had malicious intentions towards our author, there cannot be said to be really any question at all. Davenant was one of the numerous Catholic perverts of the time; and it is notorious with what feelings of enmity this class regarded the author of 'The Religion of Protestants,' whose own experience of Romanism and subsequent refutation of it had so much damaged their cause. The "great asperity and reproaches" of the Roman

Catholic faction against him was a matter of common remark.[1] It was Chillingworth's fate to be thoroughly misunderstood by religious blockheads and partisans on both sides. Blind Papist and blind Puritan alike feared and disliked him, and the aptitude of both in the arts of detraction is well known. Neither certainly spared Chillingworth, as we shall find in the course of our narrative. His own personal connection with the Romanist movement, the manner in which he was hurried away by it, and then again restored to the English Church, made him a conspicuous object of attack.

Among the Roman missionaries there was one known under the name of John Fisher, a Jesuit of great acuteness and of enthusiastic ambition in the work of proselytism. He was a native of Durham, and a convert from Protestantism.[2] His proper name was Perse or Percey. He is described as "a generosus athleta Christi," who feared neither pain nor imprisonment in the service of his faith in making converts, in which he was very successful.[3] Fisher was " much conversant in Oxford." He devoted himself to the students, especially such as gave promise of future distinction. Chillingworth very soon attracted his attention, and he "used all means possible to

---

[1] Clarendon, Life, i. 63.
[2] Bibliotheca Scriptorum, Soc. Jesu, quoted by Maizeaux, p. 5.
[3] This is the same Jesuit with whom Laud had his "conference," who was instrumental in the conversion of the Duchess of Buckingham in 1622, and whose "continual cunning labours" had well-nigh seduced the Duke himself from the Church of England. See p. 74, and Laud's Diary, p. 5, and History and Trial of Arch. Laud, p. 226.

be acquainted with him."[1] He drew him into controversy, which could not have been a difficult task. Chillingworth's mind was already excited on the question of an infallible living Judge in matters of faith, and this became the great topic of dispute between them. The Jesuit was master of his controversial weapons, and succeeded in silencing Chillingworth. He found himself "unable to answer the arguments of the Jesuit;" nor was he pleased with "the solutions which were given him by those of our learned divines to whom he proposed the said arguments."[2] These "solutions" did not seem to him to meet the case; he craved, as so many minds before and since have done, for a decisive tribunal in religious controversy as the only refuge from the doubts which tormented him. Romanism alone professed to offer such a tribunal; and the consequence was, that he forsook the Anglican communion and sought satisfaction in that of Rome. He wrote a letter on the subject to his friend Sheldon, urging upon him the serious consideration of the two following queries: "1st, Whether it be evident from Scripture and Fathers and reason, from the goodness of God and the necessity of mankind, that there must be some one Church infallible in matters of faith? 2d, Whether there be any other society of men in the world beside the Church of Rome, that either can upon good warrant, or indeed at all, challenge to itself the privilege of infallibility in matters of faith?"[3]

An attentive consideration of these questions

[1] Wood's Ath. Oxon., vol. ii. [2] Ibid. [3] Maizeaux, p. 8.

appeared to him, in his present state of mind, to lead necessarily to an affirmative conclusion in the first, and a negative conclusion in the second. He expressed his happiness as to the way in which he had entered, and hoped that it might please God to draw his friend after him.[1]

Fisher did not, of course, lose sight of so promising a pupil. He induced him to set down in writing his motives or reasons for embracing the Roman Catholic religion, and also to proceed to the college of the Jesuits at Douay, with a view to his more perfect training in its characteristic principles. The exact date of his journey to Douay is not ascertained; but he made only a short stay there.[2] It was a luckless step in Chillingworth's case sending him to a Jesuit seminary. Close contact with the system which he had embraced was all that was needed to arouse the higher susceptibilities of a mind like his. It had been his restlessness of inquiry, his frank fearlessness in search of truth, which had led him to Romanism. The Roman Catholic appeared to him for the time to have the best of the argument, with the fullest attention which he could give to the subject. But a mind so truth-loving, candid, and keen-sighted, could not halt in the investigation on which it had entered. He was especially ill-fitted to fall in with the routine of a "seminary," and the dialectic and practical studies by which Jesuitism sought to confirm converts and bring them under the full discipline of their new faith. Never was man less fitted to become a Jesuit priest, and give

[1] Maizeaux, p. 8.   [2] Ibid., p. 9.

up his mind to the service of others. Moreover, Laud, then Bishop of London, having heard of his conversion with great concern, entered into a correspondence with him. Chillingworth responded with "a great deal of moderation, candour, and impartiality," and the prelate continued to "press him with several arguments against the doctrine and the practice of the Romanists." The result was that Fisher's convert passed speedily out of his hands. His inquisitive, argumentative spirit. dug deeper into the heart of the subject, beneath the fallacies which had puzzled and captivated him. The atmosphere of Douay became unendurable, and he returned to England in 1631;[1] paid a visit to Laud, who welcomed him with kindness; and then, with the Bishop's approval, returned to Oxford, "in order to complete the important work he was upon—a free inquiry into religion."[2]

Such is, in brief, the outward history of Chillingworth's conversion to Rome and reconversion to the Church of England. Of his life and occupations at Douay he has not given us, nor do we possess otherwise, any account. From hints, however, that occur in his writings, there can be little doubt that his experience there was greatly disappointing.[3]

[1] Wood, vol. ii.
[2] Maizeaux, p. 13. In his trial before the House of Lords ('History of the Troubles and Tryal of William Laud,' &c., p. 227), Laud pleaded in favour of his own Protestantism his connection with Chillingworth, and the influence he had exercised in reconverting him from Romanism; and we are bound to remember this great service, whatever judgment we pronounce on Laud's ecclesiastical legislation.
[3] Aubrey, of course, has something to say on this point, so entirely like himself, and so unlike Chillingworth, that it may deserve

He found, as he says in one of his casual writings, termed 'Additional Discourses,'[1] "that the Roman religion is much more exorbitant in the general practice of it than it is in the doctrine published in books of controversy, where it is delivered with much caution and moderation—nay, cunning and dissimulation—that it may be the fitter to win and engage proselytes." The special point of which he is speaking is, as to whether incense was really offered to the Virgin Mary. The Roman Catholic disputant had maintained that this was a "foul slander," and that incensing in every case was "understood by all sorts of people to be directed to God only." He appeals to his own experience in refutation of this, and in proof of the fact that, in processions, incense was offered to the images of the saints. "I myself (unless I am very much mistaken) was present when this very thing was done to the picture of St Bennet or St Gregory, in the cloister of St Vedastus, in the monastery in Douay." In the course of his arguments in the 'Religion of Protestants' he also appeals unfavourably to his "conversation" with his Roman teachers. "I knew," he says, "a young scholar in Douay, licensed by a great casuist to

to be quoted. At Douay, he says, "they made him" (Chillingworth) "the porter (which was to trye his temper and exercise his obedience), so he stole over, and came to Trinity Coll. againe." Such statements are hardly worthy of notice, save to show how incapable a man like Aubrey was of understanding Chillingworth, and the low habits of thought which cling to him as to all gossips, literary or otherwise.

[1] 'A Conference concerning the Infallibility of the Roman Church.'—Works, Oxf. Press, iii. 325.

swear a thing as upon his certain knowledge whereof he had no knowledge, but only a great presumption, 'because (forsooth) it was the opinion of one doctor that he might do so.'"

Such allusions are sufficient to show that there were things at Douay which served to repel him; but we should mistake if we attributed too much influence to such matters, or to any external agencies whatever, in the process of religious conflict through which Chillingworth now passed. Whatever may have been the effect of arguments addressed to him from the one side or the other, or of incidents helping to enlighten his unsuspecting confidence, there can be no doubt that his motive power throughout was from within, rather than from without. This is clear to any one who really understands the character of his mind, and the account which he himself has given of the principles which continually animated and guided him. In the preface to his great work, he says, that it was his desire "to go the right way to eternal happiness; and whether this way lie on the left or straight forward, whether it be by following a living guide, or by seeking my directions in a book, or by hearkening to the secret whispers of some private friend—to me it is indifferent. And he that is otherwise affected, and hath not a traveller's indifference—which Epictetus requires in all that would find the truth—but much desires in respect of his ease or pleasure, or profit or advancement, or satisfaction of friend, or any human consideration, that one way should be true rather than other, it is odds but he will take his desire that it should be so for an assurance that it is so."[1] This was not his case unless he deceives himself. On the contrary, he is and was unwilling "to take anything upon trust, and to believe it without asking himself why." Nor was he disposed "to follow like a sheep every shepherd that should take upon him to guide; or every flock that should chance to go before; but most apt and most willing to be led by reason" this way or that—"submitting all other reasons to this one: God hath said so; therefore, it is true." He explains, further, that he did not expect "mathematical demonstrations on matters plainly incapable of them." All that he wished were "reasons" which, "being weighed in an even balance, held by an even hand with those on the other side," would turn the scale, and make the one religion "more credible than the other."[2]

He has left us, besides, a special paper which brings out clearly the self-directed and highly rational character of the arguments which influenced him on the one side and the other. The paper is entitled—"An Account of what moved the Author to turn Papist, with his own Confutation of the Arguments that persuaded him thereto."[3] He explains distinctly in the outset why he reconciled himself to the Church of Rome. He thought he had "*sufficient reason* to believe that there was and must be always in the world some church that could not err"—and that the Church of Rome was that church. He was

---

[1] Works, i. 2 — Oxford University Press.
[2] Ibid., i. 3.
[3] Ibid., iii. 386-392.

"put into doubt" of this way of thinking "by Dr Stapleton and others, who limit the Church's freedom from error to things necessary only." He alludes, no doubt, to a Roman Catholic divine of this name in the preceding century, who was for a time Professor of Divinity in the College at Douay, and whose writings were greatly esteemed there. Perron pronounced him to be the first polemical writer of his age. Dr Stapleton's writings had probably been commended to Chillingworth to establish him in the faith; and it is highly characteristic of his acute and restless intellect, that the very means adopted for strengthening his convictions should have been the means of again unsettling them. Reflecting "that most of the differences between Protestants and Roman Catholics were not touching things necessary," he concluded that he "had not sufficient ground to believe the Roman Church either could not or did not err in anything—and therefore no ground to be a Roman Catholic."

But he was not yet free from the toils of the controversy. Again he was persuaded that while it was possible for the Church to err in things not necessary, the Church itself must yet be held to be the only judge of things necessary and not necessary, and that, consequently, all must be believed which the Church teaches as matters of faith. In other words, he was brought back to the point that the Church is, and can be, our only guide in the way to heaven. He was brought to this conclusion, first, "Because there was nothing that could reasonably contest with the Church about this office but the Scripture"—and the Scripture seemed to him to depend for its authority on the Church; and secondly, Because it appeared to him, from a passage in the Epistle to the Ephesians,[1] that there must be to the world's end a succession of pastors infallibly fitted to guide men in matters of faith. And "by the confession of all other societies of pastors," there was no such succession elsewhere but in the Church of Rome.

Such was Chillingworth's second standing-ground as a Romanist. But the argumentativeness which drove him to this point soon again drove him away from it. Gradually it was demonstrated to him, in reference to the first point, that the ground on which Scripture is to be accepted as the Word of God was, not the authority of the Roman Church, but "the general consent of Christians of all nations and ages—a far greater company than that of the Church of Rome." Further, he became convinced that it was unreasonable to think that any one reading Scripture "with no other end but to find the will of God," should have it imputed to him as a fault that in any respect he mistook that will. This seemed to him inconsistent with the divine goodness. It will be afterwards seen how frequently he recurs to this thought, and draws it out in every possible form of emphasis. As to the second point, he came to see that the passage in the Epistle to the Ephesians, instead of teaching, when rightly viewed, an infallible succession of pastors, really furnished a strong argument against the idea of any such succession. St Paul there speaks of the appointment of certain officers in the Church,

[1] Eph. iv. 11-13.

but without any reference to their perpetuity; and "it is evident that God promised no such succession, because it is <u>not certain</u> that he hath made good any such promise." "The apostles, and prophets, and evangelists, and pastors, which our Saviour gave upon His ascension, were given by Him that they might consummate the saints, do the work of the ministry, edify the body of Christ, until we all come into the unity of faith; that we be not like children, wavering and carried up and down with every wind of doctrine. The apostles and prophets, &c., that then were, do not now in their own persons and by oral instruction do the work of the ministry, to the intent we may be kept from wavering, and being carried up and down with every wind of doctrine: therefore they do this some other way. Now there is no other way by which they can do it but by their writings; and therefore by their writings they do it: therefore by the writings, and believing of them, we are to be kept from wavering in matters of faith: therefore the scriptures of the apostles and prophets and evangelists are our guides: therefore not the Church of Rome."[1]

This passage, and the whole course of thought analysed in this paper, give a clear insight into the character of Chillingworth's mind, and furnish the true key to his changes of opinion at this period. Religion was from the first with him a subject of free, honest, persevering inquiry. He had no idea of attaching himself to a side or cause without a clear well-grounded conviction of the part he was acting.

[1] Ibid., iii. 391, 392.

Not only was he inaccessible to the motives of grosser self-interest of any kind, but equally so to the subtler self-interest which many minds obey in such matters—the prepossession of personal feeling, the impulse of the affections, or, in its highest form, some phase of mental passion which irresistibly impels towards conviction and faith of some kind, rather than mental light and the calm reasoning thoughtfulness which is continually asking higher questions and aiming at a clearer sight. It was his special characteristic to inquire till he reached some basis of principle on which he could rest in the full light of his own luminous reason. He has himself explained his stand-point so fully that we cannot do better than quote his own words—words bright with a Christian sense and wisdom now as much needed as ever.

A friend of the name of Lewgar, who had become with him, and according to some accounts, under his influence, a convert to Romanism, sent him a very angry letter after his reconversion, renouncing his friendship and excommunicating him. His reply is very noble. He does not conceal his pain. The loss of a friend goes very near unto his heart. But he is calmly interrogative in the face of abuse: "If this proceed from passion or weakness, I pray mend it; if from reason, I pray show it. If you think me one of those to whom St John forbids you to say, 'God *save you*,' then you are to think and prove me one of those deceivers which deny Christ Jesus to *be come in the flesh*. If you think me an heretick, and therefore to be avoided, you must prove me αὐτοκατάκριτον—condemned by my own judgment —which I know I cannot, and therefore I think you cannot. If you say, *I do not hear the Church*, and therefore am to be esteemed an heathen or publican, you are to prove that by the Church there is meant the Church of Rome; and yet when you have done so, I hope Christians are not forbidden to show humanity and civility even to *Pagans;* for God's sake, Mr Lewgar, free yourself from this blind zeal,— at least for a little space; and consider with reason and moderation what strange crime you can charge me with that should deserve this strange usage, especially from you. Is it a crime to endeavour, with all my understanding, to find your religion true, and not to be able to do so? Is it a crime to employ all my reason in justification of the *infallibility* of the Roman Church, and to find it impossible to be justified? I will call God to witness, who knows my heart better than you, that I have evened the scale of my judgment as much as possibly I could, and have not willingly allowed any one grain of worldly motives on either side, but have weighed the reasons for your religion and against, with such indifference as if there were nothing in the world but God and myself; and is it my fault that that scale goes down which hath the most weight in it?—that that building falls which hath a false foundation? Have you such power over your understanding that you can believe what you please, though you see no reason? If you have, I pray, for our old friendship's sake, teach me that trick; but until I have learned it, I pray blame me not for going the ordinary way

—I mean, for believing or not believing as I see reason. If you can convince me of wilful opposition against the known truth, of negligence in seeking it, of unwillingness to find it, of preferring temporal respects before it, or of any other fault which is in my power to amend, if I amend it not, be as angry with me as you please. But to impute to me involuntary errors; or that I do not see that which I would see, but cannot, or that I will not profess that which I do not believe—certainly this is far more unreasonable error than any which you can justly charge me with; for let me tell you, the imputing *Socinianism* to me, whosoever was the author of it, was a wicked and groundless slander."[1]

He then enters upon the great question which had been the determining one in all his investigations—the question of *infallibility* as claimed by the Church of Rome; and concludes against the claim especially on the ground that it was unknown to the primitive Church. *Scripture* and *universal tradition* appear to him the only firm and safe foundation on which to build the Christian faith. He had afterwards several discussions with his friend, who was moved by the tone of his letter. Other discussions were also forced upon him, all more or less on the same subject. He worked out in the course of these discussions many of the special trains of thought afterwards embodied in the 'Religion of Protestants.' The details of the controversy were taken up by him in succession till his mind became thoroughly imbued with them, and he was amply furnished for the great task awaiting him.

[1] Maizeaux, p. 32-34.

The occasion for the exercise of his powers soon arose. A Jesuit who went by the name of Knott, but whose true name was Wilson, a native of Northumberland, published in 1630 a little book, entitled 'Charity Mistaken,' the aim of which was to prove Protestants to be beyond the pale of salvation. Dr Potter, of Queen's College, Oxford, published in 1633 a reply to the Jesuit's pamphlet; and the Jesuit responded in the following year in a more elaborate treatise, under the title, 'Mercy and Truth, or Charity maintained by Catholics.' Chillingworth undertook to answer this reply, and set himself to his work with great earnestness. For this purpose he appears to have retired to the residence of his friend Lord Falkland, whose society we described in a former chapter, and whose library was peculiarly rich in controversial and patristic divinity. His lordship himself, also, was well versed in the literature of the controversy. Here, assisted by his friend's learning, and stimulated by the conversational brilliancy of the *convivium theologicum*, he completed, after a considerable interval, his task. It appears to have engaged him during the years 1635, 1636, and 1637. In the end of this last year it was published.

We hear little of him otherwise during these years. All that we do hear tends to show the liberal direction of his theological studies. He expresses himself in regard to Arianism as "at least no damnable heresy" in the view of the opinions of the ante-Nicene fathers—to which he gives detailed references.[1] He was offered preferment in the Church

[1] Maizeaux, p. 49-56.

of England, but felt himself unable to accept it, on the ground of inability to subscribe the Thirty-nine Articles. His position in this latter matter is interesting, particularly as he afterwards, on further consideration, abandoned it. He objected mainly to the Athanasian Creed, which, as well as the Nicene and the Apostles' Creed, it is said in the Articles, "ought thoroughly to be received and believed—for they may be proved by most certain warrants of Holy Scripture."[1] He disapproved of the damnatory clauses of this creed. He could not apprehend, and much less affirm, that anybody should perish everlastingly for not thinking of the doctrine of the Trinity as therein expounded. "He thought that it was great presumption thus to confine God's mercy, and that such a declaration tended to create animosities and divisions in the Christian Church."[2] He had difficulties also respecting the Fourth Commandment, which he did not acknowledge to be binding upon Christians as the Prayer-Book seemed to make it.[3] He wrote at length to his friend Dr Sheldon, setting forth his scruples, and declaring that he "would never do anything for preferment" which he "could not do but for preferment."[4] Sheldon re-

---

[1] Article viii.
[2] Maizeaux, p. 81.
[3] Ibid., p. 81, 82.
[4] This letter, long as it is, deserves to be quoted in full. Whatever may be thought of its arguments, and the somewhat excited tone of feeling which it betrays, it at least sets in a striking light the noble sensitiveness of Chillingworth's character. The letter is dated from Tew, Sept. 21, 1635, and is as follows:—

"GOOD DR SHELDON,—I do here send you news, as unto my best friend, of a great and happy victory, which at length with extream difficultie I have scarcely obtained over the onely enemie

plied, and several letters passed between them. Unhappily there have only been notes of these letters that can hurt me, that is, my selfe.

"Sir, so it is, that though I am in debt to your selfe and others of my friends above twenty pounds more than I know how to pay; though I am in want of many conveniences; though in great danger of falling into a chronicall infirmitie of my body; though in another thing, which you perhaps guesse at what it is, but I will not tell you, which would make me more joyfull of preferment than all these (if I could come honestly by it); though money comes to me from my father's purse like blood from his veins, or from his heart; though I am very sensible that I have been too long already an unprofitable burden to my Lord, and must not still continue so; though my refusing preferment may perhaps (which fear, I assure you, does much afflict me) be injurious to my friends and intimate acquaintance, and prejudicial to them in the way of theirs; though conscience of my own good intention and desire suggests unto me many flattering hopes of great possibilitie of doing God and His Church service, if I had that preferment which I may fairly hope for; though I may justly fear, that by refusing those preferments which I sought for, I shall gain the reputation of weaknesse and levity, and incur their displeasure, whose good opinion of me, next to God's favour, and my own good opinion of my selfe, I do esteem and desire above all things; though all these and many other *terribiles visu formæ* have represented themselves to my imagination in the most hideous manner that may be; yet I am at length firmly and unmoveably resolved, if I can have no preferment without *Subscription*, that I neither can nor will have any.

"For this resolution I have but one reason against a thousand temptations to the contrary, but it is $ἓν μέγα$, against which, if all the little reasons in the world were put in the balance, they would be lighter than vanity. In brief, this it is: as long as I keep that modest and humble assurance of God's love and favour which I now enjoy, and wherein I hope I shall be daily more and more confirmed; so long, in despite of all the world, I may and shall and will be happy. But if I once lose this; though all the world should conspire to make me happy, I shall and must be extremely miserable. Now this inestimable jewel, if I subscribe (without such a declaration as will make the subscription no subscription), I shall wittingly and willingly throw away. For though I am very well perswaded of you and my other friends, who do so with a full perswasion that you may do it lawfully; yet the case stands so with me, and I can see no remedy but for ever it will do so, that if I subscribe, I sub-

preserved; but it appears from the notes that Chillingworth, besides objecting to various details in the

scribe my own damnation. For though I do verily believe the Church of England a true member of the Church, that she wants nothing necessary to salvation, and holds nothing repugnant to it; and had thought that to think so had sufficiently qualified me for a subscription: yet now I plainly see, if I will not juggle with my conscience, and play with God Almighty, I must forbear.

"For, to say nothing of other things, which I have so well consider'd as not to be in state to sign them, and yet not so well as to declare my self against them; two points there are, wherein I am fully resolved, and therefore care not who knows my mind. One is, that to say the Fourth Commandment is a law of God appertaining to Christians, is false and unlawfull: the other, that the damning sentences in St Athanasius's Creed (as we are made to subscribe it) are most false, and also in a high degree presumptuous and schismaticall. And therefore I can neither subscribe that these things are *agreeable to the Word of God*, seeing I believe they are certainly repugnant to it: nor that the whole *Common Prayer* is *lawful to be used*, seeing I believe these parts of it certainly unlawfull: nor promise that *I my self will use it*, seeing I never intend either to read these things which I have now excepted against, or to say Amen to them.

"I shall not need to intreat you not to be offended with mee for this my most honest and (as I verily believe) most wise resolution; hoping rather you will do your endeavour, that I may neither be honest at so dear a rate, as the losse of preferment at so much dearer a rate, the losse of honesty.

"I think my selfe happy that it pleased God, when I was resolved to venture upon a subscription without full assurance of the unlawfulnesse of it, to cast in my way two unexpected impediments to divert me from accomplishing my resolution. For I profess unto you, since I entertained it, I have never enjoyed quiet day nor night, till now that I have rid my self of it again; and I plainly perceive that if I had swallowed this pill, howsoever gilded over with glosses and reservations, and wrapt up in conserves of good intentions and purposes, yet it would never have agreed nor stay'd with me, but I would have cast it up again, and with it whatsoever preferment I should have gain'd with it as the wages of unrighteousness, which would have been a great injury to you, and to my Lord Keeper: whereas now, *res est integra;* and he will not lose the gift of any preferment by bestowing it on mee, nor have any engagement to Mr Andrewes for me.

"But however this would have succeeded in case I had then sub-

Articles, objected to the principle of articles in general, "as an imposition on men's consciences,

scribed, I thank God I am now so resolved, that I will never do that while I am living and in health, which I would not do if I were dying; and this, I am sure, I would not do. I would never do anything for preferment, which I would not do but for preferment: and this, I am sure, I should not do. I will never undervalue the happiness which God's love brings to mee with it, as to put it to the least adventure in the world, for the gaining of any worldly happinesse. I remember very well *quærite primum regnum Dei, et cætera omnia adjicientur tibi:* and therefore, whenever I make such a preposterous choice, I will give you leave to think I am out of my wits, or do not beleeve in God, or at least am so unreasonable as to do a thing in hope I shall be sorry for it afterwards, and wish it undone.

"It cannot be avoided, but my Lord of Canterbury must come to know this my resolution, and, I think, the sooner the better. Let me entreat you to acquaint him with it (if you think it expedient), and let me hear from you as soon as possibly you can. But when you write, I pray remember, that my foregoing preferment (in this state wherein I am) is grief enough to me; and do not you add to it, by being angry with mee for doing that which I must do or be miserable.—I am your most loveing and true servant," &c.

It has been strangely represented in the view of this letter, and Chillingworth's subsequent statements about the meaning of subscription (Preface, p. 35), as if he had at length forced his conscience to the point desired by Sheldon, and, so to speak, gulped down all his difficulties under "a hollow compromise" with his better feelings. Is it not rather plain, in the light of such a letter, that Chillingworth must have reached his new conclusions through the exercise of the same conscientious thoughtfulness with which he held his old ones? A man does not change or lose his character when he changes his intellectual conclusions. Chillingworth's first attitude towards subscription may appear to some minds the more consistent and higher attitude. But this is no evidence that it is so in reality; and still less is it any warrant for supposing that it must have continued to seem so to Chillingworth himself, notwithstanding his change of action; and that, therefore, the only explanation of this change is to be found in his having dealt so far dishonestly with his own convictions. For this is what the charge comes to. On the contrary, nothing seems more natural or intelligible than Chillingworth's change of attitude. In his letter to Sheldon, he is in all the enthusiasm of a young inquirer. Subscription

much like that authority which the Church of Rome assumes."[1] Sheldon seems to have taken up his objections in detail, and done his best to remove them. He did not spare, at the same time, the sort of advice which is always ready on such occasions. "Be not forward, nor possessed with a spirit of contradiction."[2] We have no indication of the exact effect of his friend's arguments or advice upon Chillingworth. But his mind worked itself clear of its

appears to him to imply, not only assent to the general doctrine of the Athanasian Creed as "thoroughly to be received and believed" in the words of the eighth Article of Religion, but also personal acceptance of its damnatory clauses. The Fourth Commandment, again, appeared to him in its strict interpretation to be a merely Jewish law, and therefore "false" in its application to Christians. He was unable, in either case, to separate the "essential" from the "accidental." He had much less capacity than his friend Hales of doing this at any time; and an eager spirit of theological enthusiasm is almost always narrow in its intensity. But in the course of two years' further reflection, Chillingworth came to see these points, and probably other points, in a different light. He recognised, we may suppose, as so many have since done, that the damnatory clauses of the Athanasian Creed are not an integral part of the Creed in the sense of the eighth Article—the very attitude taken up by the highminded and thoughtful Bishop of St Davids at the time we write (see 'Guardian,' March 27, 1872). Beyond doubt, also, he came to see that subscription cannot mean to any rational and fully intelligent mind direct personal assent to all the particulars of a creed. This is really a higher and more thoughtful, if less enthusiastic, attitude than that expressed in his letter. But higher or not— is not really the question. The only question is—may it not be an equally honest attitude? And can we doubt that it was so in the case of Chillingworth, and that he was therefore as truly conscientious in ultimately consenting to subscribe, as in at first refusing to do so? Because a man changes his views of the stringency of an obligation, and adopts in the second instance what may seem to others a lower or laxer view, it is hardly fair or charitable to impugn his personal honesty. The deliberate conclusions of a great mind deserve from us a more candid judgment.

[1] Maizeaux, p. 101.
[2] Ibid., p. 103.

scruples before long. A passage in the close of the preface, to which we have already referred, probably gives us the best insight into his motives for ultimately subscribing the Articles and accepting preferment. " For the Church of England," he says, " I am persuaded that the constant doctrine of it is so pure and orthodoxe, that whosoever believes it and lives according to it, undoubtedly he shall be saved;—and that there is no error which may necessitate or warrant any man to disturb the peace or renounce the communion of it. *This in my opinion is all intended by subscription.*"[1] This practical and sensible ground he had previously repudiated in his letter to Dr Sheldon; but further reflection had convinced him of its soundness.[2] With his convictions there was indeed no other ground on which he could serve the Church of England or any other Church. There are certain minds—and Chillingworth's was one of them—that see difficulties in every argumentative form of doctrine. Their rational inquisitiveness makes them acutely sensitive to the limits of human knowledge in all directions; and the dogmatic meanings which human controversy has imposed upon the simple creed of the Gospel strongly repel and at times disturb them. These meanings may or may not be true; God alone knoweth. But what such minds feel is, that they are not for man to settle; they are in their nature not matters of faith, but matters of doubt and controversy; and they are therefore properly open questions which all should be left to settle humbly for themselves in the light of

[1] Pref. to Rel. of Protestants, i. 35. [2] See preceding note.

Holy Scripture. No Church heretofore has been so wise in this respect as the Church of England. Even Laud appreciated religious difficulties too well not to welcome such service as Chillingworth's, under whatever reserves it might be rendered. And Chillingworth felt himself at length able to serve the Church of England, notwithstanding his scruples. "I am ready to subscribe," he virtually said, "to all that in my opinion is or can be intended by subscription. I belong to the Church of England. I have not only no wish to renounce her communion, but I am willing to be her minister, supposing that it is enough that I approve generally of her doctrine. This approval is what I design by subscribing the Articles. In these Articles good men of former times have done what they could to express their highest Christian thought against the perversions of heretical curiosity. They would have succeeded better if they in their turn had been less curious—if they had refrained from defining where Scripture itself has refrained; but, upon the whole, I acknowledge their doctrine, or at least I have no wish to dispute it. I accept the Articles as articles of peace."[1] Whether subscription can ever mean more than this to certain minds, may be held doubtful. It must also be admitted that it does mean more to others, and that there are even minds which do not understand this point of view, but really see, in controversial statements of former times—every word of which to the historical theologian bears trace of forgotten conflict—an expression of devout faith, rather than a triumph of

[1] Pref. to Rel. of Protestants, i. 167.

dogma. The difficulty is as to the co-operation of these two classes in the great work of the Christian Church. The uninquisitive, unreflecting faith which accepts without hesitation the dogmatic decisions of the fourth and fifth, and even of the sixteenth and seventeenth centuries, can it harmonise with the critical faith which reads as in sunlight all the weaknesses and exaggerations of these decisions, and cannot help acknowledging them? The question is a vital one for the Christian Church. The rights of faith are beyond challenge; but criticism surely has also its rights; and if they cannot live and work together, the Church of the future seems a somewhat dark and hopeless puzzle.

Chillingworth soon began to pay the wonted penalty of having thoughts of his own about religion. This reasoner who had reasoned himself into Popery, and reasoned himself back to Protestantism, and who had doubts about the Athanasian Creed and the Fourth Commandment, and even the necessity of creeds altogether—was he not plainly a Socinian? There seemed no other way of accounting for his changes and scruples. He must certainly be held to be a dangerous person, against whom the public should be cautioned, lest he lead them astray by his arguments. Such was the device of his opponents. Hearing that he was engaged in a defence of Protestantism, it seemed an ingenious plan to prejudice the public against him by accusing him of Socinianism; and the Jesuit to whose book he was replying accordingly issued a pamphlet entitled, " Directions to be observed by N. N. if he means to proceed in answering the book entitled 'Mercy and Truth, or Charity maintained by Catholics.'"[1]

This pamphlet is little else than a series of scurrilous insinuations. Diverse common heresies, especially Socinianism, are imputed to Chillingworth, and he is counselled to "declare his own opinions plainly and particularly, and not think to satisfy by a mere destructive way of objecting such difficulties as upon examination tend to the overthrow of all religion, no less than of Catholic doctrine."[2] The trick, common to religious partisans, is cleverly employed of representing him, in virtue of his questioning convictions and rational hesitations, as being opposed to all supernatural verity and sound doctrine. He has scrupled at the Athanasian Creed; he is represented as destroying "the belief of the most blessed Trinity, the deity of our dear Lord and Saviour, and of the Holy Ghost; original sin, and diverse other doctrines which all good Christians believe; yea, and all besides that cannot be proved by natural reason."[3] He has questioned the infallibility of the Pope, and he is represented as "overthrowing the infallibility of all Scripture, both of the Old and New Testament."[4] He is asked to answer whether "his arguments lead not to prove an impossibility of all *divine, supernatural, infallible faith*, and religion that either hath been, or is, or shall be, or possibly can be." It might have been thought that it remained to later times to invent the ingenious mode of theological warfare, which consists in calling your op-

---

[1] Maizeaux, p. 106. [2] Ibid., p. 127.
[3] Ibid., p. 127. [4] Ibid., p. 128.

ponent an infidel; and because he does not accept your view of the Gospel, alleging that he does not believe the Gospel at all. But the device is really a very old one. It certainly was not unknown to the seventeenth century; and Chillingworth had to bear the brunt of it in a very painful form.

But whatever pain he may have suffered, he was not to be deterred from his task. The Jesuit had invited all to contemplate the sort of champion to which Protestantism was reduced. "What greater advantage," he asked, "could we wish against Protestants than that they should trust their cause and possibility to be saved to such a champion?" But the champion was all the while, amid the academic quiet of Oxford and the retirement of Great Tew, preparing his armoury for the encounter. He was not a man to be daunted by the mere abuse of fanaticism, Popish or Puritan. He knew his own mind too well; the subject filled and animated him by its highest inspirations; he saw in it a great argument at once for divine truth and human freedom. And at the end of 1637 he gave to the light 'The Religion of Protestants a Safe Way to Salvation; or, An Answer to a Book entitled "Mercy and Truth, or Charity maintained by Catholics."'

This great work claims a separate and detailed examination. In the mean time we follow out the thread of Chillingworth's personal history to its sad close.

After the publication of the 'Religion of Protestants'—which, strangely enough, met the approval not only of Archbishop Laud but the King—Chillingworth was offered, and accepted, the chancellorship of Sarum, along with the prebend of Brixworth[1] (Brixlesworth); and in the year 1640 he represented the Chapter of Salisbury as their proctor in Convocation.[2] In this manner he became a party to the subsidy voted to the King by Convocation, a vote which greatly incensed the House of Commons. This appears to have been his first step towards a more close association with the Royalist party in the impending troubles. It is not easy for us to analyse or appreciate all the motives which influenced Chillingworth in this great crisis. All his personal predilections and feelings, like those of his friend Lord Falkland, were strongly enlisted on the side of order; and, whatever may have been his rational distrust of many of the principles put forward by the Royalists, he was still more widely separated both by rational conviction and personal feeling from the opposite party. He failed, like his friend Hales, to appreciate the great movement of political liberty with which Puritanism was identified; he failed even more remarkably to see that there was a close affinity between this movement and the religious liberty so dear to him—an affinity equally unrecognised by the majority of Puritans themselves, but not the less real because unseen by so many on both sides. On the other hand, the characteristic dogmatisms of Puritanism were strongly distasteful to him. Its intolerance revolted him. Yet, withal, we wonder at his

[1] Maizeaux, p. 265.   [2] Ibid., p. 267.

zeal, and are touched with pity at his fate. We admire, and yet we mourn for, him, as for Falkland. Strange that the friends who had so often speculated on the course of events—who had marked the excesses and risen far above the prejudices of either side—should have been thus hurried into the thick of the conflict, and perished before its real issues had become apparent!

A sermon preached by Chillingworth before his Majesty at Oxford, in 1643-4, the first in the series of nine which form the most part of the third volume of the Oxford edition of his works, gives us the only insight into his views and feelings at this time. We can see very well from it that while there is no wavering in his personal devotion to the cause which he had embraced, and while his sentiments towards the king personally seem to have been those of true affection, he yet recognises the gloomy character of the crisis, and how much there was on both sides to alienate and offend sober-minded Christian men. "Publicans and sinners on one side," he says, "against Scribes and Pharisees on the other. On the one side hypocrisy, on the other profaneness. No honesty nor justice on the one side, and very little piety on the other. On the one side horrible oaths, curses, and blasphemies; on the other pestilent lies, calumnies, and perjury. When I see among them the pretence of reformation, if not the desire, pursued by anti-Christian, Mahometan, devilish means; and amongst us little or no zeal for reformation of what is indeed amiss; little or no care to remove the cause of God's anger towards us by just, lawful, and Christian means, I profess plainly that I cannot without trembling consider what is likely to be the event of these distractions." There is the same tone of half despair here which made Falkland lay down his life on the field of Newbury, "weary" of the times, and foreseeing much misery to his country.

It would have been well for Chillingworth if he had perished like his friend in battle. What must be considered a harder fate was reserved for him. There is something so singular in the story of his death, the persecution to which he was subjected, and the circumstances attending his burial, that we have some difficulty in comprehending and crediting them. All, however, seems to rest on undoubted evidence.

Chillingworth had accompanied the king's forces to the siege of Gloucester (Aug. 1643).[1] He was not content to be a mere spectator of the warlike movements, but, observing that the army wanted materials for carrying on the siege, he suggested the invention of some engines after the manner of the Roman *testudines cum pluteis*, in order to storm the place.[2] What might have been the effect of these engines it is impossible to tell, for the advance of the Parliamentary forces under Essex compelled the Royalists to raise the siege. In the end of the same year, Chillingworth, "out of kindness and respect to the Lord Hopton,"[3] accompanied him in a march into Sussex, where he took and garrisoned Arundel Castle. "Being indisposed by the terrible coldness of the season," Chillingworth remained with the

[1] Maizeaux, p. 280.   [2] Ibid.   [3] Clarendon, b. viii. p. 472.

garrison, which was but ill provided with supplies, and soon broke into factions. It was in consequence easily recaptured by Sir William Waller; and Chillingworth, out of health and out of spirits, became a prisoner. He continued so ill that he could not be removed with the garrison to London, but was conveyed to Chichester. This act of kindness he is said to have owed to a person painfully associated with his last days — Francis Cheynell, a noted Puritan divine of his day, but whose name is now entirely forgotten. He had been a Fellow of Merton College, and, according to Dr Calamy, possessed considerable learning and abilities. The fact of his having been appointed one of the Assembly of Divines at Westminster may perhaps be taken in evidence of this. Whatever may have been his previous training at Merton, he had now developed not merely into a zealous Presbyterian, but, as one describes him, a " rigid, zealous Presbyterian, exactly orthodox, very unwilling that any should be suffered to go to heaven but in the right way." In the beginning of this same year he had published a tract on the 'Rise, Growth, and Danger of Socinianism,'[1] in which, along with others, Chillingworth was violently assailed. The principles of the 'Religion of Protestants' are repudiated in this tract

[1] The full title of this tract is, 'The Rise, Growth, and Danger of Socinianism. Together with a plain discovery of a desperate design of corrupting the Protestant Religion, whereby it appears that the Religion which hath been so violently contended for by the Archbishop of Canterbury and his adherents is not the true, pure Protestant Religion, but an Hotchpotch of Arminianism, Socinianism, and Popery.' This pamphlet was *printed by order of the House of Commons* in 1643!

as destructive and unchristian, and the allowing a chance of salvation to the Papists is denounced as a miserable weakness. It was Chillingworth's unhappy fate to encounter this violent dogmatist after the capture of Arundel Castle; and it is to Cheynell's own pen that we owe the description of his conduct, which would be otherwise quite incredible. His narrative bears the following title, which of itself is a revelation of the character of the man: "Chillingworthi Novissima: or the sickness, heresy, death, and burial of William Chillingworth; (in his own phrase) Clerk of Oxford, and in the conceit of his fellow-soldiers, the Queen's *Arch Engineer* and *Grand Intelligencer*. Set forth in a letter to his eminent and learned friends. A relation of his apprehension at Arundel, a discovery of his errors in a brief catechism, and a short oration at the burial of his heretical book, by Francis Cheynell, late Fellow of Merton College."[1] Then a secondary and more special title is annexed to the epistle or dedication to Chillingworth's friends;—among them, Prideaux, Bishop of Worcester; Sheldon, afterwards archbishop; Dr Potter; and Morley, Canon of Christ Church;—namely, "A brief and plain relation of Mr Chillingworth's sickness, death, and burial, together with a just censure of his work, by a discovery of his errors, collected and framed into a kind of Atheistical Catechism fit for Racovia or Cracovia, and may well serve for the instruction of the Irish, Welsh, Dutch, French, Spanish army in England, and especially for the black regiment at Oxford."[2]

[1] Maizeaux, p. 315, 316.   [2] Ibid., p. 319, 320.

Such is the extraordinary title of one of the most extraordinary pamphlets that even the blind and mad rancour of religious zeal ever produced—a truly ludicrous as well as melancholy instance of religious madness. The tract sets out with a low gossiping narrative of Chillingworth's unpopularity with the officers of the royal army, as being supposed to be the Queen's intelligencer, and as interfering unnecessarily with his advice in their warlike councils. A gentleman is represented as informing Cheynell that Chillingworth was so "confident of his great wit and parts, that he conceived himself able to manage martial affairs, in which he hath no experience, by the strength of his own wit and reason. You may forgive him," adds our divine; "for though I hope to be saved by faith, yet Master Chillingworth hopes that a man may be saved by reason; and therefore you may well give him leave to fight by reason." And so on.

We are then told what care Mr Cheynell took of the poor sick man's body. There is no reason to doubt apparently his being animated by a certain kindness of heart. But while he took care of his body, he "dealt freely and plainly with his soul." "When I came again to him" (after he had given Chillingworth a brief period to refresh himself in his sickness), "I asked him whether he was fit for discourse; he told me Yes, but somewhat faintly. I certified him that I did not desire to take him at the lowest, when his spirits were flatted and his reason disturbed." Having the great reasoner in his power, he thirsted to engage him in argument, ill and feeble as he was. He would not take him at a disadvantage, yet his orthodox ardour could not be restrained. Chillingworth was not the man to shrink from argument while he could, and dying as he was, he responded to the invitation to defend himself. According to Cheynell's statement, he made various concessions regarding the war which were satisfactory, and he was moved to spare him further disputation; but, nevertheless, their controversy continued till the Puritan finally pressed Chillingworth with some statement he had made against the course taken by Parliament, that "war is not the way of Jesus Christ." "What!" asked the Puritan; "are not the saints to make war against the whore and the beast? Is it not an act of faith to wax valiant in fight for the defence of that faith which was once delivered to the saints?" "I perceived," he adds, "my gentleman somewhat puzzled, and I took my leave that he might take his rest."[1]

"I gave him many visits after this first visit," adds our pamphleteer, "but I seldom found him in a fit case for discourse, because he grew weaker and weaker." It seems a hard fate, even for a disputant like Chillingworth, to have been killed by such a merciless process. Day by day his sickness grew, and the vanity of all human talk must have seemed more and more to him; but the Puritan's voice gave him no peace; the Puritan's zeal flamed the more hotly as the great reasoner seemed passing beyond the strife of tongues—"to where, beyond those voices, there is peace."

[1] Maizeaux, p. 326.

He expressed a disinclination to argue the merits or demerits of the Book of Common Prayer. "I was sorry," says Cheynell, "to hear such an answer from a dying man." "When I found him pretty hearty one day," he pursues, "I desired him to tell me whether he conceived that a man living and dying a Turk, Papist, or Socinian, could be saved? All the answer I could gain from him was, that he did not absolve them and would not condemn,"—an indecision which was far from satisfactory. The dying man besought an interest in the charity of his disputant, for, saith he, "I was ever a charitable man." "My answer was somewhat tart, and therefore more charitable, considering his condition and the counsel of the apostle (Tit. i. 13): 'Rebuke them sharply, that they may be sound in the faith.' And I desire not to conceal my tartness. It was to this effect. 'Sir, it is confessed that you have been very excessive in your charity. You have lavished so much charity upon Turks, Socinians, Papists, that I am afraid you have very little to spare for a truly reformed Protestant.'"

It is a curious and painful picture which the zealous divine draws of himself. Seldom have the contrasts which religion may present been more singularly exhibited. Let us rejoice that it is not unmixed by some genuine traits of human kindliness. While he spared not the soul, Cheynell carefully consulted for the bodily relief of the dying theologian, whose heresies were yet so damnable to him. "I sent to a chirurgeon, one of Mr Chillingworth's belief, an able man, that pleased him well and gave him some ease, and I desired the soldiers and citizens that they would in their prayers remember the distressed state of Mr C., a sick prisoner in the city, a man very eminent for the strength of his parts, the excellency of his gifts, and the depths of his learning. We prayed heartily that God would bless all means which were used for his recovery; that He would be pleased to bestow saving graces as well as excellent gifts; that He would give him new light and new eyes that he might see, acknowledge, and recant his errors, that he might deny his carnal reason and submit to faith. I told him that I did use to pray for him in private, and asked him whether it was his desire that I should pray for him in public. He answered Yes, with all his heart; and he said, withal, that he hoped he should fare the better for my prayers."

The heart owns to some softening here. The humanity is not all absorbed, even beneath the hardening scales of such divinity as Cheynell's. Yet the tenderness is but for a moment. It soon disappears; and the very last hours of the dying man are not sacred from coarse intrusion. Nay, the theologian seems to have reinforced his own polemical energy by a "certain religious officer of Chichester garrison, who followed my suit to Mr Chillingworth, and entreated him to declare himself in point of religion; but Mr Chillingworth appealed to his book again, and said that he was settled and resolved, and therefore did not desire to be further troubled." He expressed a wish to be interred, if possible, according to the custom of the Church of England—if not, the

Lord's will be done. And so he departed into "the silent land." He fell asleep, and was taken to that rest which, like many others before and since, he had not found on earth amidst the strife of tongues and the noise of theological captains shouting for battle. He died in January 1644; the day of his death is not exactly known.

If Mr Cheynell's narrative had stopped here, it would have been painfully interesting enough, but not so absolutely startling as it really is. The most extraordinary part remains. Now that the heresiarch, who would not explicitly recant his errors on his death-bed, was dead, how was he to be buried? There were three opinions, he says: "The 1st, Negative and peremptory that he ought not to be buried like a Christian, seeing that he had refused to make a free and full confession of the Christian religion, and had taken up arms against his country. 2d, That being a member of a cathedral, he should be buried in the cathedral; being *Cancellarius* he should be *intra Cancellos*. And 3d, The opinion which prevailed that the men of his own persuasion, out of mere humanity, should be permitted to bury their dead out of our sight, and to inter him in the cloisters among the old shavelings, monks, and priests, of whom he had so good an opinion all his life."

Accordingly, Chillingworth was laid by his own people in the cloisters of Chichester Cathedral. "As devout Stephen was carried to his burial by devout men, so is it just and agreed," says Cheynell, "that malignants should carry malignants to their grave."

He takes care to tell us also that there were no torches or candles at the grave; for the Christians, according to Tertullian, "used no such custom, although the heathens did, and the anti-Christians now do." There was a scene, however, prepared by Mr Cheynell himself, far more expressive than any procession of torches or candles.

"When the malignants," says he, "brought his hearse to the burial, I met them at the grave with Master Chillingworth's book in my hand," and there, with a speech which he recounts, he buried the book while they buried its author. "If they please to undertake the burial of his corpse, I shall undertake to bury his errors, which are published in this so much admired yet unworthy book; and happy would it be for the kingdom if this book and all its fellows could be so buried. Get thee gone, thou cursed book, which hast seduced so many precious souls! get thee gone, thou corrupt rotten book! Earth to earth and dust to dust! Get thee gone into the place of rottenness, that thou mayest rot with thy author, and see corruption!"

So spoke a Christian divine, in the middle of the seventeenth century—a member of the Westminster Assembly, afterwards placed at the head of St John's College, Oxford, where Laud not many years before had been president—of the 'Religion of Protestants a Safe Way to Salvation.' Words would fail to do justice to the painfulness of the picture. Let us rather draw down on it the merciful veil of silence. It needs not criticism; it baffles it. Yet it was meet that the veil should be lifted, if only for a moment, to show how ugly religious zeal may become—how hateful it looks even across two centuries as it stood and cursed by the grave of Chillingworth!

Of Chillingworth's personal character it is unnecessary to add much. Clarendon's sketch is graphic, like all his other sketches; but it leaves a good deal to be desired, and certainly is not touched, as we have already hinted, with any special tenderness. The fondness with which he lingers over the portrait of Falkland, and even of Hales, no longer softens his pen. He does justice, however, to Chillingworth's " great subtility of understanding," his " incomparable power of reason," and " admirable eloquence of language." He commends, moreover, his " rare temper in debate." " It was impossible to provoke him into any passion;" and so, he adds, "it was very difficult to keep a man's self from being a little discomposed by his rare sharpness and quickness of argument." His almost unrivalled power of touching the weakness of other minds who ventured to dispute with him, combined with such a faculty of composure on his own side, may have made Chillingworth somewhat unpopular, and even unamiable beyond his own circle. He certainly had the capacity of exciting intense asperity in his opponents. It is impossible, withal, to doubt that he was a man of generous impulses and true warm-heartedness—an earnest, fearless, able man, with the higher tenderness which is seldom dissociated from true courage—incapable of a mean thought, and ready to make any sacrifices for what he deemed the truth. When he heard of

Falkland's death at Newbury, " he wept bitterly for the loss of his dear friend." As to what Clarendon says of his " inconstancy " and " propensity to change"—this is merely the natural view which a statesman and a man of the world takes of a restlessly inquisitive intellect, whose thoughts he cannot measure. There was no " levity" in any of Chillingworth's changes. They were only varying attitudes of spiritual aspiration. The same deep sincerity and sleepless search after truth, animate and guide him throughout.

Of his personal appearance we have indications both from Clarendon and Aubrey; but there is no portrait of him, as far as we know. He was, the former says, "of a stature little superior to Mr Hales. It was an age in which there were many great and wonderful men of that size." " He was a little man," says Aubrey, with " blackish hair, of a saturnine countenance."

II. 'The Religion of Protestants' is Chillingworth's great work, by which alone he can be said to be remembered. It sums up all his thought, and has taken its place in English literature as a monument of Christian genius. His other writings are comparatively unimportant, as they are comparatively unknown. A few sermons—nine in all; a series of tracts under the name of 'Additional Discourses'—most of them mere sketches, or studies for his great work; and a brief fragment, more significant than the rest, entitled 'The Apostolical Institution of Episcopacy Demonstrated,'—comprise the whole. The sermons are marked by the vigour both of thought and language which is always characteristic of him, but are not in any special manner interesting or valuable. They contain nothing which would have preserved his name from oblivion, and but little to remind us of the bold thought of 'The Religion of Protestants.' In a still less degree than the few sermons of Hooker attract notice beside 'The Laws of Ecclesiastical Polity,' do Chillingworth's sermons serve to draw attention away from the work with which his name has become identified.

The tract on Episcopacy possesses a distinct value, as showing the liberal direction of the author's mind on a subject in which his feelings, education, and the eventful turns of his life, strongly interested him. He had not only been trained an Episcopalian in the school of Laud, but all his natural love of order and ardent affection to the royal cause had enlisted his sympathies on behalf of the existing government of the Church. But no degree of personal prepossession is able to obscure in him the light of rational thought on this any more than on the general subject of religion. Episcopacy is to him in its essentials "no more but this"—"an appointment of one man of eminent sanctity and sufficiency to have the care of all the churches within a certain precinct or diocese, and furnishing him with authority (not absolute or arbitrary, but regulated and bounded by laws, and moderated by joining to him a convenient number of assistants), to the extent that all the churches under him may be provided of good and able pastors, and that both of pastors and people conformity to laws and performance of their duties may be required." Such a form of government, he maintains, " is *not repugnant* to the government settled in and for the Church by the Epistles," nor is it incompatible " with the reformation of any evil, either in Church or State, or the introduction of any good " which it may be desirable to introduce. The brief argument of the tract is confined to the " demonstration" of the first of these propositions, and is throughout of the most moderate and reasonable character. He quotes the evidence of " two great defenders of Presbytery," Molinæus (Dumoulin) and Beza, in favour of Episcopacy being the recognised order of Church government " presently after the apostles' times," and draws the usual inference from this admitted antiquity on behalf of its being the institution of the apostles themselves. With the validity of such an inference it is unnecessary to concern ourselves. It appeared to Chillingworth's mind in every respect a fair and dispassionate one, in the light of which the anti-Episcopal dogmatism of the Puritan Presbyterian party seemed utterly unreasonable. To vindicate the institution of Episcopacy from the abuse of this party, and show its claims to a rational historic standing, is the sole aim of his argument, in which aim he is completely successful. Any further claim for it as a positive *jus divinum* is inconsistent alike with his object in the tract, and with the whole tone of his thought and reasoning.

It now remains for us to consider his chief work, ' The Religion of Protestants a Safe Way to Salvation.' This work presents itself to our examination in two points of view : first, in its general intellectual and literary character; and, secondly, in its substantive argument and meaning, or, in other words, in reference to the great principles which it sets forth. It might be further considered in its controversial details, some of which are aside from the main purpose of the work, and well deserving of attention as illustrative of its logical method and force. But as our purpose in these sketches is not to revive controversy or to adjust rivalries long since forgotten, but only to fix the significant ideas which have influenced the course of religious thought and permanently enriched it, it is unnecessary as it would be useless for us to go over the particular points in the polemic between our author and his Jesuit opponent, further than it may be important to do so for our general purpose.

1. 'The Religion of Protestants' claims first to be considered by us as one of the most notable productions of English literature. What are its claims to occupy such a position? What are the distinguishing characteristics of its thought and style? In judging it from our modern standard in such matters, we are struck at first by a certain imperfection and clumsiness of form arising out of its controversial purpose. The reader is naturally anxious to get into the heart of the subject and see what a writer of such name has to say about it—what are the strong points of his argument—and how he lays them down and expounds them in relation to one another. In a modern book on the subject, of any remarkable ability, we would probably find ourselves thus carried to the centre of interest at once,

and made to recognise the great lines of thought characteristic of the opposing sides, and the claims that the one rather than the other has to his following. The modern mind, whatever it may have lost, has certainly gained in organising power—in the capacity of surveying a subject in its whole outline, and disposing of it in proportion to the relative importance of its details. In controversial literature particularly this has been a great gain. It has tended to fix attention upon the real differences of thought out of which all minor differences spring, and to deliver the reader from mazes of detailed argumentation, which, however ably conducted, have often little or no bearing upon the main points at issue.

In Chillingworth's time, controversy, and especially theological controversy, was still a conflict of details. It is one of his excellences that he is superior in this respect to many of his contemporaries. Yet, with all his advance, 'The Religion of Protestants' suffers greatly from being in form a detached reply to a forgotten book. The reader has to wade through, in successive chapters, the arguments of the author of 'Charity Maintained;'[1] and in many cases, also, the statements of Dr Potter, to which the Jesuit's work was a reply.[2] The real pith of the subject is only reached sometimes after all these repeated processes of statement and reply, when the author is at liberty to follow the unembarrassed course of his own thought.

The work opens with a preface addressed to the author of 'Charity Maintained,' mainly in answer to

---

[1] His Jesuit opponent, Knott.   [2] See preceding page.

a pamphlet entitled by him 'A Direction to N.N.' This preface, as we formerly remarked, is full of interest for the light which it throws on the formation of Chillingworth's opinions, and is marked by great dignity and elevation of tone. Then follows the preface of the author of 'Charity Maintained,' and Chillingworth's reply to this, anticipatory of many points upon which he afterwards dwells more fully. Then in succession, through seven chapters, the argument of his Jesuit opponent is given first, and his answer in detail follows. Every point is carefully met, and amidst so many minute particulars of argument there is necessarily a good deal of recurrence of thought. The reader gets impatient of interruptions, and of the multitude of steps by which he advances to the close of the controversy.

It is obvious that only rare attributes of thought and style could have risen above these disadvantages of form, and given unity and life to such an accumulated mass of controversy. But we have scarcely opened the book when we see evidence of these. We find ourselves in contact with an intellect of singular strength and brightness, of clearly penetrative and powerful thoughtfulness, which grasps the whole subject, and moves unconfused amidst its details. Strength and earnestness —genuine grasp of mind and large intelligence— are Chillingworth's highest characteristics. Some minds have shown more extent of scope, and certainly far more richness and glow of speculative comprehension, in conducting a great argument. In these respects Hooker is incomparably superior; and

Jeremy Taylor, in his 'Liberty of Prophesying,' moves with a freer and more sustained air. But neither Hooker nor Taylor equals our author in mere mass and energy of mind, and the masculine robustness and downright honesty generally associated with such simple strength. The very height at which more imaginative writers sometimes soar gives a certain indistinctness to their thought; it gains in colouring and impressiveness at the expense of plain outline and meaning. But the meaning of Chillingworth is always plain, and always strong. He evades no difficulties, and never flinches for fear of consequences; he grapples hardily with every statement of his opponent, meets it with the pure force of reason, and brings it to the ground without any hesitation. He is ready for battle at every point, and has never any doubt of the keenness of his weapons or the force of his blows.

Next to the strength and straightforwardness of his intellect, his most remarkable characteristic is fairness. No fairer controversialist, we believe, ever entered the lists. He never takes an undue advantage of his opponent. He is tender to him personally, while unsparing to his arguments. He had himself been caught in the toils amongst which the Jesuit was struggling, and while he pursues and unwinds the entanglements one by one, he never does so in a contemptuous spirit. His magnanimity is beautiful, considering the character of the attacks to which he was subjected by Romanists and Puritans alike. He grows warm and indignant at times, and he uses firm language, especially when he resents "the imputation of atheism and irreligion;"[1] but he never smites as they sought to smite him. We know of no personality that ever escaped his pen. A half-tender, half-compassionate "God forbid I should think the like of you," or, "For God's sake free yourself from the blind zeal for a little space,"[2] is the utmost to which he yields. Of all theologians of the seventeenth century, of any century perhaps, Chillingworth is one of the most thoroughly fair, candid, and open-minded. Temporarily a convert to Romanism, and actually for a while the inmate of a Jesuit seminary, the transparency of his manly and earnest spirit is never for a moment dimmed. The same love of the truth, and the same keenness in its search, inspire him from first to last. The idea of upholding a system merely because he had embraced it, or an institution because he happened to belong to it, would have been unintelligible to him. His mind could rest in nothing short of clear and definitely-reasoned convictions. He must see the truth for himself, and be able to give some reason for it—why he held to it and why he rejected the contrary. It was this that made men who misunderstood his point of view accuse him of inconstancy in religion, and allege that, according to his principles, "a man could be *constant in no religion.*"[3] As he could not understand a mere blind adherence to any system, merely because he had once accepted it, so they

---

[1] Vol. i. p. 8, Oxford ed. (All the references are to this edition.)
[2] Letter to Mr Lewgar, Maizeaux's Life, p. 32.
[3] Maizeaux's Life, p. 18.

could not understand his continual inquisitiveness and determination to see the truth more clearly. "Why constantly be asking what is the sense of Scripture? What religion is best? What Church purest? Come, do not wrangle, but believe." This, which is virtually what his Puritan opponent said to him, represents the alternative state of mind. According to a commonplace of almost all religious parties, a man is supposed to be unsettled in religion if he is constantly asking questions, if his mind is restlessly moving towards what seems to him a higher light; while the religious inquirer, on the other hand, has no idea of religion which does not involve constant inquest and movement. It is to him of the very nature of religious thought to be always moving—to be always rising, and so changing its relation to human systems. Certainly Chillingworth's mind was of this order. Truth was to him one, but its very simplicity made it all the more difficult to seize; and while he kept his eye steadily fixed on it, he was constantly readapting his attitude towards it, and trying to get a clearer sight of it.[1]

---

[1] He thus describes his own changes in religion, very much in the spirit we have described them here and in the preceding pages: "I know of a man that of a moderate Protestant turned a Papist, and the day that he did so (as all things that are done are perfected some day or other) was convicted in conscience that his yesterday's opinion was an error; and yet, methinks, he was no schismatic for doing so, and desires to be informed by you whether or no he was mistaken. The same man afterwards, upon better consideration, became a doubting Papist, and of a doubting Papist a confirmed Protestant. Even yet this man thinks himself no more to blame for all these changes than a traveller, who, using all diligence to find the right way to some remote city, where he had never been (as this party I speak of had never been in heaven), did yet mistake it, and after find his error and amend it. Nay, he

It is this earnest high-mindedness, this spirit of healthy rationality, which gives such elevation, purity, and dignity to Chillingworth's thought. He is superior to all commonplace of his Church or school—all mere professionalism. And nothing perhaps more marks the great writer in any department than this superiority. A writer who is unable to rise above the level of his profession may be acute, learned, and able; he may be a great authority on his own subject; but he will never take a place in the world of thought and literature. In order to do this, he must show himself capable of rising above traditional or official limits, and of perceiving the truth in its own light, and vindicating it on the highest grounds of reason. In all special departments of intellectual work, and particularly in theology, the highest minds have been of this order. They have been thoroughly competent in their own department, but also marked by a healthy openness of thought in other directions. They have always recognised something higher than professional canons of opinion, and carried the breath of nature, so to

stands upon his justification so far as to maintain that his alterations were the most satisfactory actions to himself that ever he did, and the greatest victory that ever he obtained over himself and his affections to those things which in this world are most precious; as whereas for God's sake, and (as he was really persuaded) out of love to the truth, he went upon a certain expectation of these inconveniences, which to ungenerous natures are of all the most terrible; so that although there was much weakness in some of these alterations, yet certainly there was no wickedness. Neither does he yield his weakness altogether without apology, seeing his *deductions were rational* and out of some principles commonly received by Protestants as well as Papists,— and which by his education had got possession of his understanding."—Vol. ii. chap. v. p. 259.

speak, and of universal reason, into their work. It is this which makes the distinction between such a writer as Hooker and Andrews, for example; the latter—a man apparently of far more special ability than Hooker (he is said to have been master of fifteen languages), but infinitely inferior in breadth and capacity of thought—forgotten, except by a few theological students who turn occasionally to his sermons; while Hooker continues, and will ever continue, one of the great classics of English literature. It is this which distinguishes our author, and sets him far above most of his theological contemporaries, either Anglican or Puritan—Hammond or Sanderson on the one side, and Owen, to take the very highest example, on the other. In contrast to such writers, Chillingworth is a man of general and not merely of special theological culture. He shows himself capable not merely of handling particular doctrinal points after the best manner of his school, and of bringing logical skill and erudition to bear upon their support and illustration, but, moreover, of dealing with questions in their most generalised intellectual shape, and of bringing them to the test of the higher reason of all men. And so it is that 'The Religion of Protestants,' like 'The Laws of Ecclesiastical Polity,' has an unfading interest to the common educated intellect, and not merely to the theological student. It remains, although in a less degree than the great work of Hooker, a living force in general literature—a permanent monument of thought marking the advance of the human mind in the loftiest of all directions.

It is especially this higher thoughtfulness, this touch of light from the altitudes of a divine philosophy, which gives any life to theological polemics. However able, ingenious, or successful for the time an argumentative work may be, if it have nothing of this — if it never soar beyond the confines of its special subject, nor start any principles of general application—it will be found to lose hold of the succeeding generations, and gradually to pass from the ranks of literature. It may be sought after and highly prized by certain minds; but the progressive intelligence finds no meaning in it. It may have served a cause, silenced an enemy, and even gained a distinguished victory; but it has done nothing to advance the course of thought; it has opened no tracks which have been further cleared and expanded; and so it passes out of sight, and deserves to do so, great as may have been its temporary reputation. It is a distinct gain to literature that an oblivion—frequently rapid, always sure—should thus overtake the great mass of controversial writings, which contain so little that is fitted to elevate or enrich human thought. To be forgotten is their happiest fate. But let a fair, generous, and noble reason—like Hooker's or Chillingworth's—irradiate a controversy, and it acquires permanent life and interest. It becomes a mirror of higher truth, and men return to it in after-generations to study the principles which it helped to elucidate, and to refresh themselves in its light.

The style of Chillingworth is the natural expression of his thought — simple, strong, and earnest, occasionally rugged and vehement. Particularly like his thought, it is without any artifice. He is concerned with what he has to say, not with his mode of saying it; and having thrown aside almost all the scholastic pedantries which in his time still clung to theological style, he gives fair play to his native sense and vigour. His vehemence is apt to hurry him into disorder, but also often breaks into passages of lofty and powerful eloquence. If we compare his style with that of Hooker or Bacon, it is inferior in richness, compass, and power, but superior in flexibility, rapidity, and point. It turns and doubles upon his adversary with an impetuosity and energy that carry the reader along, and serve to relieve the tedious levels of the argument. If he must be ranked, upon the whole, greatly below such writers as we have mentioned, he is yet in this, as in other respects, much above most of his contemporary divines. The pages of Laud, or of his biographer Heylin, or even of Hammond, are barren and unreadable beside those of 'The Religion of Protestants;' and even the richer beauties of Taylor, embedded amidst many pedantries and affectations, pall in comparison with his robust simplicity and energy. With writers of the ordinary Westminster school, like his opponent Cheynell, it would be absurd to compare him : they are utterly without grace, life, or power. Even the best Puritan writers, like Howe and Baxter, scarcely reach, in their best passages, his manly and inspiring eloquence.

2. Let us now turn to the argument of his work, and especially to the principles on which it rests.

The main question which it raises is the always vital one as to the *grounds of religious certitude*. How are we to know the truth in religion? On what basis must faith rest? Who or what is the arbiter of religious opinion? This is the great issue between him and his Romanist opponent. It is unnecessary for us, we have already said, to take up the successive details of assault and retort between them; but it is important, for the sake of clearness, to understand the manner in which they approach each other—the line of their controversial march towards the great principles in which the chief interest of the discussion lies.

After a detailed answer to the preface of the author of 'Charity Maintained,' the argument opens with the question of charity as between the two sides. Is it uncharitable for Papists to maintain that Protestants cannot be saved? This had been the special question between Knott the Jesuit and Dr Potter—the one maintaining that "Protestancy unrepented destroys salvation;" the other, that "want of charity is justly charged on all Romanists" who affirm this proposition. Chillingworth takes up the controversy from this point. The first pamphlet of Knott was published in 1630; Potter's answer in 1633; and then in the following year the Jesuit returned to the charge in 'Mercy and Truth, or Charity maintained by Catholics;' and it is to the successive chapters of this book, printed in front of his own, that Chillingworth replies.

In his opening chapter the Jesuit holds to his point, but not without the qualifications repeated to our own day by all exclusive sacerdotalists, Anglican or Roman: " Our meaning is not that we give Protestants over to reprobation. We hope, we pray for their conversion. . . . Neither is our censure directed to particular persons. The tribunal of particular judgments is God's alone." Want of opportunity of knowing Catholic truth, want of capacity to understand it, "light declaring to men their errors or contrition, retracting them in the moment of death," are allowed as excuses. " In such particular cases," says Knott, " we wish more apparent signs of salvation, but do not give any dogmatical sentence of perdition."

In his answer, Chillingworth makes good use of the concessions of his opponent as to the salvability of Protestants. The question is no longer, he says, " simply whether Protestancy unrepented destroys salvation, as it was at first proposed, but whether Protestancy in itself, apart from ignorance and contrition, destroys salvation." Knott has admitted, in short, that a Protestant may be saved, if he be either an ignorant Protestant—not having had the means or capacity of knowing any better—or if he join with his Protestantism the "antidote of a general repentance." Though Protestants may not be saved at so easy a rate as Papists, yet (even Papists being the judges) they may obtain salvation. " Heaven is not inaccessible." " Their errors are not impracticable isthmuses between them and salvation." Nothing can be finer than the courteous sneer with which Chillingworth points his reply here; all the more impressive that he seldom indulges in this vein. "For my part," he says, "such is my charity to you, that considering what great necessity you have, as much as any Christian society in the world, that the sanctuaries of ignorance and dependence should always stand open, I can hardly persuade myself, so much as in my most sacred consideration to divest you of these so needful qualifications; but whensoever your errors, superstitions, and impieties come on to my mind, my only comfort is that the doctrine and practice too of repentance is yet remaining in your Church; and that though you put on a face of confidence of your innocence in point of doctrine, yet you will be glad to stand in the eye of many as well as your fellows, and not be so stout as to refuse either God's pardon or the king's."

He then engages to meet his opponent on the more limited question — as he concludes it to be — whether Protestantism possesses so much natural malignity as to be in itself, apart from ignorance and contrition, destructive of salvation?

The combatants start with an acknowledged proposition on both sides. Chillingworth grants that there must be a " visible Church stored with all helps necessary to salvation;" and further, that the Church must have " sufficient means of determining all controversies in religion which are necessary to be determined." But "sufficient" is not with him the same as " effectual"—a distinction, he urges, which his opponent cannot overlook; " for that the same means may be sufficient for the compassing an end, and not effectual, you must not deny, who hold that God gives to all men sufficient means of salvation, and yet that all are not saved." Nor is it requisite that all controversies whatsoever, but only *such as involve salvation should be determined.* Here, where so much of the general argument is to rest, he discriminates his ground carefully from the first. The end, he says, must be the measure of the means here and everywhere. "If I have no need to be at London, I have no need of a horse to carry me thither. If I have no need to fly, I have no need of wings. So if I can be saved without knowing this or that definitely, I have no need to know it. The Church needs no means for determining points in which salvation is not involved. Is it necessary that all controversies in religion should be determined, or is it not?" The question plainly put contains its own answer even to the Romanist, in whose Church, as in all Churches, many questions remain undetermined, or open questions.

So far, therefore, there is common ground between Chillingworth and his opponent. They advance up to a certain point on the same line of argument. There must be a visible Church in possession of the means of salvation. This primary generality raises no discussion. Further, they agree that there must be within the Church an arbiter of religious truth, some "infallible" means of religious certitude. The latter expression, with both writers, comes to the same thing as the former: where there are "means of religious certitude" there are "means of salvation;" and Chillingworth is content to use the word "infallible" no less than his opponent.[1] But here the apparent

---

[1] The "means of deciding controversies on faith and religion," he grants, "must be endued with a universal infallibility *in what it propoundeth for a divine truth.*" P. i. c. i. Answer; vol. i. p. 113.

agreement between them proves to be entirely hollow. The words they use have not the same meaning. Religious truth is not the same thing to each. Their mode of reaching it is entirely different. The question, in short, of the determination of religious truth, or what is necessary to salvation, opens up their antagonism from its roots. All the other points of their argument branch off from this, and are virtually settled by the conclusions to which they come here. While avoiding the details of the controversy, it may be useful to exhibit in a table the course of discussion as it unfolds itself in successive chapters. This may be stated as follows, confining ourselves as much as possible to the language used by Chillingworth and his opponent :—

I. The question as to religious certitude, or "the means whereby the truths of revelation are conveyed to our understanding," and controversies in faith and religion are determined.

II. The distinction of points fundamental and not fundamental, whether it is pertinent in the controversy.

III. The question whether the Apostles' Creed contains all fundamental points, or "all points necessary to be believed."

IV. and V. Whether separation from the Church of Rome constitutes schism and heresy; and

VI. (which is a mere corollary from IV. and V.), Whether Protestants are bound in charity to themselves to become reunited to the Roman Church.

A mere glance at this table serves to show how the whole controversy is really summed up in the twofold question as to the source of religious truth, and the character or sum of this truth. To this question, therefore, as handled by our controversialists, we address ourselves. It assumes a very speedy and direct issue. The source of religious certitude—the infallible means of determining religious truth—Knott says, is the Church; by which, of course, he means the Roman Catholic Church. Take away the Roman principle of infallibility, and all religion falls to the ground. "None can deny the infallible authority of the Church," are his words; "but he must abandon all inspired faith and true religion, if he but understand himself." Again—" If the infallibility of such a public authority be once impeached, what remains but that every man is given over to his own wit and discourse?" The principle of Knott, therefore, was the principle of the *Church's infallible voice.* Is any man in doubt?—let him ask the Church. The Church is divinely authorised to pronounce what is true, and what every man is therefore bound to believe. This principle, whatever practical difficulties may be involved in it, is at least, in its generality, intelligible and consistent.

The position of Chillingworth as opposed to this principle is the well-known Protestant adage, so often quoted in his own words,[1] "*The Bible, and the Bible only, is the religion of Protestants.*" The Bible, not the Church, is the organ of religious

[1] Vol. ii. chap. vi. p. 410.

truth, and the only rule of faith. This is the Protestant principle, asserted by our author and professed by all Protestant Churches in its *generality*. But the merit of Chillingworth, of course, does not consist in his having enunciated this general principle. It did not remain for him to do this. It is his interpretation of the principle which constitutes all his distinction as a religious thinker — which could alone have given him any distinction. It is plain, for example, that when it is said to a man, the voice of the Church is authoritative, or, on the other hand, the voice of Scripture is authoritative, that the man is not greatly helped in a practical point of view. For he must then immediately ask, How am I to be sure of the voice of the Church, or how am I to be sure of the voice of Scripture? It is here that the real pinch lies. To take an illustration, there are ultra Anglo-Catholics who start from the same principle as the Roman Catholics, with both of whom the *Church is always the last word;* but then the question arises, Which *is the Church?* and here the Anglican High Churchman and the Roman High Churchman separate. In a similar manner with the Presbyterian and Independent, or still more strikingly with the Calvinist and Arminian, and even Socinian of the old type, alike, the Bible is the last word—only the Bible. But then, not to speak of the modern question, untouched by Chillingworth, What is the Bible? the further question at once arises, What is the voice of the Bible? what its true meaning? and here these several classes of Protestants separate. After having gained an apparent certainty in the assertion of a general principle, uncertainty again begins. Admitting Scripture to be the rule of faith, how are we to know the meaning of Scripture? Now it is here that Chillingworth has done real service. Here, where the real difficulty lies, he has cleared up the question, and settled it in the only way in which it can ever be consistently settled by Protestants. We will endeavour first to state his conclusions in our own language as briefly as possible, and then quote several passages from his work which set forth his views fully.

Chillingworth has virtually said, There is no real difficulty as to the meaning of Scripture. The great principles of religion—what we are to believe concerning God, and what duty God requires of us—are clearly revealed in the Bible. All Protestant Churches have seen and acknowledged them. The Apostles' Creed embraces them. They are patent to the "right reason" (the expression is his own) and judgment of every man. The matters that separate Christians, or at least Protestant Christians, are not matters of faith—necessary elements of religious truth pertaining to salvation—but matters of speculation on which Christians may differ safely or without any detriment to their spiritual condition. Such is the position laid down by Chillingworth. He disposes, in short, of the question of religious certitude, by reducing it to its simplest dimensions. The proper objects—the only valid objects of religious belief—according to him, are certain great facts or principles which are plainly revealed or made known to every open intelligence in Scripture. What lies beyond these facts or principles is either in its nature uncertain, or in its bearing unimportant. Religious certitude, in short, can be reached by every honest mind with Scripture before it. Where such certitude is impossible, it is unnecessary.

Let us now attend to Chillingworth's own statements, many of which are very significant. They are scattered over a wide surface, but we will endeavour to exhibit them in such an order as to bring out his meaning fully, and yet without exaggeration.

Speaking of Scripture in his second chapter as "the only rule whereby to judge of controversies," he says that it is "sufficiently perfect and sufficiently intelligible to all that have understanding, whether they be learned or unlearned. And my reason hereof is convincing and demonstrative, because nothing is necessary *to be believed but what is plainly revealed.* For to say that where a place, by reason of ambiguous terms, lies indifferent between divers senses whereof one is true and the other is false, that God obliges man, under pain of damnation, not to mistake through error and human frailty, is to make God a tyrant; and to say that he requires us certainly to attain that end, for the attaining whereof we have no certain means, which is to say that, like Pharaoh, He gives no straw, and requires brick; that He reaps where He sows not; that He gathers where He strews not; that He will not accept of us according to that which we have, but requireth of us what we have not. . . . Shall we not tremble to impute that to God which we would take as foul scorn if it were imputed to ourselves? Certainly I for my part fear I should not love God if I should think so strangely of Him."[1]

"Again," he continues, addressing his opponent, "when you say 'that unlearned and ignorant men cannot understand Scripture,' I would desire you to come out of the clouds and tell us what you mean; whether that they cannot understand all Scripture, or that they cannot understand any Scripture, or that they cannot understand so much as is sufficient for their direction to heaven. If the first,—I believe the learned are in the same case. If the second,—every man's experience will confute you; for who is there who is not capable of a sufficient understanding of the story, the precepts, the promises, and the threats of the Gospel? If the third,—that they may understand something, but not enough for their salvations; I ask you, why then doth St Paul say to Timothy, '*The Scriptures are able to make him wise unto salvation*'? Why doth St Austin say, *Ea quæ manifeste posita sunt in Sacris Scripturis omnia continent quæ pertinent ad fidem moresque vivendi?* Why does every one of the four evangelists entitle their book, The Gospel, if any necessary and essential part of the Gospel were left out of it? Can we imagine that either they omitted something necessary out of ignorance, not knowing it to be necessary? or, knowing it to be so, maliciously concealed it? or, out of negligence, did the work they had undertaken by

[1] i. 230, 231.

halves? If none of these things can be imputed to them, then certainly it must naturally follow that every one writ the whole Gospel of Christ; I mean all the essential and necessary parts of it. So that if we had no other book of Scripture than one of them alone, we should not want anything necessary to salvation."[1]

Elsewhere, in a previous part of the same chapter, in reference to the statement that Scripture—admitting it to be a rule or law of faith—" is no more fit to end controversies *without* a living judge, than the law is alone to end such," he answers: " If the law were plain and perfect, and men honest and desirous to understand aright and obey it, he that says it were not fit to end controversies, must either want understanding himself, or think the world wants it. Now the Scriptures, we pretend, in things necessary, is plain and perfect. Such a law, therefore, cannot but be very fit to end all controversies necessary to be ended. For others that are not so, they will end when the world ends, and that is time enough."[2]

He repudiates the necessity of any judge to interpret Scripture. " Every man is to judge for himself with the judgment of discretion." "For if the Scripture (as it is in things necessary) be plain, why should it be more necessary to have a judge to interpret it in plain places than to have a judge to interpret the meaning of a councillor's decrees, and others to interpret their interpretations, and others to interpret them, and so on for ever? And when they are not plain, then if we, using diligence to find the truth, do yet miss of

[1] i. 232.   [2] ii. 169.

it, and fall into error, there is no danger in it. *They that err and they that do not err may both be saved. So that those places which contain things necessary, and where no error was dangerous, need no infallible interpreter, because they are plain: and those that are obscure need none, because they contain not things necessary; neither is error in them dangerous."*[1]

With such confidence does Chillingworth lay down the principle of the sufficiency of Scripture, and of its plainness and intelligibility in all things necessary for salvation, and therefore necessary to be believed. He adverts over and over again to the great principle that the responsibility of faith is to be measured by the clearness and simplicity of the divine revelation. If God has spoken plainly, and man refuse to receive the divine testimony, he has no excuse to offer for him. This were to give God the lie, he says, and "questionless damnable."[2] But as for other things "which lie without the covenant,"[3] following his own expression—that is to say, which are either obscure in themselves or capable of different interpretations, according to the variety of tempers, abilities, educations, and unavoidable prejudices whereby men's understandings are variously formed and fashioned—" to say that God will damn men for errors as to such things, who are lovers of him and lovers of truth, is to rob man of his comfort and God of his goodness; is to make man desperate and God a tyrant." "When you can show," he adds in the same place, in a passage of great emphasis,—"When you can show that God hath interposed His testimony

[1] ii. 170.   [2] Answer to Preface, p. 80.   [3] Ibid., p. 80.

on one side or another, so that either they do see it and will not—or were it not for their own voluntary and avoidable fault might and should see it and do not—let all such errors be as damnable as you please to make them." But "if they suffer themselves neither to be betrayed into their errors, nor kept in them by any sin of their will; if they do their best endeavour to free themselves from all errors, and yet fail of it through human frailty, so well am I persuaded of the goodness of God, that if in me alone should meet a confluence of all such errors of all the Protestants of the world that were thus qualified, I should not be so much afraid of them all as I should be to ask pardon for them."[1]

Scripture on the one hand, therefore, and the free, honest, open mind on the other hand—these are, with Chillingworth, the factors, and the only factors, of religious truth—the essential elements of religious certitude. Scripture is an open mirror in which every intelligence may see the truth if it only look for it. There is no necessity for any medium to transfer it, or any judge to interpret it to the understanding. It lies open to all in the simple statements of the Gospels—of any one of the Gospels. It is not to be supposed that Chillingworth, in thus nakedly asserting the sufficiency of the individual judgment or reason to find the meaning of Scripture for itself, puts aside or rejects the necessity of divine influence in reaching divine truth. This special point was not in question between the two disputants. They alike recognised the reality of divine revela-

[1] Answer to Preface, p. 14.

tion and the necessity of the divine Spirit. What they differed about was as to the medium of the revelation and the organ of the Spirit. To the Jesuit, the Church was both the one and the other—the revealing medium and the interpreting spirit. Scripture was merely a help to the Church. To Chillingworth, Scripture and reason were the twofold source of the truth—the one external, the other internal. We have seen sufficiently what he says as to the first. Let us observe now what he says as to the second.

Knott had said that if the notion of Papal infallibility were given up, every man was given over to his own wit and discourse. Chillingworth replies: " If you mean by *discourse* right reason grounded on divine revelation, and common notions written by God in the hearts of all men, and deducing, according to the never-failing rules of logic, consequent deductions from them;—if this be it which you mean by discourse, it is very meet and reasonable and necessary that men, as in all their actions, so especially in that of greatest importance, the choice of their way to happiness, should be left unto it; and he that follows this in all his opinions and actions, and does not only seem to do so, follows always God."[1]

Again: " For my part, I am certain that God hath given us our reason to discern between truth and falsehood; and he that makes not this use of it, but believes things he knows not why, I say that it is by chance that he believes the truth, and not by choice; and that I cannot but fear that God will not

[1] Answer to Preface, p. 14.

accept the *sacrifice of fools*. But you that would not have men follow their reason, what would you have them follow?—their passions?—to pluck out their eyes and go blindfold? No; you would have them follow authority. In God's name let them. We also would have them follow authority; for it is upon the authority of universal tradition that we should have them believe Scripture. But then as for the authority which you would have them follow, you will let them see reason why they should follow it. And is not this to go a little about ;. to leave reason for a short time and then to come to it again, and to do that which you condemn in others?—it being, indeed, a plain improbability for any man to submit his reason but to reason."[1]

Every man, in short, must have some rational conviction at the root of his religion, however imperfect or concealed this conviction may be. He may accept his religion at first hand from the priest or the Church, but he must have some reason for believing the Church. He may believe that a doctrine is true because coming directly from the Spirit of God; but he must have some evidence, or, in other words, some reason, for believing that the doctrine does come from the divine Spirit. Chillingworth is quite as much opposed to a superstitious and irrational Protestantism as to a superstitious and irrational Popery. The private judgment must not merely be "a particular reason that a doctrine is true which some men pretend, but cannot prove, to come from the Spirit of God," but a rational judgment founded upon evi-

[1] i. 237, 238.

dence : "For is there not a manifest difference between saying, 'The Spirit of God tells me that this is the meaning of such a text' (which no man can possibly know to be true, it being a secret thing), and between saying, 'These and those reasons I have to show that this or that is true doctrine, or that this or that is the meaning of such a Scripture,' reason being a public and certain thing, and exposed to all men's trial and examination?"[1]

Such is the mode in which Chillingworth settles the primary question of religious certitude, or the source of religious truth. The remaining questions scarcely admit of vital controversy after laying down such a basis. It is plain that differing here, the disputants must differ throughout—as to the sum or contents of religious truth, for example, no less than its source or authority. The one question continually involves the other. Not only is the Church the authority with Knott, but all that the Church stamps with its authority is vital or fundamental. All is truth which the Church affirms to be true. Not at all, argues Chillingworth. That is truth only which is necessary to be believed in order to salvation. The Jesuit taunts him with the necessity of giving a catalogue of necessary or fundamental doctrines. This is not at all requisite, he says. "That may be fundamental and necessary to me which to another is not so." The question is one of privilege and opportunity, as the case of Cornelius shows. "In his Gentilism he was accepted for his present state; yet if he had continued in it and refused to believe in

[1] i. 235, 336.

Christ after the sufficient revelation of the Gospel to him and God's will to have him believe it, he that was accepted before would not have continued accepted."[1]

As the Romanist, therefore, thinks it enough to say in general, " That all is fundamental which the Church has defined ; " so it is enough for the Protestant to say in general, " That it is sufficient for man's salvation to believe that the Scripture is true, and contains all things necessary for salvation, and to do his best endeavour to find and believe the true sense of it." [2]

The Jesuit argues that "unless the Church be infallible in all things, we cannot believe her in any one." Chillingworth pours great contempt upon this argument. There is no more consequence in it, he says, than in this : " The devil is not infallible ; therefore, if he says there is one God, I cannot believe him. No geometrician is infallible in all things, therefore not in these things which he demonstrates." [3] If it be meant, indeed, that the Church being fallible, we cannot rationally believe her simply on her own word or authority, there is no doubt of the proposition. The Church is only to be credited—everything is only credible—on fair grounds of reason and evidence presented to the crediting intelligence. That there shall be always a Church "infallible in fundamentals," he admits ; for this is simply to say, " that there shall be always a Church." But that any given Church is always an infallible guide in fundamentals, is to say some-

[1] i. 321.   [2] Ibid., p. 322.   [3] Ibid., p. 347.

thing quite different. This statement he entirely denies. "The true Church always shall be the teacher and maintainer of all necessary truth, for it is of the essence of the Church to be so. But a man may be still a man though he want a hand or an eye. So the Church may be still a Church though it be defective in some profitable truth."[1] It follows, of course, that the simplest creed is the best creed, and that which alone offers any basis of reunion among Christians. That which is known as the Apostles' Creed best answers to this description. It has been esteemed "a sufficient summary or catalogue of fundamentals by the most learned Romanists and by antiquity." "What man or Church soever believes this Creed, and all the evident consequences of it, sincerely and heartily, cannot possibly be in any error of simple belief offensive to God."

It appears to Chillingworth that it would be of the utmost advantage for the Christian world if men would recognise the adequacy of such a creed as this, and hold all beyond as mere matters of speculation and opinion. There appears to him no other prospect of Christian union. "For this is most certain," he says, "that to reduce Christians to unity of communion there are but two ways: the one by taking away the diversity of opinions touching matters of religion; the other by showing that the diversity of opinions which is among the several sects of Christians ought to be no hindrance to their unity in communion. Now, the former of these is not to be hoped for without a

[1] i. 340.

miracle. . . . What then remains but that the other way must be taken, and Christians must be taught to set a higher value upon those points of faith and obedience in which they agree than upon those matters of less moment wherein they differ; and understand that agreement in these ought to be more effectual to join them in one communion than their difference in other things of less moment? When I say in one communion, I mean in a common profession of those articles of faith wherein all consent; a joint worship of God, after such a way as all esteem lawful, and a mutual performance of all those works of charity which Christians owe one to another. And to such a communion what better inducement could be thought of than to demonstrate that what was universally believed of all Christians, if it were joined with a love of truth and of holy obedience, was sufficient to bring men to heaven? *For why should men be more rigid than God?* Why should any error exclude any man from the Church's communion which will not deprive him of eternal salvation?" [1]

Again, he says: "If men would allow that the way to heaven is not narrower now than Christ left it, His yoke no heavier than He made it; that the belief of no more difficulties is required now to salvation than was in the primitive Church; that no error is in itself destructive and exclusive from salvation now which was not then; if, instead of being zealous Papists, earnest Calvinists, rigid Lutherans, they would become themselves, and be

[1] ii. 58, 59.

content that others should be, plain and honest Christians; if all men would believe the Scripture, and, freeing themselves from prejudice and passion, would sincerely endeavour to find the true sense of it, and live according to it, and require no more of others than to do so; nor denying their communion to any that do so, would so order their public service of God that all which do so may, without scruple, or hypocrisy, or protestation against any part of it, join with them in it,—who doth not see that, since all necessary truths are plainly and evidently set down in Scripture, there would of necessity be among all men, in all things necessary, unity of opinion? And, notwithstanding any other differences that are or could be, unity of communion, and charity, and mutual toleration, by which means all schism and heresy would be banished the world, and those wretched contentions which now rend and tear in pieces, not the coat, but the members and bowels of Christ, which mutual pride, and tyranny, and cursing, and killing, and damning, would fain make immortal, should speedily receive a most blessed catastrophe."[1]

The reader will notice the rising energy, the suppressed yet hurrying vehemence, which runs through this passage. This is Chillingworth's manner when fully under the influence of some great thought or feeling. His mind kindles, and his style catches the glow and impetuosity of a noble enthusiasm. There is no subject stirs him more readily or more loftily than religious liberty. The thought of this liberty,

[1] i. 404.

and how miserably men grudge it to each other, and Christian Churches strive to thwart and limit it instead of seeking their strength in educating it, never fails to fire his language, and makes it move with that grand, if somewhat irregular, energy which is its highest feature. He acknowledges the authority of the divine Word to control man's faith, and no other authority. " Propose to me anything out of the Bible," he says, "and require whether I believe it or no, and seem it never so incomprehensible to human reason, I will subscribe it with hand and heart, as knowing no demonstration can be stronger than this : God hath said so, therefore it is true. In other things, I will take no man's liberty of judgment from him, neither shall any man take mine from me. I will think no man the worse man nor the worse Christian,—I will love no man the less for differing in opinion from me; and what measure I mete to others I expect from them again. I am fully assured that God does not, and therefore that man ought not, to require any more of any man than this —to believe the Scripture to be God's word, to endeavour to find the true sense of it, and to live according to it." [1]

Freedom of religious opinion was thus placed by Chillingworth on its true basis more than two centuries ago—six years before the Westminster Assembly met. If anything were needed to show the height to which he rises above the divines of the time, this simple fact is enough to show it. The

[1] ii. 411.

principle of religious latitude had indeed been already laid down by the Remonstrant divines in Holland; but none had seized it more clearly or boldly than Chillingworth, and none had heretofore given such systematic expression to it in England. It is to be observed that he announces it as a principle for the direction and government of Churches, and not merely as a barren concession to the force of philosophical and religious indifference. It derives all its interest to him from its connection with religious earnestness and its seeming to open up the way for the reconstitution and advancement of the Christian Church. The idea of religious latitude being something very good outside the Church, but an impossibility within it, is opposed to his whole conception. According to him, on the contrary, the only valid basis for the Church, the only hope of its ever becoming what it professes to be—*catholic*—is the utmost freedom in the light of Scripture. Whatever tends to limit or control religious faith beyond the one controlling authority of the divine Word is evil. This is absolute when we recognise it. But whatever tends to interfere with the simplicity of this absolute spiritual authority is a source of ecclesiastical disorganisation —of unchristian disorder. It is when he touches this strain that his language rises to indignant eloquence.

"This presumptuous imposing of the senses of men upon the words of God,—the special senses of men upon the general words of God, and laying them upon men's consciences together, under the equal penalty of death and damnation; this vain conceit, that we can speak of the things of God better than in the words of God ; thus deifying our own interpretations, and tyrannous enforcing them upon others ; this restraining of the Word of God from that latitude and generality, and the understandings of men from that liberty wherein Christ and the apostles left them, is and hath been the only fountain of all the schisms of the Church, and that which makes them immortal; the common incendiary of Christendom, and that which tears in pieces not the coat, but the bowels and members of Christ. *Ridente Turca nec dolente Judæo.* Take away these walls of separation, and all will quickly be one. Take away this persecuting, burning, cursing, damning of men for not subscribing to the words of men as the words of God ; require of Christians only to believe Christ, and to call no man master but Him only ; let those leave claiming infallibility that have no title to it, and let them that in their word disclaim it, disclaim it likewise in their actions. In a word, take away tyranny, which is the devil's instrument to support errors and superstitions and impieties in the several parts of the world, which could not otherwise long withstand the power of truth ; I say, take away tyranny, and restore Christians to their just and full liberty of captivating their understanding to Scripture only, and as rivers, when they have a free passage, run all to the ocean, so it may well be hoped, by God's blessing, that universal liberty, thus unrestricted, may quickly reduce Christendom to truth and unity."[1]

It is unnecessary to carry our exposition further. These extracts render Chillingworth's principles sufficiently apparent. They are the principles evidently neither of the Laudian school, with which he was personally associated, nor of the Puritan school, to which he was opposed. He stands aloof from both, on a higher platform. From the school of Laud he is separated by his elevation of Scripture, not only into the supreme, but into the only authority in religious opinion and controversy; and while the mere general assertion of this principle might seem to place him on the same level with the Puritan, the manner in which he maintains and interprets the principle separates him widely from it. While he recognises the Bible as the only authority in religion, he recognises at the same time the free right of the individual reason to interpret the Bible. Nor does he acknowledge this merely as a generality which Puritanism may be also said to do, but he accepts it as a living practical principle in all its consequences. The right of free Scriptural interpretation, for example, implies the right of religious difference. Beyond an obvious round of great facts and truths, to be found everywhere plainly revealed in Scripture,—to be found complete in any one of the Gospels,—there is no unity of religious belief possible or desirable among Christians. Beyond such facts—of which the Apostles' Creed is the his-

[1] ii. 38, 39.

torical summary—he proclaims the principle of religious latitude. This is his distinction : Christianity is with him belief in Christ—the great facts of Christ's life and death for man's salvation—without either a Sacramentarian, or a Calvinistic, or an Arminian theory of the mode in which this salvation is made effectual to man. He requires of Christians, in his own language, " to believe only in Christ," " and will damn no man or doctrine without express and certain warrant from God's Word." He recognises the authority of God in religion, and no other. This authority is addressed in Scripture to the individual reason and conscience, so that the humblest intelligence may see and own it. There is no second authority entitled to speak for the divine voice, or to interfere between it and the individual. The voice of the Church, the voice of creeds and of councils, should be reverently listened to, but they possess no binding authority in themselves over the Christian conscience. In so far as they express the truth of Scripture we are to be thankful for them, accept and use them; but what we acknowledge in them is not the human expressions or temporary form of doctrine, but the divine substance and meaning which they have sought to render. " By the ' Religion of Protestants,' I do not understand the doctrine of Luther or Calvin or Melanchthon, nor the Confession of Augusta or Geneva, nor the Catechism of Heidelberg, nor the Articles of the Church of England—no, nor the harmony of Protestant confessions; but that wherein they all agree, and which they all subscribe with a greater harmony as a perfect rule of their faith and actions—that is, the *Bible*."[1]

Chillingworth was thus a Protestant truly and consistently. He recognised, and, for the first time in English theological literature, fully expounded, the meaning of Protestantism and its logical corollary, the principle of religious latitude, or of "agreeing to differ" in all matters of religious theory in which the varying tastes, tempers, and judgments of men necessarily create difference. He held fast to the supremacy of Scripture, the great watchword of the sixteenth century against Popery; but he appreciated as the sixteenth century had not done, the free action of reason upon Scripture. To the cause of Protestantism and of liberal theology he has thus rendered an abiding service. There are few names, upon the whole, even in a history so fruitful in great names as that of the Church of England, which more excite our admiration, or which claim a higher place in the development of religious thought.

[1] ii. 410.

VI.

JEREMY TAYLOR — LIBERTY OF CHRISTIAN TEACHING WITHIN THE CHURCH.

I. IN preceding sketches we have traced the rise and development of a spirit of rational inquiry within the Church of England. This spirit is more or less connected with the movement of liberal opinion in Holland; but it is also the result of internal forces working in the Church itself, torn by the conflicting tendencies which it embraced, and the invasion of Romanist influences once more assailing it. The religious contentions of the time, and the extreme and violent forms towards which they were advancing under the excitement of political interests, drove a few thoughtful minds to seek a higher solution of spiritual questions than had hitherto been imagined by any political or religious party. Hales and Chillingworth are the most prominent representatives of this higher religious thoughtfulness: the former owing his theological bias in some degree directly to contact with the liberal theology of Holland; the latter drawing his liberal inspiration more from the struggles of his own bold and independent spirit. Both men are thinkers characteristically; they belong to the same phase of the movement, and the remarkable group of writers and distinguished Oxford men who gathered around Falkland at Tew. Their whole intellectual life is summed up in what they did to advance the movement. Their connection with it gives them their position in the history of the Church of England. We have therefore presented full sketches of these two men,—of their life and character, as well as of their opinions. Their attitude as the leaders of liberal theological opinion in England in the first half of the seventeenth century, when the great currents of theological thought were running past them in opposite directions, and the significance of their attitude was but little understood and heeded, gives them a claim to full recognition both in their personal and theological character.

After these writers there are two names which stand in a peculiar relation to the history of religious thought in England—the names of Jeremy Taylor and Edward Stillingfleet. They belong to the liberal movement of the seventeenth century, in so far as they contributed by distinct and important works to its advancement; yet neither their special reputation nor the prevailing character of their theological activity has identified them with it. Jeremy Taylor's 'Liberty of Prophesying' is among the most remarkable works of the century. Stillingfleet's 'Irenicum' is of less significance, because less distinguished by genius and interest; and in our day it is comparatively forgotten. Yet it too claims to be remembered as marking the height to which the wave of liberal Churchmanship had risen before the reaction which set in with the Restoration. The first of these works appeared in 1647—exactly ten years later than the 'Religion of Protestants;' the second in 1659, on the eve of the Restoration.

Both Taylor and Stillingfleet only belong to our history in so far as these works are concerned. Their best-known writings are of a different, and, in some respects, contrasted mode of thought. At the same time, their consistency is not rashly to be questioned. Taylor was no longer a youth when he published the 'Liberty of Prophesying,' being, in 1647, thirty-four years of age; nor can he be said avowedly to have abandoned the principles which it advocated. He even expresses general adherence to them as late as 1662, in a famous sermon[1] preached before the University of Dublin. Still, it is only one side, and perhaps not the most characteristic side, of his intellectual and Christian activity which is represented in the 'Liberty of Prophesying.' Taylor is much more, and much besides, in the history of English theological literature, than the advocate of a liberal, eclectic theology, and of a Church based upon broad and comprehensive principles. Stillingfleet is possibly more open to the charge of inconsistency. He was comparatively a young man— only twenty-four—when the 'Irenicum' was first published; and in his later years he is represented as saying that " there are many things in it which, if he were to write again, he would not say—some which

---

[1] Published among his other works, under the title of 'Via Intelligentiæ,' Heber's ed., vi. Yet the tone of Taylor, if not also his principles, are very different in this sermon. Coleridge (Notes, &c., p. 208, 209) is unduly severe; yet Taylor's consistency can hardly be defended—his manliness certainly not.

show his youth and want of consideration, others which he yielded too far, in the hopes of gaining the Dissenting parties to the Church of England."[1]

Neither of these writers, in short, comes before us in his complete personality. Although they both helped the movement, and came under its influence, they do not as men characteristically belong to it. Their spirit is not essentially philosophic, rational, or liberal. Taylor is medieval, ascetic, casuistic in his mature type of thought. He is a scholastic in argument, a pietist in feeling, a poet in fancy and expression; he is not a thinker. He seldom moves in an atmosphere of purely rational light; and even when his instincts are liberal and his reasoning highly rational in its results, he brings but a slight force of thought, of luminous and direct comprehension, to bear upon his work. Stillingfleet, again, is antiquarian, formal, and controversial. His intellect is acute, hard, and ingenious, ready to cope with any subject and any opponent that may cross his path, or may seem to him inimical to the Church. He is alert alike against the Romanist, the Separatist, and the Rationalist—one of a common type of theologians bred by all Churches, who delight to go forth with weapons of war against all assailants of official orthodoxy and official privilege. They have their own merits, this class of writers; and Stillingfleet, as well as Jeremy Taylor, is a name of which the

---

[1] Life, 1710. He is supposed himself to be speaking in the person of P. D., in one of his controversial writings—' Conference between a Romish priest,' &c. He says something to the same effect in his preface to ' The Unreasonableness of Separation,' 1680.

Church of England has reason to be proud. Her great roll of illustrious writers would be much poorer if they were gone. There are few names, upon the whole, which shine with a richer or grander lustre than that of Taylor. But to our list they only belong in part—at one point of their lives—and in virtue of the works which we have mentioned. We shall therefore content ourselves with a comparatively brief sketch of both—of Stillingfleet in particular—and dwell mainly on the works by which they have advanced the cause of liberal Church opinion.

It is also to be remarked, that in dealing with these writers we get so far into a new sphere, and even traverse slightly the line of thought to which our second volume is devoted. Yet it seems better, in the view of the definite crisis which the Church question may be said to have reached at the Restoration, to follow out so far in this volume the series of rational arguments raised by it. Although Taylor and Stillingfleet are separated from our foregoing group, and proceed from another university, it was the special type of liberalism begun by Hales which they carried forward. With the later Platonic type their connection is less essential than has been sometimes supposed. Taylor, moreover, is brought into the direct vicinity of the Oxford set which surrounded Falkland. In short, these two writers, or rather their respective works to which we confine attention, carry out in its purely intellectual form that earlier phase of the rational movement which was ecclesiastical rather than philosophical in its character and tendency. Subsequent controversy added but little to the theory of a comprehensive Church.

Jeremy Taylor was educated at Cambridge, of which he was a native. His parents are said to have been of good descent—to have traced their lineage to the famous martyr, Rowland Taylor, who suffered in the reign of Mary; but they occupied a humble position, and were glad to receive assistance in the education of their son. Their son was entered as a sizar, or poor scholar, at Caius College in 1626, a year after Milton entered at Christ's College. There appears to be no record of his career as a student.[1] One of his biographers[2] has drawn a picture of the course of study he was likely to pursue, and professed to trace the influence of Bacon in some of the aspects of his mental development. But there is no evidence whatever that the Baconian philosophy had obtained any footing at Cambridge at this time, nor is there in the characteristics of Taylor's genius any trace of the higher culture which he would have derived from it. So far as we can trust Milton, and other authorities probably less preju-

---

[1] The sources of Taylor's biography are Heber's well-known Life, prefixed to the edition of his works published in 1822; and a Life by Archdeacon Bonney, an interleaved copy of which, "corrected, with many valuable notes," was consulted by Heber. A descendant of Taylor, William Todd Jones, had made a large collection of materials for a biography of the bishop, among which there was "a family book in his own handwriting, giving an account of his parentage and the principal events of his life;" but this, with other MSS. of Taylor, is supposed to have been destroyed in a fire that consumed the London Custom-House.

[2] Archdeacon Bonney.

diced, the scholastic system, with its singular subtleties, still held sway in the university; and fertile and unrestrained as Taylor's mental activity was in many directions, there is no influence of which it bears more trace than that of the scholasticism still prevailing in his youth. He is one of several examples in his generation of a singular combination of poetic imaginativeness, exuberant in its wantonness, with an arid scholasticism tedious in its love of trifles and distinctions. A medieval culture overlaid his native richness of fancy and feeling, without moulding and educating it. The imaginative fruitfulness survives; but it is not well mixed—it is hardly mixed at all—with the harder intellectual grain developed by the scholastic discipline. And so, like some other writers of the seventeenth century,[1] he seems almost to have

[1] Samuel Rutherford, the well-known Scotch Puritan divine, who replied in an elaborate volume to Taylor and "other authors contending for lawless liberty or licentious toleration of sects and heresies," is an instance of the same poetic and scholastic qualities ill combined, or rather not combined at all. In Rutherford, indeed, both the poetry and the logic must be admitted to be of very inferior quality. Yet the same contrast of mental character is presented. He is scarcely the same writer in his 'Letters,' the only productions of his pen now known, and in his argumentative treatises. The 'Letters' are marked by the extravagances of a fancy lawless in its exuberance. The treatises are dull, barren, operose, and unillumined in argument to a frightful degree. Nobody without an effort can read them. And if it may seem too great a disparity to compare Rutherford in any respect with Taylor (although their controversial relation suggests the comparison), we may point to the greatest literary name of the age as illustrative of the same fact. Marvellous as are Milton's prose works, they are, especially the treatise on Divorce, lacking in lofty rationality and consistency of argument. The poet is revealed in the splendour of occasional thoughts and in passages of noble eloquence; but the imagination has not blended with the understanding so as to give insight, comprehension, and light to the general train of reasoning.

two minds: one tender, sweet, and luxuriant to excess; the other hard, subtle, formal, prone to definition and logomachy. He is, at the same time, poet and casuist, orator and ascetic. The poetic, rhetorical elements lie alongside the dialectic in his genius, without blending, or fusing and strengthening into a thorough rational faculty.

Taylor became Bachelor of Arts in 1631, and is stated by his panegyrist Rust to have been chosen Fellow of Caius immediately afterwards. There appear, however, to be some doubts of this circumstance, which is distrusted by Heber. It is not till 1633, when he became Master of Arts, that Taylor's name occurs in the list of Fellows. He had then been admitted into holy orders, and appears from the first to have attracted attention as a preacher. It was his powers in this respect that brought him under the knowledge of Laud, and opened up for him a new career. One of his fellow-students, of the name of Risden, had become lecturer in St Paul's Cathedral, and wished Taylor to supply his place for a short time. Here his eloquence and graceful person, aided, no doubt, by the interest attaching to his youth, made a lively impression, and speedily procured him friends and admirers. He appeared, in the language of Rust, as "some young angel newly descended from the visions of glory." The fame of the youthful preacher was carried to Laud, just then elevated to the see of Canterbury, and, with that remarkable appreciation of genius which we have already noticed both in the case of Hales and Chillingworth, he sent for Taylor to preach before him at Lambeth. He was highly satisfied with his sermon, and immediately interested himself in his advancement. The story is that he wished to rescue so promising a preacher from the snares of a premature popularity in London. He thought him too young for such a sphere as St Paul's, and that it was "for the advantage of the world that such mighty parts should be afforded better opportunities of study and improvement than a course of constant preaching would allow of."[1] Taylor, of course, begged his Grace's pardon for the fault of his youth, and promised, "if he lived, he would amend it." Such is the manner in which Bishop Rust represents this turning-point in Taylor's career; and there is no reason to doubt his substantial accuracy, however much his admiring fancy may have embellished the event. Laud was greatly attracted by Taylor, and used his influence in establishing him at Oxford. After some difficulty, he was able to secure him a Fellowship at All Souls'. Sheldon, who was warden of the college, interposed to prevent his immediate appointment, notwithstanding the choice of the Fellows at Laud's instance; but the nomination devolving in due course to the archbishop as visitor, he carried out his intentions by his own authority: Taylor became a Fellow of All Souls' on the 14th of January 1636.

This is a curious and significant step in Taylor's career. It is singular, first of all, to find him, no less than Hales and Chillingworth, in immediate connection with Laud. At this early period, Taylor's mind had probably not opened to the deeper questions of his time. There was nothing about him, except his undoubted ability, to attract the archbishop. This

[1] Rust.

CHRISTIAN TEACHING WITHIN THE CHURCH. 353

credit must be given to Laud, whatever we may think of his ecclesiastical policy: he had an eye for theological genius. The active patron of Hales and Chillingworth and Taylor cannot be accused of intellectual meanness, or of entire misapprehension of the spiritual forces of his time. Probably, as is often found to be the case with extreme ecclesiastics, Laud had no objection to an active and even liberal spirit of theological inquiry, where there was no tendency to practical insubordination or political restlessness. He may have guessed instinctively that none of these men would be likely to prove keen opponents of his ritualistic policy. Their spirit of conciliatory doctrinism made them indifferent, if not in some degree disposed, to ceremonies which must have appeared to them mere matters of expediency, while to the Puritan they savoured of idolatry. Their broad sense acknowledged no reason for repudiating a certain richness and elaboration of worship. And in Taylor's case, while his speculative liberality can hardly have appeared as yet, there may have been already some trace of those casuistic tendencies which afterwards matured and gave complexion to his theological culture. There is no difficulty in understanding the sympathy between Laud and the author of the 'Ductor Dubitantium,' and the 'Holy Living' and 'Holy Dying,' however imperceptible may seem the links of association between him and the author of the 'Liberty of Prophesying.'

But it is further singular to find Taylor, born and brought up as he was in Cambridge—at a distance from the band of active theological spirits that sur-founded Falkland at Oxford—suddenly thrown into their very heart in the college of which Sheldon was warden, and at the time that Chillingworth was busy with the composition of the 'Religion of Protestants.' Chillingworth belonged to Trinity, where Sheldon also had been educated, and we cannot tell whether he and Taylor came into contact. It is possible that they would not have greatly attracted each other if they did. Sheldon's opposition to his appointment naturally produced a coldness between the warden and the new Fellow, thrust upon him from Cambridge, against the statutes of the college.[1] This coldness is alluded to in a letter, many years after, from Taylor to Sheldon, in which he thanks him for forgiving two debts, " one of money, and the other of unkindness;" the latter being contracted when he did not know Sheldon, and "less understood" himself. In such circumstances he probably saw little of Sheldon, and hence little of Chillingworth, the two being at this time fast friends, as they had been fellow-students. Yet we cannot help thinking that such a moving spirit as Chillingworth would make his influence in some degree felt within the college of which his friend was the head; and, in any case, the publication of the ' Religion of Protestants,' in the following year (1637), could scarcely be without effect on a mind so open and impressionable as Taylor's.

[1] The statutes of All Souls' distinctly required candidates for Fellowships to be of three years' standing in the university. Taylor was not admitted to Oxford *ad eundem* till October 1635, so that he had only been a few months in the university when Laud appointed him to All Souls'.

After his appointment at All Souls' he continued his intimacy with Laud, who made him one of his chaplains. He himself tells us that he was a "most observant and obliged chaplain," and his duties in this capacity frequently carried him away from Oxford. In the spring of 1638 he was presented to the rectory of Uppingham, in Rutlandshire, the patron of which was Juxon, Bishop of London, who was probably glad to promote the young friend of the archbishop. In November of the following year, Taylor was selected to preach at St Mary's the sermon on the anniversary of the Gunpowder Plot; and there is a story in connection with this event, of his having made advances to the Church of Rome, which were brought to an end by the hard things which he was forced to say in the sermon against the Roman Catholics. There appears to have been no foundation for the story beyond his intimacy with a Franciscan of the name of Christopher Davenport, who was better known by the pseudonym of Francis a Sancta Clara, a chaplain to Queen Henrietta, and one of the numerous Popish missionaries whom we have so often traced as then labouring secretly in England for the overthrow of the Protestant faith. Davenport was a man of a higher stamp than was usual with this class of missionaries, and had imperilled his own orthodoxy by his liberality. Taylor's friendship with him was no evidence whatever of a tendency to Rome; but it was enough to excite suspicion and jealousy in such a time, especially in combination with his relation to Laud, and his own ritual and ascetic tastes. He continued through life, as Heber says, to be haunted by a suspicion of a concealed attachment to the Roman communion.

About a year after his settlement at Uppingham he married. Little is known of his wife, or her relatives, beyond the fact that she appears to have resided with her mother in the parish, and that her brother was a physician in Gainsborough, and subsequently in Leeds, where he died in 1683. There is an affectionate letter from Taylor to him in the year 1643, congratulating him on his recovery from illness, and bespeaking very affectionate and cordial relations between the families at Uppingham and Gainsborough. He had three sons by this wife, one of whom died in 1642; and the mother does not seem to have long survived her infant.

Taylor's life had hitherto been a prosperous and happy one. The times were troubled, but he had secured powerful friends; his genius was acknowledged; and his success had been considerable. Up to this point we have little insight into his opinions. His connection with Laud, no doubt, is sufficiently significant as to his general leanings in Church and State. His sermon before the University of Oxford, on the 5th November (1638), had vindicated his Protestantism; but of the deep and broader thoughts passing in his mind regarding the conflicts around him we learn nothing. A mind like his, however, must have been greatly moved by the aspect of the times, and he was now about to break silence. His patron had been committed to the Tower at the close of 1640, and there he lay awaiting his trial at the time that Taylor was feeling the first bitterness of domestic sorrow in his parsonage at Uppingham. It may have been partly to relieve his mind under the pressure of this sorrow, but no doubt mainly to vindicate a cause dear to him, that Taylor took up his pen in defence of Episcopacy, and sent forth the first of his many works, 'Episcopacy Asserted against the Acephali and Aerians, new and old.'

This treatise was published at Oxford, "by his Majesty's command," in 1642. Before this time Taylor appears to have quitted his parsonage and joined the king. His connection with Laud had been too conspicuous, and his partisanship was too vehement, to enable him to hope that he would remain unmolested at Uppingham. There is no evidence, however, that at this time he was subjected to any active persecution. Probably he fled before the decree of the Parliament, in the autumn of 1642, to sequester the livings of the loyal clergy.

During the two years following the opening of the Long Parliament, the air was filled with ecclesiastical pamphlets. The long-pent-up rage against the abuses of the Anglican hierarchy had burst forth with irrepressible energy, Milton leading the van in his bulky argument on 'Reformation in England, and the Causes that hitherto have hindered it.' The bishops were specially attacked as an order inimical to the Scriptural simplicity of the Church, and the main cause of its corruptions and tyrannies in England. Many sincere and devout Churchmen were honestly astonished at the vehemence of the assaults made upon the Episcopal order. Both Hall and Usher entered the lists in its defence. They bore the heat and burden of the fray in conflict with the " Smectymnuans,"[1] and their great champion, whose genius was happily destined to much higher work. Taylor's treatise may be allowed to rank him along with these illustrious defenders of their order; but he scarcely emerges into public notice as a combatant; nor is there anything in his treatise itself that gives it special claims to recognition. It can hardly be said to be quite worthy of the subject, or to meet its real difficulties. It gives no indication of the liberal and comprehensive spirit which was by-and-by to expand into the 'Liberty of Prophesying.' Instead of resting the defence of Episcopacy on the rational grounds of Hooker, which still interest and impress all true thinkers, Taylor is content with nothing less than taking up the narrow principle of the Puritans, and arguing that the plan of Church government must be necessarily "platformed in Scripture." The result is very unsatisfactory. Neither the statements nor the arguments of the treatise will bear examination. They are marked by uncritical assumptions and a mass of traditional pedantries which look imposing, but which weaken and obscure rather than strengthen or throw light upon his conclusions. Its chief excellence consists in the concise and rapid divisions into which he throws his reasoning, so as to bring all his points successively in good order before the reader. We have no evidence of

---

[1] Five Puritan ministers, the initials of whose names formed the word Smectymnus, who published a reply to Hall's Humble Remonstrance in favour of Episcopacy, and whose work Milton defended against the moderate yet powerful criticism of Usher.

how it was received; but no doubt it contributed, along with his active partisanship, to expose him to the severity of persecution which awaited him after the downfall of the royal cause. It was dedicated, like the 'Liberty of Prophesying,' to one who was henceforth one of his most active and liberal patrons —Christopher Lord Hatton of Kirby, who had been his neighbour at Uppingham, and who, after the king's retirement to Oxford, acted as Comptroller of his Household, in which capacity "he possessed," says Clarendon,[1] "a great reputation, which in a few years he found a way to diminish."

Taylor had spent five years in pleasant rural retirement. During the next few years he led a wandering and unsettled life — now with the king at Oxford, now following the royal army in the capacity of chaplain, and now, apparently for a brief space, as his letters (November 24, 1643) show, with his mother-in-law, the place of whose residence at this time is uncertain. Like Chillingworth, he appears to have been involved in the actual disasters of the war, and to have suffered for a time imprisonment. The foundation for this is a passage in Whitelock,[2] in which he states that the royal forces under Colonel Gerard having been routed before the castle of Cardigan, which they were besieging, there were one hundred and fifty prisoners taken, and among them Dr Taylor. It is presumed that there was no other Dr Taylor among the Royalists who was likely to be mentioned in this conspicuous manner.

[1] Hist. Rebell., ii. 156.
[2] Memor., p. 130, referred to by Heber, p. xxiii.

This occurred in February 1644; and during the same year there appeared at Oxford a 'Defence of the Liturgy,' which he afterwards published in an enlarged form. There also appeared, under his friend Hatton's name, an edition of the Psalter, with Collects affixed, which he subsequently incorporated in his works. The substitution of Hatton's name appears to Heber evidence of Taylor being a prisoner at the time; and, except for some purpose of concealment, it is difficult to account for such a substitution. Nothing, however, is clearly known as to his movements at this period, during which he married his second wife. Heber's idea is, that he was already married in the end of 1643 or the beginning of 1644, and settled for a brief space of happiness in Wales, when the evils of the war extending, again involved him in its vortex. To this temporary period of repose he is supposed to allude in the well-known dedication of the 'Liberty of Prophesying.' " In the great storm," he says, "which dashed the vessel of the Church in pieces, I was cast on the coast of Wales; and in a little boat thought to have enjoyed that rest and quietness which in England I could not hope for. Here I cast anchor; and thinking to ride safely, the storm followed me with so impetuous a violence that it broke a cable, and I lost my anchor. And here again I was exposed to the mercy of the sea, and the gentleness of an element that could neither distinguish things nor persons. And but that He who stilleth the raging of the sea and the noise of the waves, and the madness of the people, had provided a plank for me, I had been lost to all the opportunities of content or study. But I know not whether I have been more preserved by the courtesies of my friends or the gentleness and mercies of a noble enemy."

There is difficulty in carrying back the space of temporary quietness to which Taylor here alludes so far as 1643, or even 1644; but there can be no doubt that the description gives us, upon the whole, the best general idea of his mode of life during this interval. He was caught in "the great storm" in which so many fortunes were ruined; and after remaining for some time in active service with the royal forces, he returned into Wales, there married a second time, and settled on his wife's property. The story is that his wife was a natural daughter of King Charles I., and that she bore a strong resemblance to his well-known countenance, as presented by Vandyke. Either because the evils of the war again overtook him in his Welsh retreat, or because whatever property his wife may have had proved insufficient for his increasing wants, or for both reasons, he is found, about 1646 and 1647, keeping a school in the parish of Llanvihangel-Aberbythic. Associated with him in this task were two scholars, also suffering from the disasters of the time, William Nicholson and William Wyatt. The former afterwards became Bishop of Gloucester, and the other a prebendary of Lincoln. From this scholastic retreat appeared, in 1647, 'A New and Easy Institution of Grammar,' which is reckoned among Taylor's works, but the chief authorship of which has been ascribed to Wyatt. It has two epistles dedicatory: the one by Wyatt, in Latin, addressed to Lord Hatton; and the other in English by Taylor, addressed to Hatton's son, then in his fifteenth year. In the same year appeared his great work, the subject of our special criticism.

Of the remaining events in Taylor's life we can only give a brief summary. His successive publications, in fact, constitute its chief interest. Nothing could damp the ardour and productivity of his genius; and during the whole period from 1647 to 1660, he continued to send forth from his prolific pen, practical, devotional, and argumentative treatises. In the year 1648 he published, in an enlarged form, his 'Defence of the Liturgy;' then, in the same year, his 'Life of Christ, the great Exemplar,' one of the most solid and interesting of his works. The three following years gave to the light his well-known 'Twenty-seven Sermons' and the devotional manuals—perhaps the best known, and still the most widely read of all his works—'Holy Living' and 'Holy Dying.' In 1654 he put forth a controversial treatise against the Roman Catholics, on the subject of the Eucharist; and in the same year the beautiful manual of daily prayers and litanies, &c., which he entitled 'Golden Grove,' in honour of the hospitable seat of his friend and patron, Lord Carberry. More Sermons followed in the succeeding year; and, at the same time, his famous work on the 'Doctrine and Practice of Repentance,'[1] which presents him in

---

[1] 'Unum Necessarium; or the Doctrine and Practice of Repentance, describing the necessity and measure of a strict, a holy, and a Christian life, and rescued from popular errors.'

a new theological aspect as an original speculator on the great subjects of Christian dogma. The views as to original sin which he propounded in this treatise drew wide attention, and called down hostile criticism, not only from the Calvinistic and Puritan theologians of the day, upon which he no doubt reckoned, but from his own theological friends. The venerable Sanderson, in particular, was greatly distressed by his novel speculations. He deplored, it is said, "with much warmth, and even with tears, Taylor's departure from the cautious and Scriptural decision of the Church of England, and bewailed the misery of the times which did not admit of suppressing by authority so perilous and unseasonable novelties."[1] The times had brought personal honour and credit to Sanderson, whose conscientiousness was conspicuous in the resignation of his Divinity Professorship at Oxford; but they had not taught him toleration or wisdom. He had not read, or at least, as Heber suggests, had not profited by Taylor's argument in his 'Liberty of Prophesying.' His mind, indeed, was of a narrow if subtle cast; and Taylor's originality, both as a thinker and writer, could have been very little appreciated by him. In recent years Taylor's views on original sin have attracted renewed attention in the criticism of Samuel Taylor Coleridge. The weakness and inconsequence of his theory, as well as of the extreme Calvinistic theory which he designed to supersede, have been set forth in the 'Aids to Reflection'[2] with acuteness and force, although with something also

[1] Heber, Life, p. xlii.   [2] i. 208-230.

of the wordy and pretentious amplitude of the writer on such subjects. It is not difficult, indeed, to hit the weakness in Taylor's theory. In addition to the intrinsic difficulties of theorising on such a topic, Taylor's tendency to illustration and exuberance of statement on this, as on other topics, leads him constantly into extravagance. His imagination is but rarely under the severe control necessary to fortify an argument at all points, and to exhibit it at once with due discrimination and force.

In the year 1659 he republished several of his former works in folio, and among them ' The Liberty of Prophesying,' under the title Σύμβολον Ηθικο-πολεμικόν, with a dedication to Lord Hatton, in which he defends the consistency of his views regarding the Fathers, whose authority he had appeared to some " to pull down with one hand " and " to build with the other." Finally, in 1660, was published his great work, which he had been long preparing, and which he himself was disposed to esteem the chief pillar of his fame—his ' Ductor Dubitantium,' or extended treatise on Casuistic Divinity. With this work his career as an author does not, indeed, terminate, but his significance as a theological writer reaches its highest point. His ' Dissuasives from Popery,' the second part of which was only completed in the year of his death (1667), and an important sermon, under the title of " Via Intelligentiæ," which he preached before the University of Dublin in 1662, are the only writings of his later years that demand special notice. The sermon in question is intimately related to the views expounded in the 'Liberty of Prophesying,' and generally reasserts the liberal principles of this work, with modifications which were not new, but which received from him a new and special prominence in the different circumstances in which he was placed.

To this brief sketch of Taylor's literary and theological activity during the twenty years which elapsed from the publication of his 'Liberty of Prophesying' till his death, little remains to be added, as to his external life and circumstances. He remained in Wales, making occasional visits to London and its neighbourhood, especially to see his friend Evelyn, until the year 1658. Notwithstanding his misfortunes and losses in the commotions of the time, Taylor seems to have had a great faculty of acquiring friends of rank and wealth who were able to assist him, and to whom he in return acted as a spiritual counsellor, both privately by personal advice or letter, and publicly, so far as his ministrations could be conducted with any safety under the restrictions of the time. We have already alluded to his friend Lord Carberry, whose seat of Golden Grove, in the same parish in Wales where Taylor's lot was cast, gave the name to one of his most attractive devotional works. Richard Vaughan, Earl of Carberry, had distinguished himself as a military commander on the king's side, and survived to be rewarded for his loyal service at the Restoration. He and his wife were both warm friends of Taylor, and he repaid their friendship by an enthusiastic devotion. When the first Lady Carberry died, he preached her funeral sermon, and drew a portrait of her which, as Heber says, "belongs rather to an angelic than a human character." The second Lady Carberry, who was a daughter of the Earl of Bridgewater, was no less friendly to Taylor, and had the singular fortune of not only being eulogised by him, but of forming the original of the "Lady" in Milton's "Comus." In the happy mansion of this family Taylor not only spent many pleasant hours, but was able to carry on his ministry when the neighbouring churches were shut against him. He preached here his "yearly course" of Sermons.[1] His friendship with Evelyn, which was ultimately of material assistance to him, began about 1654, apparently in one of his visits to London. About this time Taylor was in difficulties, and appears to have been, within a year, twice imprisoned in connection with some of his publications. His imprisonment, however, was of short duration on both occasions. It is possible that Evelyn was of service in procuring his liberation; for Evelyn's position, character, and moderate opinions, although a sincere Royalist, like his friend, gave him influence with the parties in power.[2] Certainly, from this

---

[1] 'Ενιαυτός,—the title by which he himself designated the first series of his published Sermons; although, as Heber remarks, with one or two exceptions, they have no reference to the yearly festivals of the Church.

[2] John Evelyn is a conspicuous figure in the literary and philosophical society of the seventeenth century. He is now chiefly remembered by his works on Gardening and Forestry, especially his great work, 'Sylva; or a Discourse of Forest-Trees.' He had returned from a prolonged residence abroad in the beginning of 1652, and settled on his wife's property at Sayes-Court, near Deptford.

time Taylor and Evelyn continued warm friends. During four years, from 1655 to 1658, their correspondence, which had previously begun, continues frequent, and gives us the best insight we have into Taylor's personal life. The picture has not much colour; but we can see, with sufficient distinctness, on the one hand, the earnest hard-working theologian and spiritual counsellor, depressed by the *res angusta domi* of which he often complains; and, on the other hand, the kind-hearted, amiable scholar and Christian philosopher, always urging his hospitality at Sayes-Court, near Deptford, upon his friend, and wishing him to settle in London. Taylor expresses, in July 1656, great anxiety to comply with his friend's wish, that he may "receive advantage of society and books to enable him better to serve God and the interest of souls;" but says that he is hindered by the straitness of his means. It seems to be doubtful whether he ever removed to London with his family; but he is represented as officiating to private congregations of Episcopalians there, and as officiating at the baptism of Evelyn's fourth son at Sayes-Court, in the spring of 1657. In the same year Evelyn seems to have granted him a yearly pension, in acknowledgment of which Taylor's thanks are affluent.

In 1658 another powerful friend of Taylor's comes upon the scene, Edward, Earl of Conway; and he, in conjunction with Evelyn, induced the neglected divine, for whom England at this time could furnish no post, to accept a lectureship at Lisburn, in the north of Ireland. At first Taylor did not like the offer, which presented few attractions. The stipend is "so considerable," he says, that it will not pay the charge and trouble of removing himself and his family, and the duty is to be shared by a Presbyterian. "I like not," he writes to Evelyn in May 1658, "the condition of being a lecturer under the dispose of another, nor to serve in any semicircle where a Presbyterian and myself shall be, like Castor and Pollux, the one up and the other down." His scruples, however, were overcome, and in the summer of the same year we find him settled at Portmore, about eight miles distant from Lisburn. Portmore was the seat of Lord Conway, his friend and patron, and was charmingly situated on Lough Neagh. Here, under the shadow of a princely mansion, "built after a plan by Inigo Jones," and amidst scenes "where a painter, a poet, or a devout contemplatist might alike delight to linger," Taylor appears to have fixed his final residence. His subsequent elevation to the bishopric of the province made no change, or at least no permanent change, in his place of abode. He clung to the sequestered charm of the place, with its cluster of "romantic islets lying near," to some of which, according to tradition, it was his practice to retire, for purposes of study or devotion. It was a fitting retreat for his closing years.

When Episcopacy was restored in 1660, it might have been supposed that so distinguished a champion of it as Taylor would have been called to some post of honour and activity in England; but, from whatever cause, he received no such call. He was elevated to episcopal dignity, however, within the district where he was. On the 6th of August, after the king's return, he was appointed Bishop of Down and Connor, and shortly afterwards he was elected Vice-Chancellor of the University of Dublin.

Of Taylor's episcopate there is not much to say. The difficulties which surrounded him were extreme. On one side the Roman Catholics, on the other side the Puritans, regarded him with disfavour. The latter had obtained great ascendancy, particularly in his diocese, during the Commonwealth. They were generally of the most extreme Calvinistic and Covenanting type; and Taylor's liberalism in theology, no less than his devotion to the ritual and government of the Church of England, were deeply distasteful to them. It is impossible to read his sermon before the two Houses of Parliament in May 1661, or his still more famous sermon before the University of Dublin, published in the following year, without perceiving traces of his disappointment at the conduct of this ecclesiastical faction. His principles were strained to the utmost in speaking of them, and some of his expressions regarding the duty of obedience to ecclesiastical superiors, and the over-doing of respect for "weak consciences," when it is evidently "not their consciences, but their profits," that are in question, are barely within those laws of toleration and charity of which he had written so earnestly and so beautifully.

As for the Roman Catholics, he found himself in face of them as "a faction and a state party," whose design was, according to his own statement, "to recover their old laws and barbarous manner of living, and so to be 'populus unius labii,' a people of one language, and unmingled with others." Unhappily, neither the political nor ecclesiastical authorities of the time fully appreciated the nature of the people whom they sought to govern and instruct. Neither penalties nor 'Dissuasives from Popery' were the means to reach an ignorant, enthusiastic, naturally patriotic race. Teachers and preachers in their own language, the systematic and patient carrying out of the policy pursued by Usher and Bedell at an earlier period might have been crowned with some measure of success. But nothing of this sort was attempted. The Irish language was in every way discountenanced. Neither Scripture nor the Liturgy was translated; while the people were yet bound to give attendance at the parish churches. The fatal results of such a policy have only reached their climax in our own day. Not even a bishop like Taylor could stem the evil influences that flowed from it. The most enlightened toleration and the purest and most benevolent character might relieve the darkness of the general system of civil and ecclesiastical government set up in Ireland, no less than in Scotland, at the Restoration, but they could do no more. The name of Taylor, like that of Leighton, serves to show how the noblest and most Christian aspirations may be bound up with a base and unjust cause. They are spots of beauty in an ugly picture, on which men look back with shame and sorrow, but in no respect do they redeem the cause with which they were identified.

They do not even cast respectability around it. On the contrary, it requires the impartial charity of the historian to lift the name of either clear from the bad system of ecclesiastical and political tyranny to which they respectively belonged, and which derived in its time some credit from their connection.

Taylor survived his elevation to the episcopate only seven years—years of severe personal trial, as well as of painful public responsibility. Of his two surviving sons, one fell in a duel; and the other, who was intended for the Church, came under the profligate influence of the Duke of Buckingham, lost his health as the result of his excesses, and died in August 1667. In the same month the father, who had felt bitterly the conduct of his sons, and been broken in spirit by the sad fate of the eldest (it is doubtful whether he survived to hear of the death of the second), was seized with fever, and died at Lisburn, after ten days' illness, in the fifty-fifth year of his age.

Those who have looked at Taylor's portraits will have been struck by the beauty and grace of his personal appearance. There is a ripe and somewhat soft freshness of health in his face, "with his hair long and gracefully curling on his cheeks, large dark eyes full of sweetness, an aquiline nose," and an open earnest expression. He is said not to have been without consciousness of his personal beauty, and to have frequently introduced his portraits in different attitudes in his various writings.[1]

[1] Heber, i. cxxv.

II. The 'Discourse on the Liberty of Prophesying' was published in 1647; and it is important to fix attention upon this particular date in the great crisis of events through which the country was passing. In the ten years which had elapsed since the publication of the 'Religion of Protestants,' momentous changes had occurred. The government of the king had been subverted, the Church overthrown, Laud beheaded. Puritanism was everywhere triumphant. The fear of Popery, which had goaded the nation into frenzy, and the intolerant claims of which had provoked Chillingworth's great work, had entirely passed away. The question was no longer as to the validity of Protestantism. The Reforming passions of the nation, long held in check by arbitrary power, had burst forth and carried all before them; and, as always happens in such crises, it was the extreme force of the reaction which had gradually acquired ascendancy. It is singular and somewhat mournful to contemplate the manner in which the national enthusiasm swept away the successive stands or rallying-points which the early friends of the movement sought to make. At first, when the Long Parliament met (November 1640), all the representatives of the national patriotism may be said to have been arrayed against the king—Clarendon and Falkland, no less than Pym and Hampden. But with the overthrow of the great abuses and agencies of tyranny which had grown up under Charles, a schism occurred in the popular party. Pym and Hampden carried forward the revolutionary movement; but

Falkland and his friends drew off, and formed that new or middle party of which we have already spoken. Falkland was the soul of this party, and its best, if not its stoutest, representative. A Constitutionalist in politics, and a Moderate in doctrine and Church government, he would have arrested the revolution, if he could have done so, by the pure operation of Parliamentary government on the one hand, and on the other hand by a reasonable reform of the Church, so as to give scope at once to freedom of opinion and a fair order of service without Popish adjuncts or Episcopal intermeddling. In this latter respect his friend Chillingworth would have been found ranked by his side. This is the very ideal of doctrinal moderation and Church order and service which he has drawn in his third chapter, on "Points Fundamental and not Fundamental."[1] There is reason to believe that, so far as reform of the Church was concerned, Pym himself was not disposed at first to go further than this. The Constitutional Moderates in Church and State, however, were rapidly swept away. They can scarcely be said even to have made a serious stand betwixt the extreme influences that were hurrying the nation into conflict. Pym, who alone had the strength of brain and the Parliamentary influence to have converted them into a party, was himself hurried by the violence of his political resentments, and his too-well-founded suspicions of the king, into an increasing hostility to the royal cause. No Puritan himself, he yet laid the foundations of the

[1] i. 404, Oxford ed.

triumph of Puritanism. He headed the forces which were destined to subvert the Church to which he professed attachment.

When, with the progress of events, power passed into the hands of the Presbyterians, they sought to make a definite and authoritative stand for their principles. They were a compact and closely organised party, fully understanding what they meant, both in reference to Church and State. Constitutionalists in politics, dogmatists in religion, even more decisively than the Laudians whose excesses had done so much to provoke hostilities, they sought to stem the advancing tide of the revolution as soon as they had secured their religious ends. And if Charles had yielded sooner the demands of Scotland, and thrown himself upon the loyalty of the Presbyterian interest in both countries, it is probable that he might still have secured his throne and life, and the course of the revolution have been stayed. But the fanaticism of Charles played into the hands of the more powerful fanaticism which animated the soldiers of the Commonwealth, and left him a prey to their ambitious energy and fierce passion for rule. Presbyterianism in its turn was swept aside, and the revolution reached its height in the triumph of the army which its necessities had called into existence.

In the years 1646 and 1647, however, it was still uncertain what course things would take. Presbyterianism, as represented by the Parliaments in both kingdoms, had begun to lose credit; but it was still powerful. Some of the military chiefs, like Essex, still clung to it. The Westminster Assembly, the embodiment of its higher spiritual wisdom, still met and gave forth from time to time their deliverances. Especially the Scottish army in the north of England was unanimously and intensely Presbyterian, and would have been quite ready, as future events proved, to turn its arms against the revolution which it had done so much to advance, if the king would only have consented to its terms and accepted the Covenant, at least for Scotland. Charles, whose own forces had been entirely ruined after the battle of Naseby (June 1645), sought refuge in the Scottish camp in May 1646. The negotiations respecting the Covenant having failed with him, he was delivered under orders from the Scottish Parliament to the commissioners of the English Parliament on the 30th of January 1647. In the following June he was forcibly taken possession of by the English army, which had now turned its forces against the Parliament.

The summer of 1647 was therefore, as Heber indicates, a critical turning-point in the great struggle. There were at least three parties in the field—the King, the Presbyterians, and the Independents, represented by Cromwell and the army. Religious confusion imbittered civil discord. Sects were rising on all sides unfamiliar alike to Presbytery and Episcopacy. Out of the very growth of religious differences there had sprung a spirit of religious latitude. The Independents, whilst claiming freedom for themselves against the Presbyterians, could not deny some measure of the same freedom to Episcopalians. And accordingly, when they obtained possession of the king, they at once showed a greater deference to his religious scruples than the Parliament had done. His chaplains were admitted free access to his presence, and were allowed to conduct service before him according to the Book of Common Prayer. It seemed for a while as if there were an opening for general pacification through some adjustment of religious differences. It is, at any rate, to the immortal credit of Taylor that such a vision of religious accommodation, based on the most profound principles of religious truth and freedom, took hold on his mind and inspired his great work. Even such a voice as his was too feeble to quell the rage of contending factions, and to breathe toleration and charity into sternly agitated minds; but it remains, nevertheless, a living voice of wisdom long after the intolerant cries on one side and another have died away. It is only the natural fate of such a voice to be unheard in its first utterance; but the cause of truth, freedom, and charity, for which it pleads, is not destroyed, although resisted. "No truth spoken by God's Spirit," as Taylor himself says, "returns unperformed and ineffectual;" and therefore he adds :[1] — " I thought it might not misbecome my duty and endeavours to plead for peace and charity and forgiveness and permissions mutual; although I had reason to believe that, such is the iniquity of men, and they so indisposed to receive such impresses, that I had as good plough the sands, or till the air, as persuade such doctrines which destroy men's interests, and serve no end but the

[1] The Epistle Dedicatory, p. cccxcv., Heber's edition.

great end of a happy eternity, and what is in order to it. But because the events of things are in God's disposition, and I knew them not—and because, if I had known, my good purposes would be totally ineffectual as to others—yet my own designation and purpose would be of advantage to myself, who might, from God's mercy, expect the retribution which He is pleased to promise to all pious intendments; I resolved to encounter with all objections, and to do something to which I should be determined by the consideration of the present distemperatures and necessities, by my own thoughts, by the questions and scruples, the sects and names, the interests and animosities, which at this day, and for some years past, have exercised and disquieted Christendom."

Such, then, was the origin of the 'Liberty of Prophesying.' It sprang directly out of the necessities of the time,—out of those public concernments which, as Taylor says, in the same dedicatory epistle, so fixed his thoughts "that besides them he could not go." He could not keep his mind off the religious conflicts on which he looked; he saw nothing but prolonged confusion and an increase of enmities in the prevalent ways "of promoting the several opinions" which were then in vogue. In the rise of the Independents and their more liberal treatment of religious questions he may have seen an opening more favourable to his views than he even confesses; and he gave, if not with hopefulness, yet with a strong confidence in the righteousness and charity of his cause, his views to the public.

The substance of the argument of the 'Liberty of

Prophesying' is contained in the first two chapters of the work on the 'Nature of Faith' and the 'Nature of Heresy.' The principles which underlie his system of religious latitude or comprehension are fully unfolded in these chapters, and most of the remaining chapters are devoted to show the weakness of any other grounds of religious certitude and agreement than those which he has set forth. One of these chapters, however, on the "Practice of the Primitive Church," has a more practical and significant bearing. It treats of the rise of the idea of persecution in the Christian Church, and shows how greatly at variance it was with the course of Christian thought in the first ages and for long afterwards. In his lengthened dedicatory epistle he recurs to this subject, and brings forth more ample evidence bearing upon it. His whole treatment of this important subject is highly interesting and satisfactory. Then, his chapter on the "Case of the Anabaptists" deserves special mention. It is an admirable piece of pleading on behalf of a sect generally repudiated and condemned; and, indeed, with such a firm and even hand did Taylor hold the balance in estimating the arguments regarding baptism on either side, that many of his friends seem to have been doubtful to which side he himself inclined, and he was obliged to add an appendix containing " the Anabaptists' arguments " (as he had himself put them) "answered."

We shall do most justice to his argument by exhibiting, in the first instance, the principles on which it rests, and which appeared to him to form the only rational basis of religious certitude; and then by reviewing briefly, according to his own order and exposition, the several false or uncertain standards of religious truth which had been set up by contending parties.

Taylor opens his treatise with a brief statement of his general position, which is plainly identical with that of Chillingworth. Differences in religious opinion are declared to be inevitable. "So long as men had such variety of principles, such several constitutions, educations, tempers and distempers, hopes, interests, and weaknesses, degrees of light and degrees of understanding, it was impossible all should be of one mind. And what is impossible to be done is not necessary it should be done."[1] Variety of opinion must subsist in the nature of things; but variety of opinion need not breed, and cannot justify, the virulent hostilities of religious parties. It is quite possible for men to differ on really important questions, such as the validity or invalidity of a death-bed repentance, or the consequences of the doctrine of predetermination, and yet not fall into sects or break up communion on this account. The source of mischief is not in the diversity of thought, but in the want of charity and breadth of mind. Men are "so in love with their own fancies and opinions as to think faith and all Christendom are concerned in their support;" and so a theological dispute grows into "a quarrel in religion, and God is entitled to it;" and the person with whom we differ becomes to us an "enemy of God," whom we

[1] Introd.

think that it is a good service to God to persecute "even to death." "It is not the variety of understandings, but the disunion of wills and affections; it is not the several principles, but the several ends, that cause our miseries; our opinions commence and are upheld according as our turns are served, and our interests are preserved, and there is no cure for us but piety and charity."[1] The mischiefs which he deplores "proceed not from this, that all men are not of one mind, for that is neither necessary nor possible, but that every opinion is made an article of faith, every article a ground of quarrel, every quarrel makes a faction, every faction is zealous, and all zeal pretends for God, and whatsoever is for God cannot be too much; we by this time are come to that pass, we think we love not God except we hate our brother, and we have not the virtue of religion unless we persecute all religions but our own."[2] The "purpose of his discourse" is to discover the origin of such "errors and mischiefs," and so to indicate their cure and remedy.

1. The first and most important point to be considered is the "nature of faith;" for it is here that "the first and great mistake" of religious parties begins. Faith, he says, is not an "intellectual habit" directed towards certain doctrines or propositions, but simply a personal acceptance of Jesus Christ, and Him crucified. We may indifferently doubt or believe many things concerning God, "when the question is not concerning God's veracity" (for every Christian accepts what he knows to be re-

[1] Ibid. [2] Ibid.

vealed of God), "but whether God hath said so or no." "That which is of the foundation of faith, that only is necessary." The primitive creed was nothing more than belief in Jesus Christ as the Son of God and our Saviour. He quotes various texts in proof of this, from the enunciation of St Peter in Matt. xvi. 16, "We believe and are sure that Thou art Christ, the Son of the living God," to the "admirable creed" of St Paul, "This is the word of faith which we preach, that if thou shalt confess with thy mouth the Lord Jesus, and shalt believe in thine heart that God hath raised Him from the dead, thou shalt be saved."[1] These and many other instances show that the "entire complexion" of a Christian faith is contained in such a creed. The "act of believing" propositions has no "excellency" in itself; faith is only valuable as a means to an end. We are bound, indeed, to believe all "which we know our Great Master hath taught;" but salvation specially flows from belief in the great Gospel verities—"which have in them the endearments of our services, or the support of our confidence, or the satisfaction of our hopes; such as are—Jesus Christ, the Son of the living God, the crucifixion and resurrection of Jesus, forgiveness of sins by His blood, resurrection of the dead, and life eternal." "Salvation is promised to the explicit belief of those articles, and therefore those only are necessary, and those are sufficient."[2]

If any man will urge further, that whatsoever is deducible from these articles by necessary conse-

[1] Rom. x. 9. [2] Sect. i. 5.

quence—a favourite mode of argument with dogmatists both Puritan and sacerdotal—is necessary to be believed explicitly, Taylor answers—" It is true, if one sees the deduction and coherence of the parts; but it is not certain that any man shall be able to deduce whatsoever is immediately or certainly deducible from these premises; and then, since salvation is promised to the explicit belief of these, I see not how any man can justify the making the way to heaven narrower than Jesus Christ hath made it, it being already so narrow that there are few that find it." [1]

He then proceeds to show that the Apostles' Creed is the summary of such verities as are alone necessary for Christian salvation. He accepts the traditional view of this Creed as in the main composed by the apostles, or "holy men, their contemporaries and disciples;" but candidly admits that the clause as to Christ's descent into hell is not to be found in the original Creed, and is omitted in all the confessions of the Eastern Churches. If the Apostles' Creed contained all that was necessary to be believed in primitive times, he is quite at a loss to understand why it should not be equally adequate now. " If the apostles admitted all to their communion that believed this Creed, why shall we exclude any that preserve the same entire? Why is not our faith of these articles of as much efficacy for bringing us to heaven as it was in the churches apostolical? —who had guides more infallible, that might without error have taught them superstructures enough, if they had been necessary. And so they did; but that

[1] Sect. i. 5, 6.

they did not insert them into the Creed, when they might have done it with as much certainty as these articles, makes it clear to my understanding that other things were not necessary, but these were."[1]

He recurs to the enlargement of the Creed by deduction, and states his opinions more fully on this point. It was lawful for the apostles to draw out the "general article" of belief in Christ as the Son of God and Saviour of the world into the special clauses of the Apostles' Creed, because these are only the explicit expressions of what is contained in the general article, and they may be supposed to have had special divine guidance in what they did; but all further deductions, with a view to being made tests of communion or orthodoxy, are illegitimate. A man may, if he likes, extend his own creed. He may make "deductions" himself, but he is not bound "to follow another man's logic as an article of faith." "No such deduction is fit to be pressed on others as an article of faith." The Church, in short, "Has *power to intend our faith, but not to extend it —to make our belief more evident, but not more large and comprehensive.* For Christ and His apostles concealed nothing that was necessary to the integrity of Christian faith or salvation of our souls; Christ declared all the will of the Father, and the apostles were stewards and dispensers of the same mysteries, and were faithful in all the house, and therefore concealed nothing, but taught the whole doctrine of Christ. So they said themselves. And, indeed, if they did not teach all the doctrine of faith, an angel

[1] Sect. i. 10.

or a man might have taught us other things than what they taught, without deserving an anathema, but not without deserving a blessing for making up that faith entire which the apostles left imperfect." [1]

He entirely denies the right of the Church to add *credenda* to the Christian creed; to declare any article to be necessary " which before was not necessary." " By so doing she makes the narrow way to heaven narrower, and chalks out one path more to the devil than he had before. . . . The object of the Church's faith is in order of nature before the Church, or before the act and habit of faith, and therefore cannot be enlarged by the Church, any more than the act of the visive faculty can add visibility to the object." [2]

Such is Taylor's clear and decisive outline of the *nature* of faith, and hence of the only essential conditions of a Christian Church. All who believe in Jesus Christ as the Son of God and Saviour of the world, he was prepared to acknowledge as members of the Christian Church. Not only so, but he maintained that those who went beyond this—the ground of Christ Himself and of the apostles—were the real authors of schism and heresy. " Bodies of confession and articles," according to him, " do much hurt by becoming instruments of separating and dividing communions, and making unnecessary or uncertain propositions a certain means of schism and disunion. Men would do well to consider whether or no such proceedings do not derive the guilt of schism upon them who least think it; and whether

[1] Sect. i. 12.   [2] Ibid., p. 13.

of the two is the schismatic—he that makes unnecessary and (supposing the state of things) inconvenient impositions, or he that disobeys them, because he cannot, without doing violence to his conscience, believe them ?—he that parts communion, because without sin he could not entertain it, or they that have made it necessary for him to separate by requiring such conditions, which to no man are simply necessary, and to his particular case, either sinful or impossible ?"[1]

Profession of faith in the Apostles' Creed, therefore, constituted with Taylor the sole essential of Christian communion. He believed, indeed, Episcopacy to be a divinely sanctioned order. The Episcopal form of Church government was to him something more than it was to Chillingworth. In his view it appeared to have been committed to the apostles by Christ Himself. He had maintained as much in his 'Episcopacy Asserted.' But whatever were his own convictions on this subject, he did not press them as entering radically into the idea of the Church. In its full conception, the Church implied Episcopacy, but not in its essence. It was part of its wellbeing—its *bene esse*—but not of its mere being, or *esse*. All its essential life was to be found in *faith in Christ*. And looking forth on the wild dogmatic contentions of his time, he proclaimed this truth as one fitted to heal its divisions and enmities. If the Episcopalian, the Puritan—Presbyterian or Independent—the Sectary, whether Anabaptist or any other, could have been induced to

Sect. xxii. 1.

recognise what seemed to him so clearly true—and proved both in the light of Scripture and of apostolic practice—it might have been possible to have built up the breaches of the national Zion, or at least to have established relations of peace amidst the distracted parties into which the country was divided.

It can scarcely be doubted that Taylor, Episcopalian as he was, designed to teach his own party especially a wholesome lesson, and to lead them to recognise the validity of differences with which they could not sympathise. " It is a hard case," he says,[1] " that we should think all Papists, and Anabaptists, and Sacramentarians (Zwinglians ?) to be fools and wicked persons. Certainly among all these sects there are very many wise men and good men as well as erring." It was supercilious indifference to private opinions—or rather, a proud impatience and oppression of them—which had produced the revolution. Severe as was the education through which the national mind had to pass, it was by no means a profitless severity which had issued in the recognition of the principle so finely expressed by Taylor, that God alone is " Master of our souls, and hath a dominion over human understanding : and he that says this does not say that indifference (of religion) is persuaded, because God alone is judge of erring persons."[2]

2. Taylor follows up his explanation of faith by a very important chapter on the " Nature of Heresy." The two chapters require to be taken together in

[1] Epistle Dedicatory. [2] Ibid.

order fully to understand the eclectic spirit of his theological and ecclesiastical system. As Christ is with him the sole comprehensive object of faith, so it is opposition to Christ, or denial of Him as having come in the flesh to save sinners, which alone properly constitutes heresy. "It is observable that no heresies are noted 'signanter' in Scripture, but such as are great errors practical, 'in materia pietatis,' such whose doctrines taught impiety, or such who denied the coming of Christ directly or by consequence."[1] Heresy, in short, is "a wicked opinion, an ungodly doctrine,"[2] and is never applied to doubtful "speculative" propositions, "nor ever to pious persons." He insists greatly upon the latter point as unmistakably evident in every notice of heresy in the New Testament.

"Heresy is not an error of the understanding, but an error of the will. And this is clearly insinuated in Scripture, in the style whereof faith and a good life are made one duty, and vice is called opposite to faith, and heresy opposed to holiness and sanctity. . . . St Paul calls faith, or the form of sound words, κατ' εὐσέβειαν διδασκαλίαν—'the doctrine that is according to godliness.'"[3] And to believe in the truth, and to have pleasure in unrighteousness, are by the same apostle opposed. "If we remember that St Paul reckons heresy amongst the works of the flesh, and ranks it with all manner of practical impieties, we shall easily perceive that if a man

---

[1] Sect. ii. 2.
[2] "ἀσεβὴς δόξα καὶ ἀθέμιτος διδασκαλία."—*De Sancta Trinitate et Fide Catholica.* Ibid.
[3] 1 Tim. vi. 3; ibid., 8.

mingles not a vice with his opinion, if he be innocent in his life, although deceived in his doctrine, his error is his misery, not his crime."[1]

As the nature of faith, in short, is, so is the nature of heresy. Faith, if it be taken for an act of the understanding merely, has no value except to improve the understanding, "as strength doth the arm, or beauty the face." It is only when it mixes charity with it that it becomes moral or religious. And so error which springs from involuntary causes, from ignorance of the truth or mistake regarding it, is no heresy in the New Testament sense; but only such as springs from ambition, wilful sectarianism, love of pre-eminence as in Diotrephes, or love of lucre, "as it was in some that were of the circumcision."[2] "In all the animadversions against errors made by the apostles in the New Testament, no pious person was condemned, no man that did invincibly err, or *bona mente;* but something that was amiss in

---

[1] Ibid.
[2] Ibid., 9. Further on in the same section, he says, in a passage of sterling truth and force: "Error is not heresy formally, and an erring person may be a Catholic. A wicked person in his error becomes heretic, when the good man in the same error shall have all the rewards of faith. For whatever an ill man believes, if he therefore believe it because it serves his own ends, be his belief true or false, the man hath an heretical mind; for to serve his own ends his mind is prepared to believe a lie. But a good man that believes what, according to his light and upon the use of his moral industry, he thinks true, whether he hits upon the right or no, because he hath a mind desirous of truth, and prepared to believe every truth, is therefore acceptable to God, because nothing hindered him from it but what he could not help—his misery and his weakness, which being imperfections merely natural, which God never punishes, he stands fair for a blessing of his morality, which God always accepts." —22.

genere morum, was that which the apostles did redargue. And it is very considerable that even they of the circumcision, who, in so great numbers, did heartily believe in Christ, and yet most violently retain circumcision, and without question went to heaven in great numbers; yet of the number of these very men, when they grew covetous, and for filthy lucre's sake taught the same doctrine which others did in the simplicity of their hearts, then they turned heretics, and Titus was commanded to look to them, and to silence them."[1]

So broadly and leniently does he fix the character of heresy, that he is careful to discriminate between an obstinacy of wilful persistence of error, which is highly criminal, and such an obstinacy as may spring from a "resolution of understanding which it is not in a man's power honestly to alter."[2] If a man cannot see reason for altering his opinion, he not only may lawfully, but he must honestly maintain it; only he should do so in the spirit of love and peace, as St Cyprian did, who persisted until death in his opinion of the necessity of rebaptising heretics, but in such a way as not to have "his obstinacy called criminal, or his own error turned into heresy."[3] "No man is a heretic against his will."[4] And if it be pretended that "every man that is deceived is therefore proud, because he does not submit his understanding to the authority of God, and so his error becomes heresy," to this he answers, just as Chillingworth did in the same case, "that there is no Christian man but will submit his understanding to God, always provided

[1] Titus, i. 10, 11; ibid., 7. [2] Ibid., 10. [3] Ibid. [4] Ibid., 12.

he knows that God hath said so."[1] Submission to authority, in short, is a good principle, which every Christian man recognises; but the recognition of the principle is no warrant of any special application made of it. All the force of the principle depends in every case upon the character of the authority. Is it truly divine? then it claims universal submission. All who acknowledge God will acknowledge God's authority. But then it must be evident that the authority *is divine*, and nothing short of this, or different from this. And so " the whole business of submitting our understanding to human authority comes to nothing; for either it resolves itself into the direct duty of submitting to God, or, if it be spoken of abstractedly, it is no duty at all." [2]

Having thus defined the nature of heresy, he occupies the rest of the chapter with a somewhat detailed review of the various heresies in the early Christian centuries. Even after the apostolic time, he shows that no men were really esteemed heretics unless they either " taught practical impieties or denied an article of the Creed."[3] So long as the " foundation " was preserved entire, great liberty of opinion was permitted, and no man's error was condemned as heresy. But the further men went from the apostles, " the more forward were they in numbering heresies."[4] And the state of the Church in the second and third centuries appears to Taylor to have promoted this growth of heresies; for as yet there was no general court or council of appeal on disputed questions. Bishops were, for the most part,

[1] Ibid., 12.   [2] Ibid.   [3] Ibid., 14.   [4] Ibid., 17.

independent in their respective provinces, and there was no principle or criterion of Christian judgment "besides the single dictates or decretals of private bishops." Scripture was professed to be authoritative by all, but the question was, as to the meaning of it. This multiplication of episcopal authority, in matters of opinion, has led, according to him, to great confusion and misconception in the traditional lists or catalogues of heretics; some men being condemned for opinions the very reverse of what they held, as Montanus is by Epiphanius and others, as Nicholas the Deacon of Antioch is by Jerome, having their views completely misrepresented by a perversion or exaggeration of their language. The example of Cyprian, however, shows that there was no curtailment of Christian liberty within the Church even during the third century. A liberty of prophesying or of interpretation was not forbidden to any one, "if he transgressed not the foundation of faith and the Creed of the Apostles."[1]

The first violation of this freedom was "when general councils came in, and the symbols were enlarged, and new articles were made as much of necessity to be believed as the Creed of the Apostles, and damnation threatened to them that did dissent." He expresses this opinion all the more forcibly because he has no quarrel with "the enlarging of the Creed which the Council of Nice made." It appears to him to have been an enlargement in the true sense of the apostles. But to others it appears in a different light. They think that the Church would

[1] Ibid., 23.

have been more happy "if she had not been in some sense constrained to alter the simplicity of her faith, and make it more curious and articulate, so much that he had need to be a subtle man to understand the very words of the new determinations." According to them, and evidently also according to his own view, "Those creeds are best which keep the very words of Scripture; and that faith is best which hath greatest simplicity; and it is better in all cases humbly to submit, than curiously to inquire and pry into the mystery under the cloud, and to hazard our faith by improving our knowledge."[1] The Nicene Fathers are admitted to have done well in their peculiar circumstances in enlarging and defining the Creed; yet they would have done still better, Taylor thinks, in leaving it undefined. For an authoritative definition, as in the case of the ὁμοούσιον, although it may be of good use "to determine the judgment of indifferent persons," is apt to be "a weapon of affront" against the scrupulous in the hands of "persons of confident and imperious understandings;" while "they against whom the decision is do the more readily betake themselves to the defensive, and are engaged upon contestation and public enmities for such articles which either might safely be unknown or with much charity disputed."[2] "Therefore," he adds, "the Nicene Council, although it have the advantage of an acquired and prescribing authority, yet it must not become a precedent to others; lest the inconveniences of multiplying more articles upon as great pretence of reason as then,

[1] Ibid., 27.   [2] Ibid., 33.

make the act of the Nicene Fathers, in straitening prophesying and enlarging the Creed, become accidentally an inconvenience."[1]

The power is a dangerous one, although in this case it was well exercised. It is like an arbitrary power, which, so long as it takes only sixpence from the subject, produces no inconvenience, but which, by the same reason, may take a hundred pounds, and then a thousand. And so sensible of this were the early Fathers themselves, that, as is well known, they pronounced at the Council of Ephesus anathema on all those who should add anything to the Creed.[2] "And yet for all this," he continues, "the Church of Rome added the clause 'Filioque' to the article of the procession of the Holy Ghost, and what they have done since all the world knows. All men were persuaded that it was most reasonable the limits of faith should be no more enlarged, but yet enlarged it themselves, and bound others from doing it, like an intemperate father, who, because he knows he does ill himself, enjoins temper-

---

[1] Ibid., 33.

[2] Taylor says "the Creed of Constantinople," following the common tradition which ascribes the enlargement of the third part of the Creed to the second Ecumenical Council which met at Constantinople in 381. But it is now well known that in the records of this council there is no trace of any additions having been proposed or made to the Creed of Nicæa. This Creed, on the contrary, is appealed to in its primary form as adequate for all theological purposes. It was not till the fourth general council, in 451, that the Creed now known as "that of Constantinople," or sometimes spoken of as the "Niceno-Constantinopolitan," crept into use, and became generally professed by the Christian Church, with the exception of the Nestorians, who had been previously separated from the general Church at Chalcedon in 431.

ance to his son, but continues to be intemperate himself." [1]

Of the Athanasian Creed it may be supposed Taylor expresses a very modified approval. For the articles themselves, he is persuaded of their truth; yet he admits that to many people they are unintelligible, contrary to reason, and in their "curiosities of explication unwarranted by Scripture." The "damnatory appendix" is entirely unjustifiable; "because 'citra hoc symbolum,' the faith of the apostles is entire; and 'he that believeth and is baptised shall be saved.'" [2] Admitting the Creed to be the production of Athanasius, there is no evidence that he designed it as a symbol of communion. According to Aquinas it was made "non per modum symboli, sed per modum doctrinæ," that it is "not with a purpose to impose it upon others, but with confidence to declare his own belief." To prescribe it to others as a creed was the act of the bishops of Rome. But it is doubtful, Taylor recognises, whether it be the Creed of Athanasius at all, the original being evidently Latin, and not Greek.[3] He affirms, at the same time, that even the Athanasian Creed makes no pretence of adding any new articles to the Christian faith, but simply of explaining further the "articles apostolical." If it be maintained that the explanations are to be received as necessarily "of faith" as the dogmatical articles of the Apostles' Creed," Taylor abandons their defence. But the

[1] Ibid., 35.
[2] Ibid., 36.
[3] Ibid. His words are—" This Creed was written originally in Latin, which in all reason Athanasius did not, it being apparent that the Latin copy is but one, but the Greek is various."

saying of Athanasius, " This is the Catholic faith," is at least a warrant that " no man can say of any other article that it is a part of the Catholic faith, or that the Catholic faith can be enlarged beyond the contents of that symbol."

In conclusion, he recurs to the Apostles' Creed as the only necessary symbol of Christian communion. It was so in the early Christian age; and "dare any man tax that proceeding of remissness and indifference in religion?" The Creed is an adequate security of faith. It contains implicitly, if not explicitly, all other articles; and "it is better the implication should continue than that by an explication the Church should be troubled with questions and uncertain determinations, and factions enkindled, and animosities set on foot, and men's souls endangered, who before were secure by the explicit belief of all that the apostles required as necessary."[1]

The sum of his argument is, that whereas the nature of faith is in all cases moral, and not merely intellectual, binding us to honour Christ, and to obey Him, so heresy "is to be judged by its proportion and analogy to faith." Heresy is only that which is against faith in the true sense—that is to say, which strikes at the foundation of Christianity embodied in the Apostles' Creed, or "teaches ill life." All other propositions which are "extrinsical to these two considerations," whether they be true or false, are not heretical.

3. In the six following sections of his work, Taylor

[1] Ibid., 40.

passes under review the alleged special sources of authority in religious opinion: Scripture, Tradition, Ecclesiastical Councils, the Pope, and the Fathers. He adds a brief section on the "Church in its diffusive capacity," and the "Pretence of the Spirit." But he thinks it unnecessary to consider these at length. For the Church must either "speak by tradition, or by a representative body in a council, by Popes, or by the Fathers."[1] It is not "a chimera or shadow,[2] but a company of men believing in Jesus Christ," whose opinions can only be known by one or other of those channels. The pretence of the Spirit, again, even if admissible, is "impertinent" to the question, because in its nature it is only of private application. Such "infallible assistance," he says, "may determine my own assent, but shall not enable me to prescribe to others."[3] The other professed sources of infallibility deserve more particular consideration, and may be viewed together as a distinct division of his work.

(a.) All "necessary" articles of faith, as well as of practice, are "plainly and clearly set down in Scripture." The Gospel is not hid except to them

---

[1] Sect. ix. 1.

[2] Coleridge quarrels with Taylor as to these expressions, in his peculiar manner (Notes, &c., i. 225.) But here as elsewhere in his elaborate "notes" on the 'Liberty of Prophesying,' he mistakes Taylor, and makes no allowance for his special point of view and the context of the argument. Taylor had no intention of denying the substantive entity of the Church, but merely wished to make it clear that its voice could only be known through some definite channel. Coleridge is thinking more of himself and of his own transcendentalism, than of doing justice to Taylor; and this pretentious egoism runs unpleasantly through all his 'Notes on English Divines.'

[3] Ibid., 3.

who refuse to see and acknowledge it. But beyond such a simple knowledge of the truth as makes us "wise unto salvation," there is no infallible declaration of theological opinion in Scripture, or, at least, men have no infallible means of determining what this opinion is. "Besides those things which are so plainly set down, 'some for doctrine,' as St Paul says—that is, for articles and foundation of faith—some for instruction, some for reproof, some for comfort—that is, in matters practical and speculative—of several tempers and constitutions; there are innumerable places, containing in them great mysteries, but yet either so enwrapped with a cloud, or so darkened with umbrages, or heightened with expressions, or so covered with allegories and garments of rhetoric, so profound in the matter, or so altered or made intricate in the manner, in the clothing and dressing, that God may seem to have left them as trials of our industry, and arguments of our imperfections, and incentives to the longings after heaven, and the clearest revelations of eternity, and as occasions and opportunities of our mutual charity, and toleration to each other, and humility in ourselves, rather than the repositories of faith and furniture of creeds and articles of belief."[1]

He dwells at some length on the varieties of copies and readings of Holy Scripture, on the many senses and designs of expounding it, its figurative and double meanings. What he says on these subjects is not much to the point, and modern criticism would not stumble at some of the difficulties he sets

[1] Sect. iii. 2.

forth. His general argument, however, remains quite untouched by any progress of criticism. Where a question arises as to the meaning of Scripture, we have no means of determining it "infallibly and certainly." No one is entitled to dictate to another as to what he shall accept as the meaning of Scripture, and the necessity hence arises of "allowing a liberty in prophesying without prescribing authoritatively to other men's consciences, and becoming lords and masters of their faith." After explaining various ways of reaching the meaning of Scripture, by " the context and connection of the parts," by "the conference of places," by "a proportion and analogy of reason," by "the analogy of faith," and, lastly, by "consulting the originals," he concludes that all these ways— "Which of themselves are good helps, are made, either by design or by our infirmities, ways of intricating and involving Scripture in greater difficulty—because men do not learn their doctrines from Scripture, but come to the understanding of Scripture with preconceptions and ideas of doctrines of their own; and then no wonder that Scriptures look like pictures, wherein every man in the room believes that they look on him only, and that wheresoever he stands, or how often soever he changes his station. So that now what was intended for a remedy becomes the promoter of our disease, and our meat becomes the matter of sickness; and the mischief is, the wit of man cannot find a remedy for it; for there is no rule, no limit, no certain principle by which all men may be guided to a certain and so infallible an interpretation that he can with any equity prescribe to others to believe his interpretations in places of controversy or ambiguity."[1]

And in evidence of this, Taylor proceeds to show that, even in the case of what appears to many so clear and determinate a prophecy as that of Jacob about the sceptre not departing from Judah "till Shiloh come," the Jews have no fewer than twenty-six explanations; while in reference to the diversity of St James and St Paul regarding Justification—a diversity, he adds, "to my understanding, very easy to reconcile"—Osiander observes, in his confutation of the book which Melanchthon wrote against him, that there are twenty several opinions concerning Justification, all drawn from the Scriptures by men only of the Augustine Confession." "There are," Taylor adds, "sixteen several opinions concerning Original Sin, and as many definitions of the Sacraments as there are sects of men that disagree about them."[1] The result of the two chapters which he devotes to the consideration of Holy Scripture is, that, while it contains plainly, in a manner apparent to all, the articles of the Apostles' Creed, which are therefore of "simple and prime necessity," there is nothing further which "a wise man" would wish to have imposed upon himself, or which "a just man" would wish to impose upon others. A liberty of prophesying and interpreting Scripture is, therefore, the right of every man—"a necessity derived from the consideration of the difficulty of Scripture in

[1] Sect. iv. 6.   [2] Ibid.

questions controverted, and the uncertainty of any internal medium of interpretation." [1]

(*b.*) Tradition, which he next considers, is affirmed to be as fallible as anything else. The Fathers themselves possessed no consistent traditional guide. On the contrary, they were "infinitely deceived in their account and enumerations of traditions." [2] And the further we descend from the fountain-head of the Christian revelation, the more varying and contradictory is found to be the course of tradition. Augustine maintained the communicating of infants to be an apostolic tradition; and many other things, notoriously of later and corrupt growth, were traced back to a primitive sanction. On the other hand, many things of apostolic custom have "expired and gone out in a desuetude—such as abstinence from blood and things strangled—the cœnobitic life of secular persons—the college of widows—to worship standing upon the Lord's Day—to give milk and honey to the newly baptised—and many more of the like nature." [3] Moreover, the Fathers themselves are found to appeal from tradition and custom to Holy Scripture. Irenæus, Basil, Jerome, Augustine, Athanasius, and divers others, all unite in the saying of St Paul, "nemo sentiat super quod scriptum est." [4] All, in effect, maintain that every article of faith is sufficiently recorded in Holy Scripture, and that "the judgment of faith and heresy is to be derived from thence" alone.[5]

[1] Sect. iv. 8.
[2] Sect. v. 3.
[3] Ibid., 8.
[4] Ibid., 11.
[5] Ibid.

CHRISTIAN TEACHING WITHIN THE CHURCH. 401

(*c.*) The judgment of general councils carries with them no further weight than belongs to their intrinsic reasonableness. They have no promise of supernatural direction beyond what belongs to every individual. Every private man will be assisted sufficiently by the Holy Spirit "in order to that end to which he needs assistance; and therefore much more shall general councils, in order to that end for which they convene, and to which they need assistance—that is, in order to the conservation of faith, for the doctrinal rules of good life, and all that concerns the essential duty of a Christian, but not in deciding questions to satisfy contentious or curious or presumptuous spirits."[1] He explains how general councils have never been pronounced by the Church and never been accepted as infallible; how they have contradicted each other, and in some cases been notoriously corrupt. The opinion of Gregory Nazianzen is quoted to the effect that he had such a poor opinion of councils of bishops that he had "never known one of them come to any good and prosperous issue, or which did not rather tend to the increase than the diminution of wickedness."[2] He refrains, at the same time, from endorsing this opinion, and sets forth in a fair and discriminating manner what he conceives to be the true uses of Church councils. They may be "excellent instruments of peace," "rare sermons for determining a point in controversy," and possess "the greatest probability from human authority;" but further he knew nothing they can pretend to be, "with reason and argument

---
[1] Sect. vi. I.   [2] Epistle to Procopius; ibid., 11.

sufficient to satisfy any wise man." There never was any council so general that it might not have been more general, in respect of the whole Church. Even that of Nice itself was but a small assembly. There is no decree so well constituted but it may be proved by an argument higher than the authority of a council. General councils are therefore, in their several degrees, "excellent guides for the prophets, and directions and instructions for their prophesying; but not of weight and authority to restrain their liberty so wholly but that they may dissent where they see a reason strong enough to persuade them."[1]

(d.) It is unnecessary to dwell upon his special argument respecting the claim of Papal infallibility. He first deals with the usual Scriptural argument as to the special powers alleged to be vested in the apostle Peter, and then, making the supposition that there is something in these arguments, which he does not allow, he points out the absurdity of the Pope claiming to represent St Peter. So far from the Popes or their successors having any claim to expound the truth infallibly, there have been among them some "notorious heretics and preachers of false doctrines; some that made impious decrees, both in faith and manners; some that have determined questions with egregious ignorance and stupidity; some with apparent sophistry, and many to serve their own ends most openly."[2] In short, he comes to the conclusion that, if he were bound to call any man master upon earth, he would, "of all men, least follow him that pretends he is infallible,

[1] Ibid., 12.   [2] Sect. vii. 15.

and cannot prove it. For that he cannot prove it makes me as uncertain as ever; and that he pretends to infallibility makes him careless of using such means which will morally secure those wise persons who, knowing their own aptness to be deceived, use what endeavours they can to secure themselves from error, and so become the better and more probable guides."[1]

(*e.*) The inconsistencies of the Fathers, and their consequent disability to determine questions with certainty and truth, are next insisted upon in a separate section. He points out the various topics on which they have disagreed, and the errors, such as Chiliasm and infant-communicating, which have widely prevailed among them. He alludes to Daillé's well-known work, 'Du vrai Usage des Pères,' then lately published, and seems to coincide with its general conclusions. At the same time he abstains from "all disparagement of these worthy personages, who were excellent lights to their several dioceses and cures. . . . It is not to be denied but that great advantages are to be made by their writings, 'all of them containing some probable things, according to their wisdom.' If one wise man," he adds forcibly, "says a thing, it is an argument to me to believe in its degree of probation—that is, proportionable to such an assent as the authority of a wise man can produce, and when there is nothing against it that is greater. But that which I complain of is, that we look upon wise men that lived long ago with so much veneration, and mistake that we reverence

[1] Ibid., 18.

them not for having been wise men, but that they lived long since."[1]

4. Having thus examined and discarded all these several sources of pretended authority in theological opinion, he turns, in a very pregnant and interesting section,[2] to discuss "the authority of reason, and that it, proceeding upon best grounds, is the best judge." His conclusions here are substantially the same as those of Chillingworth. Reason and private judgment must be the last authority of every man in the face of Scripture. Both of them would have strongly repudiated what in our days is known as Rationalism, or the exaltation of the private understanding in the place of divine revelation. It never occurred to them to doubt the reality of revelation, and its supremacy over the conscience and reason. The question is not one as to the ultimate source of religious truth. This was admitted beyond doubt to be the divine revelation in Scripture. But, admitting this, there remained the question as to the interpretation of this revelation; and here it is that both Chillingworth and Taylor assert in the strongest manner the claims of reason. What the truth is as revealed in Scripture every man must "be trusted to judge for himself. I say," he adds, "every man that can judge at all; as for others, they are to be saved as it pleaseth God." "He that follows his own reason, not guided only by natural arguments, but by divine revelation and all other good means, hath great advantages over him that follows any human guide whatsoever, because he follows all

[1] Sect. viii. 3.   [2] Sect. x.

their reason and his own too."[1] In the conscientious exercise of private judgment there is, in short, the best security for right religious opinions; and if, with all our pains and diligence to investigate the truth, we should, after all, fall into error, it is to be borne in mind that "it is not required of us not to be in error, but that we may endeavour to avoid it." This last touch is extremely like Chillingworth. It is the very echo of his manly sense and charity; and the whole of the section reminds us of some of the best passages in the 'Religion of Protestants.' Intelligent inquiry is enforced as a Christian duty no less than intelligent obedience. We are commanded to "search the Scriptures," to "try the spirits, whether they be of God or no; to try all things, and to retain that which is best. For he that resolves not to consider, resolves not to be careful whether he hath truth or no, and therefore hath an affection indifferent to truth or falsehood, which is all one as if he did choose amiss." And not only is inquiry a duty, it is a necessity for every man. All men really follow the guidance of their own judgment in some degree, although they may profess to follow other guides. If they accept the Church on tradition or a certain sense of Scripture, it is because they have some reason for what they do. "Although all men are not wise, and proceed discreetly, yet all make their choice some way or other. He that chooses to please his fancy takes his choice as much as he that chooses prudently. And no man speaks more unreasonably than he that denies to

[1] Sect. v. 2.

men the use of their reason in choice of their religion."[1]

It will be seen, therefore, that the general position of Taylor in the 'Liberty of Prophesying' is identical with that of Chillingworth in the 'Religion of Protestants.' The conclusions which the latter reaches in a special conflict with the resurgent spirit of Romanism in England in the time of Laud, the former maintains professedly in a treatise written with a view to still the strife of ecclesiastical bigotry and faction in the time of the civil war. Chillingworth shows a firmer mastery of principles, a more downright and vigorous thoughtfulness, in the midst of all the special details of his argument; but Taylor draws out his principles with a more comprehensive range and purpose, and sets the problem of his time —the reconstitution of the Church on an evangelical yet tolerant basis—in a more definite light. This problem appears in Chillingworth's pages only indirectly. But this is expressly the question which Taylor set himself to solve in the view of the jarring parties of his time. His solution is that the Church should rest on the Apostles' Creed—neither more nor less; and that there should be the widest toleration of opinions ranging from Anabaptism to Popery. He devotes a special section to the discussion of the case of the Anabaptists, and concludes that as " there is no direct impiety in their opinion," and so much which may be fairly urged in its defence, they are to be " redargued or instructed," but in

[1] Ibid., 5.

no respect to be coerced. His liberality towards a sect so hateful to all classes of dogmatists in the seventeenth century, and the extremely impartial manner in which he had set forth what might tend in behalf of their opinions, involved him in special suspicion, and he felt himself under the necessity of answering, in an appendix, his own arguments on behalf of this sect. Nothing is more creditable to Taylor than his frank liberality in this case, as nothing can better illustrate the intolerant spirit of the seventeenth century dogmatism than the obligation under which he felt of showing that his "meaning" was "innocent;" and that while maintaining that an ample case could be made out for the toleration of the Anabaptists, he did not mean in any respect to weaken what he believed to be the truth, or "to discourage the right side." To Taylor there was no error intolerable which was not impious or licentious, opposed to the fundamental principles of the Christian religion or to good morals and government; and the Christian Church, instead of seeking to narrow its terms of communion, was bound by every consideration of Christian truth and policy to open its doors as widely as possible for all who would come in. The "faith of the apostles" entitles all who hold it to "the communion of saints." "To make the way to heaven straiter than God made it, or to deny to communicate with those whom God will vouchsafe to be invited, and to refuse our charity to those who have the same faith because they have not all our opinions, is impious and schismatical; it infers tyranny on one part, and persuades and tempts to uncharitableness and animosities on both."[1]

There is no reason why individual Christians should not communicate with Churches of "different persuasions." If they require no impiety or anything unlawful as the condition of their communion, communion with them merely implies that we acknowledge them "as servants of Christ, as disciples of His doctrine, and subjects to His laws," while their "particular distinguishing doctrine" has no effect with us.

Beyond the primitive *facts* of the Gospel, in short, Taylor does not recognise any valid basis for the Christian Church, or any valid terms of Christian communion. He was, no doubt, as we have seen, himself an earnest defender of Episcopacy. For the perfect order of the Church he would certainly have maintained the necessity of Episcopal government and of liturgical worship. His writings leave this beyond question. But that Episcopacy or a liturgy has anything to do essentially with a man being a Christian, or with the recognition of Christian brotherhood, is an opinion opposed to the whole spirit of his great treatise, and to many of its express statements. A Christian is one who accepts Christ as his Saviour and Lord, and orders his life under the inspiration of this simple but mighty faith; a Christian Church is a society of men who acknowledge the same faith and walk by the same rule. These are the essentials; all else is accidental. No error is damnable which may be held with an honest

[1] Sect. xxi. 1.

mind. " It concerns all persons to see that they do their best to find out truth; and if they do, it is certain that, let the error be never so damnable, they shall escape the error or the misery of being damned for it. And if God will not be angry with men for being invincibly deceived, why should men be angry one at another?"[1] "All opinions in which the public interests of the commonwealth, and the foundation of faith and a good life, are not concerned, are to be permitted freely. 'Let every one be persuaded in his own mind,' was the doctrine of St Paul, and that is argument and conclusion too; and they were excellent words which St Ambrose said in attestation of this great truth,—' Imperial authority has no right to interdict the liberty of speaking, or sacerdotal authority to prevent the speaking of what you think."[2]

Nothing can be more beautiful than the close of Taylor's treatise. It condenses in a parable the whole pith of his argument; and the effect lingers in the memory as a lofty strain of music which has melted into pathos ere it dies. " I end with a story," he says, "which I find in the Jews' books." It was long doubtful whether Taylor did not mean under this indefinite nomenclature to hide an invention of his own rich and beautiful fancy; but, as Heber explains, the source of the story has at length been discovered, not in a Jewish work, but in a tale of the Persian poet Saadi. The story is as follows: "When Abraham sat at his tent-door, according to

---

[1] Sect. xxii. 3.
[2] "Nec imperiale est, libertatem dicendi negare; nec sacerdotale quod sentias non dicere."—Ibid.

his custom, waiting to entertain strangers, he espied an old man stooping and leaning on his staff, weary with age and travail, coming towards him, who was an hundred years of age. He received him kindly, washed his feet, provided supper, caused him to sit down; but observing that the old man sat and prayed not, nor begged for a blessing on his meat, he asked him why he did not worship the God of heaven. The old man told him that he worshipped the fire only, and acknowledged no other God. At which answer Abraham grew so zealously angry that he thrust the old man out of his tent, and exposed him to all the evils of the night and an unguarded condition. When the old man was gone, God called to Abraham and asked him where the stranger was; he replied, 'I thrust him away because he did not worship Thee.' God answered him, 'I have suffered him these hundred years, although he dishonoured me; and couldst not thou endure him one night, when he gave thee no trouble?' Upon this, saith the story, Abraham fetched him back again, and gave him hospitable entertainment and wise instruction." "Go thou and do likewise," he adds, "and thy charity will be rewarded by the God of Abraham."

The lesson is one, unhappily, which requires constant repetition in the history of the Christian Church.

VII.

EDWARD STILLINGFLEET—THE IRENICUM OF A COMPREHENSIVE CHURCH.

THE life of Stillingfleet does not belong to our subject. His main activity as a theological writer and as a Churchman is associated with the Church of the Restoration and Revolution, to the defence and maintenance of which he brought something of the tolerant and enlightened spirit which he had learned at Cambridge, and which finds expression in the 'Irenicum,' but with whose narrowness and meanness of policy he was, upon the whole, identified. In a certain measure he remained true to his early convictions, as the lengthened preface to the treatise on the 'Unreasonableness of Separation' shows. He had nothing to do with the Act of Uniformity (his youth happily saved him from this), or with any of the persecuting Acts of the reign of Charles II. Even in his controversy with Owen and Baxter he cannot be said to have occupied the illiberal side. But withal he lacked vitality of liberal conviction, and a generous trust in his own principles to save and bless the Church for which he was so zealous. He was a specimen, in short, of many men, both Churchmen and politicians, whose early liberalism degenerates with their advancement in life, under the pressure of those class feelings which grow with the growth of all but the most open, honest, and rational natures. Their liberalism is the result of education, or of temporary enthusiasm, or the excitement of the times in which they live; but it never works thoroughly into their reason so as to illuminate, control, and guide it. Traditionalism, in consequence, by-and-by regains ascendancy over them. The snares of office or the deceitfulness of party choke the good seed of liberal feeling, and gradually it wears away. And men of this stamp, who gloried in their youth in bearing some banner of reform, often become at last the most jealous guardians of official dogma, and the most unreasoning critics of new ideas.

If Stillingfleet cannot be accused of formal apostasy from his early principles, his career as a rising Churchman, his natural temper, and his somewhat cold, hard, and argumentative, rather than rational turn of mind, easily inclined him to the winning side in his time, and made him in his later years look back upon the 'Irenicum' as a mere youthful essay, conceived rather out of "tenderness towards the Dissenters"[1] than in the interests of truth and peace. This is not the language of a man who thoroughly understood and prized the principles of religious liberty. Nor does the life, which narrowed rather than broadened in sympathy, and which grew more

---

[1] "A book written twenty years since with great tenderness towards Dissenters *before the laws* *were established.*"—Preface to the 'Unreasonableness of Separation,' 1680.

limited and precise instead of more profound and comprehensive in its intellectual range, mingle in the thread of our history.

The following bare statement of facts, therefore, must suffice as an introduction to our review of the 'Irenicum.'

Edward Stillingfleet was a native of Cranbourne, in Dorsetshire, where he was born in the year 1635. He was educated at St John's College, Cambridge, and distinguished himself by " his singular ingenuity and constant improvement." His course of study extended from 1648 to 1655, when the new school of Cambridge divines, represented by Whichcote, and John Smith, and Cudworth, was in the full height of its activity. This of itself is sufficient to account for Stillingfleet's liberal leanings. Cambridge was now, rather than Oxford, the centre of the liberal theological movement. The wave of rational thought had, in the course of ten eventful years, passed from the one university to the other, and there taken a wider shape and influence, extending not merely to ecclesiastical questions, but to the whole field of religion and the sources of philosophical and moral truth. The rise, progress, and results of the school known as the Cambridge Platonists, await investigation. In the mean time, it is enough to fix and mark the significance of the fact that Stillingfleet was educated in the midst of it. He could not help catching something of the spirit which pervaded the place; and if he did not come under its deeper influences, yet both the 'Origines Sacræ' and 'Irenicum' show that his mind had been thoroughly awakened to the religious problems of his time, and that he had learned something of the rational Christian eclecticism, through which alone these problems could have been solved fairly, and the country saved from the disgraceful iniquities of the Restoration.

Stillingfleet passed from Cambridge to be tutor to the family of Sir Francis Burgoin, in Warwickshire, and subsequently to Nottingham, as tutor to the eldest son of a Mr Pierrepoint, connected with the Marquis of Dorchester. Here he is said to have begun—presumably in 1656—the 'Irenicum.' It was not completed, however, till three years later, and probably he made little progress with it till settled as rector of Sutton, to which living he was appointed by his earliest patron, Sir Francis Burgoin, in 1657. He was episcopally ordained by Dr Brownrig, one of the ejected bishops, a fact of which much is made by the panegyrical biographer, who has sketched his life in very dull and unmeaning outline as an introduction to the folio edition of his works.[1] The young rector of Sutton was in the full flush of his well-trained faculties, fresh from the generous intellectual life of Cambridge, with his mind keenly alive to the ecclesiastical difficulties of the age. He felt that he could do something to help these difficulties. The 'Irenicum' was the result. It was published in 1659, on the eve of the Restoration, and reprinted three years later, in 1662, the year in which the Act of Uniformity was passed. This was the answer which the age gave by a severe irony of

[1] 1710.

criticism to his eclectic proposal. In the same year appeared his 'Origines Sacræ, or a Rational Account of the Christian Faith as to the Truth and Divine Authority of the Scriptures, and the matter therein contained.'

The chief events of Stillingfleet's life henceforth are summed up in his successive promotions and controversies. He was appointed Rector of St Andrew's, Holborn, in 1665; first a Canon, and then Dean of St Paul's (1680?); and, finally, Bishop of Worcester, 1689. He distinguished himself in conflict with the Papists, the Deists and Atheists of the time, the Socinians, and the new school of philosophy represented by Locke. It is impossible not to admire with Clarendon "the strength and vigour of ratiocination and the clearness of style and expression" in his several writings. He is a skilful, well-trained, powerful controversialist. Whether he appears as a pseudonymous assailant of the Papal religion and policy, or as an advocate of the foundations of Christian belief, or as a defender of the doctrine of the Atonement or the doctrine of the Trinity, which he considered to be imperilled by Locke's theory of ideas, he shows the facility, vigour, and hopefulness of a well-disciplined intellect, and a copious store of argumentative resources. He is a theological champion, an ecclesiastical giant-killer, who watches continually from the sacred ramparts for the foes of the Church —Papal, Separatist, Philosophical—and goes forth with elate and joyous heart to meet and overthrow them. But with all his vigour and clearness there are none of his writings which have much life of thought. They are clever, able, and were eminently successful in their day; but they lack the vital interest which only some spark of nature, some fire of passion, or some glow of meditative or speculative genius can give to theological polemics. His youthful essay is, in many respects, his highest work. It possesses nearly all the argumentative force, the masterly logic, of his later writings; while it is distinguished above them all by catholicity of spirit, by rapidity, animation, and concinnity of treatment.

The full title of the essay is ' Irenicum, a Weapon Salve for the Church's Wound; or, the Divine Right of Particular Forms of Church Government, discussed and examined according to the principles of the Law of Nature, the positive Law of God, the practice of the Apostles and the primitive Church, and the judgment of Reformed Divines. Whereby a foundation is laid for the Church's peace, and the accommodation of our present differences.' The key-note is effectively struck in the succession of mottoes which follow on the title-page: first, from the Epistle to the Philippians,—" Let your moderation be known unto all men;"[1] then from the letter of Isaac Casaubon to Cardinal Perron; and, lastly, from the treatise of Grotius on the relation of civil and ecclesiastical authority—pointing to the great distinction betwixt a *jus divinum* in the Church, and an authority which is merely regulative or expedient.[2]

---

[1] iv. 5.
[2] " Si ad decidendas hodiernas controversias—jus divinum à positivo seu Ecclesiastico candide separaretur; non videretur de iis quæ sunt absolute necessaria inter pios aut moderatos longa aut acris contentio futura."— Isaac Casaubon, Ep. ad Card. Perron.
" Multum refert ad retinendam

The year 1659, in which the 'Irenicum' was published, was a year of political perplexity, and of the forecasts of coming change. The great Protector had died in the previous autumn, and the reins of government were already falling from the hands of his feeble son. Before the spring was over, he had signed his demission, and retired into the private life for which alone nature had fitted him. The Parliament and the army once more shared, but with very divided and jealous councils, the supreme authority. It was obvious that the period was a transitional one. Monk was already meditating his march from Scotland. Common apprehensions were drawing the Presbyterians and the older Royalists together. They remembered the miseries of misgovernment through which the country had come before the strong hand of Cromwell was laid upon it, and the special humiliations which they had both endured at the hands of military and Parliamentary officers, who valued neither Presbytery nor Episcopacy. They began to feel the necessity of common action, and even of softening in some degree their mutual asperities.

It was in such circumstances that the old idea of "accommodation," which Usher had conceived and Hales and Chillingworth would have welcomed, once more revived, and that Stillingfleet became its expositor. The character of the political situation suggested anew to thoughtful minds the possibility

Ecclesiarum pacem inter ea quæ jure divino præceptæ sunt et quæ non sunt accurate distinguere."— Grotius de Imper. sum. Potestat. circa Sacra, cap. ii.

of an ecclesiastical compromise. Could not the advantages of Episcopacy and Presbytery be united on some rational basis of expediency? Is there anything so exclusively divine in either as to prevent this? Is there any *jus divinum* in Church government at all in such a sense as to hinder wise men from acknowledging the force of circumstances, and composing their religious differences? This was the important question which, in the face of approaching changes, Stillingfleet set himself to re-examine.

In his preface he draws a highly-coloured picture of the evils which the long-protracted religious discord had produced: " Controversies about religion had increased till they had brought religion itself into a controversy. Religion hath been so much rarefied into airy notions and speculations by the distempered zeal of men's spirits, that its inward strength and the vitals of it have been much consumed. *Curiosity*, that green-sickness of the soul, whereby it longs for novelties and loathes sound wholesome truths, hath been the epidemical distemper of the age we live in; of which it may be as truly said, as ever yet of any, that it was *sæculum fertile religionis sterile pietatis*. I fear this will be the character whereby our age will be known to posterity, that it was the age wherein men talked of religion most, and lived it least."—" Men being loath to put themselves to the trouble of a holy life, readily embrace anything which may dispense with that," and hence enrol themselves as parties, and attach a religious importance to the most trifling party distinctions. " All the several parties among us," he continues, "have given such glorious names only to the outward government of the Church—'the undeniable practice of the apostles,' 'the discipline of Christ,' 'the order of the Gospel'—and account only that the Church where their own method of government is observed."—" From this monopolising of Churches to parties" hath proceeded the uncharitableness which was constantly "breaking out into open flame," and the most violent "heart-burning and contentions."[1] The only effectual remedy appeared to Stillingfleet to be "an infusion of the true spirit of religion—the revulsion of the extravasated blood into its proper channels, thereby taking men off from their eager pursuit after ways and parties, notions and opinions, and bringing them back to a right understanding of the nature, design, and principles of Christianity."

He explains Christianity as a religion of peace and tolerance, and sets forth, in the spirit of Chillingworth and Taylor, that the design of Christ was "to ease men of their former burdens, and not to lay on more." For the Church, therefore, to "require more than Christ Himself did," or "make other conditions of her communion than our Saviour did of discipleship, is wholly unwarrantable." "What possible reason can be assigned or given why such things should not be sufficient for communion with a Church which are sufficient for eternal salvation? And certainly those things are sufficient for that which are laid down as the necessary duties of Christianity by our Lord and Saviour in His Word.

[1] Preface to the Reader.

What ground can there be why Christians should not stand upon the same terms now which they did in the time of Christ and His apostles? Was not religion sufficiently guarded and fenced in by him? The grand commission the apostles were sent out with, was only to teach what Christ had commanded them,—Not the least intimation of any power given them to impose or require anything beyond what Himself had spoken to them, or they were directed to by the immediate guidance of the Spirit of God. It is not whether the things required be lawful or no, it is not whether indifferences be determined or no, it is not how far Christians are bound to submit to a restraint of their Christian liberty, which I now inquire after (of these things in the treatise itself), but whether they do consult for the Church's peace and unity who suspend it upon such things. . . . Without all controversy, the main inlet of all the distractions, confusions, and divisions of the Christian world hath been by adding other conditions of Church communion than Christ hath done. . . . Would there ever be the less peace and unity in a Church if a diversity were allowed as to practices supposed indifferent? Yea, there would be so much more as there was a mutual forbearance and condescension as to such things. The unity of the Church is a unity of love and affection, and not a bare uniformity of practice or opinion. . . . There is nothing the primitive Church deserves greater imitation by us in than in that admirable temper, moderation, and condescension which was used in it towards all the members of it. It was never thought worth the while to make any standing laws for rites and customs that had no other original but tradition, much less to suspend men her communion for not observing them."

On the contrary, the greatest latitude was allowed in the Church of the first ages, and he appeals with confidence to the well-known testimony of Sozomen,[1] of Cyprian, Augustine, Jerome, and others. "The first," he says, "who brake this order in the Church were the Arians, Donatists, and Circumcellians, while the true Church was still known by its pristine moderation and sweetness of deportment towards all its members." He expresses a hope that the Church of England may evince its conformity to the primitive Church, "not so much in using the same rites that were in use then, as in not imposing them, but leaving men to be won by observing the true decency and order of Churches, whereby those who act upon a true principle of Christian ingenuity, may be sooner drawn to a compliance in all lawful things than by force and rigorous imposition, which make men suspect the weight of the thing itself when such force is used to make it enter."

---

[1] Hist. Eccles., I. vii. c. 19. The passage from Sozomen to which reference is made is often quoted. It is as follows: "Εὔηθες γὰρ καὶ μάλα δικαίως ὑπέλαβον ἐθῶν ἕνεκεν ἀλλήλων χωρίζεσθαι, περὶ τὰ καίρια τῆς θρησκείας συμφωνοῦντες. Οὐ γὰρ δὴ τὰς αὐτὰς Παραδόσεις περὶ πάντα ὁμοίας, κἂν ὁμόδοξοι εἶεν, ἐν πάσαις ταῖς ἐκκλησίαις εὑρεῖν ἐστίν." Stillingfleet translates: "They judged it, and that very justly, a foolish and frivolous thing for those that agree in the weighty matters of religion to separate from one another's communion for the sake of some petty customs and observations. For Churches agreeing in the same faith often differ in their rites and customs."—Preface.

Sentiments of such sound wisdom and sense, uttered by a clever young ecclesiastic on the eve of the Restoration, show how far a higher spirit prevailed in many minds at this time. A rational theology had not been without its effect upon the country. Amidst the strife of opposing factions its voice had been heard. For Stillingfleet is not to be supposed a man standing very much above or apart from his age, — of independent and exceptional thoughtfulness. He was rather then, as he always was, a man with his eyes open to the signs of his time, and the influences moving men's minds. We may fairly conclude, therefore, that there was not merely in Cambridge, but amongst many of the more generous and active-minded of the younger clergy everywhere at this period, an earnest desire for some compromise amongst religious parties, whereby peace might be secured, and the Church reconstructed upon a larger and a firmer basis than ever. The government of the Church was, as it had been since the Reformation, the special difficulty; "an unhappy controversy to us in England," Stillingfleet says, "if ever there were any in the world." "And this chiefly," he adds, because so few really "understood the matter they so eagerly contended about. For the state of the controversy as it concerns us lies not here, as it is generally mistaken, what form of government comes the nearest to apostolical practice, but whether any one individual form be founded so upon divine right that all ages and Churches are bound unalterably to observe it?" This is the important question. Let it only appear that there is no form of Church government unalterably binding, and the way is cleared for a compromise on the basis of expediency.

"Certainly, they who have espoused the most the interest of a *jus divinum* cannot yet but say, that if the opinion I maintain be true, it doth exceedingly conduce to a present settlement of the differences that are among us. For then all parties may retain their different opinions concerning the primitive form, and yet agree and pitch upon a form compounded of all together as most suitable to the state and condition of the Church among us; that so the people's interest be secured by consent and suffrage, which is the pretence of the Congregational way; the due power of presbyteries, asserted by their joint concurrence with the bishop, as it is laid down in that excellent model of the late incomparable Primate of Armagh; and the just honour and dignity of the bishop asserted as a very laudable and ancient constitution for preserving the peace and unity of the Church."

This was the ideal of a Church advocated by many, and amongst others by the learned Casaubon in a passage which he quotes.[1]

Such is the general design of the treatise—to show that "there can be no argument drawn from any pretence of a divine right that may hinder men

---

[1] The passage is from the elder Casaubon, of course, and will be found in his 'Exercit. de Rebus Sacris et Eccles.' (xv. s. xi.) p. 360, published at London, 1614. "Episcopi in singulis Ecclesiis constituti cum suis Presbyteriis et propriam sibi quisque peculiari cura, et universam omnes in commune curantes admirabilis cujusdam aristocratiæ speciem referebant."

from consenting and yielding to such a form of government in the Church as may bear the greatest correspondency to the primitive Church," and be most likely to heal the divisions of the Church of England. Abuses must be removed, and he " dare not harbour so low apprehensions of persons enjoying so great dignity and honour in the Church, that they will in any wise be unwilling of themselves to reduce the form of Church government among us to its primitive state and order, by retrenching all exorbitances of power, and restoring those presbyteries which no law hath forbidden, but only through disuse have been laid aside." He is sanguine enough not only to anticipate such " self-denial" and " Christian prudence" on the part of the bishops, but to believe that the dogmatic Presbyterians and Congregationalists will be thereby so softened as to look with respect to an order which they " have hitherto the most slighted." There is something pathetic in this dream of the youthful rector of Sutton in the light of the facts which so soon followed. If anything could make us think worse than we do of the Restoration bishops, and of all the legislation of that unhappy time, it would be the thought that there may have been many who then shared Stillingfleet's sentiments, who honestly desired to see the Church of England reconstructed, not on a hierarchical, but on a practically efficient basis. The presumption we fear must be that, after all, the wise and moderate Churchmen were greatly outnumbered by the violent, the arbitrary, and the ignorant. So it has always hitherto been at every great crisis; and the dream of a truly catholic Church, which should give play to every healthy energy of government, as well as to every honest instinct of faith, remains a dream. Stillingfleet was haunted with the idea of failure even while he wrote: "I make no other account but that it will fall out with me as it doth commonly with him that offers to part a fray; both parties will perhaps drive at me for wishing them no worse than peace. My ambition," he adds, in a spirit of apostolic meekness, "shall willingly carry me through this hazard. Let them both beat me, so their quarrel may cease. I shall rejoice in those blows and scars which I shall take for the Church's safety."

I. Stillingfleet's argument is conducted in two parts, the special purport of each of which will appear in the sequel. In the first chapter, which is properly an introduction to the whole argument, he lays down his plan in a somewhat abstract manner, raising the question of what constitutes the nature of a divine right from the foundation, and following out the general train of thought to its close with a view to all his subsequent course of discussion. The nature of a divine right, according to him, is twofold. "*Jus* is first that which is *justum*. Whatever is just, men have a right to do it." In order to make a thing lawful or a right to men, it is not necessary that it be expressly commanded, but only that it be not expressly probibited. "According to the sense of *jus*," to use his own language, "those things may be said to be *jure divino* which are not determined one way or other by any positive law of God, but are left wholly as things lawful to the prudence of men to determine them in a way agreeable to natural light and the general rules of the Word of God."[1]

Having laid down this principle, he runs out into special illustrations of it anticipatory of his argument in a somewhat confused manner. His conclusion, however, is pertinent and forcible—namely, that the reason or ground of Church government, the *ratio regiminis ecclesiastici*, is of divine right, but that the special mode or system of it is left to human discretion. In other words, it is a thing for ever and immutably right that the Church should be under a definite form of government. This is undoubtedly *justum*. In no other way can the peace and unity of the Church be secured. But it is by no means equally indubitable what this form of government must be. The necessary end may be secured under diverse forms, as in the case of civil government. "Though the end of all be the same, yet monarchy, aristocracy, and democracy are in themselves lawful means for attaining the same common end. . . . So the same reason of Church government may call for an equality in the persons acting as governors of the Church in one place, which may call for superiority and subordination in another."[2]

But *jus* is not only that which is *justum*—a thing lawfully within man's power; but, moreover, that

---

[1] Chap. i. p. 9. The edition quoted throughout is that of 1662, "printed at the Phœnix, in St Paul's Churchyard, near the little northe door."

[2] Chap. i. p. 11.

which is *jussum*, a thing ordered to a man, and so made a *debitum*, or constituted a duty by the force and virtue of a divine command. And it is in this sense of a *jus divinum* Stillingfleet admits that the special controversy before him lies. He proceeds, therefore, to expound the nature of a divine right in this sense. Such a right presupposes "both legislation and promulgation." There must be an authority entitled to issue the law or command, and the fact of its issue must be beyond doubt. "Whatsoever binds Christians as a universal standing law, must be clearly revealed as such. . . . Nothing is founded upon a divine right, nor can bind Christians directly or consequently as a positive law, but what may be certainly known to have come from God, with an intention to oblige believers to the world's end."[1].

There are only two ways in which a thing may be thus clearly known to come from God with an intention to bind all perpetually—viz., "either by the law of nature, or by some positive law of God." "The law of nature binds indispensably, as it depends not upon any arbitrary constitutions; but is founded on the intrinsical nature of good and evil in things themselves." Reason is the chief instrument of discovering the "necessary duties of human nature," and hence Aristotle defines a natural law as that which has everywhere the same force;[2] yet it is not "bare reason" which enforces such a law, for every natural obligation is "expressive of an eternal

[1] Chap. i. p. 14.
[2] "πανταχοῦ τὴν αὐτὴν ἔχει δύναμιν."—Eth. L. v. c. 10.

law," and deduces its true force from thence. Such a law, "if we respect the rise, extent, and immutability of it, may be called deservedly the law of nature; but if we look at the emanation, efflux, and original of it, it is a divine law. For the sanction of this law, as well as others, depends upon the will of God, and therefore an obligation must come from him." Whatever, therefore, can be deduced "from the perceptive law of nature is of divine right," because it is thereby clearly apparent, from the very nature of the law, that it is the divine intention "to oblige all persons in the world by it."

God's positive laws are to be traced to His revealed will in Scripture. But it does not follow that all divine commands in Scripture are immutable; and hence of the nature of a divine right. It must, moreover, be clear that it is the divine will that they should always continue. This is illustrated by the case of the Jews and the ceremonial law. It is necessary, therefore, to determine certain *criteria* or "notes of difference whereby to learn when positive laws bind immutably, when not." The following are the *criteria* he enumerates, viz.: First, When the original reason of the law continues to subsist, and the Sabbath is given as a special illustration of this case; secondly, When God has expressly declared any law to be binding immutably; and, thirdly, When the law or "thing commanded in particular" is necessary to the existence of the Church, "the being, succession, and continuance of such a society of men professing the Gospel as is instituted and appointed by Christ Himself." It will afterwards appear, he says, "how much these things concern the resolution of the question proposed."

Finally, he examines under this general preparatory head of discussion certain "pretences which are brought for a divine right"—viz., Scripture examples, divine acts, or divine approbation. He shows conclusively in the case of all of these that they have not necessarily any binding force in themselves. In so far as they are binding they involve either moral considerations of universal force, or carry with them an explicit sanction "binding us to follow." It is unnecessary for us to enter into his illustrations of these several "pretences." One must suffice of the nature of a divine act. "Supposing it be granted," he says, that "the apostles had superiority of order and jurisdiction over the pastors of the Church by an act of Christ," it by no means follows from this "that it was Christ's intention that superiority should continue in their successors." This intention must be specially proved before it can be allowed. Any binding force, in short, that such a divine act has, must be derived from a special declaration of the divine will, and so any law or obligation there may be in the act falls back under one of the general *criteria* or tests of a divine right already admitted.

Such is the sum of Stillingfleet's discussion as to the nature of a divine right. It is a very good specimen of the philosophical temper and skill which he had acquired at Cambridge under the influence of the new school of thought there. It is also for the most part just and admirable in itself.

In the opening of his second chapter he restates his special inquiry—viz., How far Church government is founded upon divine right as thus explained by him. But he is still detained from immediately entering upon it by a further statement of principles or hypotheses necessary to enable him to carry on his argument. These principles are, some of them, self-evident, and must be summarised in the briefest form.

They may be expressed as follows :—

1. That the law of nature, where it is clearly intelligible, is paramount, and cannot be superseded by any positive human or divine enactments. It is part of the law of nature, for example, that God be worshipped. No human law can set this aside. If the law of nature did not bind indispensably or absolutely, nothing could bind, for all human authority comes primarily out of this law. Men yield obedience to any law only in virtue of the law of nature which binds them to stand to their compacts. Nor is it less true that the clear law of nature is irreversible by divine enactment. For, although God's power is infinite, He cannot change the nature of moral obedience. He cannot make good evil, or evil good. In confirmation of which statement he quotes a succession of pregnant sentences from Origen's Treatise against Celsus.[1]

2. Things clearly deducible from the law of nature or agreeable to it may be practised in the Church, unless otherwise lawfully determined. In other words, men are perfectly free to do what the law of

[1] Lib. 3; do. 5, e Celsum.

nature dictates, except in those cases where a lawful authority has put restraints upon their natural liberty. And the very existence of men in society implies such restraints. Good and evil thereby receive special meanings. Property is regulated and civil order established, and the restrictions which thus arise are lawful determinations of man's natural liberty. The Church is just a society under such special conditions, and has its own appropriate restrictions binding all who enter into it.

3. A principle of determination or of lawful authority being recognised in the Church, the question comes to be as to its character and extent. The divine will, when clearly manifest, is an undoubted example of such an authority. And the third hypothesis accordingly is, that "where the law of nature determines a thing, and the divine law determines the manner and the circumstances of the thing, we are bound to obey the divine law in its particular determinations, by virtue of the law of nature in its general obligation."[1] The law of nature, for example, binds us to worship God; and "as we are bound by nature to worship Him, so we are bound by virtue of the same law to worship Him in the manner best pleasing to Him, by sacrifice or otherwise." Sacrifice appears to our author unaccountable except by some express divine command. This principle or hypothesis is equally clear with the two former, supposing only the will of God is plainly made manifest. In such a case there can be no question of disobedience. All the difficulty con-

[1] Chap. ii. p. 35.

sists in making it clear that the will of God has really declared itself, and to what effect.

4. Supposing that it has done so as to "the substance and morality" of certain matters, the question arises as to others left undetermined, or as to the special circumstances of those so far determined. All the practical difficulty as to Church government and worship Stillingfleet sees very well lies here in this indeterminate region—indeterminate at least in so far as any clear revelation of the divine will is concerned. And hence his next hypothesis, which leads him into a lengthened discussion. " In such a case," he says, " it is in the power of lawful authority in the Church of God to determine "[1] circumstances left undetermined either by natural law or divine positive law. The lawful authority is the authority of the magistrate. But this is a position he is well aware much controverted, some denying the magistrate any power at all in matters of religion, others granting a defensive protective power of that religion which is preferred according to the law of Christ, but denying any determining power in the magistrate concerning things left undetermined by the Scripture. And so he feels himself " landed in a field of controversy." " It is strange," he adds, that " the things men can least bear with one another in are matters of *liberty;* and those things men have divided most upon have been matters of *uniformity;* and wherein they have differed most have been pretended things of *indifferency*." He would aim by his discussion to " beget a right understanding between the adverse

[1] Chap. ii. p. 38.

parties," rather than to make his way "through any opposite party." He then proceeds to define the magistrate's power in religion, first in its character, and secondly in its extent.

It is a power pertaining to religion as publicly professed, and not to religion in itself, which is entirely an affair of the conscience. "Men may hold what opinion they will in their minds," but the magistrate must have the power of restraining the utterance of opinions inimical to the national religion or the public good, which are identified. "As a liberty of all opinions tends successfully to the subverting of a nation's peace and to the embroiling it in continual confusions, a magistrate cannot discharge his office unless he hath power to restrain such a liberty." So far Stillingfleet does not contribute much to the settlement of a difficult point; but he was, at this time at least, fully on the level of his age as to the principle of toleration.

The magistrate's power is, secondly, external and objective about matters of religion, and not internal or elicitive. "The internal elicitive power lies in the authoritative exercise of the ministerial function in preaching the Word and administering the sacraments; the external objective power, in a due care and provision for the defence, protection, and propagation of religion."[1]

Thirdly, the power is not "nomothetical" but administrative. It does not consist in making or imposing upon the Church new laws, but in carrying out recognised divine laws. The magistrate cannot

[1] Chap. ii. p. 46.

alter or repeal any positive divine enactments; he cannot add to these of his own accord; but he may incorporate them into the law of the land. Finally, in things undetermined concerning the polity of the Church, he has the power of determination agreeably to the Word of God. It is the business and duty of pastors and governors of the Church to consult with and advise the magistrate; but it is from the magistrate alone that any power of coercion or legal obligation comes. " The great use of synods and assemblies of pastors of churches is to be as the council of the Church unto the king, in matters belonging to the Church, as the Parliament is for matters of local government." All power to oblige, all force of law, is alone derived from the civil magistrate.

How far, then, does the power of the magistrate extend? What are the matters left undetermined by the Word of God which he may determine in order to the peace and government of the Church? Stillingfleet does not give any clear or complete answer to these questions. To have done so would have been to anticipate many of his subsequent conclusions. As it is, there is an anticipatory tendency in much of this general discussion which is somewhat confusing. He contents himself with maintaining that there are things left undetermined, or matters of indifferency, which may be lawfully subject to the determination of the magistrate without any real restraint being put upon religious liberty. A due observance of prescribed rites, when the observance is rationally understood as merely a deference to constituted authority, which may vary in varying places and circumstances, fetters no principle of freedom. The very character of the restriction in such a case implies the freedom which lies behind it. The very diversity of the ritual indicates that it is freely subject to regulation as may be most convenient. And hence the golden rule of Augustine,[1] in reference to religious rites, that "every man should observe those of the Church he was in." He knew no better course for a prudent Christian, for "whatsoever is observed neither against faith or manners is a matter in itself indifferent, and to be observed according to the custom of those he lives among." This Christian rule he derived from Ambrose, who pithily expressed it, "When at Rome I fast on the Sabbath; when at home (at Milan) I do not."[2]

The liberal sentiments of these great fathers inspires Stillingfleet to break forth suddenly with some of his ideas of accommodation. How happy might the nation be if the spirit of these blessed saints only animated it! How might a Church be built up, imposing nothing but what is clearly revealed in the Word of God; requiring nothing which, from its indifferent nature, may not be rendered; leaving the service of God free even from particular requirements that may seem agreeable to the divine Word, when these requirements may give offence; inflicting no mulcts or penalties on Dissenters till it be seen whether it be wilful contempt and obstinacy of spirit, or only weakness of conscience which influences them; and, lastly, divesting religion of a multitude

---

[1] Ep. i. 18 ad Januar. Ir. p. 60. Sabbato: cum hic sum, non jejuno.
[2] "Cum Romam venio, jejuno juno."—Ibid., p. 61.

of ceremonies! The ideal is fine; but, after all, he does not help us much to see how it can be worked. One interesting piece of antiquarianism he uses as an illustration. He is sure that it is contrary to the primitive practice to impose penalties for nonconformity in habits, gestures, and the like. According to Walafridus Strabo,[1] there was no distinction of habits used in the primitive Church. The presbyters did not at first wear any distinct habits from the people. It was only gradually that the *pallium philosophicum* became a distinctive clerical vestment. Even so late as the time of Origen it had not done so universally. Only when " Christianity began to lose in height what it got in breadth," did " the former simplicity of their garments, as well as manners," change amongst Christians. Not that he would thereby condemn " any distinction of habit for mere decency and order," but only show that it was contrary to the primitive times " to impose any necessity of these things upon men, or to censure them for the disuse of them."

After his lengthened discussion about the magistrate's power, Stillingfleet reverts to the principles or hypotheses which he was unfolding; and, in a few sentences, adds two others to the series—viz., that " whatever is determined by lawful authority on the Church binds the conscience of all within the Church; in other words, subject to its authority." And, lastly, that the " determinations of this lawful authority are not unalterable, but may be revoked, limited, and changed, according to circumstances."

This finishes his elaborate preliminary matter—his

[1] De Rebus Eccles., cap. 24.

"foundation," as he calls it—and he is at length at liberty to proceed with his inquiry, "How far government in the Church is founded upon an unalterable divine right?" First, in respect of the law of nature; and, secondly, in respect of Scripture, or positive divine law. No fewer than six chapters are devoted to the examination of the subject in the first of these points of view. We can only indicate in the briefest manner his course of argument. All real interest is concentrated in his final treatment of the question, "How far any definite polity of Church government is laid down in the New Testament, or in the practice of the primitive Church?"

In the six chapters in which he views the matter on the basis of natural law, he settles such questions as that there must be a Church—a "society of men joining together for the worship of God,"[1] and "that this society must be governed in the most convenient manner."[2] Both these propositions are dictates of nature, and hence, undoubtedly, of divine right. The next thing which nature dictates is, that all things pertaining to divine worship or the government of the Church be performed "with the greatest solemnity and decency that may be."[3] It is quite unnecessary to enter into particular proof of such propositions. All who recognise a spiritual power at all will acknowledge these conditions of its recognition. The remaining three dictates of the law of nature in reference to the subject are not less unchallengeable; but one of them at least raises a more curious and difficult subject of inquiry. They are as follows:—

[1] Chap. iii. p. 72.   [2] Chap. iv. p. 85.   [3] Chap. v. p. 93.

That there must be some arbiter of controversy in the religious society, or Church;[1]

That all admitted into the society must consent to be governed by its rules;[2] and, finally,—

That it must possess a power of censuring all wilful offenders against these rules, and of expelling them if necessary.[3]

These are all equally conclusions of the natural reason regarding the government of the Church. As the former conclusions were necessary to its constitution, these are necessary to its preservation. Nature dictates the existence of such a society; the general order of the government, implying authority in some, and subjection in others; but nature would be defective if it did not also imply a sufficient provision for the maintenance and preservation of the society thus formed. A power, therefore, to prevent mischief, is as necessary in the Church as a " power to settle things." There must be some way of deciding controversies which will arise to disturb the peace of it.

The necessity for some arbiter of religious controversy raises the usual question as to the limits of Church communion and toleration, so admirably discussed by Hales and Chillingworth and Taylor. The views of Stillingfleet are identical with the views, already examined, of these writers, and are, in fact, directly borrowed from Hales, whose tract 'On Schism' is largely quoted. The matters which tend to break the peace of the Church are of the nature either of *heresy* or *schism*—matters of opinion or

[1] Chap. vi. p. 104.   [2] Chap. vii. p. 132.   [3] Chap. viii. p. 141.

practice. In reference to the former, Stillingfleet repeats strongly the opinion, that mere diversity of opinion is no ground of heresy, laying men open to the censure of the Church. It is only the "endeavour, by difference of opinion, to alienate men's spirit one from another, and thereby to break the society into fractions and divisions, which makes men liable to restraint and punishment."[1] "Opinionum diversitas et opinantium unitas non sunt ἀσύστατα." "The unity of the Church is that of communion, and not that of apprehension; and different opinions are no further liable to censure than as men by the broaching of these do endeavour to disturb the peace of the Church." Schism is a more deadly evil than so-called heresy, because more immediately destructive of Church communion. And yet here, he says, quoting Hales, it is also necessary to discriminate. Schism must be judged according to its grounds and reasons. For as it is a sin, on the one hand, to divide the Church, so also it is an offence to continue communion when it is a duty to withdraw. The Separatist is not necessarily the schismatic. He lays down the following conditions as to Church membership: 1. Every Christian is bound to join in Christian society with others. 2. He is bound to maintain his Church communion so long as he can do so without sin. And the causes of legitimate offence in a Church warranting separation from it are construed very broadly. The Churches of Galatia and Corinth are examples that even the rejection of an article of faith may not demand separation. It is

[1] Chap. ii. p. 107, 108.

not enough that the Church be corrupt even in definite points of doctrine or practice. She must, moreover, require her members to own expressly these corruptions before a total and positive separation is lawful. This is the justification of separation from the Church of Rome, as explained in Chillingworth's preface, to which our author refers. In order to be a member of this Church, it is necessary to believe that all its doctrines are not only not errors, but certain and necessary truths; so that, in fact, to hold that there are errors in the Church of Rome is "actually and *ipso facto* to forsake the communion of that Church." He quotes with approval a lengthened passage from Hales, that the best way to avoid schism is to avoid "charging Churches and liturgies with things unnecessary." "To load our public forms with the private fancies upon which we differ, is the sovereign way to perpetuate schism unto the world's end. Prayer, confession, thanksgiving, reading of Scriptures in the plainest and simplest manner, were matters enough to furnish out a sufficient Liturgy."[1] In this point of view Stillingfleet strongly approves of the revisal of the Liturgy to meet the scruples of the Presbyterians. The Reformers, he argues, did not hesitate, in "composing the Liturgy," to have an eye to the Papists as the only party at that time whom they desired to draw into their communion. And the same reason should surely induce the authorities of the Church to alter or lay aside the things which gave offence to the Presbyterians at the Restoration.

[1] Hales on Schism.

Having thus dwelt on the matters which lead to controversy within the Church, he dismisses, after a comparatively brief treatment, the ways prescribed by the light of nature for ending such controversy. The minority must yield to the majority, and a right of appeal must subsist to every accused or injured person, from the lower and subordinate powers to the higher and superior. This is all. And not much more remains to be said by any one. He urges strongly the necessity of appeal and a graduation of authority in the Church against the Congregationalists, who would leave every particular society of Christians to order their affairs according to their pleasure. According to the "light and law of nature," it appears to him "that no individual company or congregation hath an absolute independent power within itself; but that for the redressing grievances happening in them, appeals are necessary to the parties aggrieved, and a subordination of that particular congregation to the government of the society in common."[1] He is equally strong that, in a State Church, "when the Church is incorporated into the commonwealth, the chief authority in a commonwealth as Christian, belongs to the same to which it doth as a commonwealth."[2] In other words, as he has already asserted in treating of the power of the magistrate, the ultimate authority, ecclesiastical as well as civil, is in the State.

II. We pass on to the second part of Stillingfleet's argument, which discusses the Scriptural evidence of

[1] Chap. vi. p. 131. [2] Ibid., p. 127.

a divinely fixed form of Church government. So far as positive divine law is concerned, there can be no other evidence for it, he maintains, but that of Scripture. "The Word of God being the only code and digest of divine laws, whatever law we look for must either be found there in express terms, or at least so couched therein, that every one, by the exercise of his understanding, may, by a certain and easy collection, gather the universal obligation of the thing inquired after."[1] When the question is as to binding men's consciences, and not merely satisfying our historical curiosity, the appeal must be to Scripture—to the authoritative words or actions of Christ or of the apostles. Traditions of apostolical practice gathered from succeeding ages may be very interesting, and may even throw real light upon the original constitution of the Church, but they can never furnish sufficient ground to "infer any divine law." It is not enough that the practice be authentic, but it must be further clear that it was the divine intention that it should continually bind the Church. "Though the matter of fact be evidenced by posterity, yet the obligatory nature of the fact must depend upon Scripture." Nor is it enough that "the apostles' intentions be built upon men's bare surmises, nor upon after practices;" but that it be clearly shown that what they did proceeded from a divine command, obligatory upon them as the Church in all future time.[1] He ridicules the reasoning of those who would infer the necessity of any form of Church government because practised by the apostles, and then prove the

[1] Part ii. chap. i. p. 151.   [2] Ibid., p. 152.

apostolical practice from that of succeeding ages. This, he says, is to "prove the same thing by itself" —to call a practice apostolical, and then pronounce it of divine authority because apostolical; whereas in any valid argument for a divinely fixed form of Church government there are two distinct things to be proved—viz., first, what the apostolic practice was; and, secondly, what was its character. Was it designed to be universally binding or not? This last point he declares, over and over again, is the really important point which it is the special object of his treatise to settle. The controversy had been hitherto on a wrong tack in trying to settle whether Independency, or Presbytery, or Episcopacy, came the nearest to apostolical practice. The really urgent question is not this; but whether any of these forms "be so settled by a *jus divinum*—that is, be so determined by a positive law of God, that all the Churches of Christ are bound to observe that one form so determined without variation from it."

We have put the question as between the three main forms of Church government which contended for the mastery in England in Stillingfleet's youth. But, in point of fact, he has already, by the course of his reasoning, reduced the question to one between Presbytery and Episcopacy; for he has already settled, and he recurs to the question specially in the first chapter of the second part of his treatise, that neither the name nor the order of a Church can be confined to "particular congregations;" but that, on the contrary, they apply with special propriety to a national society, comprehending in it many of such lesser congregations united together in one body under a form of government. Even if the primary political form of the Church were acknowledged to have been that of a "particular congregation," it is enough, he says, "that there are other Churches besides particular congregations."[1] It is enough that whole nations professing Christianity have united themselves in the participation of religious ordinances. Such a nation is undoubtedly a true Church of God; and hence it follows " that there must be a form of ecclesiastical government over a nation as a Church, as well as of civil government over it as a society governed by the same laws."[2]

Having thus disposed of Congregationalism or Independency, he disposes, in a second chapter, of Quakerism, or the dream of a *seculum spiritus sancti* —first broached, he says, by the mendicant friars. He makes no dispute that the government of the Church must " be administered by officers of divine appointment." This " is another thing I will yield to be of divine right. . . . My meaning is, that there must be a standing perpetual ministry in the Church of God, whose care and employment must be to oversee and govern the people of God, and to administer Gospel ordinances among them, and this is of divine and perpetual right "[3] It admits of no question that special officers were appointed in the primitive Church; and the original grounds for their appointment, as enumerated in many texts of the New Testament, continue in equal force. The objects of the ministerial office remaining of necessary

[1] Ibid., p. 154. [2] Ibid., p. 157. [3] Ibid., p. 158.

and perpetual use, the office itself must be held of divine perpetuity in the Church.

The way being thus cleared, he comes to "the main subject of the present controversy." Can either Presbytery or Episcopacy make out for itself a *jus divinum?* Is either form of Church government so determined by any positive law of God as to bind unalterably all Christians to its observance? The only valid plea for such a divine right is some plain institution by Christ Himself, or the obligatory nature of apostolical practice. All the pith of the argument lies within these two points, and, indeed, within the latter. He prefixes a brief discussion as to whether any of the institutions of the law have binding force under the Gospel; and he appends an interesting chapter on the opinions of the Church divines since the Reformation on the subject of Church government. But the force of his argument is quite independent of these considerations.

1. So far as any express command of Christ Himself is concerned, there is nothing can be quoted bearing on the subject. It is of no avail to argue, as many had done, from the analogy of Moses, that Christ must have instituted a special form of government for the Church.[1] Not to insist on the difference be-

---

[1] The absurd presumption of arguing in favour of a divinely constituted form of Church government, that it was necessary for Christ, like any other legislator, to appoint a definite constitution for the society which He established, is well ridiculed by Stillingfleet as by Hooker, from whom he quotes an admirable passage on this point (Eccles. Polity, lib. iii. sect. 2): "In matters which concern the action of God, the most dutiful way on our

twixt the law and the Gospel, it is enough to say that not only has Christ not laid down any special rules for the constitution of the New Testament Church, but that there are no such rules found in any part of the New Testament. There are, indeed, "general rules of direction" given in the apostolical writings, of which the following four are enumerated by Stillingfleet: "All things to be done decently and in order. All to be done for edification. Give no offence. Do all to the glory of God."[1] But the very statement of these principles in their extreme generality brings out in the clearest manner the scantiness of the New Testament information regarding the constitution of the Church. All the laws occurring in Scripture respecting Church government may be applied with equal force to several forms of government. It is not designed to characterise or define the *form*, but only the spirit or principles which should animate the various officers in the discharge of their duties. Such rules, for example, as are contained in the Epistles to Timothy and Titus are *moral*, and not *institutional* or *ritual*. They tell us what bishops and deacons ought to be in character, but they do not tell us the relation which these two classes of officers were to bear to one another, and still less do they tell us as to the relations of bishops and presbyters. It is plain, in fact, to every unprejudiced reader, that the distinction of bishop and presbyter, as afterwards recognised by the Church,

part is to search what God hath done, and with meekness to admire that rather than to dispute what He, in congruity of reason, ought to do."

[1] Part ii. chap. iv. p. 178.

had not then emerged. The author of these epistles would not have understood the question which agitated the seventeenth century, and has not ceased to agitate the nineteenth.

It is not to be denied that Timothy and Titus occupied special positions of superiority in the primitive Church; and two indisputable inferences may be drawn from this which may be turned in favour of Episcopacy—viz., that the superiority of some Church officers over others is not inconsistent with the New Testament; and, secondly, that it is not repugnant to the primitive Church for certain officers to have power over more than one congregation. But, upon the whole, the examples of Timothy and Titus decide nothing definitely in favour of either of the disputed forms of Church government. The mere fact that it is fairly questioned whether their office was that of temporary evangelists or of fixed bishops is enough to invalidate the authoritative character of their examples. "If they acted not as bishops, nothing can be drawn from their example necessarily enforcing the continuance of the superiority which they enjoyed."[1] To those who argue "that Timothy and Titus might ordain and appoint others to succeed them in their places," he replies that the question is not, "what they might do, but what they did." "Neither," he adds, "is what they did the whole question, but what they did with an opinion of the necessity of doing it." Whether they were bound to do it or not? If the former view be taken, the binding law

[1] Ibid., p. 186.

or command must be produced, "which will hardly be if we embrace only the received canon of Scripture." "Thus we see, then," Stillingfleet concludes, in very emphatic terms, this part of his argument, "that neither the qualifications of the persons nor the commands for a right exercise of the office committed to them, nor the whole Epistles to Timothy and Titus, do determine any one form of government to be necessary in the Church of God."[1]

The special actions of our Lord which may be supposed to have any bearing on the subject are examined.[2] The mission of the apostles, as described in the Gospels (Matt. x.; Luke, vi.), the alleged primacy of St Peter, and the relation between the twelve and the seventy disciples, along with some other details,—all are discussed with a similar conclusion. Nowhere is there any evidence of any intention on the part of Christ to fix the special form of government for the Church. Nothing is said or appointed by Him which is not equally applicable to a "diversity of particular forms." There is, therefore, nothing in any of our Lord's actions, or in any special rules laid down in Scripture, which determines the necessity of a particular form of Church government.

2. The only remaining argument to be considered is that which arises out of *the practice of the apostles*. Stillingfleet has bestowed great pains upon this part of his argument; and, notwithstanding certain irrelevancies which mark more or less the whole progress of his reasoning, we do not know that there is

[1] Ibid., p. 188.   [2] Ibid., chap. v.

anything in English theological literature at once more compact and exhaustive on the subject. It divides itself into two inquiries—What the apostolic practice really was? and, secondly, How far it is binding upon us; or, in his own words, "how far they acted for the determining any one form of government as necessary for the Church?"[1]

In carrying out the first of these inquiries it is especially necessary to free ourselves from prepossessions. "Nothing has been a more fruitful mother of mistakes and errors than the looking upon the practice of the Primitive Church through the glass of our own customs." In illustration of this, he quotes the Roman Catholic use of the word *missa*, whenever they meet with it, as applying to the sacrifice of the altar; whereas it originally meant only the public service of the Church, so called from the dismission of the people after it with an *ite, missa est*, and was equally applied to the service of the catechumens *(missa catechumenorum)* and the service of the communicants *(missa fidelium)*, "which afterwards (the former discipline of the Church decaying) engrossed the name *missa* to itself, and when the sacrifice of the altar came up among the Papists it was appropriated to that."[2] In the same way the Romanists pervert the meaning of the word λειτουργεῖν, translating the phrase λειτουργούντων αὐτῶν, *sacrificantibus illis*, "although it be not only contrary to the sense of the word in the New Testament, but to the exposition of Chrysostom" and others. But it is unnecessary, he says, "to search curiously for

[1] Ibid., vi. 232.   [2] Ibid., p. 238.

examples of this abusive mode of argument." The subject itself is full of them—" as the argument for the popular election of pastors from the grammatical sense of the word χειροτονία, for lay-elders from the name πρεσβύτεροι, and modern Episcopacy from the use of the word ἐπίσκοπος in Scripture."[1] It is important, therefore, to discriminate accurately the use of names, and to draw conclusions only " from the undoubted practice of the apostolic times, if that can be made appear what it was."

The only real guide to us in such an inquiry is the customs of the Jewish synagogue, to which the apostles, beyond question, conformed in planting Christian Churches. This is argued at great length, and the various points of analogy betwixt the Jewish synagogue and the Primitive Church brought out in detail. These are found to consist in the general character of the public service, the ordination of Church officers, the formation of presbyteries in the several Churches, and the mode of government of those presbyteries. The primitive order of public worship corresponded to that of the synagogue in the following essential particulars :—(1.) Public fellowship (κοινωνία) ; (2.) Solemn prayers ; and, (3.) Reading and exposition of Scripture. The wellknown passage from the 'Second Apology of Justin Martyr,' respecting the primitive worship, is quoted with the remark, " What could have been spoken with greater congruity and correspondency to the synagogue, abating the necessary observation of the Eucharist as proper to Christianity?"[2] The prac-

[1] Ibid., p. 239. [2] Ibid., p. 262, 263.

tice of ordination was plainly derived from the synagogue. " The priests under the law were never ordained by imposition of hands, as the elders and rulers of the synagogue were; and if any of them came to that office, they, as well as others, had peculiar designation and appointment to it. It is, then, a common mistake to think that the ministers of the Gospel succeed by vows of correspondence and analogy to the priest under the law—which mistake hath been the original of many errors."[1]

The application of the name of priests to Christian ministers, naturally following the usage of the term among both Jews and Gentiles, has led in process of time to all the sacrificial ideas connected with it, and, finally, to the mass itself. So he argues. As the fact of ordination was derived from the synagogue, so the special mode of it, by the laying on of hands, the number of persons authorised to confer it, and its supposed effect, were all drawn from the same source. These features of the Christian Church were originally nothing more than copies from the Jewish Church. The one grew out of the other in a natural manner —the younger institution out of the old, taking some of its most characteristic peculiarities and stamping them with a new life and meaning. The very same process of development was repeated in both cases. The right of ordination, for example, was at first common to any presbyter among the Jews. Every one, himself regularly ordained, had the power of ordaining disciples, as Maimonides expressly affirms,

[1] Ibid., p. 265.

and also the *Gemara Babylonia*, as quoted by Selden.[1] But in course of time this liberty was restrained, and it was agreed that none should ordain others without the presence, or at least the sanction, of the Prince of the Sanhedrim—the ἀρχισυνάγωγος. The same change gradually sprang up in the Christian Church. At first, as Jerome tells us,[2] "the presbyters did rule the Church in common—communi presbyterorum concilio Ecclesiæ gubernantur." They enjoyed alike the power of ordaining other presbyters. Stillingfleet gives abundant evidence of this from patristic and even Papal authority, and especially enters into a long discussion as to the consistency of Jerome and the true opinions of Aërius, both of whom appear so prominent in the controversy respecting Presbytery and Episcopacy. There can be no fair question, he thinks, that Jerome consistently maintains the original identity of presbyters and bishops, while asserting at the same time that the superiority of the bishop was an "apostolical tradition," or a custom which might be traced to the apostolic age. The truth was, that the exercise of the right of ordination by all presbyters alike had a tendency to create division, and so the right became restricted as previously among the Jews.

"The main controversy is where this restraint began, and by whose act; whether by any act of the apostles, or only by the prudence of the Church itself, as it was with the Sanhedrim. But in order to our peace," he adds,[3] "I see no such necessity of

[1] Ibid., p. 272.   [2] Hieronym. in. 1 Tit., quoted ibid., p. 273.
[3] Chap. vi. p. 276.

deciding it, both parties granting that in the Church such a restraint was laid upon the liberty of ordaining presbyters; and the exercise of that power may be restrained still, granting it to be radically and intrinsically in them."

To hold it expedient, notwithstanding this radical power of ordination in presbyters, that the right should only be exercised by a superior order in the Church, and to hold that Presbyterian ordination is in itself essentially unlawful, are two entirely distinct propositions; and the latter opinion he " dares with some confidence assert to be a stranger to our Church of England," as he promises to show more fully afterwards. Concerning Aërius, he maintains that his special heresy was not at all the assertion of the identity in order of presbyters and bishops, in which respect he only agreed with Jerome, Augustine, Ambrose, Chrysostom, Theodoret, Theophylact; but his having carried out this opinion to the extent of "separating from bishops and their churches because they were bishops:"—"Whereas had his mere opinion about bishops been the ground of his being condemned, there can be no reason assigned why this heresy, if it were then thought so, was not mentioned either by Socrates, Theodoret, Sozomen, or Evagrius, before whose time he lived. But for Epiphanius and Augustine, who have listed him in the roll of heretics, it either was for other heretical opinions maintained by him—or they took the name *heretic* (and it is evident they often did) for one who upon a matter of different opinion from the present sense of the Church did proceed to make separations from the unity of the Catholic Church, which I take to be the truest account of the reputed heresy of Aërius."[1]

After dwelling briefly upon the number of persons required to perform the ceremony of ordination among the Jews and equally in the Primitive Church —three in each case—and also of the supposed effect of the reception of the divine presence or the Holy Spirit, Stillingfleet proceeds to draw his argument to a close in three propositions, which embrace at the same time, he says, "the full resolution" of all the points corresponding betwixt the Sanhedrim and the Primitive Church. He introduces his propositions by a statement as to the original meaning of Ἐπίσκοπος, the intention of which, he says, was "to qualify the importance of the word *presbyter* to a sense proper to the Gospel state." Primarily the word imported "duty more than honour," and was "not a title above presbyter, but rather used by way of diminution and qualification of the power implied in the name of presbyter." Having cleared this point, all that he has to say concerning the settlement of the Primitive Church by the apostles may be summed up as follows :—First, that we have no such certainty of apostolical practices as can constitute a divine right; secondly, that there is no evidence that the apostles bound themselves to any one fixed course in modelling Churches; and, thirdly, that even if it could be proved that they did this, their example would not necessarily bind us.[2]

He argues the first of these points at considerable

[1] Ibid., p. 277.   [2] Ibid., p. 287.

length, from the equivalency of the names of bishop and presbyter in the New Testament (Acts, xi. 30, xiv. 23, xxviii. 17; 1 Tim. iii. 1; Titus, i. 5); from the "defectiveness, ambiguity, partiality, and repugnancy" of the records of the ages immediately succeeding that of the apostles.[1] The clear impossibility of making out any *jus divinum* for Church government from Scripture has driven controversialists, he says, "to follow the scent of the game into this wood of antiquity, where it is easier to lose ourselves than to find that which we are upon the pursuit of." He has, perhaps, coloured strongly his picture of the uncertainty of ecclesiastical tradition; but those who have most critically examined the subject will be the most likely to agree with him. He speaks with peculiar force of the sub-apostolic age, from the close of the Acts of the apostles to "the middle of Trajan," as a *tempus* ἄδηλον, in the words of Scaliger.[2] Christian antiquity is then most defective, unhappily, when its light would have been most useful. The lists or catalogues of bishops set down by many ecclesiastical annalists are treated very slightly. Eusebius[3] found it no easy matter "to find out who succeeded the apostles in the churches planted by them." What becomes then of the "unquestionable line of succession and the large diagrams made of the apostolical churches, with every one's name set down in his order?"[4] Irenæus is found attributing the tradition of apostolical doctrine "to the suc-

[1] Ibid., p. 294.
[2] Ibid., p. 298.
[3] Lib. iii. c. iv.
[4] Ibid., p. 297.

cession of presbyters which before he had done to bishops."[1] He asserts not only "the succession of presbyters to the apostles, but likewise attributes the *successio Episcopatus* to these very presbyters. What strange confusion must this raise in any one's mind that seeks for a succession of episcopal power above presbyters from the apostles by the testimony of Irenæus, when he so plainly attributes both the succession to presbyters and the episcopacy too which he speaks of? . . . But it is not Irenæus alone who tells us that presbyters succeed the apostles. Even Cyprian, who pleads so much for obedience to the bishops, as they were then constituted in the Church, yet speaks often of his *Compresbyteri;* and in his Epistle to Florentius Papianus he attributes apostolic succession to all that were Præpositi, which name implies not the relation (of bishops) to presbyters as over them, but to the people, and is therefore common both to bishops and presbyters. Jerome saith that presbyters are *loco Apostolorum*, and that they do *Apostolico gradui succedere;* and the so much magnified Ignatius πρεσβύτεροι εἰς τόπον συνεδρίου τῶν ἀποστόλων, that *the presbyters succeeded in the place of the bench of apostles.*"[2]

The sum of his argument is, that no clear line of *Episcopal* succession can be traced in many cases. The claim of a *jus divinum* for Episcopacy implies

[1] Lib. iv. cap. iii. The passage of Irenæus is as follows:—"Quapropter iis qui in Ecclesia sunt Presbyteris obaudire oportet, his qui successionem habent ab Apostolis, sicut, ostendimus, qui cum Episcopatus successione, charisma veritatis certum secundum placitum Patris acceperunt."—Iren., p. 307.
[2] Ibid., p. 308.

that in all cases the apostles in "withdrawing from the government of churches did substitute single persons to succeed them." But the evidence for this egregiously fails even in the most conspicuous churches. In Rome, for example, "the succession is as muddy as the Tiber itself, for here Tertullian, Rufinus, and several others, place Clement next to Peter; Irenæus and Eusebius set Anacletus before him; Epiphanius and Optatus, both Anacletus and Cletus; Augustinus and Damasus, with others, make Anacletus, Cletus, and Linus all to precede him. What way shall we find to extricate ourselves out of this labyrinth, so as to reconcile it with the certainty of the form of government in the apostles' times?"[1]

Having shown how little certainty there is of any divinely-fixed form of Church government in the apostolic age, he proceeds to show how the apostles probably acted "according to the several circumstances of places and persons which they had to deal with." He sketches, in other words, the formation of the Christian Church according to the natural law of development which it appears to him to have followed. His idea is the genuinely historic one, that the government of the Church adapted itself to circumstances, and the varying increase of the community of believers in different districts. A small number of believers did not require the same number of teachers and governors as "a great Church did." In some cases a single pastor, with deacons under him, was all that was needed; and "every such single pastor was a bishop, in the sense that he

[1] Ibid., p. 322.

had none above to command him," but not, of course, in the special sense of having presbyters under him. In larger churches, consisting of a multitude of deacons, he supposes that the government was settled in "a college of presbyters." This is his interpretation of the apostles' "ordaining elders in every city, and Paul's calling for the elders from Ephesus, and his writing to the bishops (presbyters) and deacons of Philippi."[1] "We have many remaining footsteps," he says, "of such a college of presbyters established in the most populous churches in the apostolical times." Among these presbyters some attended most to ruling, others laboured most in preaching, but none of them were *lay elders* in the dogmatic Presbyterian sense. For any presbyter in the New Testament sense is also a bishop, and is described as having pastoral charge over a flock, which is inconsistent with the notion of a lay elder.[2]

Thus far he supposes the Church to have developed in the apostolic age; and in a subsequent chapter[3] he traces its further development in the institution of a president, or bishop in the special sense, over each college of presbyters. In the second century this manner of government in the Church appears clearly: "the bishop sitting as the נשיא ('prince' or 'chief') in the Sanhedrim, and the presbyters, as Ignatius expresseth it, acting as the common council of the Church to the bishop[4]—the bishop being as the ἄρχων τῆς ἐκκλησίας, answering to the ἄρχων τῆς πόλεως, and the presbyters as the βουλὴ τῆς ἐκκλησίας, answering to the βουλὴ καθ' ἑκάστην

[1] Ibid., p. 335. [2] Ibid., p. 337. [3] II. c. vii. [4] ὡς συνεδρευτοὶ τῶν ἐπισκόπων.

πολίν, as Origen compares them (c. Celsum, l. iii.), whereby he fully describes the form of government in his time in the Church, which was by an ecclesiastical senate, and a president in it, ruling the society of Christians in every city."[1] We need not trace further his historical picture, according to which churches gradually extended from cities to the surrounding villages, and thence enlarged into dioceses, and subsequently into provinces. The result of the whole is to bring out the varying human element which entered into the growth of the Church. The government was the result, not of any special divine law, but of a succession of laws, springing up "according to the several states and conditions wherein the Church was." And "as it gradually grew up, so was the power of the Church by mutual consent fitted to its state in its several ages.[2] In further evidence of which, it is found, as a matter of fact, that there were several Churches, such as the ancient Scottish Church, without any bishops for a long time; and other Churches, he alleges, " which discontinued bishops for a great while where they had been."

The final strength of his argument yet remains. Even if a stronger case could be made out for a uniform apostolical practice as to Church government, it does not follow that such a practice would be necessarily binding upon us. Many things were done by the apostles which were suitable merely to the exigencies of the Primitive Church, and carried with them no binding force after the occasion for them had passed away. " Let any one consider but these

[1] Ibid., p. 356.   [2] Ibid., p. 374.

few particulars," he says, "and judge how far the pleaders for a divine right of apostolical practice do look upon themselves as bound now to observe them; as dipping in baptism, the use of love-feasts, community of goods, the holy kiss, by Tertullian called *signaculum orationis* (de Orat.); yet none look upon themselves as bound to observe them now, and yet all acknowledge them to have been the practice of the apostles."[1]

His concluding review of the opinions of Reformed divines is extremely interesting. But we cannot do more than indicate its general purport. He shows, beyond all dispute, that the most distinguished divines of the English Reformation — Cranmer, Whitgift, Parker, Hooker, and, later, Cosins, Low, Bridges, Sutcliffe, and King James himself—were all of opinion that no definite form of Church government was laid down in Scripture, or commanded to the Church of God (very nearly Whitgift's words in his reply to Cartwright). He quotes the detailed opinions of Hales and Chillingworth to the same effect. He then adds the testimony of foreign divines in abundance, and of learned men, particularly Bacon and Grotius. All these "assert in terms that the form of Church government does not depend upon any unalterable law, but is left to the prudence and discretion of every particular Church to determine it according to its suitableness to the state, condition, and temper of the people whereof it consists, and conduceableness to the ends for which it is instituted."[2] Others, such as Calvin, Beza, Melancthon, while

Chap. vi. p. 345.   [2] Chap. vii. p. 404.

holding Presbyterian parity to be the primitive form, yet approve of Episcopacy in special circumstances as lawful and expedient. Others still, while judging Episcopacy to be the primitive form, do not hold it to be "unalterably binding, but that those churches which are without it are truly constituted churches, and their ministers lawfully ordained by mere presbyters. This is given as the opinion, not only of Jewel, but of Field, Downam, Saravia, Andrews, and others. "The stoutest champions for Episcopacy before their late unhappy divisions," he says, "acknowledged that ordination, performed by presbyters in cases of necessity, is valid, which I have already shown doth evidently prove that Episcopal government is not founded upon any unalterable divine right."[1]

This closes his lengthened argument, in which he believes that he has laid down "a sure foundation for peace and union." The result of the whole has been "to prove that the form of Church government is a mere matter of prudence, regulated by the word of God." *Prudence*, therefore, is the first principle which must be used in the resettlement of the Church. The second principle is, that that form of government is the best which, according to principles of Christian prudence, comes nearest to apostolical practice, and tends most to advance the peace and unity of the Church. What this form is he does not presume to determine; but no better key to its discovery can be given than the advice of "his late Majesty, of glorious memory," to divines of differing

[1] Chap. viii. p. 413.

opinions, to "lay aside private interests, and reduce Episcopacy and Presbytery into such a well-proportioned form of superiority and subordination as may best resemble the apostolical and primitive times, so far forth as the different conditions of the times, and the exigencies of all considerable circumstances, will admit."[1] The elements of such a Church constitution are—1. The restoration of presbyters as the senate to the bishop. 2. The contraction of dioceses, and appointment of bishops at least in every county town. 3. The constant preaching of the bishop, and residence in his diocese. 4. The solemnity of ordinations, with the consent of the people. 5. The observation of provincial synods twice every year. 6. The employment of none in judging church matters but the clergy! Finally, whatever form of government is determined upon by lawful authority, should be submitted to in so far as it contains nothing contrary to the word of God. The very fact that the determination of Church government is a matter of liberty, makes the government binding when once lawfully determined.

Such was the ideal Church of Stillingfleet, probably of many of the younger and more thoughtful clergy, on the eve of the Restoration. Unhappily, their voice was unheard, or at least uninfluential. The old parties represented by Baxter and Calamy[2]

---

[1] Charles I. Second Paper to the Ministers at Newport.

[2] Both Baxter and Calamy were in a certain sense moderate men, and, if what is known as the Worcester Declaration (October 1660) had become law, they would have probably accepted the preferment offered them in the Church of England. But they had many narrow prejudices, and neither Calamy, at Breda, nor both at the

on one side, and Sheldon and Morley on the other, exasperated and hardened by their long struggle, continued for a time to wrangle with one another. Both were alike incapable of rising above the dogmatisms which enslaved them, and which had desolated the country. The end was sufficiently mournful, and bears mournful consequences unto this day; but the time may come when thoughts of wisdom and moderation will prevail on this as on other subjects, and we may see the end, as Stillingfleet, in his concluding sentence, dares to hope, " of our strange divisions and unchristian animosities, while we pretend to serve the Prince of Peace."

Savoy Conference, can be said to have managed matters well in the interests of a Comprehensive Church.

END OF THE FIRST VOLUME.

PRINTED BY WILLIAM BLACKWOOD AND SONS, EDINBURGH.